The Dow Jones-Irwin Guide to Tax Planning

The Dow Jones-Irwin Guide to
Tax Planning

Ray M. Sommerfeld
The John Arch White Professor in Accounting
The University of Texas at Austin

Third edition

DOW JONES-IRWIN
Homewood, Illinois 60430

Also published in hard cover by Richard D. Irwin, Inc.
under the title *Federal Taxes and Management Decisions.*

© RICHARD D. IRWIN, INC., 1981

© DOW JONES-IRWIN, 1974 and 1978

All rights reserved. No part of this publication may be reproduced, stored in a retrieval system, or transmitted, in any form or by any means, electronic, mechanical, photocopying, recording, or otherwise, without the prior written permission of the publisher.

This publication is designed to provide accurate and authoritative information in regard to the subject matter covered. It is sold with the understanding that the publisher is not engaged in rendering legal, accounting, or other professional service. If legal advice or other expert assistance is required, the services of a competent professional person should be sought.

From a Declaration of Principles jointly adopted by a Committee of the American Bar Association and a Committee of Publishers.

ISBN 0-870-94-233-6

Library of Congress Catalog Card No. 80–70151

Printed in the United States of America

1 2 3 4 5 6 7 8 9 0 K 8 7 6 5 4 3 2 1

To Andrea and Kristin

Preface

This book is intended to serve the tax needs of the entrepreneurs of contemporary American society (property owners, owners and managers of businesses, and corporate executives who are responsible for the management of others' assets). In it I have attempted to explain the multitude of tax opportunities and pitfalls that surround common business transactions. Salaried employees may also be interested in this book if they can either foresee a day when they, too, will have accumulated some property, or simply because they have a nagging curiosity about how others play the tax game.

The differences between recognizing a tax problem and solving one and between recognizing a tax opportunity and exploiting it are significant. The ideas presented in this book should be applied to an actual situation in the real world only with the assistance of a qualified expert in federal taxation. Many tax planning opportunities lie in that vast wasteland of gray that separates the obviously legal from the equally obviously fradulent. In this wasteland particularly an expert's opinion and advice is indispensable.

Bearing the above caution in mind, this book should have several immediate uses. First, and most importantly, it should give the reader an appreciation of the general ways in which major tax savings are achieved so that he or she can better review their own situation and discover what might be done to realize greater tax savings in the future. Second, it ought to give the reader a starting point from which anyone can assess the quality of tax assistance they are receiving. Third, it should alert a person to the many tax traps into which the uninformed or overeager may fall. As one young but wise tax advisor commented, "If it looks too good to be true, it probably isn't."

The author would like to take this opportunity to thank the many persons who have contributed so importantly to his own education. Their patience and assistance in bringing this project to fruition is deeply appreciated.

The options expressed are, of course, those of the author and in no way represent an official position of the institution with which he is associated.

RAY M. SOMMERFELD

Contents

1. An introduction   **1**

The morality of it all. Basic Terminology: *Exclusions. Deductions. Tax base. Tax rate. Tax credit.* The more important taxes. The elements of tax planning: *The law. The facts. An administrative and/or judicial process.* Tax avoidance versus tax evasion.

2. The income concept: General rules and common misconceptions   **15**

Gross income: *The realization criterion. Accounting methods. Constructive receipt. Form of payment. Indirect benefits. Illegal gains. Source of payment. Assignment of income. Exclusions.* Deductions: *Deductions and expenses compared. Accounting methods. Losses.*

3. Taxable entities   **41**

The individual taxpayer: *The married couple. The head of household. Single persons. Definitional problems. Planning opportunities.* The corporate taxpayer: *Legal entities. Economic realities. Legal definitions.* The fiduciary taxpayer. Other entities: *Partnerships. Hybrid organizations. Subchapter S corporations.* Entities and the taxable income concept: *Special corporate considerations. Special considerations for individual taxpayers.*

4. Tax aspects of selecting a business form   **68**

The basic tax constraints: *Maximum reinvestment of income. Retention of special income characteristics. Utilization of net operating losses. Employee status. Earned income. Gaining a special tax deduction. Disposition of a business. Fluctuating income.* Special considerations for multinational businesses: *Unincorporated businesses. Corporate businesses.*

ix

5. **Capital gains and losses: Basic rules** 95

Understanding the advantages: *Individual and fiduciary taxpayers. Corporate taxpayers. Illustrating the advantages.* Defining the boundaries: *Inventory assets. Real or depreciable property used in a trade or business. Copyrights. All other exceptions.* Measuring a capital gain or loss: *The tax basis of purchased property. The tax basis of property acquired by gift. The tax basis of inherited property.* Combining short-term and long-term capital gains and losses. The correct tax treatment of net capital losses: *Individual and fiduciary taxpayers. Corporate taxpayers.*

6. **Capital gains and losses: Some applications** 116

Definitional manipulation: *Modification of use involving a single taxable entity. Modification of use involving more than one taxable entity. Favorable price allocation in property transactions. Favorable interest rate in installment sales. The corporate quagmire. Statutory exceptions to "Normal" rules.* Timing considerations: *The year-end security review. The use of installment sales.*

7. **Compensation considerations** 143

Techniques providing an immediate corporate deduction and a benefit that is never taxed to the employee: *Group term life insurance. Health and accident plans. Group legal services. Meals and lodging. Death benefits. Other employee benefits. Travel and entertainment. Automobiles (and airplanes?). Employee discounts. Interest-free loans.* Techniques providing an immediate corporate deduction and a tax-deferred benefit to the employee: *Common characteristics of all qualified pension, profit-sharing, and stock bonus plans. Some important differences in qualified plans. Related considerations.* Techniques providing an immediate corporate deduction and an immediate tax to the employee: *Cash salary. Nonqualified stock options.* Techniques providing a deferred corporate deduction and a deferred tax to the employee. Techniques providing no corporate deduction but a tax to the employee: *Disguised dividends.* Special tax considerations for self-employed taxpayers: *Individual retirement accounts.* Summary.

8. **Tax factors in the acquisition, use, and disposition of fixed assets** 177

Fundamental relationships between tax laws, the present value concept, and simple economics. Tax factors pertinent to the acquisition of fixed assets: *Direct purchases. Indirect acquisitions through stock ownership. Leasing fixed assets. Constructing or otherwise creating fixed assets. The investment credit.* Tax factors pertinent to the use of fixed assets: *Depreciation methods. Depreciation method restrictions. Other special rules related to depreciation. Depletion methods. Expenditures during use—repair or improvement?* Tax factors pertinent to the disposition of fixed assets: *Capital gain or ordinary income? Investment credit recapture. Form of disposition.* An illustrative comparison of tax effects on investment decisions.

9. **Tax shelters**   **217**

Three additional tax provisions: *The minimum tax. Interaction between tax preferences and the maximum tax. The alternative minimum tax.* The essential ingredients of a tax shelter: *Leveraging. Preferential income tax provisions. Avoiding the corporate entity.* An illustration of a tax-sheltered investment under two alternative assumptions regarding return: *Alternative 1. Alternative 2.*

10. **The nontaxable transactions**   **247**

Common characteristics of nontaxable transactions: *The potential need to recognize some gain. Transfer of basis. Time constraints.* Specific nontaxable exchange provisions: *Exchange of productive-use or investment properties. Nontaxable transactions between a corporation and its shareholders. Involuntary conversions. Residence sales. Low-income housing. Other nontaxable exchanges.* Planning considerations in nontaxable transactions: *Three-cornered exchanges. Mortgaged properties. The role of intent.*

11. **Corporate reorganizations**   **276**

Basic definitions: *The type A reorganization. The type B reorganization. The type C reorganization. The type D reorganization. The type F reorganization.* Tax consequences: *The recognition of gain or loss. Basic rules.* Special problems: *Unwanted assets. Net operating losses. Contingent acquisitions. Liquidation-reincorporation. Debt-financed acquisitions.*

12. **Family tax planning**   **295**

Federal taxation of gifts: *Basic provisions. An illustration. Planning considerations.* Federal taxation of estates: *Basic provisions. An illustration. Planning considerations.* Integrating the income, gift, and estate taxes: *The importance of the marginal tax rate. The importance of the basis rules. Charitable gifts. Retirement income funds.*

13. **Accounting method options**   **333**

General methods of accounting: *The cash method. The accrual methods. The complete contract method. The installment method.* Accounting procedures and conventions: *Inventory costing conventions. The unit of account. Other convenient tax assumptions. The fiscal year. Records: Good and bad. One-time elections. Income averaging.*

14. Common tax traps   353

Judicial tax traps: Substance over form. Business purpose. Step transactions. Statutory tax traps: The accumulated earnings tax. The personal holding company tax. Collapsible corporations. The preferred stock bailout. Constructive ownership of stock. Allocation of income and deductions.

15. The taxing process   370

Compliance considerations: Filing tax returns. Returns selected for audit. Settling disputes. A summary observation. Taxpayer assistance: Questions of competence. Questions of cost. The tax future.

Code section index   387

Topical index   389

CHAPTER 1

An Introduction

Tax planning is a complex subject. That unfortunate conclusion does not mean, however, that the average person can never understand the fundamental concepts upon which successful tax plans are based. Rather, this complexity means that the average individual will have to be satisfied with understanding general rules and allow others who are more expert in tax matters to concern themselves with the details actually needed to implement any complex tax plan. Stated in another way, tax complexity means that the average U.S. citizen will have to be satisfied with a symptom-recognition level of knowledge.

The increasing dependence on symptom recognition combined with expert assistance is by no means unique to federal taxation. In the last two or three decades, virtually all Americans have come to rely upon expert assistance in fields as diverse as automobile mechanics and medicine. What is unusual in taxation is the relative scarcity of published materials that can be used as a general guide to overall tax planning. There are literally hundreds of books published each year on tax subjects, but most of those are either written for the expert or concerned with only one aspect of tax planning, such as investing in tax shelters, providing reasons for incorporating a business, or improving executive compensation. Unlike most of the other books, this one attempts to provide the reader with the broadest possible vista of tax planning opportunities and tax traps. Simply stated, the goal of this book is symptom recognition—for those who either manage a business or control wealth—a tax equivalent of Dr. Spock's well-known book on pediatric medicine for parents. The tax-conscious businessperson and the expert tax adviser, working closely together, can very often reduce an otherwise onerous tax burden to reasonable proportions.

Once each year the daily press dutifully reports the number of individual taxpayers who earned an income of $200,000 or more in the preceding year, but paid no taxes. That annual announcement triggers two basic emotions—namely, disgust for a tax system that allows it to happen and curiosity about how it might apply to us individually. This book is intended to help you understand how and why a significant tax reduction may be possible for you. In all candor, you should understand that the probabilities of your being able to reduce your own tax liability to zero are really very limited and not terribly important. What is far more important is that there are things that you may be able to do to reduce your tax liability substantially even though they will not reduce it to zero. Headlines and political interest may focus on the few wealthy individuals who reduce their income tax to nothing; fortunately, real economic success is not so demanding.

Before we go farther, the reader should understand that this book has limited immediate impact for the nonpropertied, salaried employee of a large corporation. The only reason for neglecting this person is the cold fact that relatively little can be done to save him or her significant amounts of taxes. Our income tax bears most heavily upon wage and salary earners simply because they have so few options available and because the tax laws have taken the necessary precautions to block most of those. Self-employed people, and especially people with substantial amounts of property, have an almost endless number of options, and because of the magnitude of those options, such people have many important opportunities for tax saving. Our primary concern will be with those opportunities.

The Morality of It All

No socially sensitive reader can escape subtle doubts about the morality of finding more and better ways to reduce his or her own tax liability when taxes are supposedly collected and then expended for the greatest common good. These doubts, however, might be resolved on at least two grounds. First, tax avoidance has been found by the courts to be wholly legal. Perhaps the most celebrated statement on this point was delivered in 1947 in the case of *Commissioner v. Newman.* In a dissenting opinion, Justice Learned Hand wrote: "Over and over again courts have said that there is nothing sinister in so arranging one's affairs as to keep taxes as low as possible. Everybody does so, rich or poor, and all do right, for nobody owes any public duty to pay more than the law demands: taxes are enforced exactions, not voluntary contributions. To demand more in the name of morals is mere cant."[1] Even though Justice Hand's words are from a dissenting opinion, and therefore of no legal value as precedent, they have been widely quoted as authoritative. Other legal opinions have reached the same conclusion, but have stated it in less colorful language.

Granting the legality of tax avoidance does not necessarily lead to the conclusion that it is in the country's best interest that knowledge of tax opportunities be more widely disseminated. However, there is even less to be said for restricting the knowledge of tax opportunities to any select few. All validated observations support the conclusion that the rich have been substantially more successful than the poor in tax avoidance. Nothing in this book is going to change that result because, as noted earlier, the mere ownership of property gives the wealthy taxpayer the large number of alternatives that make substantial tax savings possible. To the extent that this book facilitates greater utilization of existing tax opportunities, it will serve to diffuse the benefits of tax avoidance among a larger number of less wealthy people. If the results of these tax opportunities are finally deemed to be socially unacceptable by the masses, the widest possible dispersion of knowledge about them can only hasten the adoption of corrective political mechanisms.

Basic Terminology

Taxation, like every other discipline, relies upon some basic terminology to convey fundamental ideas. In tax plan-

---

[1] *Commissioner v. Newman,* 159 F. 2d 848 (CCA–2, 1947).

ning, understanding a few common terms is essential. Among the most critical words and phrases are the following: *exclusion, deduction, tax base, tax rate,* and *tax credit.* Virtually every successful plan to save taxes is based on the manipulation of one or more of these variables. Because the concepts behind these words and phrases are so critical to tax-saving opportunities, it seems advisable to clarify their meaning before we turn our attention to more specific details.

Exclusions

In tax parlance the word *exclusion* is used to refer to any item that, in ordinary English usage, would be considered part of a more general class of items or events that has been made the basis for a tax but has been specifically removed from the tax base by law. For example, the sales tax imposed by most of the states in the United States is technically imposed on all retail sales. At the same time, virtually all of the state legislatures have decided to exclude from the sales tax base all sales of foodstuffs for off-premise consumption. Thus, the retail sales of food items in a grocery store frequently constitute an exclusion from the more general retail sales tax base.

In tax planning, one of the simplest and most effective methods of tax minimization involves the maximization of exclusions. As you might suspect, the list of exclusions is typically very brief, and therefore the amount of tax-planning potential in this area is rather limited. Our federal income tax does provide one very major exclusion. It does not tax the interest earned by taxpayers who invest their capital in a state or local government's bonds. Consequently, investors can reduce their federal income tax liability on passive income to zero simply by switching their investment portfolios from corporate stocks and securities to state and local government bonds. The major economic cost that attaches to this simple tax-saving plan is the reduced earnings that usually result because of the tax-exempt feature. That is, state and local government bonds typically pay lower rates of interest than do bonds of equivalent risk precisely because high-tax-bracket investors are willing to accept lower rates of interest that go tax-free in preference to higher rates of interest that produce a lower aftertax return on their investment. To illustrate, the taxpayer in a 50 percent marginal tax bracket is better off investing in 6 percent state bonds than in 10 percent commercial paper because his or her aftertax return remains at 6 percent in the former instance but is reduced to 5 percent in the latter case. A taxpayer in the 30 percent marginal tax bracket would not, of course, reach the same conclusion.

Deductions

In tax literature, the word *deduction* is used to refer to any item that the law authorizes as a reduction of a gross quantity to a net quantity designated as a tax base. Because both exclusions and deductions serve to reduce the net tax base, it is very easy to confuse the two concepts. For purposes of interpreting and applying certain tax rules, however, it is important that a clear distinction be maintained. As a simple illustration of this difference, consider the need of two taxpayers to file a federal income tax return. Taxpayer A earns $50,000 in interest on State of California bonds but incurs no authorized expenses in connection with that income. Taxpayer B earns $50,000 in rents from an apartment house and incurs $50,000 in deductions for depreciation, property taxes, interest, maintenance costs, and so forth. The law provides that a single taxpayer must generally file an income tax return if his or her gross income exceeds some *de minimus* amount, currently $3,300. Application of this filing requirement provision means that taxpayer A need *not* file a return but that taxpayer B must. A has a gross income of zero because his or her income can be excluded from the gross tax base by definition. B has a gross income of $50,000 since his or her expenses are only deductions from the gross tax base. Neither A nor B, of course, will pay income tax if this is their only source of income, since both will have a net tax base of zero.

Obviously, taxes can be minimized to the extent that deductions can be maximized. The first step in maximizing deductions consists of learning which items are deductible simply to avoid overlooking one or more authorized deductions. Sometimes maximizing deductions may also require the rearrangement of one's business affairs and the creation of a particular form of business organization. The tax-saving value of a deduction is also directly related to the marginal tax bracket of the taxpayer incurring it. Thus a taxpayer in the 70 percent marginal tax bracket will save $7,000 in income taxes for every additional $10,000 in deductions that he or she may claim; a taxpayer in the 22 percent marginal tax bracket would save only $2,200 in taxes from an equivalent deduction. It is therefore important that the taxpayer ensure, to the extent possible, that all authorized deductions are incurred at the most advantageous time (for example, in an unusually high income year) or by the most advantageous taxpayer (for example, by an individual rather than a corporation under certain circumstances).

Tax Base

The term *tax base* simply refers to the net quantity on which any particular tax is levied. For purposes of income taxation that net quantity is called *taxable income;* for estate taxation, *taxable estate;* and for gift taxation, *taxable gifts.* The key word in each instance is the adjective *taxable.* What it connotes, of course, is that the residual quantity is the dollar value that remains after the taxpayer has given adequate consideration to all pertinent definitional problems, exclusions, and deductions. Careful attention to these three items makes possible the minimization of any tax base.

A taxpayer may be able to further minimize a tax liability by making certain that the tax base is divided among the maximum number of taxable entities. Because the tax rates utilized in income and estate and gift taxation are progressive rates—that is, the marginal tax rates get higher as the tax base increases in amount—it is generally to the taxpayer's benefit to split a tax base among a number of taxable entities. Each reporting unit may therefore begin by applying the rates at the lowest possible level rather than have a single entity report the entire tax base and thus be forced to apply higher and higher marginal tax rates to the same aggregate amount of tax base.

Tax Rate

A *tax rate* is a specified percentage, or series of percentages in the case of a progressive tax, which the law stipulates as the appropriate multiplier in the determination of a gross tax liability. Stated another way, any tax liability is calculated by multiplying the tax base by the statutory tax rate(s). For example, a state legislature may stipulate that it will utilize a 5 percent tax rate in determining the retail sales tax liability in a particular year. In that event anyone who purchases a $100 item that is subject to the retail sales tax will pay a sales tax of $5 on his purchase ($100 × 5 percent).

In income taxation, Congress has specified four different rate schedules for individual taxpayers (one each for single persons, heads of households, married persons filing jointly, and married persons filing separately), another totally different rate structure for corporate taxpayers, and yet another rate schedule for fiduciaries (i.e., for estates and trusts). Obviously, then, the tax liability of a taxpayer with a given amount of income will change automatically any time that the taxpayer rearranges his or her affairs so that a different rate schedule will be applied to that amount of income. Perhaps the most obvious rearrangement is marriage: a single individual earning a taxable income of $60,000 can currently reduce his or her annual tax liability from $23,943 to $19,678 simply by getting married *to a person who has no taxable income to report*. This illustration also demonstrates clearly the importance and complexity of the nontax considerations that must often be weighed before rushing headlong into perfectly legal tax-planning ideas. In addition, this illustration emphasizes the importance of details to tax conclusions because, for example, the marriage of two single persons, each earning a $30,000 taxable income, will actually increase their combined tax liability from $15,924 to $19,678.

Congress has also designated that certain special "kinds" of income shall be eligible for special tax rates. For individual taxpayers, income can be classified in one of three ways: personal service income, certain capital gain income, or other income. The special rates that are available for special kinds of income differ for different taxpayers. Furthermore, each special rate necessitates a special definition of exactly which income items shall be eligible for that rate and which shall be excluded from it. Several tax-saving opportunities exist because taxpayers may be able to achieve a reclassification of their income from a less privileged to a more privileged class.

Tax Credit

A *tax credit* is any specially authorized reduction in a gross tax liability. Note that tax credits are fundamentally different from deductions and exclusions even though all three items are subtracted at one point or another in the tax calculation procedure. A $500 tax credit reduces a gross tax liability by the full $500; a $500 deduction will reduce a tax liability by some smaller amount, the specific reduction being determined by the marginal tax rate of the taxpayer authorized to claim the deduction. Once again the list of tax credits is typically small. For the entrepreneur, the most important tax credit is the investment credit. At present the income tax law authorizes a variable tax credit based on purchases of specified assets. By a careful selection of assets, by giving attention to the determination of those assets' estimated life, and by carefully timing their disposition, a taxpayer can change the dollar amount of the investment credit and thus substantially modify a tax liability.

To summarize the basic terminology introduced in this chapter, we might construct the following simple computational guide to illustrate the various steps followed in the tax determination process.

> A gross measure of any general class of items or events declared a tax base by legislative action minus *exclusions* equals the gross tax base.
>
> The gross tax base minus *deductions* equals the *net tax base*.
>
> The *net tax base* multiplied by the *specified tax rate(s)* equals the gross tax liability.
>
> The gross tax liability minus *tax credits* equals the net tax payable to the government.

As you consider the various tax-saving propositions detailed in the remaining chapters, you should attempt to categorize each one in the context of this computational guide. In other words, you should ask yourself exactly why that particular tax saving is made possible. You will very often discover that the answer depends upon the combined effect of two or more variables; for example, by a timely maximization of deductions, the taxpayer may be able to modify the effective tax rate in a most favorable manner. The reason for attempting to place each idea in this perspective is simply that, by the act of analyzing each illustration carefully, you will become attuned to the often simple differences that constitute a common thread among all tax-saving opportunities. The sooner you can identify these common threads, the sooner you will be able to apply the same basic idea to your own particular situation.

The More Important Taxes

The U.S. tax structure differs significantly from those in most other countries because it depends so heavily on the income tax. Excluding social insurance contributions—more commonly known as Social Security taxes—approximately 63 percent of all tax revenues collected in the United States come from an income tax, 19 percent from sales tax, 12 percent from property taxes, and the remaining 6 percent from all other taxes combined. In most other countries, the indirect taxes—that is, the sales, property, and excise taxes—play the dominant role, while the income tax is of lesser importance. Because the federal income tax plays such a dominant role in the United States, and because it is so readily subject to managerial manipulation, our primary attention in this book will be given to that one tax, which, incidentally, provides nearly $1 billion in federal revenue every day of the year! Most other taxes—such as state and city income taxes, sales taxes, property taxes, real estate transfer taxes, customs duties, and excise taxes—will be wholly dismissed from consideration. The only nonincome tax discussed here is the federal donative transfers tax, which, until 1976, was really two separate taxes: the federal estate tax and the federal gift tax. Although the federal donative transfers tax plays a modest role in our total tax structure, it can be of major significance to those few people who either inherit or accumulate substantial amounts of wealth. Furthermore, it too is generally amenable to successful tax planning techniques. We will, therefore, consider the fundamentals of tax planning for the federal donative transfers tax in

Chapter 12. With that one major exception, however, all the remaining chapters of this book are primarily concerned with tax planning for the U.S. federal income tax.

The Elements of Tax Planning

An *element* may be defined as the fundamental unit that, singly or in combination with other elements, constitutes all matter. Using that definition, the world of tax planning might be divided into three elements:

1. The law.
2. The facts.
3. An administrative and (sometimes) judicial process.

Singly, or in combination, these three elements constitute the essential ingredients of every tax plan.

The Law

The current statutory law of federal income taxation is technically known as the Internal Revenue Code of 1954 (as amended to date). Unfortunately, that legal document is approximately 1,700 pages long. To make matters worse, some portions of the code are nearly unintelligible, even for those whose native tongue is English. As one example, consider the first sentence of Section 2613(a)(1), which reads as follows:

> The term "taxable distribution" means any distribution which is not out of the income of the trust (within the meaning of section 643(b)) from a generation-skipping trust to any younger generation beneficiary who is assigned to a generation younger than the generation assignment of any other person who is a younger generation beneficiary.

Because the code is filled with such obtuse language, and because the primary objective of this book is restricted to the recognition of major income tax opportunities, we fortunately will devote minimal attention to the exact words of the statute. Nevertheless, in following this approach, you should always remember two things. First, even the best paraphrased general rules are not the words of the code, and they may be misleading in a few circumstances. Second, the law itself is constantly being revised by the Congress. The latter observation is important for two reasons. First, it means that one or more tax planning ideas discussed here could be made obsolete at any time. It also implies one legal, albeit unusual, method of tax planning: In rare circumstances, a few persons may actually get Congress to change the extant law so that it will be more favorable to their situation. The second element in tax planning is more readily modified by anyone.

The Facts

Most successful tax planning involves nothing more sophisticated than a rearrangement of some intended events. Taxpayers who enter into unfamiliar business transactions without the aid of a competent tax adviser very frequently reach an unfavorable tax result. Tax liabilities ordinarily depend upon what taxpayers actually do, not on what they intended to do. Because competent tax advisers understand the importance of facts to tax results, they frequently are able to recommend a method of achieving a tax-preferred result by a sometimes simple rearrangement of facts *before* they transpire. For example, the distribution of $1 million in corporate assets by a financially successful corporation to its owners might be subject to an individual income tax of anything from zero (i.e., no tax) to $700,000. If the distribution is a repayment of a corporate security—created through foresight when the business was first incorporated—there would be no income tax to the recipient because the $1 million would represent a return of capital. On the other hand, if the original incorporators failed to include adequate debt in the original capital structure of the corporation, the subsequent distribution of $1 million would very likely be treated as an ordinary dividend and be subject to an individual income tax of up to 70 percent. As this one illustration suggests, the importance of facts to tax planning can never be overestimated.

An Administrative and/or Judicial Process

No system of taxation will function smoothly without independent administrative and judicial authorities. By definition, a tax necessarily transfers control over a certain amount of wealth from the private to the public sector. Because taxpayers nearly always desire to minimize their own tax liability, and thereby maximize their personal wealth, someone must enforce the laws that accomplish this transfer. Furthermore, because the code is so complex, someone must officially interpret and translate that document for public consumption. These basic tasks of law enforcement and interpretation have been assigned to the Internal Revenue Service, which is part of the Treasury Department.

The administrative interpretations that ordinarily carry the greatest authority are known as Treasury regulations. They represent the government's interpretation of the Internal Revenue Code, stated in general terms that are intended to have broad application to many taxpayers. The government will also respond to an inquiry from a specific taxpayer asking for an interpretation of the law in very detailed circumstances. These latter interpretations take the form of private letter rulings and sometimes revenue rulings. In the last few years, all the private rulings have been made available to the general public, but only the revenue rulings are published and distributed by the Government Printing Office. Although everyone can rely on Treasury regulations as authoritative, only the taxpayer who made the request for a private ruling can firmly rely on that interpretation, and, even in that instance, the private ruling will be deemed authoritative (i.e., controlling) only if the taxpayer revealed all facts openly and in complete detail.

Taxpayers frequently disagree with the IRS interpretation of the code; if carried to their extreme, such disagreements can only lead to litigation. As explained in Chapter 15, tax litigation can be initiated in any one of three courts: the Tax Court, a federal district court, or the Court of Claims. The decisions of the first two courts can be further appealed to a circuit court of appeals. And, finally, the decisions of both the Court of Claims and any circuit court of appeals may be appealed to the U.S. Supreme Court. Thus a diverse array of interpretative authority exists on tax matters, and all of this is properly considered a part of the tax law. The initial interpretation, however, remains within the province of the IRS.

The IRS is not, however, given carte blanche in matters of taxation. It does represent the government's interest, but its interpretations and administrative actions are also subject to judicial review whenever challenged by a taxpayer. Even though the administrative and judicial processes are not ordinarily subject to manipulation in the same manner as the law and the facts, every taxpayer should carefully consider the very human nature of the administrative and judicial processes in tax planning. This warning may translate simply as "too much is still too much." In other words, even if a tax plan seems otherwise to be entirely within the law, if it is abhorrent to human sensitivities, it just *may* fail when put to the human test implicit in every administrative or judicial hearing. This element in tax planning will be examined in greater detail in Chapter 15. In all the other chapters, we will constrain our attention to matters of fact and law, the two more malleable elements.

Tax Avoidance versus Tax Evasion

Finally, every reader should understand that the contents of this book are restricted to wholly legal methods of tax minimization. Legitimate means of reducing taxes are known as tax avoidance; illegal means to the same end are called tax evasion. Thus, for example, this book does not recommend that a taxpayer simply fail to report an income-producing cash transaction, even though the low probability of an IRS audit that might uncover such a transaction is noted in the final chapter. Tax evasion is characterized by fraud and deceit; tax avoidance, by open and full disclosure. That difference does not imply, however, that legal tax planning is always a cut and dried affair. Many tax avoidance plans involve major questions of judgment; the conclusions of the IRS agents and those of the taxpayer may very well differ. Those who engage in tax planning must assume the potential risk of litigation if they are to be successful in some circumstances. The areas of tax avoidance in which disagreements are common will be discussed in this book so that a taxpayer might better assess the wisdom of proceeding with a questionable course of action.

This concludes our introduction to tax planning. Chapters 2 and 3 lay the statutory groundwork for most of the tax planning ideas developed in Chapter 4. In the same manner, Chapter 5 explains the tax law that must be understood before the ideas developed in Chapter 6 can have meaning. In most of the remaining chapters, the tax law and the planning concepts common to many specific business decisions are developed within the confines of a single chapter. These latter chapters, therefore, can be read independently. The author recommends, however, that every reader read the next two chapters before pursuing any specific topic developed later.

CHAPTER 2

The Income Concept: General Rules and Common Misconceptions

Perhaps the most accurate but least useful definition of taxable income is that attributed to unnamed skeptics who have suggested that taxable income is what the Internal Revenue Code says it is and nothing more pretentious. In lieu of such useless accuracy, this chapter will attempt to simplify and restate some of the more important general rules used to measure income for tax purposes. These general rules tend to be harsh in their application. The reader should not, however, give up hope too early. Most of the remaining chapters explain how taxpayers may be able to mitigate the generally harsh criteria established in this chapter.

Virtually all readers of this book have had some exposure to the income concept. If nothing else, most of them will have filed their own tax returns at one time or another. Some readers will have examined or even prepared an income statement for a business enterprise. Notwithstanding those experiences, this chapter will review some basic elements of the income concept as it is applied in federal income tax matters. Primary attention will be given to the basic concepts that are most frequently misunderstood or misapplied in particular circumstances. The chapter is divided into two major sections. The first section deals with gross income, the positive element in income determination. The second section deals with tax deductions, the negative element in income determination. Taxable income is, of course, the arithmetic difference between the aggregate number used to represent gross income and the aggregate number used to represent deductions.

Gross Income

Before we even attempt to define *gross income*, the reader should get accustomed to the first basic rule of federal income taxation. That is, *all income is taxable income unless the taxpayer can find good authority for excluding it*. To help the reader interpret this basic rule as it applies to gross income, the next several pages will be used to consider some of the more important corollary rules used to implement the basic rule in specific circumstances. These corollary rules explain the importance of the realization criterion, the insignificance of the form of payment, the unimportance of the direct or indirect status of a benefit received, and the relative significance of accounting methods, statutory exclusions, and assignment-of-income principles.

The Realization Criterion

Stated in its simplest form, the realization criterion says that mere appreciation in value will not be considered to constitute taxable income. Alternatively, it says that income will not be recognized for tax purposes until it has been realized. The reader must be careful to avoid misinterpretation of the alternative definition; the realization criterion does *not* say that an increase in cash, or even an increase in current assets, is a precondition to income. Income is generally associated with an increase in net wealth, and most increases in wealth, unless attributable to mere appreciation in value, do constitute taxable income. However, an increase in wealth in the current year is not essential to the presence of taxable income. To illustrate this conclusion, assume that a taxpayer purchased common stocks 15 years ago and that these stocks steadily increased in value for the first 9 years and then remained constant in value for the next 6 years. In the first nine years of ownership, the taxpayer would not report any taxable income even though the stocks might have appreciated from their cost of $10,000 to a value of $100,000. In the next six years, the taxpayer would not perceive that he or she had any income, excluding the possibility of dividends, because the stock value failed to increase further. If, however, at the end of the 15th year, the taxpayer exchanged those stocks for a plot of land, for other stocks or bonds, or for almost any other property, the taxpayer would be deemed to have realized the $90,000 income that had previously gone unrecognized. Even though this taxpayer had realized no increase in net wealth during the six years prior to the exchange, and even though the property the taxpayer took in exchange for the stock was relatively unmarketable, he or she would have to recognize the entire $90,000 taxable income in the one year in which the exchange was made. That conclusion is the essence of the realization concept.

Virtually any change in the form or the substance of a property or property right is sufficient to constitute realization for income tax purposes. To the frequent surprise of taxpayers, income may be realized when others forgive their outstanding debts, when they win a prize in a contest, when they embezzle funds, when they incorporate their extant business, when they divide property with an ex-spouse in a divorce action, or when they find a treasure trove on their property. Because realization is such a pervasive concept, and because the income tax is a concomitant facet of realization, a taxpayer should always consult an adviser on the potential tax consequences that may attach to any intended action that could modify the form or the substance of any of the taxpayer's property rights.

Accounting Methods

The subject of accounting methods will be considered in greater depth in Chapter 13. At this early juncture we need only note that the code technically provides that taxable income shall be computed on the same basis of accounting as taxpayers use in maintaining their regular set of books. This provision, unfortunately, is often as misleading as it is helpful when applied to the notion of gross income. Most noncorporate taxpayers operate on a cash basis of accounting, and this sometimes causes them to conclude that they need not report any taxable income unless and until they receive cash. This conclusion is not justified in many circumstances. A taxpayer on a cash basis of accounting will utilize a cash-receipts test only to determine the proper year of reporting such routine items of income as wages, salary, interest, dividends, and rents. The same cash-receipts test will not apply to such nonrecurring transactions as the sale of an investment or the sale of a home. In all nonroutine transactions, the tax authorities will apply a *cash-equivalence* rule and proceed as if cash were received in an amount equal to the value of the noncash property received on the disposition. Return momentarily to the earlier illustration in which a taxpayer exchanged stocks worth $100,000 for, say, a plot of speculative desert land; even if that taxpayer were ordinarily a cash-basis taxpayer, the authorities would insist that the land received must have been worth $100,000 and would tax it accordingly. Tax administrators generally assume that a taxpayer will not enter into an exchange unless an equivalent value is received. Hence, they tend to value the most easily valued property and assume the value equivalence for the other item exchanged. Special rules are applied to transactions between related taxpayers where there is reason to believe that an exchange was not made at arm's length.

Constructive Receipt

A taxpayer on the cash method of accounting will occasionally attempt to postpone the recognition of even routine taxable income by refusing to exercise domination over funds received. A taxpayer might, for example, defer picking up a paycheck until January 2, refuse to open an envelope known to contain a dividend check until the first day of a new year, or fail to withdraw or record interest that had accumulated on a savings account in the current year. In each of these situations, the tax rules would find that the income in question was taxable in the current year because it had been constructively received. Whenever a taxpayer has the authority to exercise control over the income, he or she has constructively received it, regardless of when the actual exercise of power or domination is completed.

The tax authorities occasionally stretch the concept of constructive receipt well beyond the boundaries of common sense. For example, employees of many state agencies are required by law to participate in a state retirement program.

Frequently this participation requires a "contribution" from the employee, which can be regained and enjoyed only upon (1) quitting the job, (2) retiring, or (3) dying. A reasonable person might well argue that such an employee does not have constructive receipt over the withheld portion of the salary until he or she quits, retires, or dies. The tax authorities disagree, and the courts sustain their contention that the full salary, including any amounts withheld, is fully taxable when earned. Their conclusion apparently rests upon the belief that the taxpayer does receive an indirect benefit immediately (the knowledge that he or she is covered by a retirement program) and that the value of the benefit is equal to the amount withheld from the salary. Alternatively, the true rationale may be that the taxing authorities and the courts realize that any other interpretation would be very costly to the government, as well as highly inflationary. Since it may be unduly costly to correct an error of long standing, bad decisions may become permanent decisions.

Form of Payment

As previously observed, the asset form in which a taxpayer receives income is wholly immaterial to the tax consequence. A wage is equally taxable whether it is paid in the form of a case of good scotch, a book, or cash. Noncash payments necessitate the determination of a fair market value. This may create administrative problems in obtaining agreement between the taxpayer and the Internal Revenue Service (IRS) agent. Typically the taxpayer will undervalue the asset received and the IRS agent will overvalue it. Both parties realize that a reasonable estimate can usually be agreed upon during the administrative or judicial proceedings that accompany a tax dispute.

The author has known numerous instances in which taxpayers erroneously believed that they had cleverly avoided the income tax by taking their rewards in noncash forms. Three illustrations may be helpful. In one instance, a university professor took pride in the fact that he always elected to receive the honorarium for speeches in the form of personally selected books, which he added to his library. In the second instance, a dentist exchanged services with his laundryman neighbor.

That is, the dentist kept the teeth of the laundryman and his family in good repair in exchange for free laundry and drycleaning services for the dentist and his family. The third instance involved a new corporate venture in which the young entrepreneurs took their compensation in the form of corporate stocks. Legally the professor, the dentist, and the entrepreneurs all realized taxable income in an amount equal to the fair market value of the goods or services that they received. In each instance the taxpayer erroneously failed to report the income received, and in each instance the error went undetected by the IRS. The chances of the IRS uncovering such an error are admittedly small. Nevertheless, the reader should understand clearly that each of these intended tax-saving plans could be considered fraudulent and that each of the taxpayers could end up in a federal penitentiary for tax evasion. Any tax adviser who condones or recommends such tax planning is grossly incompetent, as well as a party to fraud, and should be dismissed immediately.

Indirect Benefits

The relative insignificance in tax matters of the form of payment also extends to the direct or indirect status of any benefit received. A taxpayer must recognize as part of his or her own taxable income any amounts earned that are paid directly to another person. Suppose, for example, that a physician were to direct a patient to make his or her payment directly to the physician's grandchild. Even though the physician never received any cash for the service rendered, he or she would be taxed fully on the amount paid to the grandchild by the patient. The tax authorities would determine the tax liability just as if the physician had received the fee and had immediately made a gift of it to the grandchild.

The indirect-benefit concept is sometimes more difficult to apply than the previous illustration would suggest. Corporations often expend rather large sums of money for the apparent benefit of their employees. The corporation may purchase, for example, life, health, and accident insurance policies, recreational facilities, pension plans, and other perquisites. Whether or not the indirect benefits from these corporate purchases will be taxed to the employee depends upon a host of special rules.

In general it is safest to assume that all benefits received, directly and indirectly, do constitute gross income. In Chapter 6, we will learn why and how employee benefits in particular may be one of the most promising ways for many taxpayers to achieve substantial tax savings in a wholly legal fashion.

Illegal Gains

Profits obtained from illegal activities are just as taxable as those earned from legitimate activities. As a matter of fact, income tax evasion has been made the basis for legal prosecution in instances where the government seemed unable to obtain a conviction on other grounds. In recognition of this fact, some underworld characters take unusual precautions to maintain an excellent set of financial records. In the absence of good records, the IRS is authorized to use relatively crude methods of estimating a taxpayer's income, and, just to be safe, these estimates are often on the high side. To illustrate, the income of a house of prostitution has been estimated on the basis of a commercial laundry's records, apparently after an IRS special agent determined the modus operandi of the house. In any legal dispute over a tax liability, the burden of proving the IRS estimates wrong usually rests with the taxpayer. Without records, the taxpayer is hard pressed to defeat the commissioner's estimates of gross income.

Although well beyond the scope of this book, and beyond the expertise of the author, the concurrent legal problems created by the need to report illegal gains for income tax purposes appear to be substantial. To what extent the Justice Department should be given access to tax files for purposes other than tax litigation is an interesting question. The danger of self-incrimination is obvious. Any taxpayer receiving illegal gains—whether from the sale of narcotics, gambling, extortion, embezzlement, or air piracy—should realize that he or she badly needs a good tax *attorney* as well as a good criminal lawyer.

The word *attorney* was italicized in the prior sentence for good reason. In Chapter 1 the need for a good tax *adviser* was emphasized. Most qualified tax advisers are either lawyers or certified public accountants. To date, the concept of privileged communication has not been extended under federal law to the

CPA. It is extremely important, therefore, that income tax records from *criminal* activities be handled initially by an attorney. The attorney can engage a CPA on behalf of a client if appropriate and thereby extend the attorney's privileged communication to the accountant's workpapers.

Source of Payment

Even well-educated taxpayers occasionally get the notion that certain receipts will not be taxed if they are paid by a particular kind of taxpayer. A prominent university professor, for example, believed that he was correct in not reporting his summer compensation for income tax purposes because it had been paid to him by a tax-exempt research organization. As a matter of fact, the taxable status of the organization making a payment is seldom of significance in determining the tax consequences of the payment to the recipient. In the case of this professor, a portion of the money received could be excluded under some very special rules for fellowship grants, but not simply because they were paid by a tax-exempt organization.

Other taxpayers have been amazed to learn that income paid by a foreign entity and received in a foreign country may be subject to the U.S. income tax. We have what is known as a global income tax. This means that U.S. citizens and resident aliens, including all domestic corporations, are generally subject to the U.S. income tax regardless of where their income is earned, paid, or received. Nonresident aliens—that is, citizens of another country who are not physically in the United States and who may never have been here—are also subject to the U.S. income tax, but only on their income from U.S. sources. Needless to say, the rules applicable to the taxation of multinational transactions are doubly complex. Often a single income stream is subject to taxation by more than one country. This necessitates a series of tax treaties and other tax credit provisions to avoid double taxation. The code does provide limited relief for income earned abroad by individual taxpayers under prescribed conditions. A few of the more important aspects of multinational transactions will be discussed later in this book. Suffice it to observe here that the source of an income payment is generally not pertinent to the determination of tax consequences to the recipient.

Assignment of Income

Sometimes the most difficult tax problem is not in determining whether or not a particular receipt constitutes gross income but in identifying whose income it is. Because the detailed discussion of taxable entities is deferred to Chapter 3, this discussion of assignment-of-income problems will necessarily be very brief. Income ordinarily derives from one or more of three events: (1) the rendering of a service, (2) the disposition of a property, or (3) the payment by one person for the use of another's property. For some analytic purposes, we combine the last two notions into a single class and say that income is derived either from services or from property (or capital).

Initially it seems clear that income derived from the rendering of a service must be reported by the person rendering that service and that income derived from property must be reported by the person who owns (or holds legal title to) that property. One need not venture far into the world of business to discover how useless these concepts are for determining tax consequences. Applied literally, they would say that every employee should report the gross value of his or her services notwithstanding the fact that he or she personally may receive only some fractional share of that value. A study of taxation would further prove that our concepts of property and services are amazingly ill-defined. Much of the intrigue of tax planning comes from the sometimes deliberate confusion of those ill-defined concepts.

To illustrate this tax confusion briefly, consider the income earned by an entertainer or an athlete. If this individual goes about the conduct of his or her business simply and solely as an individual, there is not much doubt that any fees received for services rendered will be attributed and taxed to him or her personally. If this same individual incorporates his or her talent, and then the corporation negotiates for all appearance contracts, is the income received by the corporation taxable to it or to the person as an individual?

Or take another example. If an individual spends his or her time writing music or tinkering with mechanical devices, and if he or she subsequently obtains a copyright for a musical score or a patent for a gadget, is the income received attributable to a service (writing music or tinkering with mechanical devices) or to a property (a copyright or a patent)?

Finally, consider the father who clipped a series of interest coupons from some bonds and made a gift of those coupons, but not of the bonds, to his son. Is the interest paid to the son, at the maturity date of the interest coupons, taxable to the son as the owner of the coupons or to the father as the owner of the bonds from which the coupons were clipped?

These three brief illustrations suggest both the breadth of opportunity for tax planning and the need for expert assistance. The answers to the questions are not always clear-cut. As you will discover later in this book, the corporate veil is sometimes, but not always, pierced, so that the income earned by a corporation may or may not be attributed and taxed to the individual owner. Gains from the sale of patents get a favorable tax treatment, as a capital gain from a property disposition, whereas gains from the sale of a copyright are taxed in the same way as income earned directly by an individual. Income from property may be transferred to another taxpayer without transferring the basic property, but only if several special conditions are met. All of these problems are discussed later in more depth.

Exclusions

Our final consideration pertinent to the gross income concept will consist of a brief review of the items of economic income that are not deemed to constitute gross income for tax purposes. The vast majority of these exclusions are statutory in origin. Before we turn our attention to the statutory exclusions, however, we might note in passing the few exclusions that exist by judicial or administrative interpretation. As a class, virtually no items of imputed income are deemed to constitute gross income. Economists in particular like to point out the reality of such items of imputed income as owner-occupied homes, home-produced and home-consumed foods, and the services of the housewife. Even though the value of these items could be imputed, and even though not taxing them may create an inequity between homeowners and renters, between farmer-gardeners and city dwellers, and between housewives and career wives, the U.S. income tax has never been extended to items of imputed income on the ground that such an extension would be administratively difficult to implement.

Administrative interpretation has also excluded from the tax base social security payments (unless received from a foreign government) and most public assistance payments. Tax administrators apparently believe that it would not constitute desirable government policy to tax away part of the payments made by welfare agencies designed to help people deemed to be in particular need.

Most statutory exclusions are contained in Sections 101 through 128. Even a cursory reading of the section titles will suggest how narrow in application some of the exclusions really are. Because this book is intended as a layperson's introduction to tax planning, rather than as a complete treatise on tax rules, many of these items will not be discussed. Consideration of the exclusions of more general interest to tax planning is deferred to subsequent chapters for pedagogic reasons. For example, the discussion of all exclusions requiring that the recipient be an employee is deferred to Chapter 6, where these exclusions can be treated as part of the larger problem of compensation considerations. Before we begin a discussion of the remaining items of general interest, it may be desirable for the reader to review the titles of the sections that create the statutory exclusions. These titles are:

Sec. 101. Certain death payments.
Sec. 102. Gifts and inheritances.
Sec. 103. Interest on certain governmental obligations.
Sec. 104. Compensation for injuries or sickness.
Sec. 105. Amounts received under accident and health plans.
Sec. 106. Contributions by employer to accident and health plans.
Sec. 107. Rental value of parsonages.
Sec. 108. Income from discharge of indebtedness.
Sec. 109. Improvements by lessee on lessor's property.
Sec. 110. Income taxes paid by lessee corporation.
Sec. 111. Recovery of bad debts, prior taxes, and delinquency amounts.
Sec. 112. Certain combat pay of members of the armed forces.
Sec. 113. Mustering-out payments for members of the armed forces.

Sec. 114. Sports programs conducted for the American National Red Cross.
Sec. 115. Income of states, municipalities, and so on.
Sec. 116. Partial exclusion of dividends received by individuals.
Sec. 117. Scholarships and fellowship grants.
Sec. 118. Contributions to the capital of a corporation.
Sec. 119. Meals or lodging furnished for the convenience of the employer.
Sec. 120. Amounts received under qualified group legal service plans.
Sec. 121. Gain from sale or exchange of residence of individual who has attained age 55.
Sec. 122. Certain reduced uniformed services retirement pay.
Sec. 123. Amounts received under insurance contracts for certain living expenses.
Sec. 124. Qualified transportation provided by employer.
Sec. 125. Cafeteria plans.
Sec. 126. Certain cost—sharing payments.
Sec. 127. Educational assistance programs.
Sec. 128. Cross references to other acts.

Other statutory exclusions are scattered throughout the code in such diverse sections as:

Sec. 37. Retirement income. (Technically this provision is worded as a tax credit for the elderly, rather than as an exclusion, but it has the same effect as an exclusion.)
Sec. 74(b). Prizes and awards. (The exception, which is tantamount to an exclusion, is contained in subsection [b].)
Sec. 79(a). Group-term life insurance purchased for employees.
Sec. 621. Payments to encourage exploration, development, and mining for defense purposes.
Sec. 872(b). Gross income. (Subsection [b] deals with special exclusions for nonresident aliens.)
Sec. 892. Income of foreign governments and of international organizations.
Sec. 893. Compensation of employees of foreign governments or international organizations.
Sec. 911. Income earned by individuals in certain camps.

Sec. 912. Exemptions for certain allowances. (This section contains special rules for foreign service officers and Peace Corps volunteers.)

Sec. 933. Income from sources within Puerto Rico.

Simply reading this list should help to sensitize the reader to any personal situation for which an unusual exclusion may apply. It should also emphasize the relatively restricted scope of most exclusion provisions. The most common exclusions will be discussed in greater detail in later chapters. In this chapter, we will consider briefly the exclusions for prizes, gifts and bequests, state and local bond interest, scholarship and fellowship grants, and the rental value of parsonages.

Prizes. Section 74(b) provides an exception to the general rule that gross income includes any amounts received as a prize or award. That general rule is stated in subsection (a). The exception reads as follows:

> Gross income does not include amounts received as prizes and awards made primarily in recognition of religious, charitable, scientific, educational, artistic, literary, or civic achievement, but only if (1) the recipient was selected without any action on his part to enter the contest or proceeding; and (2) the recipient is not required to render substantial future services as a condition to receiving the prize or award.

The general rule of subsection (a) clearly makes taxable such awards as door prizes, raffles, and television quiz show bounty. Equally clearly, the exception in subsection (b) excludes from gross income the stipend attached to a Pulitzer or Nobel prize. As our introduction to the vast wasteland of statutory interpretation, however, let us consider a real problem that lies somewhere between the more obvious extremes. Paul Hornung was given an automobile by a publishing company because of his prowess on the football field. Could the value of this automobile be excluded by Hornung under the authority of subsection (b)? In other words, would such an award be considered to be an "award . . . in recognition of . . . artistic . . . achievement"? The court said no. Apparently the court concluded that playing football—even the way Paul Hornung played it—was not an artistic achievement within the meaning of the code. Could it, then, be excluded as a gift?

Gifts and inheritances. Section 102 provides that "gross income does not include the value of property acquired by gift, bequest, devise, or inheritance." The major problem involved in the interpretation of this brief section is the difficulty of distinguishing on any operational basis between transfers that are truly gratuitous and those made for other reasons. In Paul Hornung's case, the court believed that the transfer was not gratuitous, but that it was made with the hope that it either had provided or would provide better sports stories, and, therefore, greater magazine sales.

In general, if the recipient has rendered (or will render) any service to the apparent donor, the tax authorities find that the transfer is not gratuitous and, therefore, that any amount received constitutes gross income. Under this interpretation, ordinary tips given to waiters and waitresses, bellhops, and other service personnel are includable in gross income. So are traditional gifts to members of the clergy following weddings and other religious ceremonies. A more delicate problem of statutory interpretation was presented to the courts in the cases of *Greta Starks* and *Everett Brizendine.* To state the essential fact of those two cases succinctly, each involved a "kept" woman. The delicate tax question involved the need to distinguish between a gift and compensation for services rendered. After "all of the facts and circumstances" were examined, the amount received was classified as ordinary income in one case and as a tax-free gift in the other.

Relative to inheritances, the reader should be cautioned to observe the difference between a basic bequest and income that may accrue on that bequest. Generally only the former can be excluded from gross income. For example, a taxpayer can generally exclude from taxable income any amount that he or she receives as the beneficiary of a life insurance policy purchased by another individual. The income derived from the inheritance, however, is as taxable to the heir as is income derived from property that he or she has personally accumulated. Only the basic bequest or inheritance can be excluded because of Section 102. Under Section 101(d) a surviving spouse may also be entitled to an annual exclusion for $1,000 in interest earned on life insurance proceeds left with an insurance company to be paid as an annuity. With that exception, however, virtually all other income earned on inherited property will be taxed to the heir.

State and local bond interest. As noted in Chapter 1, any interest derived from bonds issued by a state or local government is generally excluded from gross income for federal income tax purposes. Upper-bracket taxpayers consequently find it financially advantageous to invest large sums in state and local government bonds. The governments issuing these bonds are able to float them at lower rates of interest because of the tax shelter they provide the purchaser. Tax reformers have contended for many years that this exclusion should be ended because the results are highly inequitable in that they benefit most the wealthiest segment of our society. The tax reformers usually cite estimates to support the contention that the federal government could increase its *net* tax revenues even if it were to grant direct subsidies to the state and local governments in an amount sufficient to compensate them for any increase in interest costs. Whether or not the estimates are realistic, Congress thus far has refused to terminate this statutory exclusion both because of genuine concern for the greater bureaucracy that would attend a direct subsidy and because of pressures brought by governors, mayors, and investment bankers.

Scholarship and fellowship grants. Section 117 excludes from gross income amounts received by an individual as a scholarship or fellowship grant. The amount that can be excluded depends on whether or not the recipient is a degree candidate. In general, degree candidates are not subject to limits, whereas nondegree persons can exclude a maximum of $300 per month for 36 months. The exclusion also extends to amounts received for travel, research, clerical assistance, and equipment that are incidental to the scholarship or fellowship grant.

Implementation of this exclusion is made difficult by the definitional imprecision common to the terms *scholarship* and *fellowship grant.* In any instance where a specific service is required of the grantee, the tax authorities are inclined to argue that the grant is compensation for services rendered, and therefore included in gross income. For example, the stipends paid to medical residents and interns, teaching and research assistants, and other graduate students who render a service to their educational institution are often found to constitute taxable income rather than an exclusion. The difficulty in statutory interpretation is compounded by the fact that the work experience is an important and integral part of the student's education, and for this reason the stipend could reasonably be considered to be a scholarship even though a service is rendered. Perhaps the most unfortunate aspect of this exclusion is the fact that it is being administered differently in various sections of the country.

Rental value of parsonages. Section 107 excludes from gross income the fair market value of a home furnished to a "minister of the gospel" as part of his or her compensation (or the rental allowance paid in lieu of a parsonage, to the extent used to rent or purchase a home). This section would not be worthy of specific comment in a book on general tax planning were it not for the fact that some of the more radical elements in our society have seized upon this and related sections as their legal basis for paying no income tax to the federal government. In a nutshell, this radical element typically recommends that every reluctant taxpayer create a "church" and proclaim himself or herself to be a "minister of the gospel." For the more reluctant, the radical group will sell, at a bargain price, appropriate degrees and clerical titles in their own organizations. The advertisements and "news" reports that extol these tax plans typically fail to report the ease with which the IRS and the courts have seen through the deceit implicit in most of these schemes. The courts have consistently held that they have no status as a religious organization or as "a minister of the gospel."

The recent activity in this area does serve, however, to emphasize an important aspect of all legitimate tax planning—namely, the importance of statutory interpretation. It is extremely difficult to define with any precision many words and phrases in the code. For example, precisely who should qualify as a minister of the gospel? Should it include the "minister of music" or "minister of youth" in a large congregation? Should it include only ordained persons; and, if so, what minimal requirements should exist for ordination? Should it include ordained ministers temporarily serving in a purely administrative capacity? These questions related to

Section 107 are typical of those found in virtually every other section of the code. The tax expert must know how to locate and interpret authority to answer these and similar questions if he or she does not already know the answers.

Exclusions and deductions both reduce the size of the income tax base and therefore the tax liability. The list of possible income tax deductions is considerably longer than the list of statutory exclusions. Deduction rules are additionally confused by frequent limitations and options. The remainder of this chapter is devoted to an elaboration of the general rules governing the deductions authorized in the computation of taxable income.

Deductions

Deductions may be defined only as those items that collectively constitute the difference between the quantity called gross income and the quantity called taxable income. The basic rule applicable to deductions is just the opposite of that stated earlier for gross income—that is, *nothing is deductible unless the taxpayer can find good authority for deducting it.* Even momentary reflection on the general proposition just stated should cause the reader some concern, because income is generally thought to be a net concept. In accounting, *income* is usually defined as the difference between properly matched revenues and expenses. A tax on income, therefore, seems to provide implicitly for an automatic deduction of all properly matched expenses. Technically this is not true for income tax purposes. The code does include a provision (Section 162) that authorizes the deduction of all ordinary and necessary expenses paid or incurred in carrying on any trade or business. Nevertheless, some items that are deductible in computing financial accounting income are not deductible in computing taxable income, and a few items that are not deductible in computing financial accounting income are deductible in computing taxable income. Especially as used in the income taxation of an individual, the word *deduction* is a much broader, more legalistic word than the word *expense.*

In addition to the provision authorizing the deduction of all ordinary and necessary business expenses, the code authorizes many other more restrictive deductions. These include a zero bracket amount for individual taxpayers only; a personal and dependent exemption deduction; deductions for interest, taxes, losses, bad debts, depreciation, and charitable contributions, for research and experimental expenditures, and for soil and water conservation expenditures; and a dividend-received deduction for corporate taxpayers only. In addition, there are many other special deductions. For example, some deductions are restricted to certain industries, such as railroads, the extractive industries, exempt organizations, banks, and insurance companies. As noted earlier, the details of all tax provisions cannot be examined in this book. Only the more important deductions for tax-planning purposes will be considered here. The important thing for the reader to remember at this point is that unless an expenditure fits the definition of an ordinary and necessary expense incurred in a trade or business, it generally cannot be deducted without very specific authorization in the code.

The rules applicable to tax deductions are complicated by the need to distinguish carefully among expenditures incurred in a trade, business, or profession, expenditures incurred in an income-producing venture that cannot be deemed to constitute a trade or business, either because of its special nature or because of its limited size, and expenditures of a purely personal nature. The first of these three classes of expenditures is usually deductible without limit; the second is probably deductible, but sometimes only in an amount that does not exceed the income produced; and the last is not deductible at all unless a very specific provision authorizes its deduction, notwithstanding its purely personal character.

The difficulty of distinguishing between a trade or business and an income-producing venture is well demonstrated by many hobbies. The breeding of animals, the racing of horses and automobiles, the restoration of antiques, and even farming may be a primary source of recreation for a harried taxpayer. The same activities usually produce some gross income. Because the rule applicable to gross income says that all receipts must be included in gross income, it seems only fair that the related expenses should be tax deductible. On the other hand, since most purely personal expenditures are not deductible, it seems equally unfair to authorize the deduction of expenses related to certain hobbies and not to others just because some occasionally produce income. Thus the tax authorities are frequently faced with the need to determine whether or not a particular activity constitutes a full-fledged trade or business or something else. To assist in making this decision, the code was amended to include a statutory presumption, subject to rebuttal by the taxpayer, that any activity that does not produce a profit in any two of five consecutive years will be deemed to constitute a hobby. Expenses related to a hobby may be deductible, but only to the extent that gross income is reported. If we assume for the time being that we can distinguish between hobbies and real trades or businesses, we can proceed to examine more carefully the general rules applicable to trade and business expenses.

Deductions and Expenses Compared

The basic criteria that must be considered before assuming that an expenditure directly related to a trade or business can be deducted can be separated into three positive and three negative tests. That is, an expenditure incurred in a trade, business, or profession will generally be deductible if:

1. It is "ordinary," which has been interpreted to mean that it is common to other taxpayers who find themselves in similar circumstances.
2. It is "necessary," which has been interpreted to mean that it is helpful to the conduct of the taxpayer's trade or business.
3. It is "reasonable in amount," which has been interpreted to mean that any other taxpayer would pay an equivalent sum for an equivalent good or service.
4. It is *not* a personal expense.
5. It is *not* a capital expenditure.
6. It does *not* relate to tax-exempt income.

Unlike taxation, accounting has no explicit rule that says that an expense must be reasonable in amount. This difference occasionally accounts for reported differences between financial accounting income and taxable income, especially in closely held corporations. Owners of these corporations often overstate their own salaries, as well as the salaries paid to other members of their immediate family, for tax reasons that will become clearer in the next two chapters. Whenever this happens, the authorities may find that what purported to be a salary must be treated as if it were a dividend, a gift, or some other distribution, and taxed accordingly. The reasonableness criterion has been applied in the opposite direction as well. A salary paid to Victor Borge by his own corporation was found to be unreasonably small, with the unpleasant consequence that the corporation ended up being treated as one engaged in a hobby rather than in a *bona fide* business. Mr. Borge, the famous pianist-comic, probably did not find it funny that this meant paying a personal income tax on the extra salary attributed to him, in addition to finding that the expenses incurred by his Rock Cornish hen (farm) corporation were nondeductible.

The rule that precludes the deduction of expenses related to the production of tax-exempt income may also explain some differences between the income reported by financial accounting and by taxation. Businesses very often insure the lives of the owners to guarantee the availability of a sufficient amount of cash to purchase any deceased owner's share of the business from his or her estate. As noted earlier, the insurance proceeds received following the death of an owner would be excluded from gross income by Section 102. Consequently, the premiums paid to obtain the insurance are not deductible by businesses for tax purposes in the years preceding the owner's death. Accounting, on the other hand, generally reports some or all of the insurance premium as an expense of doing business. Accounting may also report some portions of the insurance proceeds as income.

Some deductions are subject to limitations for tax purposes. For example, charitable contributions made by corporations are limited to 5 percent of the corporations' adjusted taxable income; percentage depletion (when allowed at all) is limited to 50 percent of the net income from the depletable property; and corporate capital losses are deductible only to the extent of capital gains in any one year. Because there is no financial accounting convention that similarly limits any of these items, the amounts deducted for financial accounting purposes in any given year may vary substantially from those deducted for income tax purposes. The major differences between these two figures, however, are attributable to tax provisions which have been written into the code for economic, national defense, or social reasons.

Economic policy considerations. During the past two decades, Congress has enacted several major tax provisions relating to deductions with the apparent intention of promoting economic growth, maintaining reasonable price stability, and/or reducing unemployment. Still other tax measures have been justified on the ground that they are essential to the maintenance of a strong national defense. When these policy considerations are deemed sufficiently important, the implications of the tax provision for the traditional conventions used to measure income are not given much weight. Thus it is not unusual to discover that in instances where economic or defense considerations are primary, tax rules differ substantially from accounting rules for essentially identical expense items.

Among the list of accounting and tax differences that can be attributed to economic motivation are the following: rapid depreciation allowances, first-year depreciation allowances, percentage depletion, and the investment credit. Three of these four produce tax deductions larger than the usual measure of the comparable expense for financial accounting purposes. The fourth provides a direct tax credit. Recent changes in the tax rates have also been motivated by economic considerations. Some of the tax provisions motivated by economic objectives will be considered in subsequent chapters because they represent important opportunities to achieve major tax savings through careful planning.

Social policy considerations. The primary objective of other tax provisions that seem peculiar in light of accounting conventions may also be related in some way to a social goal. Such sociological factors as family size, blindness, old age, marital status, or condition of health have little or nothing to do with problems of income measurement for financial accounting purposes. Income is simply the difference between revenues and the properly matched expenses incurred to produce those revenues. Special problems peculiar to a person earning an income may influence his or her disposition of that income, but these problems in no way influence the size of the income measure. For tax purposes, however, sociological factors are often important to the procedure used to measure the size of the income stream. Congress tries, sometimes in an obscure manner, to recognize that equal financial accounting incomes need not represent equal taxpaying abilities. To achieve a degree of social equity, the code recognizes some of the differences in the ability to pay taxes by allowing special deductions for large families, for blind taxpayers, for persons 65 or older, for persons who incur large medical expenses, and for a host of other persons in special circumstances. In a few instances, these provisions intended to achieve a higher degree of interpersonal tax equity can be used to benefit taxpayers whom they were not intended to benefit.

Accounting Methods

We observed earlier in this chapter that the code provides that taxable income shall be computed on the same method of accounting as the taxpayer uses in maintaining his or her regular books. The cash-basis method of accounting for expenses produces relatively few problems pertinent to tax deductions since both financial and tax accounting require that no deduction be made until cash is actually paid. The accrual method of accounting, however, presents more serious problems in application. That method of accounting is based on the notion that expenses should be deducted in the same year that the revenue which they produce is reported. Accountants refer to this notion as the matching concept. Application of that concept often necessitates the estimation of expenses in advance of the time that they are actually known with certainty. The expense associated with a guarantee or warranty, for example, is typically not known with precision until several years after the sale of the guaranteed product. Good financial accounting requires that such expenses be estimated in advance and that they be deducted in the same year in which the gross revenue from the sale is reported. With major exceptions for the estimation of depreciation of fixed assets and for doubtful accounts, the code generally forbids the deduction of any expense for tax purposes until the amount of that expense is fixed by more objective evidence than statistical estimates based on historical records.

The absence of a strict matching concept in taxation, especially for taxpayers reporting their income on a cash method of accounting, explains a number of important tax-saving opportunities. These opportunities are expanded when the deduction item is treated in one way and the related gross income item is reported in another, more favored way. To illustrate this important difference, consider the tax-saving potential associated with the immediate deduction of interest expense for borrowed funds that are invested in a way that will yield only a long-term capital gain at some time in the future. For reasons that will become clearer in the next few chapters, this means that the cost associated with the borrowing may be shared by the government on a 70–30 basis—that is, an individual in a 70 percent marginal tax bracket will discover that the government effectively pays 70 percent of his or her interest expense, through the reduction of tax liability, if the interest can be deducted from ordinary income—whereas the fruit of an investment may be shared with the government on a 28–72 basis—that is, the government may demand no more than 28 percent of the profit back in income tax if the profit from the investment can be categorized as a long term capital gain. Adding to the taxpayer's delight until recently was the fact that the interest could be deducted when paid, whereas the capital gain tax could be deferred until realized. This particular opportunity to achieve tax savings was so widely abused that Congress first put some limitations on the deduction of "excess investment interest" for the years beginning after 1971. The original statutory limitations were so generous, however, that they affected only a very few persons. Consequently these provisions were drastically revised in the Tax Reform Act of 1976, which placed a much more severe limit on the opportunity of individual taxpayers to benefit by manipulating investment interest expenses. Furthermore, new rules generally require that any interest—investment or personal—be allocated over the period of the loan without regard to the date it is paid, even if the taxpayer generally uses a cash method of accounting.

Losses

The proper tax treatment of losses is often confusing. In this introductory chapter we can do little more than get acquainted with some of the more important general distinctions pertaining to the tax treatment of losses. Additional details of some of these distinctions will be discussed later, whereas other details will have to remain outside the confines of this work. To begin with, we might distinguish between (1) the loss attributable to a specific transaction and a specific property, and (2) the loss more generally associated with the nonprofitable conduct of a trade or business, considering all of the many transactions common to that business.

The correct tax treatment of a loss derived from a specific transaction and a specific property is determined primarily by the purpose for which the property was held. If it was held for the production of income in an ordinary trade or business, any loss associated with the disposition of the property will generally be fully deductible for tax purposes. If the property was held solely as an investment, any loss associated with the disposition of the investment will generally be deductible, but will be subject to special limitations applicable only to capital losses. If the property was held solely for personal purposes, any loss associated with the disposition of the property will generally not be deductible unless the disposition is attributable to a casualty or a theft. According to these diverse rules, the loss on the sale of a machine used in a business would be fully deductible; the loss associated with the sale of a common stock would be deductible only as a capital loss; and the loss associated with the sale of a personal residence would not be deductible (even though a gain on the sale of that same residence would be taxable). But note that the loss associated with the destruction of a personal residence by fire would be deductible as a casualty.

The general loss associated with the nonprofitable conduct of a business, considering the effect of all transactions common to that business, is called a *net operating loss* (or *NOL*). If the authorized deductions exceed the gross income, the negative difference between the two sums effectively eliminates any tax for the current year. The question remains, however: What, if anything, can be done with that excess to offset taxable income in other years? The answer is that, after making several possible adjustments to the amount of this difference, the taxpayer may carry the net operating loss back three years and treat it as a newly discovered deduction to be subtracted from the gross income reported in that year. If the taxpayer reported a taxable income in that year and paid a tax, the new NOL deduction will create a refund of some or all of the tax paid three years ago. This refund even includes interest for the interim years. If the NOL deduction is larger than the taxable income of the third prior year, the taxpayer treats any remaining loss as a deduction in the second prior year. If that is still insufficient to absorb the loss, the taxpayer proceeds to offset it against the income of the immediately preceding year. Finally, if that is still insufficient to absorb the total net operating loss, the taxpayer is allowed to carry the remaining NOL forward and to offset it against any gross income earned in the next seven years.

In lieu of the tax treatment described in the prior paragraph, the code gives every taxpayer another option. Instead of carrying the NOL back and offsetting it against the taxable income of the three prior years, a taxpayer may now elect to forego the carry-*back* and opt only for a seven-year carry-forward. Whether or not this new election is advantageous depends largely on the marginal tax rates applicable in the various years involved.

Special problems are created when one taxable entity tries to utilize another taxable entity's net operating loss. Thus if corporation A acquires all of the stock or assets of corporation B, and if corporation B had an unused net operating loss carry-forward, special rules must be applied to determine whether or not the surviving corporation is entitled to the losses originally incurred by corporation B. Before these special rules were enacted, there was a brisk business in our country for worthless corporate shells because they provided valuable tax deductions for the acquiring taxpayer. The Catch-22 tax effect was to make the most socially worthless corporation the most valuable one! For the same reason, unlucky persons with accumulated net operating losses might make an excellent marriage prospect, financially speaking, for the more fortunate taxpayer who has need of some big tax deductions.

Whether or not one corporation can claim the NOL deduction of a second corporation, accumulated prior to the acquisition of the second corporation by the other corporation, depends largely on the requirements of Section 382. Currently the NOL deduction of an acquired corporation can be claimed by a successor only if there has *not* been both (1) a "major change of ownership" within the two prior years and (2) a change in the business of the acquired corporation. If some 1976 changes are ever allowed to go into effect, in the future the NOL deduction will be denied strictly on the basis of a major change in ownership. The old change-of-business test proved to be too difficult to administer satisfactorily. Under the revised rules, however, the change-of-ownership test will cover three years (rather than two), and will consider the ownership of the 15 largest shareholders (rather than only the 10 largest shareholders). The major impact of the new provisions can be summarized as follows: whales (large corporations) can no longer swallow minnows (small corporations) to take advantage of the minnows' NOL. Whales may continue to swallow whales, and minnows may swallow minnows, in the NOL game, but those are the outer boundaries under the current rules for NOL deductions.[1]

In summary, the reader should remember two very important rules of income taxation. First, remember that all income is deemed to constitute taxable income unless you (or your tax adviser) can find good authority for excluding it. Second, remember that nothing is deductible in the computation of taxable income unless you (or that same adviser) can find good authority for deducting it. In the remaining chapters we will discover how the apparently harsh results of these two rules are mitigated by many taxpayers.

---

[1] The author is indebted for this handy analogy to Prof. Boris Bittker and James Eustice.

CHAPTER 3

Taxable Entities

The Internal Revenue Code technically acknowledges the existence of only three taxable entities. They are the individual, the corporation, and the fiduciary. All taxable income recognized in a single year must be attributed to some individual, corporation, or fiduciary. This means, of course, that the taxable income recognized by other entities—for example, that recognized by a sole proprietorship, a partnership, or a joint venture—must be allocated annually to one of the three entities that are acknowledged for tax purposes. In some cases the code may require a nontaxable entity to file a return, but this return is for information purposes only, and it does not, of itself, create an income tax liability.

The Individual Taxpayer

Theoretically, every living person is a separate and distinct taxable entity. Age is of no significance: A two-year-old child who "models" baby clothes or "acts" in a television production is legally responsible for the payment of taxes and is as much a taxable entity as is each of the child's parents. In the case of the incapacitated or of very young children, the law provides, of course, that the parent or guardian may be equally liable for the filing of the return and the payment of the tax liability. The important point is that the individual, rather than the family unit, is the taxable entity. As a practical matter, however, the technical point just stated is, at best, a half-truth.

The Married Couple

The code has provided since 1948 for something known as the "joint return" of married persons. The effect of the joint return provision is to decrease the effective tax rate for literally millions of married persons. The reason for initiation of the joint return was to establish some reasonable degree of federal income tax equity between taxpayers who lived in community property states and taxpayers who lived in common-law states. The inequity of the situation that existed prior to 1948 can be demonstrated by the use of a simple graph. If there were only one progressive income tax rate schedule (as there was prior to 1948), and if the entire income of a married couple were earned by one spouse in a community property state, that income could be treated for federal tax purposes as if half of it had been earned by each of the two partners to the marriage (which was and is the general result of those state laws). Consequently the tax would be equal to two times the tax on an income of an amount equal to distance *ab* in Figure 3–1, not on one amount equal to distance *ac*. The tax saving available to a married couple residing in a community property state, as compared to a married couple in identical circumstances but residing in a common-law state, can be represented by the crosshatched area in Figure 3–1. To reduce this inequality and

FIGURE 3–1

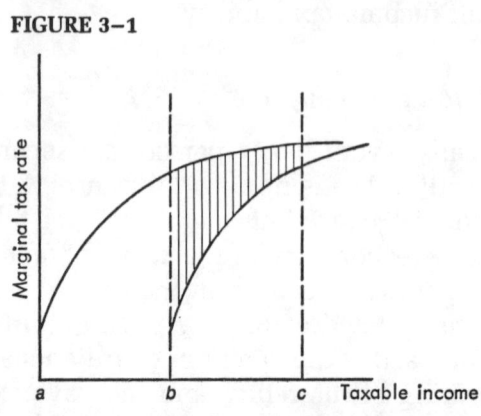

Where *ab* equals *bc* and joint income equals *ac*

to stop a movement by all of the states to adopt community property laws, Congress made provision in 1948 for the joint return of married persons. The important effect of this change was to do for others exactly what the community property laws had done earlier for others. That is, it effectively assumed that one half of the income earned by any married person was earned by each spouse and then permitted the federal income tax computation to be made accordingly. In order to simplify the administration of the law—by avoiding the assumed division of each spouse's income and subsequently by the addition of the two independently determined income taxes—the IRS created a second tax rate schedule, which could be applied only once to the combined incomes of the married couple. To achieve the congressional objective, this new rate schedule was necessarily designed so that the marginal tax brackets were exactly twice as wide as those applied to income earned by single persons. In other words, if the first $500 of taxable income of a single person were to be taxed at the marginal rate of 14 percent, then the first $1,000 (2 × $500) of taxable income of the married couple had to be taxed at 14 percent.

The Head of Household

As a consequence of the introduction of the joint return, the basic entity for individual income tax purposes after 1948 remained the individual only for single persons; most married persons filed as a husband-wife team. In the mid-1950s, Congress decided to add a third category of individual taxpayers by creating a "head-of-household" status. The thought behind the creation of this third subcase of the individual was that for tax purposes some persons were really more like married persons than they were like single persons and that, under these circumstances, they ought to be entitled to some of the tax advantages that attached to matrimony. The basic idea was that if a single person—in most instances, a person who was once married but was no longer in that status—retained the responsibility of supporting one or more dependent relatives, even though he or she were no longer married, then that taxpayer should be entitled to some tax relief. The relief decided upon took the form of a new rate schedule whose brackets and marginal tax rates were arranged in such a manner as to give this person approximately one half of the tax advantage of being married.

Single Persons

Although the joint return and the head-of-household rates reduced the tax inequities that had existed between married persons living in different states and, to a lesser degree, between married persons and heads of households, these same tax innovations magnified the tax inequity between single and married individuals. In 1970, the tax on a $32,000 taxable income earned by a married couple was $8,660, whereas the tax on the same income earned by a single person was $12,210, a difference of $3,550 (or an increase of 41 percent) per year. Sufficient pressures were again brought on Congress, and in 1971 a fourth tax rate schedule was introduced for single individuals only. This new schedule was deliberately constructed in such a manner that the tax paid by a single person on any amount of taxable income would never be more than 120 percent of the tax paid by a married couple on the same amount of taxable income. At the same time, the rates applicable to heads of households were also adjusted downward so that they remained approximately midway between the single and the joint return rates. In order to avoid a return to the community property problem that had existed 22 years earlier, Congress required that married persons filing separate returns use a rate schedule that was not the same as that applicable to single persons. The rates were generally higher for married persons filing separately than for single persons earning the same taxable income.

The most interesting consequence of this latest revision has been to introduce a new tax inequity for married persons who *independently* earn a substantial and approximately equal taxable income. This result has been dubbed a tax on marriage. The real inequity that results can be simply illustrated. Using the current tax rate schedules, which appear at the end of this chapter, we can determine that the tax paid by a single person on a $34,100 taxable income is $9,7666. If two persons each earning a $34,100 taxable income were to marry, their joint liability would increase to $24,754, which is $5,222 more annually than they were paying separately before saying

"I do." How and when Congress will solve this last inequity remains to be seen. Since the number of married couples with working wives is growing rapidly, the chances for a prompt solution are politically improved. In addition, many young couples continue to live openly "in sin" to gain a tax advantage. Since the communications media found their problem newsworthy, another solution may be found to this problem before long.

A graphic presentation of two of the four tax rate schedules currently applicable to individual taxpayers is contained in Figure 3–2. The rates for heads of households and for mar-

FIGURE 3–2
1980 Tax Rates

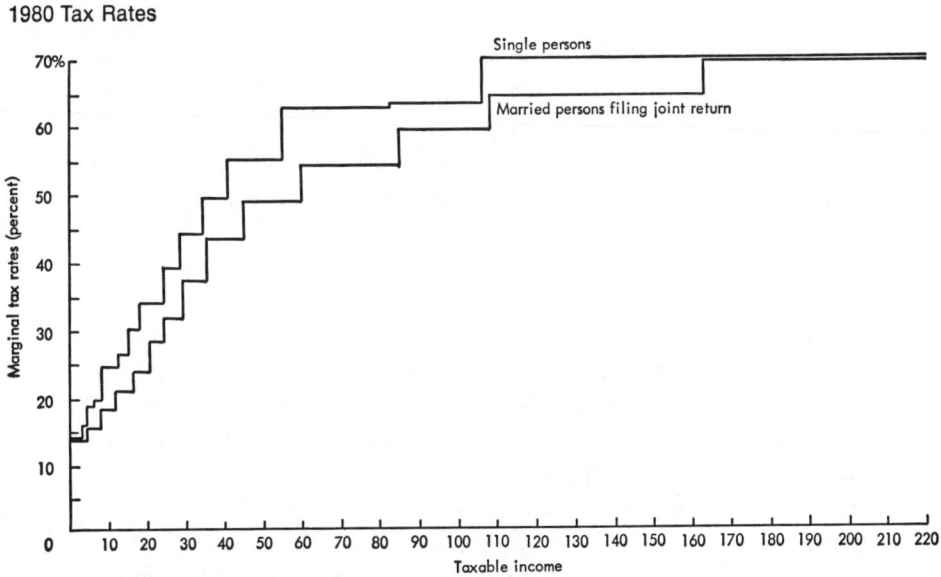

* Code *only* for (1) married persons filing jointly and (2) single persons.

ried persons filing separately were omitted from Figure 3–2 simply because they make reading the graph difficult. The tax rate function for these persons frequently overlaps one of the others. Two very important aspects of the federal income taxation of individual taxpayers should be evident from even the most cursory examination of these two curves. *First, observe that the tax rates applicable to individual taxpayers are highly progressive. Second, observe that most of the progression takes* *place in the first $50,000 of taxable income.* That is, the marginal tax rates move rapidly from 14 percent to about 50 percent in the first $50,000 of taxable income. The increase for the second $50,000 of taxable income is substantially less. The progression for the third $50,000 is still smaller; in fact, there is almost no further progression for the single individual. *These two important facts explain why some tax-saving ideas are especially meaningful in the relatively lower income brackets.* A single movement of $10,000 in taxable income from the $40,000-to-$50,000 bracket to the zero-to-$10,000 brackets can mean sizable tax savings precisely because of the degree of progression in the marginal rates at these relatively low income levels.

Definitional Problems

Before returning to our major concern—that is, the importance of the taxable entity to tax-planning ideas—a final word of caution is in order. The precise definitions necessary to determine whether or not a particular taxpayer is eligible to use any given rate schedule are not as straightforward as the common words used to describe them would seem to imply. For example, a taxpayer may be eligible to use the rate schedule for married persons filing jointly even though his or her spouse died a year or two earlier. This opportunity exists whenever the taxpayer can qualify for status as a *surviving spouse,* another technical income tax term requiring more than simply outliving the person to whom you were once married. Similarly, status as head of household is determined by some very specific, and sometimes apparently inequitable, criteria. In keeping with the objectives of this book, no details of the pertinent definitions will be examined here. The taxpayer having a personal interest in such definitional problems ought to consult the current tax return instructional booklet, a reliable tax reference work, or a competent tax adviser.

Planning Opportunities

To return to the fundamental discussion of the individual as a separate taxpaying entity, we discover that a family unit may be able to lower its aggregate tax liability by dividing up the total income earned between a maximum number of family members. Just as the husband-wife team found it advantageous, prior to the days of the joint return, to split income between themselves, so also we find today that many wealthy individuals transfer property to minor children, grandchildren, or elderly relatives, in order to relieve themselves of the higher tax liability that would attach to the same income stream had it been retained by the donor. Notice that this generally requires the transfer of an income-producing property. It cannot be accomplished through the transfer of only the income that stems from a property, and it is very difficult to accomplish with income from personal services. In other words, a father generally could *not* for income tax purposes give his son either part of his salary or the interest income he derives from selected corporate bonds unless, in the latter instance, the father is willing to actually transfer ownership of the bonds to the son. In reality, a less-than-complete transfer of property can achieve the desired income tax objective. If the father creates a trust with those bonds, and if that trust satisfies certain rules (the most important one being that the father cannot revoke the trust and regain the bonds in less than ten years), then the father can effectively divert the income derived from the property from himself to another designated person. The details of these and other tax-saving opportunities that involve the careful selection of the entity to be taxed will be considered presently. Before looking at the opportunities, we must consider some of the general rules applicable to the other two taxable entities.

The Corporate Taxpayer

The corporation, like the individual, has for many years been recognized as one of the basic entities for income tax purposes. Recently, Congress has been reconsidering the wisdom of this tradition. However, even though this treatment of corporations could change in the future, at the moment we must continue to assume that the corporation will remain a separate taxable entity. This fact creates about as many tax opportunities as it does tax traps. Most of the traps that it creates revolve around the obvious fact that a corporation is nothing but a legal fiction that is responsible ultimately to the people who own the shares of stock that represent the corporate entity; when a small group of people, or even a single individual, owns all of the shares, it becomes exceedingly difficult to distinguish between personal and corporate interests.

Legal Entities

The propriety of taxing a purely legal entity seems, at first blush, to be questionable. Legal entities, after all, cannot consume the incomes they earn because consumption is a purely human opportunity. Corporations and other legal entities can reinvest the incomes they earn, and they can transform resources into (one hopes) more valuable forms, but they cannot destroy or consume these resources if they want to survive. Why, then, should these entities be taxed? Many people delight in pointing out that the taxation of income earned by any nonhuman entity necessarily means that a single income stream faces double income taxation. In the case of the corporation, that income stream must first be taxed as part of the corporation's taxable income and later as part of the stockholders' taxable incomes when whatever is left after corporate income tax is distributed as a dividend. This double tax observation is generally applicable to the large, publicly held corporation, but the smaller, closely held corporation finds it quite easy to circumvent much of the double tax.

Among the alternatives to the double tax is the option of ignoring the corporate entity and allocating all corporate income immediately and directly to the stockholders, whether or not the corporation distributes any of its earnings. This alternative would be administratively cumbersome for large, publicly held corporations since ownership of these corporations changes on a daily basis and income simply cannot be measured that frequently. In addition, this alternative could create major hardships were the corporation to earn a large income and distribute none of it; under these conditions, a stockholder could discover that he or she had a large tax liability with very limited funds to pay the income tax. As a consequence, if this alternative were enacted, corporate boards would be under tremendous pressure from stockholders to distribute all or most of the corporation's income as dividends. For this reason alone, corporate boards are not likely to give much support to an early demise of the corporate income tax. Another extreme alternative would permit the corporation's income to remain untaxed until distributed to the owners. If applied to a corporation, this would result in vast hoarding of corporate earnings and in widespread tax evasion. After all, anyone can create a corporation for $500 or less, and even persons of very modest means would find that cost immaterial if there were no tax on corporate income until that income was distributed. Although other intermediate positions can be designed to overcome most of the objections stated to each of these alternatives, none of them have ever gained the support of a majority of Congress. Options currently available to the small, closely held corporation are explained later in this chapter.

To note that the corporation, like the individual, is recognized as a separate taxable entity is to tell only half the story. The tax rate structure applicable to a corporation's taxable income is significantly different from the tax rate structure applied to an individual's income. In the absence of any complications, a corporate entity currently pays an income tax of 17 percent of its first $25,000 in taxable income, 20 percent of its second $25,000 in taxable income, 30 percent of its third $25,000 in taxable income, 40 percent of its fourth $25,000 in taxable income, and 46 percent of any remaining taxable income. For most practical purposes, therefore, we can generally assume that a large corporation—that is, a corporation with a very large taxable income—will generally pay 46 percent of its taxable income in federal income taxes, whereas a small corporation will generally pay something like 20 to 30 percent of its income in federal income tax. In summary, the corporate tax has five major steps or brackets; the personal income tax, 15. Figure 3–3 illustrates the essential features of the current corporate tax rate structure.

The reader should begin immediately to see possible corporate tax-saving ideas, given only the two fundamental facts just stated. If each corporation is recognized as a separate taxable entity, and if the corporate tax rate structure contains five progressive brackets, it should be possible for the owners of middle-sized firms to split their business ventures in a most tax advantageous way. Suppose, for example, that a businessman owned a venture that provided him with a

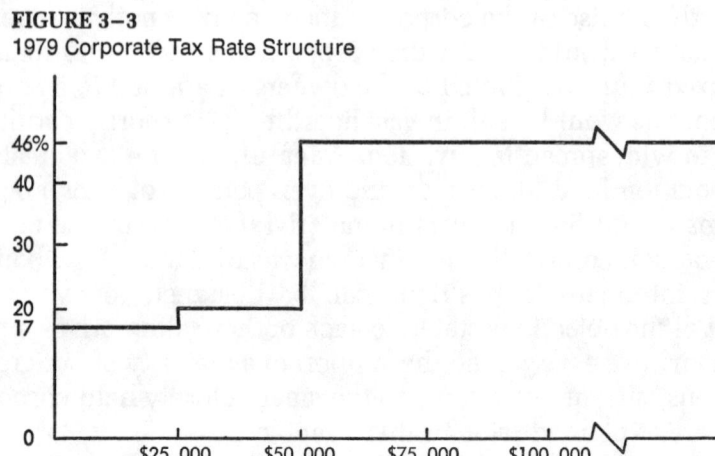

FIGURE 3-3
1979 Corporate Tax Rate Structure

$200,000 annual taxable income. If this businessman elected to incorporate his business venture, should he attempt to form four corporations of approximately equal size or should he put the entire operation into a single corporate shell? Considering only tax factors and ignoring for the moment any possible complications in making this choice, it should be immediately evident that major tax savings would attach to the four-corporation alternative. That is, the corporate income tax on four equal incomes of $50,000, earned by separate legal entities, would appear to be $37,000 [4 × (17% × $25,000 + 20% × $25,000)], whereas the corporate income tax on a single income of $200,000 would appear to be $72,750 [(17% × $25,000) + (20% × $25,000) + (30% × $25,000) + (40% × $25,000) + (46% × $100,000)], an increase of $35,750 (or over 96 percent) per year! Ventures earning more than $200,000 in taxable income should, of course, be able to increase their tax saving even more by creating an appropriately larger number of corporate entities.

Regardless of the details of the corporate tax rate structure, so long as the corporation remains a separate taxable entity, and so long as the corporate tax rate structure remains lower than that applied to the individual taxpayer, the general tax-planning notion discussed here is certain to remain valid. Only the detailed calculations—and the point at which each idea becomes viable—change. Accordingly, the author urges each reader to concentrate his or her attention on the basic ideas rather than on the arithmetic of a specific example.

Economic Realities

The simple tax-planning opportunity noted in the preceding paragraph was widely observed and utilized in the United States for decades. The practical consequence was that literally thousands of small corporations were formed, where fewer would otherwise have sufficed, primarily to achieve the substantial tax benefits that were available. It is still not uncommon to discover that one person remains president and chairman of the board not of one corporation but of ten or more corporations, all of which are closely related in operation and none of which is very large. In some cases, this is a historical anachronism; in other cases, it is a recent change undertaken because of changes in the 1978 Revenue Act.

A critical change, introduced in the 1969 Tax Reform Act, provided that, after December 31, 1974, controlled groups of corporations must be treated for most tax purposes as if they were a single taxable entity. In effect, for a few years it appeared that economic realities won out over legal fictions when tax avoidance reached epidemic proportions. The definition of a controlled group of corporations was concurrently expanded so that most corporations that were created previously for tax avoidance reasons (as well as some others) were caught in the definitional web. That definition of controlled corporations encompasses both brother-sister and parent-subsidiary ownership arrangements. The basic differences between these two can be illustrated simply, as shown in Figures 3–4 and 3–5. Figure 3–4 represents a brother-sister ownership

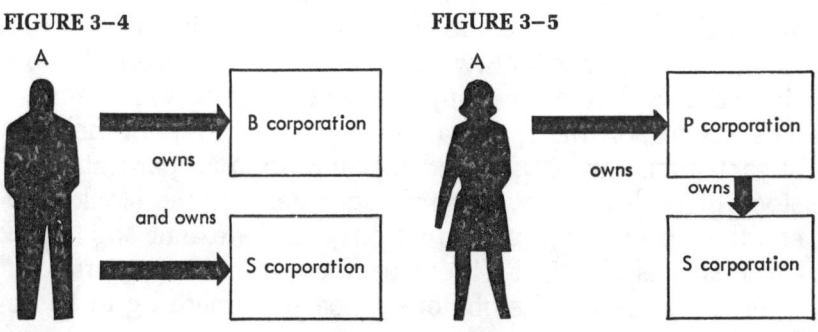

FIGURE 3–4

FIGURE 3–5

arrangement; Figure 3–5, a parent-subsidiary arrangement. If we assume in Figure 3–4 that person A owns all of the stock of both corporations B and S, and if we assume in Figure 3–5 that person A owns all the stock of corporation P and that corporation P owns all the stock of corporation S, then it is very easy to see why it may be more appropriate to tax the corporations on the basis of economic realities rather than legal fictions. To do otherwise permits widespread tax avoidance possibilities.

Legal Definitions

When Congress tried to close this tax loophole, it created some entirely new problems in statutory interpretation. The 1969 statutory definition of the parent-subsidiary form of the controlled group proved to cause little difficulty. It provides that there will be a parent-subsidiary controlled group any time that a parent corporation owns equal to or greater than 80 percent of one or more subsidiary corporation's stock (determined by vote or by value, whichever yields the greater percentage). The parent's ownership interest can be direct or indirect, through third- or fourth-tier corporate structures. For example, corporations A, B, C, and D would constitute a single parent-subsidiary controlled group of corporations if their ownership were distributed as in Figure 3–6.

FIGURE 3–6

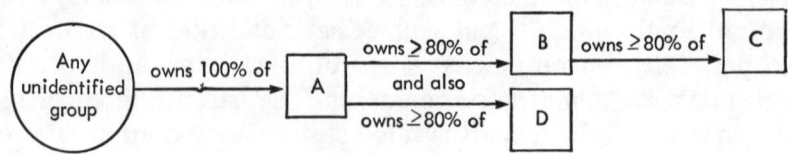

The interpretation of the new brother-sister controlled group definition proved to be much more difficult. Section 1563(a)(2) provides that two or more corporations will be considered a brother-sister group if five or fewer persons (individuals, estates, or trusts) own (1) 80 percent or more of the stock of each such corporation *and* (2) more than 50 percent of the stock of each such corporation considering "the stock ownership of each such individual only to the extent such stock ownership is identical with respect to each such corporation." This last phrase, quite obviously, leaves something to be desired in terms of lucidity. Nevertheless, Treasury regulations were promptly issued to help taxpayers understand what Congress supposedly intended. For example, according to the regulations, corporations A and B are considered members of a brother-sister controlled group if their ownership interests are divided between two unrelated shareholders, as indicated in Figure 3–7.

FIGURE 3–7

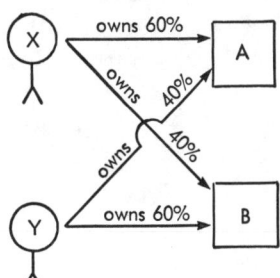

In diagram format

In tableau format

Owner	Percent owned in:		Identical ownership
	A	B	
X......	60	40	40
Y......	40	60	40
Total	100	100	80

In words, in Figure 3–7 two individuals (X and Y) own (1) 100 percent of corporations A and B and (2) 80 percent of those same corporations considering only their "identical ownership"—at least as that phrase is interpreted by the Treasury regulations, the courts, and the congressional committee reports.

On the other hand, according to these same authorities, corporations C and D would *not* be considered members of a brother-sister controlled group if they were owned by three unrelated individuals, as depicted in Figure 3–8.

FIGURE 3–8

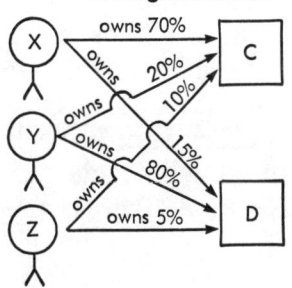

In diagram format

In tableau format

Owner	Percent owned in:		Identical ownership
	C	D	
X......	70	15	15
Y......	20	80	20
Z......	10	5	5
Total	100	100	40

In Figure 3–8, three individuals (X, Y, and Z) own 100 percent of corporations C and D; hence, the first (or 80-percent) test *is* satisfied. The second (or 50-percent) test, however, *is not* satisfied. The identical ownership of X, Y, and Z is only 40 percent in this example. The code requires that it be *more than* 50 percent if a brother-sister group is to exist.

Unfortunately, the difficulties of statutory interpretation do not end with the identical ownership phrase. Another particularly troublesome issue has been determining whether or not every stockholder must own some minimum number of shares in each corporation in order for that corporation to be included in any controlled group. For example, the authorities currently are divided on the issue of whether or not the corporations depicted in Figure 3–9 constitute a brother-sister controlled group.

FIGURE 3–9

In diagram format

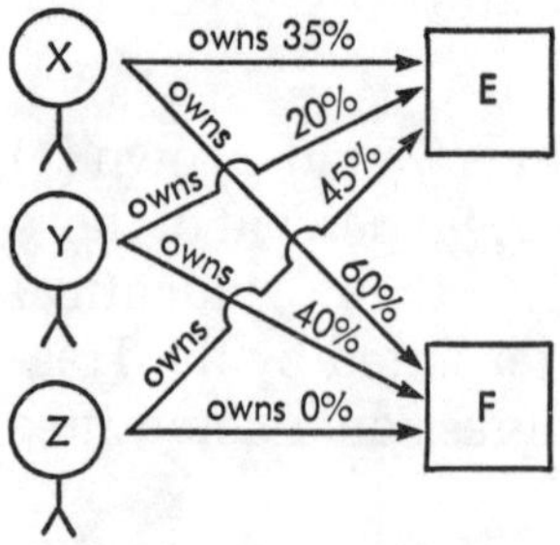

X owns 35% → E
X owns 20%
X owns 45%
Y owns 60%
Y owns 40%
Z owns 0% → F

In tableau format

Owner	Percent owned in: E	F	Identical ownership
X	35	60	35
Y	20	40	20
Z	45	0	0
Total	55 or 100?	100	55

A majority of the Tax Court contends that corporations E and F *cannot* be a controlled group because individual Z owns no part of corporation F. In other words, even though the second (or 50-percent) test is satisfied, the first (or 80-percent) test is not satisfied. Whether the 80-percent test is or is not satisfied depends, of course, on whether or not you include stockholder Z in making the percentage determinations. Treasury regulations, the IRS, and several Circuit Courts of Appeals say that the Tax Court is incorrectly interpreting the code and, therefore, that corporations E and F (in Figure 3–9) are members of a controlled group.

Unfortunately for the taxpayer, the definitional complications of controlled groups of corporations do not end with the considerations already discussed. This definition is further complicated by both some overlapping group problems and a maze of constructive ownership rules. Because this book is intended only as a recognition-oriented effort, we will forgo any detailed review of further definitional complications and get directly to the heart of the current tax planning matter. What is evident today is that the 1969 tax law changes are not as harsh as they first appeared to be. Two statutory details are particularly important:

1. The 50-percent identical-ownership test requires that the five or fewer persons own *more than* 50 percent of the corporations before the law makes them members of a brother-sister controlled group.
2. There is no attribution between a parent and any *adult* (defined to be persons 21 years of age or older) child so long as neither owns *more than* 50 percent of the jointly owned corporation.

As a consequence of these two details, a family unit consisting of only one parent and two adult children can own 100 percent of six corporations and not have a single controlled group. To achieve that tax magic, the family would have to be willing to divide its ownership interest *exactly* as depicted in Figure 3–10. A deviation of even one percentage point

FIGURE 3–10

Owner	Percent owned in					
	A	B	C	D	E	F
Parent	100	50	—	50	—	—
Adult child 1	—	50	100	—	—	50
Adult child 2	—	—	—	50	100	50

would create entirely different results. In Figure 3–10, there are several potential groups of corporations in which the identical ownership is equal to exactly 50 percent; there is no possible combination in which the identical ownership is *more than* 50 percent.

For reasons too complex to explain at this juncture, after the Tax Reform Act of 1969 and before the Revenue Act of 1978, most tax advisers acted as if the golden era of multiple corporations had ended forever. After ten years of living with the "new" provisions, and after some important changes in the 1978 Act, however, there suddenly appears to be a rebirth of multiple-family corporations. In other words, within the very recent past, we are once again finding that what is really a single closely held business is being divided up among a greater number of corporate entities, largely for tax reasons. To be sure, the owners of these newest corporations are having to take much greater care than they did in the pre-1970 era when distributing the stock ownership among family members. What is important, however, is that it is happening, and happening for good reason. If a single-family business that earns approximately $350,000 per year can be divided up among six closely held corporations *with equal incomes,* the family business will be worth an additional $5 million in just 25 years (assuming that the federal income tax saved in each year is reinvested at a 6 percent aftertax rate of return). Figure 3–10 illustrates how such a six-way division is possible!

Although the vast majority of taxpaying entities are either individuals or corporations, there is a third taxable entity, which we must consider briefly. That third entity is known as the *fiduciary taxpayer.*

The Fiduciary Taxpayer

The estate and the trust are the two common forms of the fiduciary taxpayer. The estate fills a necessary gap following the death of an individual taxpayer. A person's death marks the end of a final income tax period. On the final return of a decedent, taxable income is reported from the date of the last accounting, usually December 31 of the prior year, to the date of death. Years may pass, however, before the assets of a decedent are distributed to the heirs or devisees. An estate must report and pay tax on any taxable income earned on the assets in the interim period. Once a decreased taxpayer's assets have all been distributed, the estate ceases to exist, and the new owners begin to report on their own tax returns the income earned on the property transferred to them.

A *trust* is a legal relationship in which one person, called a *trustee*, holds title to property for the benefit or use of another person, called a beneficiary. The trust may be testamentary (created by a will) or *inter vivos* (created among living persons by a legal document other than a will). The latter trust will be recognized as a separate taxable entity only if it is not revocable and if the term of the trust is for a period of ten years or longer or for the life of a designated beneficiary. If these or other requirements are not satisfied, the income of the trust will continue to be taxed to the grantor (the person who created the trust through the transfer of property). If all requirements are satisfied, the trust becomes a separate taxable entity, but only to the extent that it does not distribute income to beneficiaries.

The fact that a trustee may be given an option over the distribution of income makes the trust a particularly viable vehicle for tax planning. If conditions are favorable—for example, if the income beneficiary is in a low tax bracket because of his or her age or because of an unusually large tax loss incurred from some other source—the trustee can proceed with an income distribution and avoid or minimize the income tax liability of the trust itself. If conditions are not favorable to a distribution, the trustee may be given the authority to retain the taxable income, in which case the trust pays the income tax (utilizing a special tax rate schedule roughly comparable to that used by married persons filing separately.) In summary, the trust is, for income tax purposes, something of a half-entity; it is recognized as a taxable entity only if and to the extent that it does not distribute its taxable income to the beneficiaries.

Other Entities

For financial accounting purposes, many entities are recognized in addition to the individual, the corporation, and the fiduciary. For example, in financial accounting a sole proprietorship is typically treated as an entity, separate and distinct from its owner. For income tax purposes, however, the income of a sole proprietorship simply becomes one of several schedules that collectively constitute the aggregate income picture for the owner. Except for the physical separation of financial data on Schedule C, Form 1040, the income of the proprietorship is commingled with the owner's gross income and deductions from other sources, such as interest, rents, and dividends.

Partnerships

Although a partnership is required to file an annual tax return, Form 1065, this return serves only to indicate to the Internal Revenue Service the amount and kind of income, deductions, and credits that the individual partners ought to be reporting on their individual tax returns as their share of the income from the partnership venture. Again, each partner's share of the partnership's income is commingled with his or her income from all other sources on the individual Form 1040. If the partnership elects to retain all of a sizable taxable income, a partner may owe a large tax liability with only limited resources to pay it. Under the reverse financial circumstances, a partner may discover that his or her share of a partnership's losses can be offset against income from other business ventures and therefore be of real tax advantage.

Hybrid Organizations

To posit that a partnership is not recognized as a separate taxable entity whereas a corporation is so recognized begs a very important question: What, exactly, is a corporation? Suffice it to note here that just because a business has been incorporated in compliance with state law does not of itself guarantee the recognition of this entity as a corporation for federal tax purposes. Most corporate entities organized in compliance with state law admittedly are recognized as such for tax purposes, but they need not be so recognized in unusual circumstances. In other situations, businesses that are formally organized as partnerships may discover that for tax purposes they are treated as corporate entities. And, occasionally, what is legally formed as a business trust may be taxed as a corporation. The judicial decisions in this relatively limited area seem to turn upon the presence or absence of such corporate characteristics as continuity of life, centralization of management, transferability of ownership, limited liability, and purpose of organization. The courts have carefully avoided delineation of which, how many, or what combination of corporate characteristics are sufficient to create or to destroy the business association that will be taxed as a corporation. The decisions proceed on an ad hoc basis, and the taxpayer must always be alert to avoid an inadvertent arrangement that could lead to an undesirable classification in a questionable situation.

Subchapter S Corporations

More important, it may be legally possible to organize a business venture as a corporation and then to elect to tax the organization in a manner similar to that of a partnership, assuming that the conditions for making this election can be satisfied. This provision is contained in Subchapter S of the code; consequently, such corporations are frequently referred to as Subchapter S corporations. They are alternatively called small business corporations, which is unfortunate for two reasons. First, the qualifying criteria pertinent to this option say nothing about the dollar size of the firm's net worth, sales volume, or number of employees; hence they really may be very large corporations. Second, other special kinds of corporations are also known as small business investment corporations (SBICs) and small business corporations (if their stock has been qualified under Section 1244, a special rule to be considered later). The use of very similar terminology for essentially different kinds of organizations only tends to confuse the uninitiated.

Until 1966, it was legally possible for a business to operate as a sole proprietorship or as a partnership but to elect, under Subchapter R, to be taxed as if it were a corporation. This option was terminated and all prior elections expired on January 1, 1969.

Before a corporation can elect Subchapter S treatment it must meet all of the qualifications set out in the code. Among the more important of these qualifications are the following:

1. There can be no more than 15 shareholders, and each must consent to the election.
2. Only individuals, estates, and certain trusts can hold stock in the electing corporation (that is, there can be no corporate or partnership shareholders).

3. There can be only one class of stock.
4. All shareholders must be either U.S. citizens or resident aliens.
5. Not more than 80 percent of the firm's gross receipts may come from sources outside the United States.
6. Not more than 20 percent of the firm's gross receipts may come from interest, dividends, rents, royalties, annuities, and gains from the sale or exchange of securities.

The first four of these criteria must be satisfied before a firm can make a valid election; failure to meet any of the six criteria during a year will automatically terminate an otherwise valid election.

In addition to the taxable entities already discussed in this chapter, numerous other special tax situations exist that bear upon the entity problem. The regulated investment company, the real estate investment trust, the domestic international sales corporation (or DISC), and the possessions corporation are four such special cases. Rather than belabor these special cases here, we will conclude this chapter with a brief discussion relating the tax formula introduced in Chapters 1 and 2 to the basic entity concepts introduced in this chapter.

Entities and the Taxable Income Concept

The calculation of taxable income proceeds on a slightly different basis for corporations than it does for individuals and fiduciaries. The differences in question are sometimes of importance to the achievement of success in tax avoidance ideas. Consequently, these differences will be examined briefly in the remaining pages of this chapter. To introduce the important differences, let us expand the general formula used to determine the federal income tax liability as it was presented on page 8. The expanded formula can be summarized as illustrated in Figure 3–11.

Special Corporate Considerations

Relative to the corporate entity, only one additional comment is deemed necessary at this point. Among the "special deductions" (those available only to the corporate entity)

FIGURE 3-11

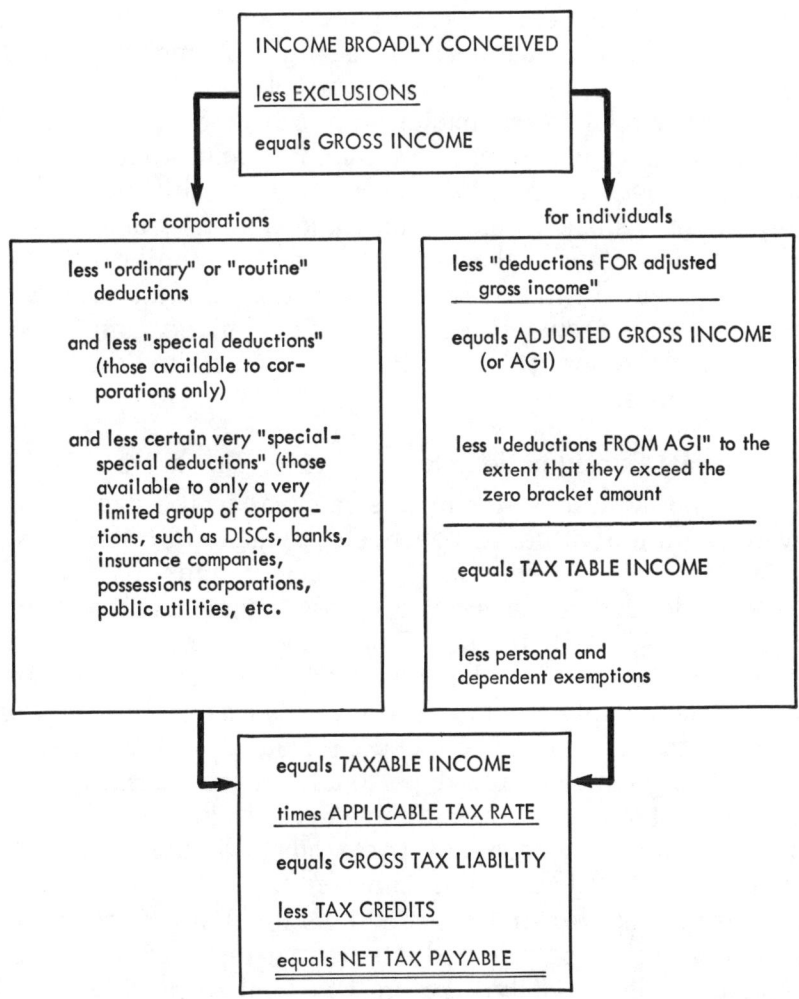

is a dividend-received deduction. A corporation can generally deduct, in the calculation of its taxable income, 85 percent of the dividends it receives during a year from other domestic corporate entities. In the case of controlled groups of corporations, 100 percent of the dividends received from other corporations in the same controlled group may be deducted. The reason for this special corporate deduction is relatively obvious if we reconsider a point made earlier in this chapter: Income earned in the first instance by a corporate entity may be subject to a double tax. If one corporation owns another corporation's stock, does that mean that a single income stream will be subject to a triple tax? In the absence of a dividend-received deduction, or of a special exclusion rule available to the corporate entity, that would be the unhappy circumstance. In the absence of such a provision, corporate ownership of another corporation's stock would be of dubious value since the tax consequence would make such relationships prohibitively expensive. To avoid this serious intervention in multicorporate ownership arrangements common to a modern economy, Congress elected to grant the dividend-received deduction to corporate entities.

Special Considerations for Individual Taxpayers

A few additional comments relevant to the deductions available to individual taxpayers also seem appropriate. First, note that every individual's tax deductions must be divided between deductions *for* adjusted gross income (AGI) and deductions *from* AGI. In the former category, no options are available, and therefore the only question is one of definition. Which deductions are properly classified as deductions for AGI? In the category of deductions from AGI, the taxpayer must determine if itemized personal deductions exceed the zero bracket amount. Thus, relative to the individual's deductions from AGI, we encounter two kinds of problems: the definitional ones and the maximizing ones.

Deductions for AGI. Deductions for AGI are, generally speaking, the taxpayer's deductions that relate to a trade or business. Unfortunately, like most general rules, this one is replete with exceptions and a satisfactory definition would require a time-consuming investigation of Section 62. In lieu of such an investigation, try to understand the following restatement of the more important limits that apply to deductions *for* adjusted gross income.

1. All deductions that can be classified as
    a. *Nonemployee* trade or business expenses (for example, all routine business expenses associated with the operation of a sole proprietorship).

b. Expenses associated with the production of rents and royalties, whether or not that activity constitutes a "trade or business."
2. Only certain expenses incurred as an *employee*, including
   a. All expenses of travel away from home.
   b. All transportation expenses (which classification excludes both the cost of travel away from home and the nondeductible personal cost of commuting from home to work).
   c. Any reimbursed business expenses, but only to the extent of the reimbursement.
   d. All expenses associated with activities conducted as an outside salesperson.
3. The long-term capital gain deduction (explained in Chapter 5).
4. Certain losses from the sale or exchange of trade, business, investment, or "nonbusiness" assets (not including personal assets).
5. The moving expense deduction.
6. Certain contributions to pension or profit-sharing plans.
7. Alimony.
8. Penalties forfeited because of early withdrawals from savings accounts.
9. Certain expenses for living overseas.
10. A few miscellaneous items.

Any legitimate income tax deduction not within one of the above classifications must be a deduction *from* the adjusted gross income of the individual taxpayer.

Deductions from AGI. An individual taxpayer's deductions from AGI can be subdivided into two major groups: the $1,000 personal and dependent exemption deductions and all other deductions. As noted earlier, personal deductions must exceed the zero bracket amount if the taxpayer is itemizing deductions. The zero bracket amount is automatically built into the current tax rate schedules. For single persons and heads of households, it currently amounts to $2,300; for married persons filing jointly, it is $3,400; and for married persons filing separately, it is $1,700. If itemized deductions exceed these amounts, the excess may be claimed as a deduction from AGI. No dollar limit is applicable to itemized deductions.

For most individual taxpayers, the important personal or itemized deductions are the medical expense deduction, the charitable contribution deduction, the interest expense deduction, and the deduction for certain taxes. To the extent that these items can be manipulated individually in successful tax avoidance, they will be discussed later. However, one very simple tax avoidance idea ought to be noted here since it depends upon aggregate deductions from AGI.

It is not unusual to discover that a salaried individual taxpayer in the lower income brackets finds that his or her legitimate itemized deductions are about equal to the zero bracket amount. This individual often concludes that itemizing his or her deductions is not advisable because it permits him or her to forget record keeping and costs little if anything in additional taxes. Actually this individual may be missing the only opportunity for tax planning available. Because the cash-basis taxpayer has a great deal of control over the timing of expenditures, he or she can often accelerate or postpone the incurrence of a tax-deductible item. To minimize the tax liability, a taxpayer may elect to itemize deductions only in alternate years. In the year in which he or she itemizes deductions, the taxpayer can accelerate all charitable contributions, incur and pay larger medical and dental expenses (for example, schedule an annual physical examination late in December to facilitate payment in December or in January, as best suits the tax plan), pay interest and possibly, to a limited extent, prepay property taxes. In the year in which this taxpayer claims only the zero bracket amount, he or she should delay (at least in the last four months of the year) the payment of any medical or dental bills, the making of any charitable contributions, and the payment of any taxes or interest. These expenditures could be paid early in the following year, which would be another itemizing year. By this simple application of careful timing, the salaried taxpayer may be able to increase aggregate deductions and minimize the net tax liability over several years.

We should also note that to whatever extent a taxpayer can legally classify deductions as deductions for AGI, it may pay to do so. This is especially true if the zero bracket amount exceeds itemized deductions. That is, if a taxpayer could legally arrange to incur all deductible expenses as deductions for AGI, he or she would gain to the extent of the zero bracket amount. Obviously, the reclassification of deductions is not at the option of the taxpayer and the definitional problems are substantial. Suffice it to note here that the self-employed taxpayer engaged in a trade or business is frequently at an advantage in this regard, as compared to an employee.

1980 Tax Rate Schedules: Unmarried Individuals (other than surviving spouses and heads of households)

If taxable income is:		Then the gross tax payable is:		
Over	But not over	Amount (dollars)	Plus (percent)	Of the amount over
$ 0	$ 2,300	No tax		
2,300	3,400	$ 0	14%	$ 2,300
3,400	4,400	154	16	3,400
4,400	6,500	314	18	4,400
6,500	8,500	692	19	6,500
8,500	10,800	1,072	21	8,500
10,800	12,900	1,555	24	10,800
12,900	15,000	2,059	26	12,900
15,000	18,200	2,605	30	15,000
18,200	23,500	3,565	34	18,200
23,500	28,800	5,367	39	23,500
28,800	34,100	7,434	44	28,800
34,100	41,500	9,766	49	34,100
41,500	55,300	13,392	55	41,500
55,300	81,800	20,982	63	55,300
81,800	108,300	37,677	68	81,800
108,300	—	55,697	70	108,300

1980 Tax Rate Schedules: Married Individuals Filing Joint Returns and Surviving Spouses

If taxable income is:		Then the gross tax payable is:		
Over	But not over	Amount (dollars)	Plus (percent)	Of the amount over
$ 0	$ 3,400	No tax		
3,400	5,500	$ 0	14%	$ 3,400
5,500	7,600	294	16	5,500
7,600	11,900	630	18	7,600
11,900	16,000	1,404	21	11,900
16,000	20,200	2,265	24	16,000
20,200	24,600	3,273	28	20,200
24,600	29,900	4,505	32	24,600
29,900	35,200	6,201	37	29,900
35,200	45,800	8,162	43	35,200
45,800	60,000	12,720	49	45,800
60,000	85,600	19,678	54	60,000
85,600	109,400	33,502	59	85,600
109,400	162,400	47,544	64	109,400
162,400	215,400	81,464	68	162,400
215,400	—	117,504	70	215,400

1980 Tax Rate Schedules: Married Individuals Filing Separate Returns

If taxable income is:		Then the gross tax payable is:		
Over	But not over	Amount (dollars)	Plus (percent)	Of the amount over
$ 0	$ 1,700	No tax		
1,700	2,750	$ 0	14%	$ 1,700
2,750	3,800	147.00	16	2,750
3,800	5,950	315.00	18	3,800
5,950	8,000	702.00	21	5,950
8,000	10,100	1,132.50	24	8,000
10,100	12,300	1,636.50	28	10,100
12,300	14,950	2,252.50	32	12,300
14,950	17,600	3,100.50	37	14,950
17,600	22,900	4,081.00	43	17,600
22,900	30,000	6,360.00	49	22,900
30,000	42,800	9,839.00	54	30,000
42,800	54,700	16,751.00	59	42,800
54,700	81,200	23,772.00	64	54,700
81,200	107,700	40,732.00	68	81,200
107,700	—	58,752.00	70	107,700

1980 Tax Rate Schedules: Heads of Households

If taxable income is:		Then the gross tax payable is:		
Over	But not over	Amount (dollars)	Plus (percent)	Of the amount over
$ 0	$ 2,300	No tax		
2,300	4,400	$ 0	14%	$ 2,300
4,400	6,500	294	16	4,400
6,500	8,700	630	18	6,500
8,700	11,800	1,026	22	8,700
11,800	15,000	1,708	24	11,800
15,000	18,200	2,476	26	15,000
18,200	23,500	3,308	31	18,200
23,500	28,800	4,951	36	23,500
28,800	34,100	6,859	42	28,800
34,100	44,700	9,085	46	34,100
44,700	60,600	13,961	54	44,700
60,600	81,800	22,547	59	60,600
81,800	108,300	35,055	63	81,800
108,300	161,300	51,750	68	108,300
161,300	—	87,790	70	161,300

1980 Tax Rate Schedules: Fiduciary Taxpayers

If taxable income is:		Then the gross tax payable is:		
Over	But not over	Amount (dollars)	Plus (percent)	Of the amount over
$ 0	$ 1,050	No tax	14%	$ 0
1,050	2,100	$ 147.00	16	1,050
2,100	4,250	315.00	18	2,100
4,250	6,300	702.00	21	4,250
6,300	8,400	1,132.50	24	6,300
8,400	10,600	1,636.50	28	8,400
10,600	13,250	2,252.50	32	10,600
13,250	15,900	3,100.50	37	13,250
15,900	21,200	4,081.00	43	15,900
21,200	28,300	6,360.00	49	21,200
28,300	41,100	9,839.00	54	28,300
41,100	53,000	16,751.00	59	41,100
53,000	79,500	23,772.00	64	53,000
79,500	106,000	40,732.00	68	79,500
106,000	—	58,752.00	70	106,000

CHAPTER 4

Tax Aspects of Selecting a Business Form

Successful tax planning is dependent upon a timely selection of the most advantageous alternative. The tax problem is not unlike the problem of transporting oneself or some other object from, say, New York City to Chicago. There are an almost infinite number of alternatives for both problems. Considering the transportation problem, we could begin with such obvious alternatives as flying, driving, taking a bus, riding a bicycle, walking, or even going by ship (up the Atlantic and down the St. Lawrence Seaway). Upon further investigation each of those alternatives yields many further choices. For example, if we elect to fly, will it be by commercial or private plane? By jet, propjet, or propeller-driven aircraft? First class, day coach, economy, or night coach? On United, American, TWA, or some other airline? A morning, afternoon, or evening flight? Do we want to go directly or stop over? If we stop over, should we go via Boston, Philadelphia, Miami, Dallas, Los Angeles, San Francisco, or Seattle?

Planning a trip, fortunately, is typically not all that complicated because we have some general constraints that grossly simplify our decision. For example, we may want to go the fastest, most direct, and cheapest way that will get us to our destination by 10 A.M. and allow us to leave from a specified airport. Alternatively, we may want to drive and take the "most scenic route," allowing a maximum of eight days en route. In some tax problems, as in transportation problems, the constraints often dictate a specific answer. In other tax problems, they allow us greater though limited leeway. Fortunately, the number of overriding tax constraints is sufficiently small for us to deal with them adequately in this book. The myriad of possible tax details can be left to the volumes written for professional tax advisers.

The Basic Tax Constraints

Most business-oriented people are at one time or another introduced to the nontax advantages and disadvantages of the various forms of business organizations. They learn, for example, that the corporate form of organization provides numerous opportunities for raising large sums of capital, limits the financial liability of the owner to the amount invested in the corporate stock (in most instances), provides for unrestricted transferability of the ownership interest, and makes possible an unlimited life of the business entity. They also know that the sole proprietorship and the partnership are much easier to create than the corporation, but that these business forms also provide for the unlimited liability of the owners; that they may be terminated in numerous ways, sometimes at a most disadvantageous time; and that the transferability of their ownership may be restricted.

In many situations these nontax considerations are of paramount importance in the selection of a business form for a particular enterprise. However, in an equally large number of small to medium-sized business ventures this is not the case, particularly in ventures owned by a small number of individuals. Here tax considerations commonly play a dominant role in the process of selecting the business form. Unfortunately, some owners form and operate businesses without giving adequate thought to the pertinent tax considerations. This chapter is concerned with precisely those considerations. It will introduce some basic tax-planning ideas; concomitant details will be considered in subsequent chapters. Consequently, it might be advisable to read this chapter twice; once now, and again on completion of the book. It is hoped that, on the second reading, the significance of many items that may seem remote after the first reading will have become obvious.

Maximum Reinvestment of Income

Many businesses, especially new ventures, want to maximize the capital available for reinvestment in the business. The amount of income that is available for reinvestment is closely related to the taxation of the earnings stream. Obviously, a person can reinvest only aftertax profits. As a consequence, it is particularly important to consider the tax rate that will be applied to a given income stream if the aftertax income and the reinvestment potential are to be maximized. As noted in Chapter 3, the marginal tax rates applied to individual taxable income currently range from a low of 14 percent to a high of 70 percent. The marginal tax rates applied to corporate taxable incomes are 17, 20, 30, 40, or 46 percent. It is apparent, therefore, that one of the prime criteria in the selection of a business form is the aggregate income of the owner of the business. If he or she earns an income subject to a marginal tax bracket that exceeds 17, 20, 30, 40, or 46 percent, as the case may be, that taxpayer may very well elect to arrange all business affairs in such a way that a corporate entity may be used to shield the income from higher personal tax rates. Observe that this consideration becomes a pertinent factor at relatively low levels of income: the single taxpayer is subject to a *marginal* tax rate of more than 17 percent on all taxable income in excess of $4,400 per year; the married taxpayer filing a joint return pays more than 17 percent when taxable income exceeds $7,600 annually. The 46 percent marginal corporate tax bracket becomes preferable when taxable income exceeds $34,100 for the single individual and $45,800 for the married person filing jointly. Hence, it is possible to maximize the income available for reinvestment by splitting an income between a corporation and an individual even at relatively modest incomes. As an overriding practical constraint, of course, the diversion of any income into a corporate entity for reinvestment presupposes that the individual taxpayer has sufficient personal income to satisfy personal financial needs.

Some readers will have serious misgivings about the point just made. That is, they may have observed that income earned by the corporate entity must sooner or later be taxed twice and therefore conclude that a better comparison might match the two taxes (corporate plus personal) of the incorporated business to the single tax of the unincorporated business. On further examination, however, the reader will find that, for the small, closely held corporation, this double tax problem is just about as much myth as it is reality.

First, note that the owner of a closely held business can avoid any double tax on much of the corporation's income by the use of any of several simple expedients. For example, the owner may pay himself or herself a salary for the service performed in the corporate employ. This salary, so long as it is reasonable in amount, is deductible by the corporation in the calculation of taxable income. Consequently, the salary is taxed only once to the individual owner, as personal compensation. Small corporations may reduce their taxable income to zero, virtually at the owner's discretion, by a simple adjustment of the owner-employee's salary. If the salary reaches the unreasonable range, and the corporation desires to reduce its taxable income still more, it may rent property from the owner and pay a reasonable rent, pay interest on money borrowed, or pay a royalty for the corporation's use of the owner's patent or copyright. Any reasonable amounts paid for these items become a corporate tax deduction at the same time that they create additional gross income for the owner. As illustrated, the closely held corporation may be able to distribute a substantial portion of its income to the owner without incurring a double tax. The only time a double tax is incurred is when the corporation accumulates the income and subsequently distributes corporate assets to the owner *as a dividend*. Dividends paid are *not* deductible by the corporation in the determination of corporate taxable income even though dividends received by the individual stockholder are generally taxable as ordinary income. Admittedly, individual stockholders are authorized to exclude $200 in dividends annually, but this exclusion does not provide them with any great opportunity for large tax savings.[1]

---

[1] For years after 1982, the $200 dividend—interest exclusion is scheduled to return to $100 per year. Whether or not that will happen remains to be seen.

To summarize, we might think of every person as having direct or indirect command over an annual stream of income, which can be represented by the size of an arrow. If that income is derived from anything other than a salary paid by a noncontrolled corporation, the owner typically has a great deal of discretion over how the income stream should be diffused among business organizations and how, therefore, it will be taxed. The problem can be depicted as shown in Figure 4–1.

FIGURE 4–1

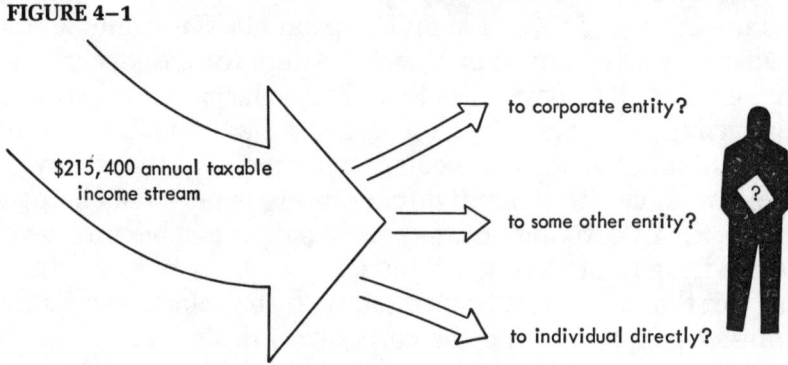

The person shown in the figure would be in a high marginal income tax bracket because of the size of the annual income stream. If this person wants to maximize the reinvestment potential, he or she might consider the distribution shown in Figure 4–2 as desirable. If this owner had selected any form of

FIGURE 4–2

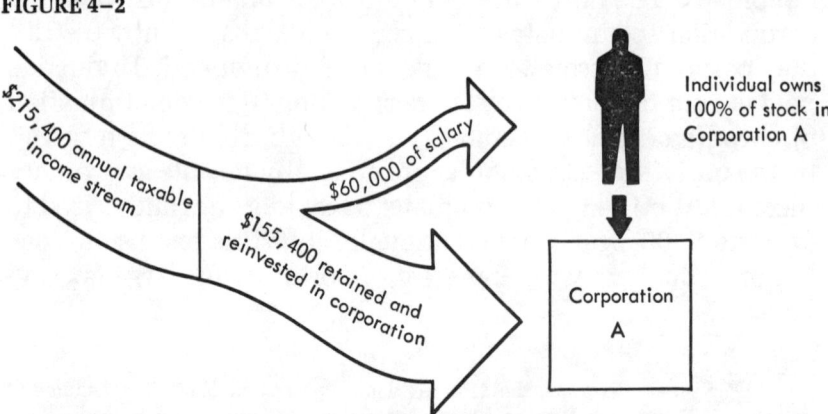

business organization other than a corporation, he or she would have been treated as if the $215,400 had been received directly, and would have paid an individual income tax of $117,504 (assuming that the owner was married and filed a joint return with a spouse). This alternative leaves the owner with only $97,896 for consumption spending plus reinvestment in a business. Given the arrangement suggested in the second diagram, the corporation would pay an income tax of $52,234 and the owner would pay an income tax of $19,678. By this simple rearrangement of business affairs, this taxpayer has reduced the total income tax liability by $45,592 per year and thereby increased the annual opportunity to reinvest in a business by that same amount. To quantify the importance of this difference we need but observe that an annual tax saving of this size, reinvested at a 5 percent after-tax rate of return, accumulates to something like *$5.5 million* over a 40-year period! Given this fact, is it any wonder that more than 1.9 million corporate income tax returns are filed annually in the United States, even though less than 5,000 corporations account for two thirds of all corporate taxable income?

Perhaps an early word of caution is in order. The owner of a closely held corporation must take care to avoid the incurrence of an accumulated earnings tax. This income-related tax was instituted by Congress to control the abuse of the corporate tax rate shelter—a fancy name for the tax avoidance opportunity just explained. That is, Congress did not want wealthy individuals transferring most of their income-earning assets into a corporate shell *solely* for the purpose of avoiding higher personal income tax rates. To control this abuse, Congress instituted the accumulated earnings tax, which applies to all *unreasonable* accumulations of income (in excess of a $150,000 exemption). The details of this penalty tax are discussed much later in this book. Suffice it to note here that only unreasonable accumulations are taxed and that accumulations of corporate income are generally not found to be unreasonable so long as the owner puts them to good use rather than permitting them to lie relatively idle, simply reinvesting them in high-grade securities, or lending them back to the corporate stockholders.

Retention of Special Income Characteristics

A second important tax factor pertinent to selecting a business form concerns the desirability of retaining certain tax characteristics that are attributed to select "kinds" of income. The notion of exclusions was introduced in Chapter 1 and explained further in Chapter 2. What was not noted, however, was that the designation of certain income as exempt income may be lost when this income is commingled with other income in a corporate entity. That is, if a corporation earns interest on state or local government bonds, the corporation, like the individual, need not report this interest as part of its taxable income for the year. Suppose, however, that, after the corporation earned this interest, the corporate board voted to distribute this same income as a dividend to the stockholders. Would the cash distributed retain its tax-exempt characteristic? No. So long as the distributing corporation had either current earnings and profits or earnings and profits accumulated after March 1, 1913, the distribution would be taxed as ordinary dividend income. Even if the corporation had no such earnings, any distribution of that same income as a salary would be subject to tax by the employee receiving it. There is nothing that the corporate board could do by way of isolating or separating this income from other corporate income to make it retain its tax-free characteristics.

The rule just stated is not restricted to tax-exempt income. It applies equally to other tax-advantageous forms of income, such as long-term capital gain. Suppose, for example, that a small corporation realizes a large amount of long-term capital gain in a particular year. Although the corporation can claim the tax benefits extended to long-term capital gain, the corporate board generally can do nothing to pass this tax advantage along to the owners if and when they choose to distribute the gain.

Based on even this limited discussion, it is apparent that whenever a business venture earns a significant amount of tax-favored income it is generally desirable to have that venture organized in such a form that the tax laws will treat it as a conduit rather than as a separate entity. This result is generally possible if the venture is organized as a sole proprietorship, a partnership, or a Subchapter S corporation. It is not possible when the business venture is incorporated unless the Subchapter S option can be exercised, and even then special limits become applicable in some instances.

Utilization of Net Operating Losses

Net operating losses present a tax situation very similar to that of the tax-favored income items mentioned in the preceding paragraphs. That is, it is generally desirable for a business venture that incurs a loss to be organized as a tax conduit rather than as a separate taxable entity. This is true because the owner can often use the operating loss from one venture to offset taxable income from another venture on his or her individual tax return. If the loss is incurred in a separate corporate entity, the owner cannot pass the loss through the entity and utilize it on his or her personal tax return. In that case, the loss can be used only to offset prior or subsequent income of the corporation, as suggested on pages 39 and 40.

Business entities that frequently or continually incur tax losses are usually organized as sole proprietorships, partnerships, or Subchapter S corporations so that the owners can take maximum advantage of the tax loss on their personal tax returns. This consideration is also pertinent in the formation of a new business venture since it is commonplace for new ventures to incur losses during the first several years of operation. The Subchapter S corporation may be particularly useful in this instance since the new corporation that subsequently becomes profitable may elect to terminate the Subchapter S election at a most advantageous time.

The conclusion suggesting that loss operations are best organized in noncorporate forms presumes, of course, that the individual owner(s) would be in a higher marginal tax bracket than the corporation. If this presumption is not valid, an opposite conclusion is correct. In other words, if a net operating loss can be carried back by a corporation and offset against its own taxable income of prior years that was taxed at 46 percent, this alternative is preferable any time the owner will have to utilize that same net operating loss in offsetting his or her own taxable income that was taxed at a marginal rate of less than 46 percent.

A second aspect of net operating losses is also pertinent to the business-form question. The owner of corporate stock generally gets no personal tax advantage from the corporation's losses until he or she elects to sell some or all of the shares. At that time, the shares presumably will be worth less because of the losses incurred by the corporation. If the stockholder does sell the shares at a loss, he or she will discover that such a loss is a capital loss and, as such, is restricted in the amount deductible in a particular year. As a general rule, an individual taxpayer cannot deduct more than $3,000 per year in capital losses against ordinary income. Admittedly, a taxpayer may use capital losses to offset capital gains without limit, but most taxpayers would prefer to deduct capital losses against ordinary income and recognize the larger amount of capital gain since that gain carries significant tax advantages with it. As explained above, the owner of a sole proprietorship or partnership interest is not faced with the necessity of disposing of part or all of a business interest before reaping the tax benefit of the loss incurred by the business. In addition, such an owner gets that loss as an ordinary loss rather than as a capital loss in most instances.

Employee Status

The owner of a sole proprietorship or a partnership interest is generally not considered to be an employee of his or her own firm for tax purposes. The owner of a corporate entity may, however, be an employee of his or her own corporation. This difference constitutes another major consideration in selecting from among alternative business forms. Generally speaking, significant tax advantages are available to an employee that are not available to a self-employed individual. In a limited number of cases, however, it may be to a particular taxpayer's advantage to avoid employee status.

Among the tax advantages granted an employee but denied to the self-employed person are tax-free group life, health, and wage-continuation insurance plans, certain death benefits, and the chance to receive meals, lodging, and recreational facilities without increasing taxable income. In addition, the tax advantages hidden in the deferred compensation plans that may be granted to employees, including pension and profit-sharing opportunities, typically are more generous than are the tax benefits available under similar plans granted to self-employed individuals.

In a closely held corporation, these employee benefits may provide the best of all possible tax worlds. This happy result occurs whenever the corporate entity is permitted a tax deduction for an item that need not be reported as gross income by the owner-employee recipient. In effect, the owner's left pocket (the corporation) has obtained a tax deduction for an item that the right pocket (the individual owner) may treat as an exclusion. A next-best alternative is to get the corporation an immediate tax deduction for an item of gross income that the individual owner need not report for a number of years and then, perhaps, only as a capital gain.

A corporate owner-employee may also be in a position to take advantage of an entertainment allowance, travel opportunities, or a company car. Because these items are difficult to separate from personal expenses that frequently would not constitute a deductible item if incurred directly by a taxpayer at his or her own expense, the IRS pays particular attention to audit returns that indicate possible misuse in this manner. The remaining opportunities are, however, sufficiently great that Chapter 7 is entirely devoted to this topic.

The major tax disadvantage that may attach to classification as an employee stems from the deduction problem discussed in Chapter 3. An employee is more restricted than the self-employed person in deducting items *for* adjusted gross income. Many trade or business expenses incurred by an employee must be categorized as deductions *from* adjusted gross income. Since itemized deductions are of no tax value except to the extent that they exceed the zero bracket amount, the employee in a very few instances may find that it would be preferable to be self-employed. On the whole, however, the majority of the tax advantages rest with the *owner-employee* status that can be achieved only through incorporation.

Earned Income

Another possible tax reason for selecting the corporate form of business organization pertains to the ease with which a businessperson can create "personal service taxable income" through the payment of salaries to the corporate executive. To explain the importance of this change, we must revert briefly to a discussion of the individual tax rate schedules introduced in Chapter 3. Those tax rate schedules are subject to at least two major aberrations: (1) the 50 percent maximum tax on personal service taxable income and (2) the special tax treatment given certain long-term capital gains. The former aberration will be discussed here; the latter, in the next chapter.

Abstracting from certain calculational details, the maximum tax on personal service income simply says that the *marginal* tax rate to be applied to personal service taxable income of an individual taxpayer cannot exceed 50 percent. Application of this provision obviously necessitates the separation of taxable income into two component parts, which can be labeled *earned* (or, more accurately, personal service taxable income) and *unearned* income. The distinction intended by these terms is essentially the difference between (1) income derived from the rendering of personal service and (2) income derived from property. At the margin, the former will not be taxed at more than 50 percent; the latter may be taxed at rates up to 70 percent. This departure from the tax rate schedules plotted in Figure 3–2 can be depicted conceptually as shown in Figure 4–3, where the distance *ac* equals total taxable in-

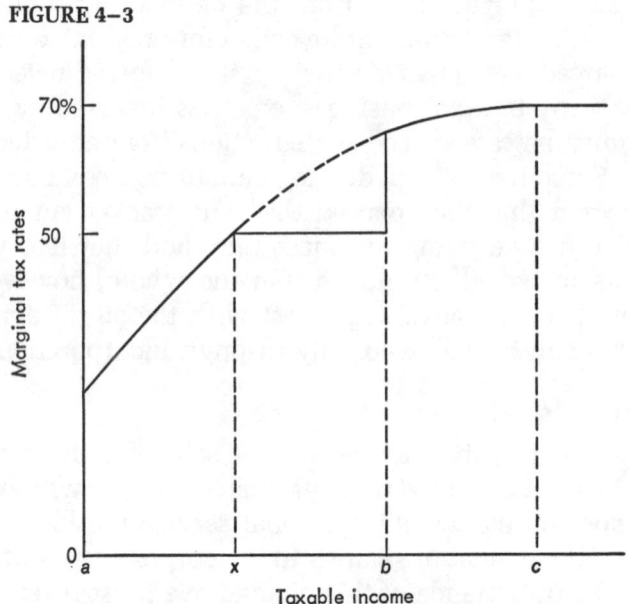

FIGURE 4–3

come, ab represents personal service taxable income, and bc represents unearned income. Distance ax represents the portion of personal service taxable income (ab) that would be taxed at a marginal rate of less than 50 percent because of the normal progression in the regular rate schedule. The exact dollar amount of distance ax depends, of course, on the particular rate schedule in question. For single taxpayers the maximum tax on earned income becomes operative whenever the taxpayer's personal service taxable income exceeds $41,500. In other words, for single taxpayers, the distance ax is $41,500. For married taxpayers filing jointly, it is $60,000; for married persons filing separately, it is $30,000; and for heads of households, $44,700.

The critical aspect of the business-form alternative is related to the separation of taxable income into its personal service and unearned components. The taxable income of many businesses is attributable jointly to the presence of a service and of capital. For example, the income derived from operating a grocery store, an automobile dealership, a gasoline station, a drugstore, a farm, a truck line, a shrimp boat, or literally hundreds of other businesses is typically a combination of the taxable income attributable to the service rendered by the owner and the taxable income attributable to the capital that that owner has invested in the business. If the taxable income is sufficiently large, the maximum tax on personal service taxable income will require that a taxpayer distinguish between these two component elements in the application of the appropriate tax rate.

Prior to 1980, for unincorporated businesses only, the Internal Revenue Code arbitrarily provided that, whenever income was derived from a business in which capital was a material income-producing factor, not more than 30 percent of the business income could be reported as personal service income. This arbitrary statutory rule provided an excellent reason for incorporating a business because it facilitated the transformation of unearned income into personal service income. In other words, by the mere act of incorporating a business and distributing the corporation's income as a salary to the owner-employee, what otherwise might have been unearned income was suddenly personal service income. Since January 1, 1980, the 30 percent statutory rule is no longer in effect. Nevertheless, at least for the next several years, the author believes that the existence of a corporate entity will continue to help minimize arguments with IRS agents over what portion of a business income is unearned income, attributable to the owner's capital investment. Agents are only human, and it takes humans many years to break old habits.

To illustrate the tax planning potential of the maximum tax on earned income in combination with the benefits of splitting a single income stream between two entities—one individual, the other corporate—consider the tax liability that would apply to the owner of a business in which capital was a material income-producing factor and that produced a $150,000 annual taxable income. If that business were not incorporated, a liberal agent today might disregard the old 30 percent rule and permit 50 percent of the business income to be treated as personal service income. What would that mean for the owner of this business? Ignoring several possible complications, that means the owner could report $75,000 as personal service taxable income and another $75,000 as unearned income. Using the current tax rates for married persons filing a joint return, the federal income tax would be computed as follows:

"Regular" tax on first $60,000		$19,678
Plus 50 percent of next $15,000		7,500
Plus "regular" tax on the last $75,000 of unearned income, determined as follows:		
"Regular" tax on $150,000	$73,528	
Less "regular" tax on $75,000	27,778	
Difference		45,750
Total federal income tax on $150,000 earned		$72,928

If this same businessperson were to incorporate the business, have the corporation distribute $100,000 to the owner as salary, and have the corporation retain the remaining $50,000 within the corporate entity, the federal income tax liability for that business would be computed as follows:

Personal income tax liability of the owner:		
"Regular" tax on first $60,000	$19,678	
Plus 50 percent of the next $40,000	20,000	
Total individual income tax		$39,678
Corporate income tax on the retained income:		
First $25,000 × 17 percent	$ 4,250	
Plus second $25,000 × 20 percent	5,000	
Total corporate income tax		9,250
Total federal income tax on $150,000 earned		$48,928

Obviously, the two total tax liabilities determined in the prior paragraph are not wholly comparable. In the first example, the owner has $77,072 in aftertax income completely available for personal consumption or investment needs. In the second example, the owner has only $35,322 in aftertax income available to satisfy personal consumption needs; the remaining $65,750 in aftertax income is tied up within the corporate entity. That sum is generally free for additional investment, but it is severely restricted when it comes to consumption spending for the owner. As we will discover in Chapter 7, some consumption needs may be satisfied through tax-deductible executive "perks" provided by the corporation for its owner. Not all consumption needs, however, are so readily accommodated. In summary, whether or not this tax plan is desirable depends upon the portion of the business income that the owner desires to consume individually and the portion that he or she is willing to reinvest. The greater the latter amount, the more desirable the tax plan. If the owner of the business is willing to forgo immediate consumption and invests the $24,000 in federal income taxes saved each year for 40 years in an investment that returns just slightly over 5 percent after taxes, the tax saving alone will increase the value of the owner's wealth by $3 million! The additional value attributable to the annual reinvestment of $65,750 in the corporation will, of course, dwarf even that impressive sum.

    A word of caution might also be in order. The success of the tax plan just explained will depend upon the ability of the owner-employee to sustain a $100,000 annual salary as "reasonable" in amount. Although a few years ago salaries of $100,000 were rare, the introduction of the maximum tax on personal service income—along with some other changes in the code—made even much larger salaries commonplace. The tendency to increase salaries is apparent in some of the aggregate data released in the IRS commissioner's IRS report to Congress. In 1972, the first year that the maximum tax was fully integrated into the law in its present form, only 88,085 individuals took advantage of this option. In 1976, the last year for which data are available, 231,877 individuals claimed the right to utilize the maximum tax provision. Although some of the increase is attributable to detailed changes in the law, and some to inflation during the period 1972–76, the 260 percent increase in just four years suggests that many businesspeople were responding intelligently to the major changes taking place in federal income taxation.

Prior to 1970, the owners of small and medium-sized businesses tended to accumulate all their business income beyond personal consumption needs within the corporations formed to take advantage of the lower corporate rates. As explained in Chapter 3, this was usually achieved through the use of multiple corporate entities. The 1969 Tax Reform Act changed those tendencies by concurrently (1) eliminating the possibility of multiple corporations and (2) instituting the maximum tax on personal service income. The owners of many businesses soon realized that leaving taxable income beyond approximately $50,000 in their corporations was tantamount to subjecting that income to an immediate corporate income tax of (then) 48 percent. The distribution of that same income as a salary paid to the owner meant a personal income tax of no more than 50 percent. In exchange for the penalty of only two additional percentage points in taxes, the owner could be immediately free to consume or invest the additional business income as he or she desired.

Even the retention of $50,000 per year within a corporate entity was questionable between 1970 and 1979. Prior to the 1969 Tax Reform Act, individual long-term capital gains were never taxed at more than 25 percent. After the 1969 Act and prior to 1979, the same gains were frequently taxed at rates approaching 50 percent. Thus, if even the first $50,000 of retained corporate income were eventually subject to an additional 50 percent long-term capital gain tax—when the owner sold the capital stock in the corporation that had appreciated in value because of the $50,000 retained every year—there was little tax incentive to retain any income within the corporation. An immediate distribution of the entire corporate income, as salary paid to the owner, clearly made good tax sense in many situations.

The 1978 Revenue Act changed tax planning dramatically for the closely held businesses of America. That Act changed the tax rules for long-term capital gains so that, under most circumstances today, an individual will pay no more than 28 percent on those gains. Furthermore, the 1978 Act made major changes in the corporate tax rate schedule. Prior to 1979, corporations were subject to a three-step tax rate schedule (of 20, 22, and 48 percent); in 1979, the current five-step schedule (of 17, 20, 30, 40, and 46 percent) came into effect. Thus any income retained within the corporation after 1979 (1) was immediately subject to less tax than it had been in prior years, and (2) would be subject to a much less severe capital gains tax if later realized by the owner through the sale of the corporate stock. The combined effect of these two recent changes—along with the increased realization that multiple-family corporations were only crippled, not killed in 1969—has caused many business people to rethink their income distribution policies.

To summarize, between 1969 and 1978 many businesspeople decided to distribute nearly all their corporation's income as salary; since 1979 they have once again begun to retain some of that income within multiple-family corporations. This tendency to retain income within a corporate entity gained additional strength when, as part of the 1980 Windfall Profits Tax Act, Congress changed the basis rules for inherited properties back to the rules that existed prior to the Tax Reform Act of 1976.

The several changes in capital gains taxation mentioned above will be further explained in Chapter 5. At the moment, however, we must return to the basic theme of this chapter—that is, the important tax reasons for selecting one business form rather than another.

Gaining a Special Tax Deduction

For most purposes, the individual taxpayer and the corporation are entitled to claim essentially the same deductions, at least so far as business-related expenses are concerned. A major exception to that general rule exists relative to the dividend-received deduction. As explained earlier, a corporation is granted a deduction equal to 85 percent of the dividends it receives from most other domestic corporations. An individual taxpayer gets no similar deduction, although he or she is allowed to exclude from gross income the first $200 of dividends or interest received each year.

Because of this important difference in the tax treatment of individuals and corporate entities, a major opportunity for tax avoidance exists. Any individual earning a substantial *dividend* income must consider the possibility of transferring some dividend-paying investments into a corporate entity. By doing this, the taxpayer may significantly lower the effective tax rate on the dividends received. Ignoring complications that will be discussed later, suppose for a moment that a married individual receives $60,000 in taxable income from a salary, plus $100,000 in dividends annually. This taxpayer would incur a minimum tax liability of approximately $60,000 on the dividends received. If this same individual were free to transfer the stocks that paid the dividends into a corporation (created simply to receive them), the annual tax liability on the same income could be reduced to something like $2,550 were it not for some special restrictions. This low tax liability would be the direct result of the corporate dividend-received deduction, which would operate as follows:

Dividends received by new corporation	$100,000
Less 85 percent of $100,000 dividends received	85,000
Corporate taxable income	$ 15,000
Times applicable corporate tax rate	× 17%
Equals gross tax liability	$ 2,550

Recognizing this tremendous opportunity that a corporation creates for sheltering the dividend income of wealthy persons, Congress enacted a personal holding company tax. The critical effect of this tax is to take away the tax shelter provided for dividends received by the corporation, but the special tax is applicable only in the more obvious and extreme cases. It becomes effective only when the *passive* income of a corporate entity is *relatively* more important than income earned in more *active* business endeavors. That is, if a corporation is created to do little more than collect dividends, clip interest coupons, and/or cash rent checks, the personal holding company tax will probably prevail. If, on the other hand, the dividend-rich taxpayer is careful to blend into a single corporate shell both some active business venture and some passive business investments, he or she may be able to reduce the effective tax rate paid on the dividend income to something like 2.5 percent (that is, 17 percent of 15 percent of the dividends received). This kind of tax planning once again reduces consumption options, but it obviously permits a maximization of reinvestment opportunities by gaining a tax deduction that would not be available in the absence of the corporate entity.

A second example that illustrates how a taxpayer might benefit from obtaining a special deduction does not actually require the existence of a corporate entity, but its existence certainly may facilitate the objective. This second illustration turns on the fact that every individual is ordinarily entitled to claim a $1,000 personal exemption deduction (currently) and a zero bracket amount. For many years, wealthy families were able to take advantage of the zero bracket amount originally intended for low-income people by making certain that every member of the family received a minimum income. Children and grandchildren were given sufficient property—often nonvoting, high-dividend preferred stocks in a closely held corporation—to ensure their receiving an income equal to the sum of the personal exemption deduction and the standard deduction (which is now called the *zero bracket amount*). The tax result was partially restricted after 1971 because Congress passed a rule that disallows the zero bracket amount to any individual claimed as a dependent by another taxpayer, to the extent that the dependent's income is from passive sources. Thus, it is now necessary to ensure that every child "*earns*" at least $2,300 of his or her income—perhaps as a salary paid by the family business—if the maximum tax saving is to be achieved. Although the dollar amounts are relatively small, the tax savings can still be meaningful. In an extreme situation this simple device can remove $3,300 of taxable income from the highest bracket and thereby save $2,310 in taxes each year per child, since the new recipient would pay no tax on that income. Incidentally, the parent will not lose the right to claim a second personal exemption deduction for the child if the child is under 19 or a full-time student and if a few other requirements are satisfied. This duplication of a single special deduction—that is, the claiming of a personal exemption deduction by both the child and the parent—is a rare occurrence in taxation. Typically, only one taxpayer is entitled to claim any particular tax deduction.

Disposition of a Business

The form in which a business is organized is particularly important when a taxpayer dissolves or otherwise disposes of that business. Upon disposition of a sole proprietorship, an owner is generally assumed to have disposed of the individual assets that constitute the business venture for tax purposes. The proceeds of the sale must be allocated among all of the assets, based on their relative fair market values. As a consequence of this presumption, much of the profit realized upon disposition may result in ordinary income, since the sale of those same assets individually would have produced ordinary income. By contrast, the owner of a corporate entity usually has an option: The owner can allow the corporation to sell specific assets or can personally dispose of the business by selling the corporation's stock. In most instances the owner is able to claim the tax-advantageous capital gain treatment for any gain realized from the sale of the corporation's stock.

A corporation also provides a good vehicle for partial dispositions. It is relatively cumbersome to sell a partial interest in either a sole proprietorship or a partnership. A partial interest in a corporate entity is often more marketable. Disposition of a partial business interest through the sale of some part of a larger block of stock almost guarantees that any gain will be capital gain. The ease of making stock dispositions also makes the corporate form of business organization of major importance to estate planning for wealthy taxpayers.

Corporations were once widely utilized to convert what would otherwise have been ordinary personal service income into capital gain in rather obvious situations. Perhaps the most celebrated use of the corporation for this purpose came to be known as the Hollywood corporation. Movie moguls, producers, and actors would jointly form a corporation to produce a motion picture. Each participant would contribute his or her talent and minimal capital in exchange for the corporation's stock. Then, after completion of the movie but prior to its distribution, the corporation was collapsed and the stockholders were given the movie royalty rights as a liquidating dividend. The liquidating dividend was taxed as a capital gain rather than as ordinary income. Thus, through the temporary use of the corporation, Hollywood personalities were able to convert what was essentially salary into a liquidating dividend and thereby change the applicable tax from an ordinary income tax into a capital gains tax. Congress, again at the urging of the Treasury, closed this unintended tax loophole by creating a special set of tax rules, which apply only to the disposition of stock in a *collapsible* corporation. It is sufficient to note here, without going into the definition of a collapsible corporation, that the sale or other disposition of stock in such a corporation produces ordinary income rather than capital gain. Although the definitional provisions restrict the breadth of opportunity for converting ordinary income into capital gain through the use of a corporate entity, they do not eliminate such possibilities entirely. Chapter 14, which considers selected tax traps, will examine the remaining possibilities.

Fluctuating Income

Business ventures that are characterized by wide variations in annual income may find it advantageous to incorporate for several reasons. First, the steeply progressive feature of the individual income tax rates at relatively low levels of taxable income may result in a larger tax liability over a period of years than would application of the less progressive corporate rates. Admittedly, this result has been reduced by the introduction of income-averaging provisions that are available to individual taxpayers. Second, the adjustments that are required in converting a negative taxable income into a net operating loss carry-back involve a greater chance for the loss of a tax deduction in the case of an individual taxpayer than they do in the case of a corporate taxpayer. Third, a corporation is generally presumed to be engaged in a trade or business; activities conducted directly by an individual carry no such presumption. Consequently, business ventures that could be considered hobbies (which are often characterized by widely fluctuating incomes) may be better able to withstand an IRS challenge if they are incorporated.

Although the preceding discussion is by no means exhaustive, it should give the reader some appreciation of the basic tax consequences that attach to the selection of any one of the various possible forms of business organization. What may not yet be apparent is that selecting the most advantageous organizational form is often dependent upon a diverse array of unknowns, including the amount of a taxpayer's future income or loss from all sources, the dispersion of that income or loss over several annual periods, the ultimate size of the taxpayer's family, the length of the taxpayer's life, the possibility that either the accumulated earnings tax or the personal holding company tax may be imposed, and subsequent changes in the tax laws. Recognizing the imprecision implicit in these variables, many knowledgeable taxpayers will concentrate their attention on one or two variables deemed to be of primary importance in the hope that other tax consequences can be reasonably accommodated as the business proceeds. In some circumstances, however, nontax considerations may be sufficiently dominant to override what might otherwise be preferable from a tax standpoint. Any reader contemplating a new business venture should seek competent tax advice before selecting the business form within which he or she is going to conduct that venture. Special consideration must be given to business activities that involve more than one country.

Special Considerations for Multinational Businesses

The tax rules applicable to multinational business operations are inordinately complex. What appears here is only a capsule summary of a very few of the more critical tax aspects of doing business abroad. This brief discussion has been divided into unincorporated and incorporated business activities. The more substantial tax-planning opportunities involve the utilization of a corporation.

Unincorporated Businesses

The U.S. income tax is, as previously noted, a global tax; it reaches the taxable income of all citizens and resident aliens, regardless of where that income is earned. As was also noted, the U.S. income tax does not recognize unincorporated businesses as separate taxable entities, but prefers instead to attribute any taxable income from an unincorporated business directly and immediately to the owners of the business. As a consequence of these two rules, any U.S. citizen must generally pay a U.S. income tax each year on any income earned through business operations conducted outside the United States, even though none of that income is immediately repatriated. Special rules are applicable, however, if a foreign government has blocked repatriation by currency restrictions.

Income earned in a foreign country by U.S. citizens is often taxed by the foreign government as well as by the U.S. government. To eliminate a double tax on the single income stream, the United States usually allows the taxpayer to claim a tax credit against the U.S. gross tax liability for any foreign income tax paid. The net effect of this arrangement is to tax an unincorporated business venture, operated by a U.S. citizen or resident alien, at the highest effective rate that is operative in the countries involved.

Corporate Businesses

U.S. corporations doing business abroad must reconsider the business-form question with specific reference to foreign operations. The corporation with a domestic (U.S.) charter can conduct its foreign operations as a branch of the domestic corporation, as a separate but domestic subsidiary of the U.S. parent, or as a foreign subsidiary corporation. In some instances such a corporation can also achieve its objectives through a licensing arrangement with a foreign corporation that is not a subsidiary. The tax consequences of each alternative are different and sometimes substantial.

Branch operations. Domestic corporations engaged in foreign business through branch operations are in essentially the same position as individual taxpayers conducting an unincorporated business abroad. That is, the domestic corporation must pay the U.S. income tax on all operations of a foreign branch immediately, regardless of the disposition of the taxable income earned by the branch. A tax credit may be claimed for any foreign income taxes paid by the branch.

Subsidiary corporations. A domestic corporation can, of course, create a subsidiary corporation to handle its foreign operations. This subsidiary can be either a second domestic corporation or a corporation created under the laws of a foreign country. Subject to a few major exceptions, which are discussed below, the domestic subsidiary doing business abroad will be treated with regard to taxes like most other domestic corporations. However, the creation of a foreign subsidiary gives birth to a host of new problems and opportunities.

Recall the general rules, which provide (a) that a stockholder is generally not taxed on the taxable income earned by a corporation until the corporation distributes its previously accumulated taxable income, and (b) that nonresident aliens are subject to the U.S. income tax only to the extent that they have income from U.S. sources. If applied literally, as they were until about 1962, these rules provided tremendous tax-planning opportunities for foreign subsidiary corporations. A U.S. taxpayer could create a foreign corporation (thus creating something comparable to a nonresident alien) and withhold all earnings of that corporation, until the most propitious moment, without incurring a U.S. income tax. In addition, by a careful selection of the country in which the subsidiary was incorporated, the tax on the corporation's income could be minimized or even obliterated. No less than 25 countries, most of them tiny nations, clamored for years for such corporate shells by creating the most favorable possible corporate tax laws. These became known as "tax haven countries," and the corporate shells created in such countries became known as "base country corporations."

In their heyday, these foreign operations were further

blessed by price gerrymandering of grand proportions. To glimpse briefly the glorious tax opportunities of the past, consider the corporate superstructure shown in Figure 4–4. Although goods were shipped directly from corporation P to

FIGURE 4–4

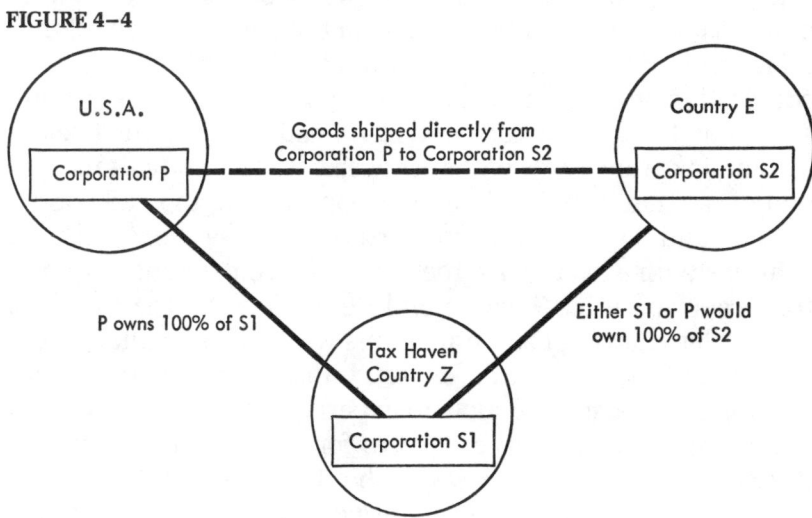

corporation S2 for sale in country E by corporation S2, the legal title to those goods passed momentarily through island empire Z (a tax haven country) and corporation S1. Corporation P would price its sales to corporation S1 at something close to its cost, thereby reducing to a minimum or even to zero the reportable taxable income on foreign sales of corporation P. Corporation S1 would resell the same goods to Corporation S2 at a price comparable to the ultimate sales price of the goods by Corporation S2 in country E (which imposed a corporate income tax), thereby reducing corporation S2's taxable income to zero. Needless to say, corporation S1, in country Z, was a fantastic financial success! The owners of corporation S1 were twice blessed by the coincidence that neither the United States nor country Z would tax those profits until corporation S1 paid corporation P a dividend or until corporation P sold its corporation S1 stock and reaped its bountiful capital gain.

So much for history. Specific statutory changes in the Internal Revenue Code, as well as more vigorous attempts by the IRS to force related taxpayers to deal with each other at something like arm's-length prices, have changed the foreign scene considerably. In the process, the IRS has also created some of the most complex tax provisions ever known to humankind. The important results of the new rules are (a) that under prescribed conditions a U.S. stockholder of a foreign corporation *may be* required to report the taxable income earned by the foreign corporation immediately (as the taxable income is earned) and without regard for any actual repatriation of income from the foreign corporation to the U.S. stockholder; and (b) that related parties must be careful in all dealings with each other if they want to avoid a reallocation of their reported gross income and deductions by the IRS. The exact rules charting these dangerous waters can be understood and interpreted only by an expert. International business ventures simply must have such an expert on board. A few special tax-saving opportunities related to foreign operations that, by design, remain in our tax code, should be examined briefly.

The DISC. In 1971, Congress created a set of special tax provisions intended to reduce the perennial balance of payments problem. These provisions established a special kind of corporation called the Domestic International Sales Corporation, or DISC. The original tax benefits available to a DISC shareholder were curtailed by changes in the Tax Reform Act of 1976. At present, the shareholder in a corporation that qualifies and elects to be taxed as a DISC need report and immediately pay tax on only 50 percent of the excess of the DISC's taxable income in the current year over its average income in a base period, unless a greater percentage is actually distributed by the DISC to the shareholder. If a larger distribution is made, that amount is immediately taxed to the shareholder. If a lesser amount is distributed, the currently untaxed portion of the DISC's taxable income will remain untaxed by the United States until the DISC distributes the income or the shareholder disposes of his or her interest in the DISC. To qualify for DISC deferral privileges, a domestic corporation must, among other things:

1. Have only one class of stock outstanding.
2. Have corporate capital of not less than $2,500.
2. Utilize 95 percent of its assets in direct export activities.
4. Obtain 95 percent of its gross receipts from specified foreign operations.

To a limited extent, therefore, the DISC opportunity returns us to the tax-saving possibilities described generally for foreign subsidiary corporations under the prior caption.

The possessions corporation. A subsidiary corporation that does most of its business in a possession of the United States may be eligible for other tax benefits. Specifically, a subsidiary corporation that earns 80 percent or more of its income from a possession and that earns 50 percent or more of its gross income from an active trade or business is eligible for a new possession tax credit (also known as a Section 936 credit), whether or not it actually pays an income tax to the possession. Some U.S. possessions, such as Puerto Rica, have deliberately excused new business ventures from any local income tax for a period of from 10 to 15 years, just to attract new business. Consequently a U.S. parent corporation that owns a subsidiary doing business in Puerto Rico might well be excused from paying any Puerto Rican income tax because of Puerto Rican law and, at the same time, be excused from paying any U.S. income tax on the income of its subsidiary because of the new possession tax credit. The U.S. tax credit is a phantom credit determined as if the subsidiary had paid a tax to the possession at the tax rate that would have prevailed had that corporation earned the same taxable income in the United States. Furthermore, because of the 100 percent corporate dividend-received deduction applying between two controlled corporations, the subsidiary can repatriate all of its current earnings to its U.S. parent tax-free. Such a dividend distribution may, however, be subject to a "tollgate" tax in Puerto Rico of from 10 to 15 percent. Although the details of these rules may be unclear, even this brief discussion should alert the reader to major tax reduction possibilities for any business which could conduct much of its business in a possession, such as Puerto Rico.

The special tax considerations for multinational business operations could be expanded to include other exotic special provisions. Because most readers could not take advantage of the tax-saving opportunities of those provisions, they are dismissed without discussion. It is hoped that this brief and limited introduction to foreign operations will trigger ideas in some readers. Imagination often pays large dividends in tax matters, and this kind of imagination sometimes involves the careful selection of both a business form and a country of incorporation. Perhaps a classic example of creative imagination came to light in the case of *U.S. Gypsum,* 304 F. Supp. 627. There the court found that a corporation created to own gypsum rock for the split second it took for the rock to fall from a related corporation's conveyor belt to the hold of a ship, which was owned by another related corporation, was not a valid Western Hemisphere Trade Corporation (or WHTC) because it was not actively involved in the conduct of a trade or business.

FIGURE 4–5

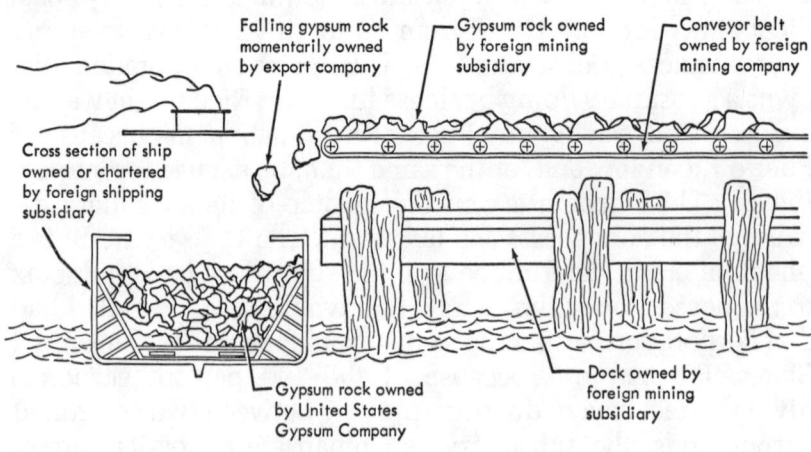

The court report's diagram of the critical facts, which is reproduced in Figure 4–5, is most informative. Although the WHTC tax advantages have been phased out, the case should stand as a monument to creativity for years to come.

CHAPTER 5

Capital Gains and Losses: Basic Rules

Most taxpayers realize that capital gains carry some form of special tax advantage in the United States. Very few taxpayers, however, can accurately explain either what those tax advantages are or exactly which gains represent capital gains. This chapter is intended to give the reader a clearer understanding of the complex rules applicable to the taxation of capital gains and losses and to illustrate the important tax differences that exist because of these complex rules. Even this rather lengthy chapter must be regarded as an incomplete discussion, and the reader must proceed cautiously in applying these rules to real-world situations unless he or she obtains competent tax advice in the process.

Before we begin our examination of the many rules that must be understood in the area of capital gains and losses, we might recall that for years Treasury Department studies have revealed that capital gains privileges constitute the single most important tax loophole in our income tax laws. It is the capital gains privileges alone that explain why a substantial majority of taxpayers earning $100,000 to $200,000 per year pay something like 30 to 35 percent of their income in income taxes rather than 60 to 70 percent, as Figure 3–1 seems to imply. Treasury data prepared in 1969 revealed that of all the tax returns in the $100,000 to $500,000 income class, 11 percent paid an effective tax rate of something between 0 and 20 percent; 60 percent paid an effective rate of between 20 and 40 percent; and only 29 percent paid an effective rate of more than 40 percent. Between 1969 and 1978 there were a number of changes in the provisions concerning capital gains taxation, which, by and large, made those provisions relatively less significant. Since 1978, however, we have largely returned to the situation that existed prior to 1969. It is, therefore, necessary to untangle the web of rules that must be followed before a taxpayer can effectively utilize the tax-saving opportunities available in the capital gain provisions.

This chapter is divided into five major parts. The first is an explanation of the ultimate tax advantages that can accrue to certain forms of income commonly known as capital gains or, more precisely, as net capital gain. The second is concerned with definitional problems necessitated by the separation of ordinary gain from capital gain for tax purposes. The third interprets the most important corollary "basis rules" critical to the measurement of any capital gain or loss. The fourth explains how short- and long-term transactions must be combined for tax purposes. The final part explains the special rules that apply when a taxpayer realizes more capital losses than capital gains in a particular year. Illustration of the many ways in which the capital gain rules can be advantageously utilized in specific situations is deferred to the next chapter.

Understanding the Advantages

Many people believe that the ultimate tax advantage that accrues to income classifiable as a long-term capital gain is that such income is taxed at a flat rate of 28 percent. This belief is at least partially incorrect. A more accurate understanding of the ultimate tax advantages of a long-term capital gain needs to be separated into two sets of rules. Individual taxpayers and fiduciaries play by one set; corporate taxpayers, by another.

Individual and Fiduciary Taxpayers

An individual taxpayer who, in any year, has realized a net long-term capital gain in excess of a net short-term capital loss—an amount that, since December 31, 1976, has technically been known as the "net capital gain"—is entitled to claim a long-term capital gain deduction.

The long-term capital gain deduction is by definition equal to 60 percent of the net capital gain. Translated into simple English, this means that an individual taxpayer can pretend that 60 percent of the gain does not really exist if it can be classified as a net capital gain rather than as ordinary gain. Although the technical computation proceeds on the basis of a special deduction that serves to reduce the tax base called taxable income, the real economic effect is equivalent to a 60 percent reduction in the applicable tax rates for certain capital gains. As a practical result, our tax rates begin at 5.6 percent and increase to a maximum of only 28 percent anytime a taxpayer is entitled to claim the privilege of the long-term capital gain deduction. The obvious advantage of those rates in comparison with the apparent 14 to 70 percent rates printed in the tax rate schedules (see again pages 70 through 74) needs no further comment.

If a taxpayer's entire taxable income does not consist of qualifying capital gains, it is necessary to tier that income before trying to determine the federal income tax liability. The Internal Revenue Code tells us, in effect, that personal service taxable income should be considered the first tier, and that the passive, or unearned, income should be considered the second tier. Since the net capital gain is part of the second tier, what really happens is that a 60 percent discount factor is applied to the net capital gain before it is combined with other forms of passive income. To illustrate this tax calculation, let us return to the concept implicit in Figure 4–3. Now, however, we must divide the second tier (represented by the distance bc) into two parts, as illustrated in Figure 5–1.

The upper portion of distance bc is the "cream" of the U.S. tax law; in other words, it represents only 40 percent of what otherwise would be subject to the highest marginal tax brackets. The lower portion of distance bc is the remaining portion of the unearned (or passive) income, which cannot qualify as a net capital gain. Except for the 60 percent dilution, which takes place before the two forms of passive income are added together, the remainder of the tax calculation is made in exactly the same manner as was illustrated in Chapter 4. The

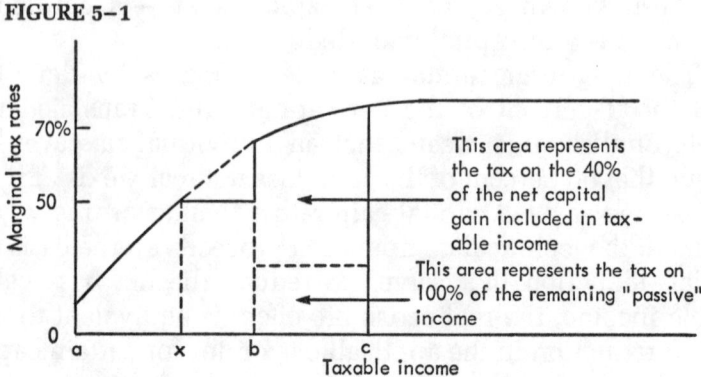

FIGURE 5-1

distance *ab* is, of course, the individual's personal service taxable income.

Corporate Taxpayers

If a corporation realizes a net capital gain in any particular year, it has the option of taxing that excess at a flat alternative rate of 28 percent. The option is in lieu of taxing that same excess in the normal way for a corporation. Since the corporate tax rate schedule involves only a five-step progression, this means that, in most instances, a corporation with a taxable income of less than $50,000 will *not* elect the 28 percent alternative tax rate, whereas a corporation with a taxable income of more than $50,000 will elect it. Because of the income mix—that is, the ratio of ordinary income to net capital gain—and because of a rule requiring that the entire net capital gain be treated in the same way, corporations with taxable incomes slightly in excess of $50,000 (*including* a net capital gain) should make both calculations to determine which alternative is more advantageous in their particular circumstances. It is important to observe that the corporation never has the option of claiming a long-term capital gain deduction; this tax privilege is restricted to individual and fiduciary taxpayers.

Illustrating the Advantages

The tax-saving potential of a net capital gain is easily demonstrated. Assume that an individual taxpayer earns a $215,400 taxable income, and that all of the income is ordinary income not eligible for any special privileges, whereas a neighbor also earns a $215,400 income, all of which can be classified as a long-term capital gain. If the first taxpayer is married and files a joint return, his or her tax liability amounts to $117,504, whereas the tax liability of the neighbor (also married and filing a joint return) amounts to only $33,832. Observe that the first person's tax liability is nearly 350 percent of the tax liability of the second! If the first taxpayer were a corporate entity, it would pay a tax of $79,834, whereas the neighboring corporation would pay $60,312. As these comparisons amply demonstrate, the potential tax advantage of a net capital gain is especially significant for individual taxpayers with substantial incomes. Because the potential for tax savings is so great, it is worthwhile reviewing the related and often complicated rules that determine exactly which gains may ascend into this tax heaven and which gains are doomed to the tax purgatory known as ordinary income.

Defining the Boundaries

Most people believe that capital gains and losses are those gains and losses attributable to transactions involving either stocks and bonds or plant-and-equipment-type assets. Once again, the common belief is both incomplete and at least partially incorrect. Fortunately, however, we do not have one set of definitions for one kind of taxpayer and another set for another kind of taxpayers. For individual, fiduciary, and corporate taxpayers alike, a capital gain or loss is simply any gain or loss attributable to the sale or exchange of a capital asset. The real question, then, becomes one of defining a capital asset.

Surprising as it may seem, the code defines capital assets by exception. That is, the code states that *all assets are capital assets unless they are specifically excluded.* The list of excluded assets is initially both limited and surprising. It includes:

1. Inventory items, "or property held by the taxpayer primarily for sale to customers in the ordinary course of his trade or business."
2. Real or depreciable property used in a trade or business.

3. A copyright, a literary, musical, or artistic composition, a letter or memorandum, "or similar property," but only if such an asset is held either by the taxpayer who created it or by one who has assumed the tax basis of that creator—in the case of letters, memorandums, and similar property, the exception also applies to the person for whom it was prepared or produced.
4. Receivables acquired in a trade or business.
5. Certain discount bonds issued on or after March 1, 1941.
6. A few miscellaneous items of limited significance.

Inventory Assets

The first group of assets excluded from the capital asset category—that is, inventory items—is self-explanatory. If such an exclusion were not made, all routine profits of a merchandising operation would be capital gains by definition. The only practical problem with this first exclusion is the difficulty in applying it to situations in which a taxpayer frequently, perhaps regularly, buys and sells certain assets, but this activity is not deemed to be a primary or even a secondary source of income. A lawyer, for example, was surprised to discover that the IRS and the courts found that his dealings in real estate constituted a trade or business even though he did not have a broker's license and did not take an active part in the sales activity. The court found that the frequency and the substantial nature of this activity were sufficient to sustain the IRS contention that such purchases and sales did constitute a trade or business, and that the profits were, therefore, ordinary income from the sale of real estate held primarily for sale rather than capital gains from investments. Just why this same criterion should not be applied to nonbroker investors who are heavily engaged in stock market transactions is not at all clear. Suffice it to say that the frequency criterion has not generally been applied when the asset in question was a security, although the literal wording of the code makes no such distinction. The IRS and the courts seem to have implicitly adopted a hands-off attitude in applying the capital gain definition to securities transactions for reasons known only to themselves. Only regular securities dealers realize ordinary income from trading transactions. With this notable exception, however, the reader should understand that there is absolutely nothing inherent in any particular kind of property that makes it capital or noncapital. That definitional result is based solely on the relationship between the taxpayer and the property: If an asset is held primarily for resale in the ordinary course of a trade or business, it is not a capital asset for that particular taxpayer. And any one taxpayer can be engaged in multiple trades or businesses at the same time.

Real or Depreciable Property Used in a Trade or Business

The second group of assets excluded from the capital asset category—that is, real or depreciable property used in a trade or business—is probably the most surprising entry in the list of noncapital assets. If the exclusion were applied without further modification, this would mean that all profits and losses from the sale of plant-and-equipment-type assets would be ordinary income or loss by definition. Stated in another way, it would mean that any profit on the sale of farmland by a farmer or a rancher, or the sale of a factory by a manufacturing corporation, or the sale of a cash register by a retail business, would be categorized as ordinary income. There are several additional sets of rules that modify this conclusion in varying circumstances.

Before we concern ourselves with those modifications, we should observe that *this exclusion applies to either real or depreciable property, but only if such property is used in a trade or business.* When the adjective *real* is used to modify the noun *property*, the expression generally means land and anything permanently attached to land. Thus the term *real property* would include most buildings and building components, a lot of heavy equipment, and fences, tanks, tracks, and other assets permanently attached to the earth, directly or indirectly. The adjective *depreciable* tries to distinguish a wasting asset from a nonwasting asset. Any property, whether realty or nonrealty, that will deteriorate over time can be considered a depreciable property. In this context, however, the code has reference to more than this physical wasting characteristic. The term *depreciable property* as used here demands wasting plus a profit motive. Thus a taxpayer's personal residence would *not* constitute a depreciable property for purposes of this definition because no profit motive is present in the taxpayer's ownership of that house. A single dwelling rented by a taxpayer to another person for a reasonable rent, however, generally constitutes a depreciable property, since the code permits that taxpayer to claim a depreciation deduction against the income derived from the property. Note that a property can be depreciable, then, without being part of a trade or business. When we classify an item for tax purposes from a profit motivation standpoint, we utilize a trichotomy, which includes (1) a full-fledged trade or business class, (2) a profit-oriented, but less than trade or business status, and (3) a wholly personal or not-for-profit category. This definitional distinction is diagramed in Figure 5–2. The term *nonbusiness* is often used in

FIGURE 5–2

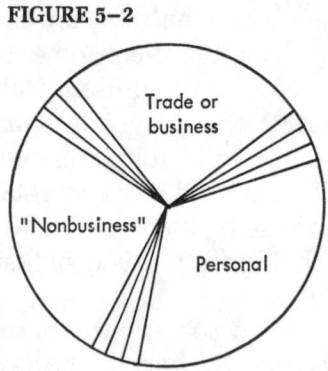

tax matters to describe something held for profit but not classifiable as a full-fledged trade or business. The definitional distinctions are sometimes very hazy, even though the distinction may be critical to the capital asset definition. Returning to our earlier illustration, if a taxpayer rents a single dwelling unit to another party and this rental activity is not deemed to constitute a trade or business, the rented unit remains a capital asset since the statutory exception applies only to real or depreciable properties *used in a trade or business.*

A book devoted to tax-planning ideas is not an appropriate place to review all of the complex rules that modify the ultimate tax treatment of even the most straightforward trade or business-type asset. Given our objective, it seems more appropriate to provide some summary statements that will usually be correct and then to remind the reader that these statements should not be used in actual circumstances without first verifying their applicability in those specific settings. Table 5–1 summarizes, correctly in most circumstances, the present

TABLE 5–1
The Usual Tax Treatment of Gain or Loss Realized on the Sale or Exchange of Real or Depreciable Property Used in a Trade or Business

Kind of property	If result is gain	If result is loss
Depreciable nonreal property (for example, car used by salesperson, office desk and typewriter, hand tools, and so on)	Ordinary income	Sec. 1231 loss
Depreciable real property (for example, retail store, warehouse, factory, and so on)		
If rapid depreciation was claimed	Partially or wholly ordinary income	Sec. 1231 loss
If straight-line depreciation was claimed	Sec. 1231 gain	Sec. 1231 loss
Nondepreciable real property (land)	Sec. 1231 gain	Sec. 1231 loss

tax treatment of the gain and loss realized on the sale or exchange of a real or depreciable property used in a trade or business. The reference to Section 1231 gain or loss will be explained immediately.

Section 1231 is a very peculiar part of our income tax law. In effect, it provides that specified items shall be brought together and their ordinary or capital character held in suspense until the end of the year when a net result can be determined. If the net result of all Section 1231 transactions is a loss, each of the items is treated as if it involved a noncapital asset; if the net result of all Section 1231 transactions is a gain, each of the items is treated as if it involved a long-term capital asset. From a tax-planning standpoint, this is most favorable to the taxpayer. A net capital gain is always preferred to equivalent amounts of ordinary income. Partially for these same reasons, and partially for reasons to be explained in the last portion of this chapter, ordinary losses are always preferred to equivalent amounts of capital losses.

Combining this terse explanation of Section 1231 with Table 5–1, we should note that a taxpayer may still be able to recognize capital gains from the sale or exchange of depreciable real property used in a trade or business. The likelihood of this result is increased if the gain is attributable to the sale or exchange of land, or if the taxpayer claimed only straight-line depreciation on depreciable real property before it was sold or exchanged. The opportunity to allocate a higher proportion of the sales price to land, and a smaller proportion to a building, may enable the taxpayer to increase the amount of a capital gain even if rapid depreciation has been utilized. Because the buyer's best interest in any allocation of the sales price is typically adverse to that of the seller's, the IRS and the courts are usually willing to accept any allocation stipulated in a sales agreement. This continuing opportunity for a knowledgeable seller to convert potential ordinary income into a capital gain will be further illustrated in the next chapter. Suffice it to note here that the exclusion of property used in a trade or business from the capital asset definition has not always meant that transactions involving such assets will necessarily produce ordinary income or loss.

Copyrights

The third group of assets excluded from the capital asset category includes copyrights, literary, musical, or artistic compositions, letters, memorandums, and similar property. The rationale for the exclusion of most of these items turns on the belief that taxpayers should not be able to reap the rewards of their individual efforts in the form of a capital gain just because those efforts culminated in the production of a property. The potential inequity between a taxpayer who rendered a personal service without the production of a property (for example, a physician, an accountant, or salesclerk) and a taxpayer whose service produced a property (for example, an author, a composer, or an artist) would be tremendous were it not for this exception. The obvious failure to include patents in this list of noncapital assets is notable. Congress apparently believes that it is preferable for our citizens to tinker and to invent machines than to spend time in other creative ways. At least the substantial tax reward of a capital gain is retained solely for such activities.

The exclusion of letters and memorandums is closely related to the tax rules applicable to the charitable contribution deduction. Without explaining these rules here, we might note that the important result of this exclusion is to deny a taxpayer a sizable tax deduction for any gift of property that would produce ordinary income if sold. As specifically applied to letters and memorandums, this means that all U.S. presidents taking office after Lyndon Johnson have been denied a substantial tax deduction for the value of the many papers they typically donate to their presidential libraries.

Note that this third category of exclusions usually applies only to persons who created the property, or to those who received it without cost from such persons. If a taxpayer purchases a copyright or a literary, musical, or artistic composition from the creator, that property may be a capital asset for the purchaser. Whether or not it will depends in large measure on the reason the purchaser had for acquiring the asset and the way it is used after acquisition. If the property was purchased with the intention of reselling it in the ordinary course of business, or if it becomes a depreciable property used in a trade or business, it will remain a noncapital asset. If, on the other hand, the purchase was made as an investment or for personal enjoyment, it will become a capital asset of the purchaser.

All Other Exceptions

Accounts and notes receivable are generally not considered to be capital assets for the same reasons that inventory assets are excluded from the capital asset definition. If the receivables are derived from the ordinary conduct of a trade or business, any gain or loss on the disposition of the receivables should be treated in the same way that the income produced by those receivables would be treated. The exception of receivables from the capital asset definition effectively accomplishes this result.

The last exclusion to be considered here—certain discount bonds—was instituted as a way of ending the conversion of ordinary interest income into capital gain. Prior to the exception of this item, it was possible for a taxpayer to purchase a noninterest-bearing security at an appropriate discount and later to sell the same security at a "profit." The discount was obviously nothing more than an alternative to paying a stipulated rate of interest. The tax result, however, would be to create a capital gain rather than ordinary interest if this special exception were not included among the list of assets not to be treated as capital assets.

In summarizing this portion of Chapter 5, we should remember that the capital or noncapital status of any asset is determined by the relationship between the asset and the taxpayer. There is no inherent characteristic in a property that leads to a correct classification. For example, a car would be a noncapital asset to an automobile dealer because it is part of the inventory; it might also be a noncapital asset to a contractor, who uses it entirely in his or her trade or business; but it would be a noncapital asset to a taxpayer who uses it solely for purposes of personal enjoyment. Actually a single property may be both a capital and a noncapital asset. If, for example, a physician used a car 80 percent of the time for business purposes and 20 percent of the time for personal purposes, that car would be both capital (20 percent) and noncapital (80 percent). The importance of the definition of a capital asset, and the complications it can create, will be demonstrated after we investigate further the rules associated with the measurement of a capital gain or loss.

Measuring a Capital Gain or Loss

The amount of a capital gain or loss is simply the difference between the "amount realized" on the sale or exchange of a capital asset and the "basis" of the capital asset surrendered. The amount realized is, in turn, the sum of (1) any cash received, (2) the fair market value of any noncash property received, and (3) the amount of any liability that the buyer assumes from the seller. To illustrate, assume that in 19x1 a taxpayer purchased, solely for investment purposes, a parcel of land for $50,000, paying $10,000 down and assuming a $40,000 mortgage for the balance. If the taxpayer sold the land in 19x6 for (1) $30,000 cash, (2) a boat worth $25,000, and (3) the purchaser's assumption of the $20,000 mortgage that remained outstanding against the property, the selling taxpayer would realize a long-term capital gain of $25,000. The amount realized would be $75,000 (that is, $30,000 + $25,000 + $20,000), and the adjusted basis of the property surrendered would be $50,000 (the original cost of the land). The difference of $25,000 represents the taxpayer's capital gain.

In the real world, of course, it may not be easy to determine the fair market value in a noncash exchange of properties. A determination of that value is, nevertheless, necessary to the measurement of the gain or loss realized, and the IRS and the courts generally insist that taxpayers make such a determination immediately. In some situations the tax authorities will infer the value of the more-difficult-to-value property on the basis of an easier-to-value property, believing that a taxpayer would not engage in an "arm's length" sale or exchange of the two properties if those values were not equal. To return to the illustration in the prior paragraph, if the value of the boat received in that exchange were difficult to determine, but the value of the land surrendered were easier to determine, the IRS and the courts would not hesitate to infer the $25,000 fair market value for the boat if they could readily determine that the land was worth $75,000 at the date of the exchange.

Another difficult problem in measuring a capital gain or loss involves the determination of the tax basis of the capital asset surrendered. This difficulty is attributable to the fact that the basis rules differ, depending upon the way in which a taxpayer acquired the capital asset. One set of basis rules is applicable to purchased property, another set to property acquired by gift, another set to inherited property, and yet another to property acquired in a "nontaxable exchange." The first three of these four sets of rules will be considered here; the basis rules applicable to property acquired in a nontaxable exchange will be deferred to Chapter 10.

The Tax Basis of Purchased Property

The tax basis of purchased property is generally equal to its cost plus the cost of any subsequent capital improvements and less the amount of depreciation (or depletion or amortization) claimed for tax purposes. The term *cost* includes both the basic purchase price and all associated costs necessary to acquire the asset and make it operative. Thus, the cost of a security includes the broker's commission; the cost of equipment includes the freight and installation charges that may be incurred before the equipment can be put to its intended use; and the cost of land may include fees paid to real estate agents and lawyers. If a taxpayer purchases more than one asset for a single purchase price, the total cost must be allocated among the assets acquired. This allocation is based on relative fair market values.

After an asset is acquired, and before it is sold or exchanged, a taxpayer typically incurs numerous costs to "keep it going." Any costs that do not extend the original estimated life of the asset are usually treated as current expenses and (if authorized) deducted immediately for tax purposes. Costs that extend a property's original life, or improve it in some material way, are called "capital expenditures," which simply means that at the time they are incurred they are properly charged to the asset account rather than to an expense account. Because of the time preference value of money, a taxpayer typically wants to expense everything (and thereby reduce an income tax liability) as soon as possible; the IRS agent seems to think that everything should be capitalized. The distinction between an expense and a capital expenditure is sometimes very hazy; in such instances, tax disputes are commonplace.

The amount of depreciation (or depletion or amortization) that a taxpayer can claim for any asset is a function of its cost, estimated life, salvage value, and depreciation method. These concepts are sufficiently complex to justify a separate discussion in Chapter 8. For our immediate purposes—the quantification of a capital gain or loss—we will avoid any problems associated with determining which costs must be capitalized and how much depreciation can be claimed, so that we may concentrate on the problems peculiar to the measurement of a capital gain or loss.

To summarize and illustrate the rules applicable to the determination of the tax basis of purchased property, consider the plight of a taxpayer who purchased land and a building in

19x1 and sold that same property in 19x9 if, during the interim period, this taxpayer incurred the following expenditures or charges:

Initial purchase price	$40,000
Legal fee associated with title search made at purchase date	1,000
Capital improvement to building made three years after purchase	8,000
Cost of routine repairs, taxes, and so on during ownership	12,000
Depreciation claimed on building during ownership	10,000

Before this taxpayer can determine the amount of gain or loss on the sale made in 19x9, it is necessary to determine the tax basis of the assets sold. This begins with a separation of the initial purchase price of $40,000 between land and buildings. Assuming that the taxpayer has good evidence of their relative fair market values, $30,000 might be allocated to the building and $10,000 to the land. Questions then arises concerning the $1,000 legal fee: Must this cost be capitalized, or could the taxpayer deduct that expenditure in 19x1? If the legal fee must be capitalized, should the cost be divided between the land and the building, or is it entirely allocable to the land? The answers to those questions are not obvious, but further investigation would probably substantiate the conclusion that the legal fee would have to be capitalized and that it should be allocated entirely to the land. Capital improvements would be added to the basis of the building; routine costs would be deducted as they were incurred. In summary, then, this taxpayer could determine the tax basis of the assets in 19x9, as follows:

Building: $30,000 + $8,000 − $10,000 = $28,000
Land: $10,000 + $1,000   = $11,000

If the taxpayer sold the land and building for $60,000 and at the time of the sale $20,000 was properly allocated to the land and $40,000 to the building, a gain of $9,000 on the land and $12,000 on the building would have been realized. By reviewing the way the taxpayer utilized this building and by reference to the rules implicit in Table 5–1, the taxpayer could finally determine the correct tax treatment of the $21,000 gain.

The Tax Basis of Property Acquired by Gift

The tax basis of property acquired by gift is usually either (a) the donor's cost basis or (b) the fair market value of the property on the date acquired. The tax basis of property acquired by gift will be the donor's cost unless the fair market value of the property on the date the gift is made is lower than that cost. In the event that the fair market value is lower than the donor's cost on the date of the gift, the basis of the property cannot be determined until the donee finally disposes of the property. In this latter instance, if the donee eventually sells the property for less than the "depreciated" value on the day the property was received, the basis becomes the value on the day it was received; if the donee eventually sells the property for more than the donor's original cost, the basis becomes the donor's cost; if the donee sells the property for any value between the value on the day it was received and the donor's cost, the taxpayer need not report either gain or loss.

These rules may seem unduly complex, and they probably are. However, they become easier to remember and to apply if the reader will but observe that the one thing the tax law will *not* tolerate is passing around a "paper loss" to a donee in a high tax bracket. In other words, if a taxpayer purchased a stock for $100,000 and that stock declined in value to $60,000, the law would not permit the original owner to transfer this $40,000 paper loss to another taxpayer in a higher marginal tax bracket prior to selling it. If the taxpayer gave the stock away and the donee sold the stock immediately after receiving it, the donee's basis would have become $60,000 and thus he or she would not realize any loss on the sale (that is, $60,000 amount realized less $60,000 basis). On the other hand, observe that the law will not penalize the donee if he or she waits and sells the shares at a date when their value has returned to something more than the donor's cost basis of $100,000. In that situation the donee's basis reverts to $100,000 and the gain is calculated from that value. If the donee sells for any price between $60,000 and $100,000, the tax rules essentially tell the taxpayer to forget it—there is neither gain nor loss to report.

Observe again that the critical fact that initially determines the tax basis of property acquired by gift is the relationship between the donor's cost and the fair market value on the date a gift is made. If the fair market value on the date of the gift is equal to or greater than the donor's cost, the donee's basis will under all possible circumstances remain the donor's cost—subject only to a relatively minor modification if the donor pays a gift tax on the transfer. As a practical matter, a taxpayer should only rarely make a gift of property that has decreased in value since it was purchased. To do so risks the possibility that an income tax loss may go forever unrecognized by anyone. Some of the important tax-saving opportunities that remain because of the basis rules will be discussed in later chapters.

The Tax Basis of Inherited Property

The basis of inherited property to the heir or devisee is determined by one of three rules. Generally, it is equal to the fair market value of the property on the date of the decedent's death. An exception to that general rule applies if the executor or executrix elects to value the decedent's property for estate tax purposes on the alternate valuation date. Stated briefly, the administrator of the estate is given an option to value the deceased's estate either on the date of death or exactly six months after death. If the administrator elects the latter date, then the heir or devisee who eventually receives the property must also take, as his or her basis, the fair market value of the property six months after the decedent's death. In the rare case in which the administrator elects the alternate valuation date but distributes a particular piece of property prior to that date, the property so distributed will take as its basis the fair market value on the date of distribution. To summarize: (1) the basis of any inherited property is generally its fair market value on the date of the decedent's death; (2) an exception exists for any property included in an estate for which the administrator elects the alternate valuation date—in this special case, the basis of any inherited property is the value of the property six months after the decedent's death; and (3) if the administrator elects the alternate value date *and also* distributes a property prior to that date, then for any property so distributed the heir's basis is the fair market value of the property on the date distributed.

For income tax planning purposes the significance of the rule just stated can hardly be overemphasized. Note that no one ever pays the *income tax* on the appreciation in the value of the property that is retained by its owner until death. Any heir can sell inherited property immediately after receiving it and report absolutely no gain or loss! If the deceased taxpayer had sold or exchanged the same property prior to death, any previous appreciation in value between the date of purchase and the date of sale would be subject to the income tax, possibly as a capital gain. In addition, the administrator of the decedent's subsequent estate would still have to pay the estate tax on the aftertax proceeds realized on the sale or exchange. Thus the tendency to retain appreciated assets and to allow them to pass through a decedent's estate is very great for persons of substantial means. This strong tendency is commonly referred to as the "locked-in effect." The lock-in has obvious reference to the wealthy, older person who feels that it would be unwise to dispose of an appreciated asset prior to death because of the extra tax that would be imposed on that disposition. People of less means have, of course, more limited opportunities. Very often they must dispose of the few appreciated properties that they have prior to death simply to live decently during their retirement years.

Application of the basis rules for property acquired by gift and for inherited property is important to family tax-planning ideas. The very large tax savings that are possible will be explained in Chapter 12, after we have reviewed the rules common to gift and estate taxes. For the moment, it is sufficient to observe that the income tax can be permanently avoided by application of the basis rules for inherited property, but that it cannot be avoided by the basis rules for property transferred by gift. Since a donee can never get a basis higher than a donor's cost (except for minor increases due to the gift tax), a donee will eventually recognize the income implicit in appreciated property that is made part of a gift.

Combining Short-term and Long-term Capital Gains and Losses

The special tax privileges explained in the first part of this chapter apply only to the excess of net long-term capital gains over net short-term capital losses (if any). Application of this rule obviously necessitates the separation of capital gains and losses into two categories—namely, short term and long term. Only capital gains and losses derived from the sale or exchange of a capital asset held for *more than* one year are categorized as long-term gains and losses; those arising from sale or exchange of capital assets held for one year or less are characterized as short-term gains and losses. Observe again that the tax benefits generally associated with capital gains are restricted to the *net* long-term gains in excess of *net* short-term losses. This means that all long-term transactions must be combined separately, and that all short-term transactions must be combined separately, before the two net amounts can be considered. We can express this in formula fashion as follows:

$$(LTCG - LTCL) - (STCL - STCG)$$

where LTCG is long-term capital gains, LTCL is long-term capital losses, and so on.

Tax benefits are possible from capital gains if and only if the quantity in the first set of parentheses in this formula is both (a) positive *and* (b) greater than the quantity in the second set of parentheses. Because this calculation is made on an annual basis, a taxpayer obviously has a great deal of opportunity to influence the net result in any particular year by a careful selection of the date on which certain gains and/or losses are recognized. By careful timing of capital gains and losses, a taxpayer can substantially change the tax liability attaching to long- and short-term transactions. Some of the tax-saving opportunities will be explained in the next chapter. Before we consider those opportunities, however, we must become familiar with one additional set of rules. These rules deal with the tax treatment of net capital losses.

The Correct Tax Treatment of Net Capital Losses

If a taxpayer realizes in the aggregate more capital losses than capital gains in any particular year, another host of special tax rules come into play. Once again, the rules for individual and fiduciary taxpayers differ from the rules for corporate taxpayers. We will review the rules applicable to individual and fiduciary taxpayers first and then consider the corporate rules.

Individual and Fiduciary Taxpayers

If an individual or fiduciary taxpayer realizes in the aggregate more capital losses than capital gains in any single year, he or she may offset a maximum of $3,000 of such losses against ordinary income in that year. To make matters worse, if the losses were derived from long-term transactions, the taxpayer can claim those losses only on a two-for-one basis, and with no option but to claim them to the maximum extent allowed. If the taxpayer has both net short- and long-term capital losses he or she must utilize the net short-term losses on a one-for-one basis before beginning to expend net long-term losses on the two-for-one basis. But what happens if the taxpayer's aggregate net capital losses exceed the $3,000 maximum?

In the case of individual and fiduciary taxpayers, any capital losses in excess of the maximum $3,000 that may be offset against ordinary income can only be carried *forward* and offset against the taxable income of future years. Short-term losses are carried forward and treated as short-term losses in subsequent years, and long-term losses are carried forward and treated as long-term losses. There is no dollar limit on the amount of capital losses that can be offset against capital gains in either the current or future years. If, however, a capital loss is carried forward and the taxpayer does not realize sufficient capital gains in the next year to offset such a carry-forward, he or she once again is limited in the next year to a maximum $3,000 offset against ordinary income. All remaining losses are carried to later years until they have finally been utilized or the taxpayer dies.

Corporate Taxpayers

If a corporation realizes in the aggregate more capital losses than it does capital gains in a single year, it cannot offset any of that capital loss against its ordinary income. However, the corporation can carry that loss *back* and offset it against any capital gain it reported in the third prior tax year. If the capital gains in that year are insufficient to absorb the current year's capital loss, the excess is carried to the second prior year and, if necessary, to the last taxable year. If the total capital loss in the current year exceeds the amount of capital gain reported by the corporation in the three prior years, any balance can be carried forward and offset against capital gains realized in the next five years. If the loss has not been utilized by the end of the fifth subsequent year, it expires without tax benefit.

Whenever a corporation carries a capital loss back or forward, that loss is magically transformed by law into a short-term loss, regardless of how it may have been characterized originally. Under the proper circumstances, this transformation of long-term loss into short-term loss can be fortunate for the corporate taxpayer, since the tax refund is based on whatever tax was paid on the capital gain thus removed from the third prior year. If it happens that the corporation reported a net short-term capital gain in that year, it may have paid as much as 46 percent of that gain to the government in income taxes. In that event, a net long-term capital loss in the current year could actually provide a refund based on a 46 percent rate when it was reclassified as short-term loss and carried back to the earlier year.

A mathematically oriented reader may see the possible number of permutations and combinations implicit in these capital gain and loss rules and seriously question the sanity of anyone who would try to plan events to take maximum advantage of them. Other readers may simply be inclined to throw up their hands in disgust and only say that they know there are so many rules that they simply cannot remember and utilize them effectively. Although it is true that the number of complex rules is inordinately large in this area of the tax law, some reasonably obvious tax-planning situations can be described and appreciated by all readers. Because the tax-saving potential in this area is significant, it will pay the reader to persevere and study the examples of the next chapter.

CHAPTER 6

Capital Gains and Losses: Some Applications

In Chapter 5, the basic rules determining the tax treatment of capital gains and losses were explained. In this chapter, we will examine several separate situations that demonstrate the need for careful tax planning so as to maximize the benefits, or minimize the detriments, that attach to transactions involving capital assets. The chapter is not exhaustive, and some portions of the discussion are necessarily superficial. Understanding the chapter is complicated by the fact that the ideas do not flow logically to culmination in one or two ideas.

This chapter has been divided into two parts in an attempt to provide some structure to the otherwise scattered illustrations. The illustrations contained in the first section depend for their success or failure upon careful attention to definitional details. The taxpayer who is appropriately attuned to the capital asset definition is often in a position to amend intended actions in a manner that will achieve personal and economic objectives and, at the same time, modify the tax consequences in a favorable manner. The success or failure of the illustrations contained in the second section of this chapter depends largely upon careful attention to the timing of transactions. In almost all instances other than casualty events, a taxpayer has domination over the exact time at which a gain or loss will be realized. When dealing with capital assets, this time dimension becomes especially critical because of the tax distinction made between short- and long-term gains and losses.

Definitional Manipulation

In the preceding chapter we learned that all assets are capital assets unless they have been specifically excepted from that classification by Internal Revenue Code provision. The most surprising exception is that of real or depreciable property used in a trade or business. That exception provides an unusual opportunity for the owner-operator of a business to modify the use of a particular asset and thereby also modify its status as a capital or noncapital asset. In determining whether or not a particular gain or loss is a capital one, the tax authorities generally look at the relationship between the taxpayer and the asset on the date the sale or exchange is completed rather than on the date the asset was acquired or on any intermediate date. By removing a depreciable asset from its original use in a trade or business and by utilizing it solely in a personal manner, a taxpayer *may be* able to change the classification of the asset from a noncapital to a capital status and thereby modify the tax result on disposition. The intended-use criterion may be subject to even greater manipulation when more than one taxable entity is involved. We will consider first the case in which only a single taxable entity is involved.

Modification of Use Involving a Single Taxable Entity

Any taxpayer who operates a trade or business in the form of a sole proprietorship, a partnership, or a joint venture has multiple opportunities to modify the use of a particular property on a timely basis and thereby to modify its status as a capital asset. To illustrate the basic idea involved in this change of status, consider the tax consequences attaching to the disposition of an automobile by a taxpayer who had used that automobile 80 percent of the time in business and 20 percent of the time in personal use from the date of acquisition until the date of disposition. If we assume that the taxpayer-owner originally paid $8,000 for the car, depreciated it a total of $5,800 for tax purposes, and finally sold it for $2,000, we might be tempted to conclude that there was a $200 loss on the sale ($2,000 amount realized − $2,200 adjusted basis) and that $160 of this loss (80 percent × $200) was ordinary loss and $40 (20 percent × $200) was capital loss. Such a conclusion would be incorrect under the circumstances described. Tax rules essentially view this transaction as involving two entirely separate assets, one capital and the other noncapital. The correct calculation of gain and loss is as follows.

To the dismay of the taxpayer, the correct determination of the tax consequences of this simple transaction would produce a $1,000 ordinary income and a nondeductible $1,200 capital loss! The tax treatment of the $1,000 "gain" is determined by the basic tax rules implicit in the preparation of Table 5–1 (page 112). Those rules provide that any gain on the sale of depreciable nonrealty used in a trade or business will probably be ordinary income. The correct tax treatment of the $1,200 loss is derived from the basic rules stated in Chapter 2. It was noted there that all income is taxable income unless the taxpayer can find some authority to exclude it; on the other hand, nothing is deductible unless the taxpayer can find some authority that makes it deductible. Search as he may, except in the case of casualty losses, the taxpayer will find no authority for the deduction of any loss incurred in the sale or exchange of purely personal assets. In other words, if a taxpayer sells a personal residence, car, or clothing at a profit, he or she must pay tax on that profit as a capital gain. However, if the taxpayer sells a personal residence, car, or clothing at a loss, such a loss is properly classified as a capital loss; but more important, it constitutes a capital loss for which no tax deduction can be claimed since no code section authorizes the deduction of losses from the sale or exchange of purely personal assets. As explained on pages 39 and 40, losses arising from the sale of specific properties are deductible if attributable to (1) properties used in a trade or business or (2) "nonbusiness" properties (that is, profit-producing properties that do not constitute a trade or business), but not if attributable to purely personal properties. The only exception for purely personal properties applies to casualty and theft losses. In our illustration, no casualty was involved in the sale of the car for $2,000, and therefore the $1,200 loss attributable to the 20 percent of the car used for personal reasons would not be deductible.

	Noncapital portion (80 percent business use)	Capital portion (20 percent personal use)	Total (100 percent)
Original cost............................	$6,400	$1,600	$8,000
Less depreciation	5,800	0*	5,800
Adjusted basis on sale...................	$ 600	$1,600	$2,200
Amount realized	$ 1600	$ 400	$2,000
Less adjusted basis	600	1,600	2,200
Gain or (loss) realized	$1,000	($1,200)	($ 200)

* Personal-use assets are not depreciable for tax purposes because they are not income-producing.

Suppose that the taxpayer had converted the car from 20 percent personal use to 100 percent personal use for one week preceding the disposition at $2,000. Would this change in use for one week magically transform the classification of the transaction to one solely involving a personal property and thereby get rid of the $1,000 ordinary gain that otherwise would attach to the 80 percent of the car that had been used previously for business purposes? A literal reading of the code might lead one to that conclusion. Anyone familiar with the tax game, however, would immediately predict that such a simple tax plan would fail, possibly on some rather nebulous judicial doctrine. On numerous occasions, the courts have not hesitated to look through a "rigged" transaction to find either that the transaction had no "business purpose" or that "form should give way to substance" in tax matters. When a court makes this finding, it usually is trying to find good authority for ignoring the code as it is literally written and to apply it as Congress probably intended it to be applied. The interesting aspect of such nebulous judicial doctrines is that they are not applied consistently and that taxpayers can help to improve their chances for nonapplication of such judicial rules by slightly modifying their own behavior.

Returning to our illustration of the car sold for $2,000 just one week after it had been converted to wholly personal use, we might note that the most "phony" aspect of that transaction involved the short time period that elapsed between the date of the alleged conversion from 20 percent to 100 percent personal use and the date of disposition. If the taxpayer had allowed one year rather than one week to elapse, several things would have happened. Most important, perhaps, the time lapse would have provided evidence that the conversion in use was "real," or "had substance," beyond its obvious tax-saving result. It is likely that this difference would have been sufficient to convince any court that such judicial doctrines as substance over form or business purpose were not applicable to this transaction. A favorable tax result would also have been buttressed by the fact that values would have changed sufficiently during the intervening time period to make any allocation of earlier and undetermined amounts difficult if not impossible—an interesting corollary of the realization criterion.

This illustration could easily be dismissed as unimportant because of the small dollar amounts involved. Such a peremptory dismissal would be unwise. The same principle can sometimes be applied in circumstances in which larger sums are involved. Consider, for example, the possibility of converting a well-depreciated rental home into a personal residence prior to sale. In this instance, the potential ordinary income to be realized on the disposition of the property at a profit would remain intact and the owner-turned-occupant might feel that he or she would have to remain in the home indefinitely for the apparent tax advantage just discussed to be achieved. Because of some rather generous rules in the area of nontaxable exchanges, however, the taxpayer could probably avoid recognition of this ordinary income permanently if he or she were willing to live in the home for at least one year. The exact details of such a plan should be checked carefully by a competent tax adviser before being implemented.

The reverse possibility is equally pertinent. Consider, for example, the plight of the taxpayer who purchased a personal residence for $80,000 and found a few years later that the home has decreased in value so that it could be sold only if the taxpayer were willing to realize a nondeductible loss on the sale. Instead, this taxpayer might convert the former home to a rental property and then, some years afterward, proceed to sell it and thereby try to convert a nondeductible personal loss to a deductible loss on rent-producing property. In this instance, the tax rules have specifically attempted to preclude the deduction of such a loss by providing that the tax basis on the date of conversion from a personal residence to a rental property must be the *lower* of (a) the owner's cost or (b) the fair market value on the date of the conversion in use. The only fact that works to the taxpayer's benefit in this circumstance is that fair market values are exceedingly difficult to determine, especially retroactively, and the taxpayer may be able to achieve the intended objective if he or she (a) is sufficiently patient and allows a reasonable time to lapse before realizing any loss, and (b) is sufficiently adamant in maintaining a position on assumed fair market values at the earlier date. At least the taxpayer has given the real economic facts a maximum opportunity to become sufficiently confused so that a revenue agent might be persuaded to yield on a debatable point that the agent recognizes as a distinct risk if the controversy proceeds to judicial settlement. Finally, even if the taxpayer cannot convince the revenue agent that the contention is reasonable, a court or jury has been given potential grounds on which to render a decision favorable to the taxpayer.

Modification of Use Involving More Than One Taxable Entity

Under some circumstances, a taxpayer may find it advisable to utilize more than a single taxable entity if a desired tax consequence is to be achieved. To illustrate this possibility, suppose that a taxpayer purchased a tract of land in 19x1 for $150,000 and that he or she held this land solely for investment purposes for the next six years. Let us assume that by 19x7 the land had increased in value to $350,000 because of the growth of a nearby city and the favorable location of a new highway. Under these circumstances, the investor-taxpayer could sell the land and realize a long-term capital gain of $200,000. The taxpayer might believe, however, that the value of the tract could be increased by another $150,000 if it were divided into smaller lots and if an additional $50,000 were expended for streets, curbs, gutters, sewers, and similar improvements. If this taxpayer proceeded with the development plans and eventually sold the smaller lots for a total of $500,000, he or she would discover that the entire $300,000 profit ($500,000 realized minus basis of $150,000 plus $50,000) was ordinary income. The IRS and the courts, with sufficient authority, would maintain that the lots were held primarily for sale to customers in the ordinary course of a trade or business venture, and the entire profit would therefore be classified as ordinary income.

If instead of developing the land, the taxpayer had sold the land to a development corporation for $350,000 before making any improvements, the right to claim the $200,000 capital gain would have been fixed. If the taxpayer also happened to own 100 percent of the purchasing corporation, he or she might eventually reap the additional $100,000 profit, even though that portion of the profit would have to be reported as ordinary income either by the corporation or by the owner (as salary). Certainly, the taxpayer would prefer to report $200,000 of long-term capital gain and $100,000 of ordinary income rather than $300,000 of ordinary income. Under these circumstances, it is again possible that the courts would look through the form of the transactions and, by ignoring the corporate entity, find that the entire income was ordinary income of the individual taxpayer. The most vulnerable aspect of the proposed tax-saving plan is the fact that the original investor also owned 100 percent of the corporation that eventually developed the property. If this owner were willing to allow a nonrelated party to own, say, 25 percent of the stock in the development corporation, he or she would have gone a long way toward ensuring the right to claim the capital gain status of the $200,000. In summary, through the creation of a viable second entity and the sale of property to that entity, the investor-taxpayer in this illustration might avoid an inadvertent conversion of a $200,000 long-term capital gain into ordinary income by making certain that the status of the property as an investment would not be lost prior to realization of the initial appreciation.

The reverse of this tax-saving idea was the basis for the collapsible corporation discussed in Chapter 4. Until the collapsible corporation provisions were enacted into law, it was possible for a taxpayer to develop land (or almost any other property) within a corporate entity and, after the increase in value had occurred but before the increase had been realized, collapse the corporation and convert the potential ordinary income attributable to the development work into a capital gain for the shareholders by virtue of the corporate liquidation provisions. Because this alternative is no longer generally available, it will not be further developed here. The possibility of converting a potential ordinary income into capital gain through the careful allocation of a selling price is much more likely to be possible today.

For many years, it appeared that the era of the collapsible corporation had ended because tax advisers rarely recommended a tax plan based on this old idea. The statutory provisions added to the law in 1950 had apparently achieved their objective because the collapsible corporation was increasingly viewed as a tax trap rather than an opportunity.

In the very recent past, however, there appears to have been a small revival of the old collapsible corporation idea. This growing revival can be attributed directly to the major changes in capital gains taxation included as part of the Revenue Act of 1978. For the first time in over a decade, capital gains are once again of major tax benefit to individual taxpayers. During the prior period, the maximum tax on personal service income provided roughly equivalent tax benefits with much less trouble and risk. Today, however, the difference between capital gains, taxed at no more than 28 percent, and personal service income, taxed at 50 percent, is sufficiently large to justify tax risks that were previously dismissed with little thought.

The current interest centers on the imprecise definition of collapsible corporation found in Section 341(b)(1)(A). There the code states, among other things, that a collapsible corporation is any corporation whose stock is sold (or otherwise disposed of) by the shareholders at any time before the corporation has realized "a *substantial part* of the taxable income" that ordinarily would accrue to the corporation if it were to dispose of the property that it was created to manufacture, construct, or produce. But exactly what is a substantial part? In 1961, the Fifth Circuit Court of Appeals concluded that 30 percent was a substantial part. Initially the IRS did not agree, but they acquiesced in 1972. Thus, today there is reasonable authority to conclude that stock in a corporation that has realized 40 to 50 percent of its total income potential can be sold without the risk of the IRS claiming that the seller must report ordinary income because the corporation was a collapsible corporation.

The most popular use today of the almost-collapsible corporation appears to be in the building trades industry. There a contractor will create a corporation for the specific purpose of converting an old apartment house into a condominium. After completing the remodeling work, the contractor's corporation will proceed to sell, for instance, all its efficiency and one-bedroom units. The income attributable to those units might represent 40 to 50 percent of the total income potential of the project. At that point, before selling the two- and three-bedroom units, the contractor sells all of his or her stock in the construction corporation created for this project. Any income realized by the corporation on the sale of the smaller units can be distributed to the contractor as salary; the unrealized income implicit in the remaining larger units, still to be sold, can thus be converted into long-term capital gain on the sale of the stock. Although this route to tax bliss is not without pitfalls, it is being traveled by more than a few hardy taxpayers. Anyone interested in joining the group should, of course, insist that his or her tax adviser go along.

Favorable Price Allocation in Property Transactions

In Chapter 5, we noted the necessity of allocating a portion of the purchase (or sales) price to land whenever a taxpayer buys or sells a parcel of realty that includes both land and buildings. In the purchase transaction, this allocation is required in order to determine what portion of the initial cost is subject to depreciation (the portion allocated to the building) and what portion must remain intact and be recovered with regard to taxes only upon disposition of the property (the portion allocated to the land). In the sales transaction, the same allocation is necessary in order to determine separately the amount of the gain or loss on the building and on the land. An examination of Table 5–1 further reveals that some or all of the profit on the sale of a building may be treated as ordinary income, if rapid depreciation has been claimed on the building, whereas any profit on the sale of the land is likely to be treated as Section 1231 gain, and therefore as long-term capital gain.

Because the interests of the buyer and the seller are generally adverse, the IRS is inclined to accept whatever allocation of the price is agreed upon by the parties to the contract. The opportunity for the buyer to make a favorable allocation is especially great when the seller has depreciated the building on a straight-line basis and therefore has no tax reason for preferring one allocation to another. Sometimes it is also possible to obtain a favorable allocation when one of the parties to the transaction fails to understand the tax significance of the agreed-upon allocation.

The cost allocation opportunity can also be combined with the change-in-use opportunity explained earlier in this chapter to achieve still greater tax savings. Suppose, for example, that you desired to acquire, at a cost of $400,000, several parcels of real estate, including numerous old buildings, with the idea that you would tear down the old buildings and erect a new office building on the same location. If you proceeded openly and directly with your plans, the IRS would have every reason for allocating the entire $400,000 purchase price to the cost of land. If, on the other hand, you adequately disguise any possible intention to erect the new building behind an apparent intention to acquire and operate the old rental properties, your tax consequences might be quite different. If you actually acquired the properties for $400,000, you might be able to find some authority—perhaps utilizing city property tax assessments—for allocating $250,000 of the $400,000 cost to the buildings and only $150,000 to the land. Then, after two or three years of rental experience, you could have a detailed study made of your rental activities that would show that you were utilizing this land ineffectively. Based on the independent study, you might have good authority for "changing your mind," tearing down the old buildings, and erecting the new office building. Under these revised facts, some portion of the $250,000 allocated to the buildings would have already been recovered with regard to taxes through depreciation deductions that were offset against the ordinary rent income in the interim years. The remaining basis allocated to the buildings would become an ordinary tax loss deductible in the year the buildings were torn down. This quick recovery of much of the initial investment through tax deductions would be significantly more favorable than would the required capitalization of the entire $400,000 purchase price contemplated earlier.

Any attempt to quantify the dollar value of the tax benefits of this alternative plan would require the selection of an appropriate discount rate, the stipulation of a useful life for the old and new buildings, the actual holding period for the old and new buildings, a marginal tax rate for the taxpayer both at present and in the future, and an estimate of the probability that the tax plan would succeed without additional cost. All of these variables are sufficiently imprecise to support the conclusion that quantification of the benefit would not be reliable enough to justify the effort required to make it here. Nevertheless, the reader should appreciate the potential dollar significance of the tax savings suggested.

Favorable Interest Rate in Installment Sales

Taxpayers often sell property under terms that require the buyer to pay for it over a period of several years. Such sales, called *installment sales*, usually provide for interest on the unpaid balance. In effect, the seller has lent the buyer a portion of the purchase price, and it is only reasonable to assume that the buyer will pay interest on the sum borrowed. From the standpoint of the seller, however, it will be preferable with regard to taxes to provide a minimum of interest and a maximum in sales price anytime that the asset sold is a capital asset that has been owned for more than one year. To illustrate, assume that a taxpayer sold a capital asset for $1 million under a contract that required a $100,000 down payment and $100,000 per year plus 9 percent interest on the unpaid balance. To simplify this illustration, let us assume that the seller had no remaining basis in the asset sold and that the entire sales price, therefore, represents long-term capital gain. Under this extreme assumption, the seller's reported income for the next ten years would be:

Year	Long-term capital gain	Ordinary income (9 percent interest)	Total received
1	$ 100,000	$ 0	$ 100,000
2	100,000	81,000	181,000
3	100,000	72,000	172,000
4	100,000	63,000	163,000
5	100,000	54,000	154,000
6	100,000	45,000	145,000
7	100,000	36,000	136,000
8	100,000	27,000	127,000
9	100,000	18,000	118,000
10	100,000	9,000	109,000
Total	$1,000,000	$405,000	$1,405,000

Even momentary reflection on these numbers will sustain the conclusion that the seller would prefer a sales contract providing for a $1,405,000 sales price and no interest to the one specified here. If this were possible, the seller could convert the $405,000 ordinary interest income into a long-term capital gain and thus reduce his or her tax liability on that income. The buyer, of course, would prefer the contract providing for a maximum rate of interest since interest payments can generally be deducted immediately for tax purposes. In this situation, the seller is often in a dominant position, and the buyer may accept almost any terms that the seller dictates. In order to reduce the conversion of ordinary income into a capital gain, Congress has authorized the imputation of interest in situations in which the taxpayer provides either no interest or an unreasonably low interest on an installment sale. The present provision, however, states that interest will not be imputed if the sales agreement provides for at least 9 percent simple interest. During all recent years, the market rate of interest has remained well in excess of 9 percent; the opportunity to convert some ordinary interest income into capital gain therefore remains a real possibility for the alert seller on an installment contract.

The Corporate Quagmire

As soon as a taxpayer transfers what were personal assets into a corporate entity, he or she has created a whole host of new tax problems and opportunities that often involve the application of capital gain and loss rules. In the space available here, we can only scratch the surface of these opportunities. Two aspects of the corporate-shareholder quagmire will be considered. First, we will consider the different tax consequences that might attach to the disposition of assets in corporate and noncorporate solution. Next, we will consider the different tax consequences that might attach to an asset distribution by a corporation to its shareholders.

The disposition of assets. If an individual taxpayer sells a bundle of assets outside a corporate entity, their capital or noncapital classification will generally be determined on an asset-by-asset basis. In other words, each asset sold will be examined in light of the capital asset definition, and the gain or loss will be classified as ordinary or capital, based on that definition. Suppose, for example, that a taxpayer owns three assets (items A, B, and C) that have the following tax basis and fair market values:

Item	Tax basis	Fair market value	Paper profit (or loss)
A	$100,000	$200,000	$100,000
B	150,000	100,000	(50,000)
C	200,000	450,000	250,000
Total	$450,000	$750,000	$300,000

If the taxpayer were to sell these assets individually, and if items B and C were *not* capital assets, the taxpayer would have to report a $100,000 capital gain and a $200,000 ordinary income.

Suppose that this taxpayer instead transferred assets A, B, and C into a new corporate entity in a nontaxable transaction. He or she would then own stocks in a new corporation rather than assets A, B, and C, and those new stocks would assume a tax basis of $450,000. What has changed is the number of options open to the taxpayer: He or she can now indirectly sell the same assets by selling a 100 percent ownership in the new corporation's stock, or he or she can allow the corporation to sell the old assets and thus have it recognize the paper gains and losses implicit in those assets. If the individual owner sells stocks, he or she will realize nothing but a capital gain and thereby will have effectively converted the potential ordinary income into a capital gain. Because of the tax differential in this example, a knowledgeable buyer might not be willing to pay $750,000 for the stock, even though everyone might agree that the assets were worth that amount. If the buyer can acquire the assets only in corporate solution, the buyer will have the new and increased tax basis in the shares of stock, not in the assets purchased indirectly. However, because of potential ignorance on the part of the buyer, or because of the possible application of other tax rules, which might be available to the buyer, a purchase price of something approaching $750,000 is not entirely impossible.

In short, an individual taxpayer might be able to convert potential ordinary income into a capital gain by transferring appreciated properties into a corporate entity and then selling the stock in the entity that owns the assets. Once again, the time horizon may be critical to the success of such a tax plan. A hasty transfer of assets followed by an immediate sale of stock is certainly subject to question by the IRS. A properly aged sale would raise fewer questions.

Extracting corporate income. In prior chapters we learned that a corporation is not entitled to a deduction for the dividends it pays, and that individual stockholders, with minor exceptions, pay ordinary income tax on all dividends received. These rules have strongly influenced the ways in which closely held corporations distribute their accumulated profits.

To begin our study of this area we need to observe that the tax treatment of values received by corporate shareholders from their corporation varies, depending on the classification of that distribution. The major classifications and the attendant tax results are as follows:

Classification of distribution	Usual tax result to shareholder
Salary, interest, rent, and so on	Ordinary income
Routine dividend	Ordinary income
Stock redemption	Ordinary income or capital gain
Partial liquidation	Capital gain
Complete liquidation	Capital gain
Repayment of debt	No tax (return of capital)

In earlier chapters we considered the first two of these six possibilities, so we will consider only the remaining four here.

A stock redemption differs from a dividend in that a redemption requires the shareholder to surrender part or all of his or her shares of stock in the corporation in exchange for the assets distributed by the corporation. This critical difference is illustrated in Figure 6–1. If there is only one shareholder, or if

FIGURE 6–1

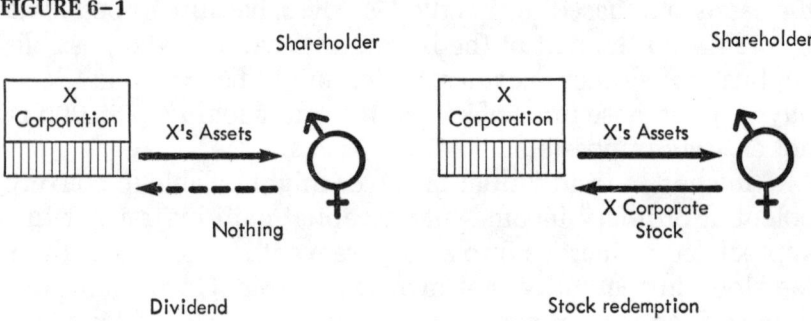

each shareholder surrenders a pro rata share of ownership, the act of surrendering shares is pointless in terms of real economic effects. The tax law has recognized this reality and provides that under these circumstances amounts received in a stock redemption will generally be treated as ordinary income. On the other hand, if one shareholder is completely removed from ownership through a stock redemption of only his or her shares, or if the redemption is substantially disproportionate among all owners, the code provides that the amount received in such a stock redemption should be treated as a capital gain.

A partial liquidation is very much like a stock redemption except that, for tax purposes, we must look to the effect of the distribution on the corporation to determine the tax consequences for the shareholder. If the assets distributed by the corporation represent a "significant corporate contraction," the distribution will be characterized as a partial liquidation and the stockholders are entitled to capital gain treatment. The corporate contraction concept implies some significant change, such as the liquidation of a branch operation, the decision not to replace a plant or division destroyed in a casualty, combined with a distribution of the insurance proceeds, or some similar contraction of genuine business operations.

A complete liquidation requires, of course, the total termination of all business operations by the corporate entity and a distribution of the remaining corporate assets to the stockholders. Unless the liquidated business is a collapsible corporation, or unless the same stockholders hastily return the operating assets of the old corporation to a new corporation and continue the business pretty much as it was before the liquidation, the amounts received in complete liquidation usually will be taxed as a capital gain.

Even this superficial review of the differences among stock redemptions, partial liquidations, and complete liquidations should indicate the need for expert tax assistance anytime a closely held corporation is considering the distribution of some or all of its assets. The way such a distribution is arranged may very easily make the difference between the shareholder's having to report ordinary income and having to report a long-term capital gain.

In limited instances, the shareholder may even be able to avoid capital gain treatment. If at the time the corporation is originally organized, the owners take sufficient care to designate some of the initial investment as a loan, and only the remainder of the investment as an equity investment, they have laid the necessary groundwork that will allow a later tax-free extraction of some of the corporation's accumulated income. In the previous paragraphs we discovered that stock redemptions and partial liquidations produce either ordinary income or capital gain for the recipient shareholder. The repayment of debt, however, creates no taxable income because in that transaction the debtor is deemed to get back only previously taxed capital. Realizing this critical difference in tax treatment, taxpayers might be tempted to create a corporation with very minimal equity and maximum debt; for example, $10 in equity and $999,990 in debt would certainly be preferred to $1 million in equity and no debt from the standpoint of the owners of a closely held corporation. Once again, the tax authorities will use administrative rules and judicial doctrines to correct such obvious abuses in "thin corporation" cases. A more reasonable allocation of debt and equity—say $250,000 equity and $750,000 debt—would very likely withstand attack by the IRS if other indications of real debt were adequately maintained. Once again, the value of expert assistance cannot be overrated. The administrative rules are currently in proposed form. If these proposals are eventually adopted—with or without modification—there should be greater certainty concerning the outer boundaries of this often difficult issue.

The preceding illustrations demonstrate sometimes subtle differences in behavior that may spell the difference between ordinary income and capital gain. In a limited number of situations, the same tax result stems from explicit statutory provisions that create special exceptions to the normal rules for specified transactions. Two such statutory exceptions will be considered here.

Statutory Exceptions to "Normal" Rules

In select instances, the code provides special rules that convert what would otherwise be ordinary income into a capital gain or what would otherwise be capital loss into an ordinary loss. Section 1231 exemplifies the former kind of special rule; Section 1244, the latter. Obviously it is to any taxpayer's benefit to take advantage of these special rules if possible. Section 1244, which is of general applicability, will be discussed first.

Section 1244. Based on the normal rules reviewed in the previous chapter, we know that a taxpayer must generally report a capital loss when he or she sells or exchanges corporate stocks or securities for an amount less than basis. We also know that capital losses are generally not as tax advantageous as ordinary losses. Section 1244 is worth investigating precisely because it allows a taxpayer to treat a loss from the disposition of certain common stock as an ordinary loss rather than a capital loss. The conditions specified before this result can obtain, include the following:

1. The taxpayer claiming the loss must be an individual.
2. The loss must be attributable to stock issued to the taxpayer by the corporation—that is, it cannot be purchased from a prior owner, acquired by gift, and so on.
3. The stock must have been issued for property—that is, shares issued for services are not eligible.

4. The corporation must qualify as a "small business corporation"—this qualification includes specified dollar limitations (generally available only to corporations with equity capital of $1 million or less) and which derive 50 percent or more of their gross receipts from any active trade or business.
5. The stock must be common stock.
6. The amount deducted as ordinary loss under this provision cannot exceed $50,000 per taxpayer per year. (Thus, on a joint return, $100,000 per year is allowable.)

Any taxpayer who is the owner-operator of a closely held corporation should make certain that a maximum amount of stock is qualified under this special provision. In the initial planning stages, the owner-operator may be so optimistic that the need for anticipating tax differences that become pertinent only if the new venture fails will be overlooked. Historical data support the conclusion, however, that many more small businesses fail than succeed. For those businesses that do fail, the opportunity to obtain a tax refund based on a $50,000 ordinary net operating loss deduction is generally more valuable than the potential use of a $50,000 net capital loss carryforward. This provision should also be of special interest to new corporations seeking venture capital. High marginal tax bracket investors are attracted by the possibility of investing in a new firm if they know that the government will share their risk of loss on a 70–30 basis but will share the potential profit on a 28–72 basis. Finally, except for knowledge of the provision and a little timely action, the cost associated with this tax-saving opportunity is essentially zero.

Section 1231. In Chapter 5, we learned that Section 1231 is the code provision that makes it possible for a taxpayer to realize capital gain on the disposition of real or depreciable property used in a trade or business, even though such property does not constitute a capital asset according to the pure statutory definition. Actually, Section 1231 is much broader than the previous discussion implied. It is also among the most complex provisions of the entire code.

Under the circumstances, it seems most appropriate to observe that Section 1231 effectively converts into long-term capital gain what would otherwise be routine operating (ordinary) income from timber, coal, and domestic iron ore operations, from livestock held for draft, breeding, dairy, or sporting purposes (if held for more than 24 months), and from the disposition of certain unharvested crops. Just why these particular forms of business activity should be able to reap the benefits of capital gains taxation, whereas other business ventures must face the higher tax consequences of ordinary income, is not at all obvious. The probable role of politics is apparent and possibly instructive—that is, for those with sufficient funds and connections, this is an alternative route to major tax savings. Because most readers are not engaged in these forms of business endeavor, we will turn our attention to more common tax-saving opportunities, which depend for their success only on the careful timing of a particular transaction by the taxpayer.

Section 1239. Section 1239 is a loophole closer! In effect, this code provision converts what would otherwise be a capital gain into an ordinary gain. If a taxpayer *sells* a capital asset (or a Section 1231 asset) at a gain to a related party, and the property sold will be subject to depreciation by the purchaser, the selling taxpayer must report any gain as ordinary income rather than capital gain. The code defines a *related-party sale* as a sale to one's spouse (husband or wife) or to a corporation that is 80 percent or more owned by the seller (and/or members of the seller's family). The reason for this provision is obvious if one will but stop and consider the tax avoidance possibilities that would exist without it. In the absence of this provision, a taxpayer could report the gain on a sale as a capital gain, tax that gain at the preferential capital gain rates, and proceed to depreciate the new purchase price (and to deduct the depreciation claimed from ordinary taxable income) via the related-party purchaser. This is, of course, too good to be true, and Section 1239 effectively put an end to all such chicanery after May 3, 1951.

Timing Considerations

Just as many physicians advocate an annual physical examination for anyone over 30 years of age, tax advisers commonly advocate an annual, year-end security examination for frequent investors. As any investor approaches the year-end, he or she typically has already realized several capital gains and losses and has, ready for disposal, a number of additional investments, which could be manipulated if there were a compelling reason for doing so. In numerous situations, the special rules applicable to the tax treatment of capital gains and losses provide such a reason, and a careful consideration of the time horizon is often the controlling variable.

The Year-End Security Review

Based on the rules explained in the previous chapter, we know that tax privileges extend to transactions in capital assets only when the taxpayer has realized a net long-term capital gain in excess of any net short-term capital loss. The year-end security review must begin, then, by quantifying the present position of the taxpayer. To illustrate this procedure, let us consider the tax position of a taxpayer who has engaged in six security transactions during the year with the following results:

Transaction no.	Long-term gain (or loss) realized	Short-term gain (or loss) realized
1	$ 60,000	
2	40,000	
3		($20,000)
4	(10,000)	
5		50,000
6	30,000	
Net position	$120,000	$30,000

Going into the end of the year, this taxpayer has realized a net long-term capital gain of $120,000 and a net short-term capital gain of $30,000. If he or she does nothing further, the $120,000 would create a $72,000 long-term capital gain deduction. The $30,000 net short-term capital gain, however, would create no special benefits and would be taxed in exactly the same way as any other $30,000 of ordinary income. A taxpayer in this situation would almost certainly be in a high marginal tax bracket; therefore, doing nothing further would result in payment of up to 70 percent of the $30,000 short-term gain to the government in the form of income taxes. Since no taxpayer likes that prospect, a search for ways of negating that tax result is commonplace.

The way to change the tax consequences might well be suggested by a careful review of this taxpayer's remaining investments with implicit or "paper" gains and losses that have not yet been brought to fruition through a sales transaction. Such a review might, for example, reveal the following:

Stock	Original cost	Present fair market value	Potential LTCG or (LTCL)	Potential STCG or (STCL)
A	$100,000	$210,000	$110,000	
B	50,000	30,000		($20,000)
C	60,000	40,000		(10,000)
D	30,000	20,000	(10,000)	
E	70,000	100,000		30,000

Under the circumstances described earlier, at a minimum it would be advisable for this taxpayer to sell all of the B and C stocks so as to realize an additional $30,000 in short-term capital loss during the current year. By making such a sale, the taxpayer could in effect offset $30,000 in short-term capital loss against ordinary income. Whether or not this taxpayer would choose to realize additional gains or losses would have to depend on further analysis of economic expectations and the potential tax effect of those transactions.

Wash sales. In the previous illustration, the taxpayer might have been convinced that the investments in stocks B and C were still desirable from an economic standpoint. That is, he or she might believe that the present paper losses were only temporary and that retention of the securities would eventually yield a profit. Under these circumstances, a taxpayer might be tempted to sell the stocks to obtain the offset of the loss against the $30,000 net short-term gain previously realized, and be further tempted to repurchase the same shares immediately to reestablish an economic position in stocks B and C. Such a sale-repurchase would become a "wash sale," which, for tax purposes, would negate the right of the taxpayer to recognize any of the loss thus realized. The applicable wash sale rule provides that no capital *loss* shall be recognized for tax purposes if the taxpayer purchases substantially identical securities during a period 30 days before or 30 days after the sale in which a loss was realized. In other words, this taxpayer would have to be willing to go without an investment in B and C for at least 31 days if he or she wants to obtain the tax advantage just described. Note, however, that the wash sale rules do not apply to transactions involving gains, and that they do permit an investment in other companies in the same industry and possibly even an investment in a different class of stock of the same corporation.

To illustrate the potential benefit of a wash sale resulting in a gain, consider the year-end security review of a taxpayer who has realized a net long-term capital gain of $20,000 and a net short-term capital loss of $60,000. If this taxpayer does nothing further, the long-term gain of $20,000 will be offset by the short-term loss of $60,000, leaving a net $40,000 short-term capital loss. Only $3,000 of that loss could be offset against the taxpayer's ordinary income in the current year, the remaining $37,000 having to be carried forward to future years. The potential tax benefit of that loss is, thus, substantially deferred. If this taxpayer had at least $37,000 in potential or "paper" short-term gains that could be realized, this would be an ideal time to do so. He or she could sell the shares with a short-term paper gain and immediately repurchase them to maintain an economic position. Such a transaction would cost only the broker's fee in exchange for the right to immediately offset the previously realized short-term capital loss against a potential item of ordinary income; in addition, the taxpayer would have increased his or her tax basis in the shares repurchased by the amount of the gain just realized. Thus, any subsequent sale at a later date could be made with less concern for tax consequences since much of the taxable gain had already been absorbed. There would be no way this taxpayer could benefit more with regard to taxes since he or she has been able to utilize a short-term loss in offsetting what is potential ordinary income (that is, the net short-term gain).

Generalizations. Obviously, there is an almost infinite array of circumstances that we could create for this kind of year-end security review. What action is preferred for any particular taxpayer will depend upon the taxpayer's present capital position, his or her anticipation of future economic events, and the marginal tax rates that will be applied to various gains and losses both now and in the future. In general, however, a taxpayer will prefer to:

1. Maximize (LTCG − LTCL).
2. Minimize (STCL − STCG).

Typically, this means that a taxpayer should allow capital gains to become long-term by holding them for more than one year. It also means that losses should be realized before they have been sustained for one year because such an early realization leaves open the possibility of offsetting those losses against short-term capital gains before they must be offset against long-term capital gains (which are the only form of tax-blessed capital gains). Finally, it usually means that short-term capital gains should be realized in any year in which the taxpayer has net long-term losses, since the failure to realize the short-term gains at that time will mean that those losses will either be utilized against known long-term gains, which, obviously, are already tax-blessed, or offset against ordinary income on a two-for-one basis. An exception to this last rule exists in any year in which a taxpayer can realize *only* net capital *losses*. In that event, the taxpayer should make certain that he or she has at least $3,000 in net short-term capital loss to offset ordinary income. If the taxpayer has only long-term capital losses available, those losses must be offset against ordinary income on a two-for-one basis. Otherwise the long-term capital losses could be carried forward and applied against capital gains of future years on a one-for-one basis. Under the most favorable conditions, a long-term loss carried into a new year could be offset against a net short-term capital gain and thus effectively reduce potential ordinary income on a one-for-one basis even though that same loss could otherwise only be offset against ordinary income on the less favorable ratio.

Short sales. Taxpayers occasionally will discover that they have so arranged their affairs that they are in the most desirable tax position, but their prediction of future economic events is such that they would very much like to "freeze" a particular economic gain or loss in the current year. If such a taxpayer proceeds to freeze this gain or loss in the usual manner, this will upset the already arranged preferable tax position. To illustrate, suppose that a taxpayer had already realized $80,000 in net long-term capital gains and that the taxpayer's net short-term position is exactly zero. The taxpayer may be very willing to pay the income tax on the $80,000 long-term capital gain, but he or she also has a $60,000 potential short-term gain, which must be realized very soon if it is not to be lost. Furthermore, the taxpayer is aware that if he or she does realize this short-term gain, there are no further short-term losses immediately available to offset the $60,000 gain.

Under the conditions just described, this taxpayer is a prime candidate for a "short sale against the box." A simple "short sale" involves the sale of something a person does not own. In the case of short sales of securities, the broker typically borrows the shares sold short for the seller, and at some future date the seller goes into the market and purchases the shares sold earlier and delivers those shares to the broker to "cover" the prior short position. If the value of the shares decreases in the interim, the seller obviously profits on the transaction, because he or she was able to sell for more than cost. If the value of the shares increases between the two dates, the seller obviously loses, having sold for less than he or she eventually paid.

The tax magic of the short sale is due entirely to noneconomic factors. The pertinent question involves the selection of a date that must control for tax *reporting* purposes. Two dates are potential candidates: the controlling date might be the date of the short sale (that is, the date on which the seller had the broker sell short), or it might be the date on which the short sale was covered (that is, the date on which the seller purchased and delivered to the broker the shares borrowed in the interim period). In a pure short sale, the amount of the gain or loss cannot, of course, be determined until the cover date. Therefore, the tax rules provide that the cover date will control for purposes of determining the correct year of reporting gain or loss.

One final twist must be clarified before we can solve this taxpayer's problem. A short sale against the box is like a pure short sale except that in this instance the seller already owns what he or she purports to sell short. However, the seller allows the broker to go out and borrow the stock temporarily, and only after the new year has dawned does the seller deliver the original shares to the broker to cover the short sale. By application of the short sale rules, this taxpayer has been able to defer the recognition of a $60,000 short-term gain into the next taxable year by withholding delivery of the shares against the earlier short sale. Through this simple device, the taxpayer has maintained a desirable tax position and put the additional short-term gain into a new tax year. This adds an entire year during which the taxpayer can again offset the gain in the most appropriate manner.

Observe that short sales *cannot* be used to convert short-term gains into long-term gains. For purposes of determining whether a capital gain or loss should be classified as short- or long-term, the pertinent time lapse is that between the date of purchase and the date of the short sale, *not* the date of covering the short sale. If one year or less has elapsed between the purchase date and the date of the short sale, the gain or loss will forever remain a short-term gain or loss, even though delivery of the shares is postponed beyond one year. In summary, a short sale is useful only in shifting the year of reporting, not in transforming short-term transactions into long-term ones.

Care must always be exercised to make certain that any gain or loss can be reported in the most desirable year. We have already considered why it may be desirable for a taxpayer to utilize a short sale to defer the tax recognition of a particular transaction. Under other circumstances, year-end sales can present similar problems or opportunities. Generally, an accrual basis taxpayer must report all gains and losses in the year in which a transaction is completed; for securities transactions, this would be the year of sale. Cash-basis taxpayers would normally expect to report gains and losses in the year they received their cash settlement. The normal rules apply for securities transactions with one major exception: Cash-basis taxpayers must report losses in the year a sale is executed, even though cash settlement is deferred until the next year. Obviously, to a limited extent, a cash-basis taxpayer can alter the year of reporting by making special arrangements with the broker to modify the usual time lapse that occurs between the sale date and the settlement date in securities transactions.

The Use of Installment Sales

A taxpayer typically has some control over the time and manner in which he or she will receive the proceeds from the sale of a capital asset. An immediate payment can be demanded, even if this necessitates borrowing by the purchaser from another source, or the purchaser can be allowed to make payments over several years. As explained earlier, the latter option is known as an installment sale. If a sale qualifies for installment treatment, this means that a taxpayer can defer recognition of any gain until the years in which the proceeds of the sale are received.

A taxpayer will typically find the installment sale to be advantageous if there is good reason to anticipate a decline in income in future years. This situation is most frequently encountered with individuals facing imminent retirement. If, for example, an individual taxpayer were in a 60 percent marginal ordinary tax bracket before retirement, and if he or she anticipated being in a 40 percent marginal ordinary tax bracket following retirement, the use of an installment sale could be highly recommended, whether the asset sold would produce ordinary income or long-term capital gain. In the former case, the effective tax rate would, of course, decline from 60 to 40 percent; in the latter case, from 24 to 16 percent.

Obviously, the opposite prescription is equally valid for the person anticipating a substantial increase in income. For example, an M.B.A. student living on the GI Bill would be ill advised to utilize an installment sale in the year preceding graduation. Under these circumstances the taxpayer-student should protect the right to report any income in a low-income year and thus ensure the application of the lowest possible marginal tax rate, whether the income be ordinary or long-term capital gain.

The application of a series of tax rules commonly known as the "nontaxable exchange provisions" may enable a taxpayer to defer recognition of a taxable gain for an even longer period. In the most favorable circumstances, a taxpayer may be able to defer recognition indefinitely. The possibility of longer-term deferrals will be considered in Chapters 10 and 11.

In summary, every taxpayer should be aware of the many ways he or she can influence the tax liability attaching to common transactions. Every taxpayer should be aware that an inadvertent action may convert what was once capital gain into ordinary income. He or she should also be aware that a deliberate action can be helpful in converting what would otherwise be ordinary income into capital gain. And a smart taxpayer should be aware that nondeductible capital losses can occasionally be turned into deductible ones, and that under still other circumstances capital losses can be turned into ordinary losses. The possible array of variations in tax consequences is almost endless. It is hoped that this chapter has helped to sensitize the reader to those situations over which he or she may have some control.

CHAPTER 7

Compensation Considerations

Employee compensation transactions have been more significantly affected by tax considerations than virtually any other common business occurrence. A majority of the tax-saving techniques available in this area demand that the employer be a corporate entity, either because the techniques depend in part for their success upon the existence of corporate stock or because the law makes the particular privilege available only to employees. Self-employed people—the proprietors of sole proprietorships and the partners of partnerships—are not considered to be employees of their own firms and, therefore, any tax shelter restricted to employee benefits is unavailable to them.

Largely because of the distinction between employees and self-employed people, and the dollar significance of the differences between the tax treatment of pensions for employees and those for self-employed people, such professions as medicine, law, accountancy, dentistry, and engineering recently brought great pressure to bear upon the state governments to pass legislation authorizing professionals to incorporate in professional service corporations. Virtually all of the states responded affirmatively to this pressure. Although the Treasury Department for some time fought the recognition of the new professional corporations, the courts were generally unsympathetic to the IRS view. The dispute was largely resolved when Congress passed new legislation providing major improvements in the tax benefits available to self-employed people. That solution is not surprising since most of the major restrictions in the area of tax-oriented compensation considerations have required legislative action to curtail their success.

The degree to which tax laws have influenced compensation packages in large corporate enterprise is hard to overestimate. A thorough study of compensation experience in large organizations was undertaken several years ago by the National Bureau of Economic Research. Wilbur Lewellen, author of the NBER studies, reported many interesting statistics in several reports. Summarizing extensive data for the period 1955–63, Lewellen found that the average before-tax cash payments to the five most highly paid corporate executives in each of the 50 large manufacturing companies studied was in the neighborhood of $135,000 per year. These cash payments, however, amounted to only 50 percent of the real remuneration of these top executives; the remaining amount went largely into tax-shielded benefits. If the employer corporations had attempted to provide the executives with a cash salary that would have been sufficiently large to allow them to purchase, from their aftertax salaries, an equivalent collection of benefits without a tax shield, their before-tax salaries would have had to increase to something like $734,000 per executive per year! In the 18 years since 1963, these salaries and benefits have increased substantially. Unfortunately, however, no equally good empirical data for the more recent period are available.

The many tax shields available in the compensation area can be classified in several different ways. One of the most meaningful ways to classify them seems to be in terms of their differential tax effect on the employer corporation and on the employee. Although equally applicable to the large corporation, the importance of the alternatives comes into particularly clear focus when we think about the small to medium-sized, owner-managed business venture. In terms of priority-ranked preferences, few owner-managers would disagree with the following preferences:

Preference ranking	Tax effect to employer corporation	Tax effect to employee recipient
1	Immediately deductible	Never taxable
2	Immediately deductible	Tax deferred and, if possible, realized in a preferential form
3	Immediately deductible	Immediately taxed
4	Deferred deduction	Deferred tax
5	Never deductible	Taxed immediately or at a later date

As a matter of fact, each of these five preferences is a viable possibility, and the specific techniques commonly used in compensation arrangements have been classified under these preferences in the remaining pages of this chapter.

Techniques Providing an Immediate Corporate Deduction and a Benefit That Is Never Taxed to the Employee

In Chapter 2, we observed that, generally speaking, individuals are taxed on any economic benefits they receive for services rendered, no matter how indirect the benefits may be. In that same chapter, however, we also observed that the Internal Revenue Code does provide a limited number of exceptions to this rule in the form of specific statutory exclusions. We further noted there that a taxpayer is entitled to deduct all ordinary and necessary business expenses incurred in a trade or business, including any reasonable compensation paid to an employee. By carefully combining the exclusion provisions with the deduction authorizations, it is possible in a limited number of circumstances to provide an employee with a real economic benefit, which is never taxed, and, at the same time, provide the employer corporation with an immediate deduction.

Group Term Life Insurance

Code Section 79(a) provides that an employee need not report as gross income the value of group term life insurance premiums paid by his or her employer so long as the insurance coverage provided under this group-term policy does not exceed $50,000. Observe that, before this special exclusion can apply, the insurance in question must be *group, term, life* insurance. Regulations issued by the Treasury Department suggest that such insurance coverage generally must include at least ten full-time employees if it is to be recognized as a legitimate group plan. For very small organizations, the group might include fewer than ten employees, but in that event the plan cannot discriminate in favor of corporate owners if it is to be recognized as a legitimate plan. If the coverage exceeds $50,000, the employee is taxed only on the cost of the premium for the excess; this cost is based on tables provided in the pertinent regulations. Suffice it to note that the tax cost of coverage in excess of $50,000 is relatively inexpensive. An obvious economic advantage attaches to tax-free life insurance in comparison with insurance purchased from aftertax salary dollars.

In the case of life insurance, a double exclusion is actually possible. Note that the employee need not report the premiums paid by his or her employer for this insurance. Furthermore, if the employee dies and the beneficiaries collect insurance under the policy, they need not report as gross income the amount they received by reason of the insured person's death.

Health and Accident Plans

Code Section 106 provides for a very similar tax treatment of health and accident insurance plans purchased by an employer for the employee. In the case of health and accident insurance, however, it is necessary to distinguish between the tax treatment of the premium payments and the tax treatment of the amounts actually received under such coverage. The cost of the premiums can be excluded by the employee under Section 106. Other sections of the code determine the tax consequence of compensation (a) for injuries and medical expenses and (b) for wage continuation payments received before age 65 but after permanent and total disablement. The employee can generally exclude the former amounts, whereas the latter are excludable only to a maximum of $100 per week, and then only to age 65 and subject to reduction if the taxpayer's adjusted gross income exceeds $15,000. The details of the many rules are best left for other books.

It is again pertinent to note that, relative to health and accident insurance, an employer corporation can provide a very real economic benefit to an employee without tax cost. If the employee were to purchase his or her own equivalent insurance coverage from aftertax salary, the employee would pay more for the same coverage; the exact amount of the increased cost depends upon the employee's marginal tax bracket. Alternatively, of course, the employee might be forced to purchase a less desirable coverage for the same dollar cost. Incidentally, this tax-saving opportunity can include the increasing cost of an annual physical examination for any employee; it can also cover the medical expenses of the employee's spouse and dependents.

Group Legal Services

Code Section 120 provides that an employee generally need not report as taxable income an amount contributed by an employer on behalf of an employee to a qualified group legal service plan. Neither will an employee have to report as gross income the value of the legal service provided to the employee, a spouse, or a dependent under a qualified group legal service plan. As usual, the code provides a list of restricting conditions—for example, the plan cannot discriminate in favor of corporate officers or shareholders—but this time, contrary to the norm, the provision was extended to self-employed individuals.

Meals and Lodging

Code Section 119 permits an employee to exclude from gross income the value of meals and lodging furnished on the employer's premises for the convenience of the employer. The potential benefit of this section seems to have gone largely unrecognized in the past, and it should be carefully examined by many more taxpayers. Apparently Section 119 is the statutory authority that explains the presence of executive dining rooms high in the metropolitan skies, as well as the authority that allows our presidents to live in regal splendor (at least for the period of their presidency) and corporate presidents and university chancellors their right to live in million-dollar homes without tax consequence. One critical nexus in succeeding with regard to taxes lies in the employer's ability to establish a valid corporate reason for insisting that an employee eat while at work or live in a particular home. In regard to company homes, the success of beer magnates Adolph and Joseph Coors is encouraging. (See *Adolph Coors Co.,* T. C. Memo, 1968–256.) The undeveloped but potential use of this section by ranchers, farmers, operators of small businesses, and professionals seems to be substantial, since many should find it easy to explain why their constant presence would be required by their own employer corporation. The economic impact of this alternative can be substantial since it effectively provides the taxpayer, through a closely held corporation, the right to deduct depreciation on a home, the cost of utilities and insurance, and many other costs not otherwise deductible. Note that, under the proper circumstances, even the cost of the food eaten by the employee becomes deductible by the employer corporation. For these plans to succeed, however, it is essential that the corporation pay the bills in the first instance. Corporate reimbursements will generally fail.

Death Benefits

Code Section 101 allows a taxpayer the right to receive up to $5,000 in tax-free death benefits paid by a deceased employee's corporate employer. The employer can also deduct the amounts paid under such a death benefit plan. Although the dollar significance of this opportunity is obviously rather limited, any taxpayer who takes the trouble to incorporate a business in order to obtain other employee tax benefits should also take the necessary action to insure the right to this small additional benefit.

Other Employee Benefits

Although it has had limited impact to date, Section 124—which was added to the code by the 1978 Revenue Act—could become important in the future. This provision excludes from the gross income of an employee the value of any qualified transportation provided by the employer between the employee's residence and place of employment. In order to qualify under this provision, the vehicle used (among other things) must seat at least eight adults, excluding the driver; it must remain at least 50 percent occupied over 80 percent of the mileage traveled; and it must not discriminate in favor of employees who are officers, shareholders, or highly compensated employees. With rapidly escalating gasoline prices, this could become a very welcome tax-free fringe benefit in the near future, especially for the smaller corporation whose employees live in a limited geographic area.

Another 1978 addition to the code that may increase in popularity is Section 127. That provision excludes from the gross income of an employee the amounts paid by the employer for educational assistance to the employee. Once again, in order for any payments to qualify for this exclusion, many specific requirements must be satisfied. Most important, perhaps, the provision requires that any educational assistance program be *nondiscriminatory* relative to employees who are officers, owners, highly compensated employees, or their dependents. If the program qualifies, the employee can receive tax-free tuition, fees, books, supplies, and equipment. The program *cannot*, however, extend to the cost of meals, lodging, or transportation; neither can it include education involving sports, games, or hobbies. Like a few of the other exclusion provisions, this one extends to self-employed people. Unlike most others, it is scheduled to terminate after December 31, 1983. That termination date, however, is very likely to be changed in the future.

Some employers provide their employees with the personal right to select from a specified group, which perquisites they would like to receive, subject to some maximum dollar amount. These programs are widely known as *cafeteria plans*, for obvious reasons. Section 125 of the code makes it clear that no otherwise tax-free benefit will become taxable merely because it is part of a cafeteria plan, or because some employees elect to receive cash or other taxable compensation. There is, however, an exception for plans that discriminate in favor of highly compensated employees; these cafeteria plans do not qualify for any tax-free status.

Some tax shelters are available not because of specific statutory exclusion provisions, but because of the way in which other code provisions are applied and interpreted. The net effect of these interpretations may be to provide an employee with the equivalent of a tax-free (or tax-cheap) economic benefit.

Travel and Entertainment

The detailed rules that regulate the correct tax treatment of travel and entertainment expenses are so lengthy that they cannot be examined here. However, it would be equally inappropriate to gloss over the obvious benefits available in this area. Country club memberships, theater tickets, admissions to athletic events, box seats in domed stadiums, elegant dining, premium-brand alcohol, and other perquisites too numerous to mention may all be deducted as reasonable entertainment expenses under the proper circumstances. Travel that combines business with pleasure is frequently rewarding from a tax standpoint.

The critical tax result is that, under prescribed conditions, travel and entertainment costs can be deducted as proper business expenses. Those who enjoy the fruits of such outlays are either (a) not required to report taxable income or (b) required to report equivalent amounts of income and deductions. Although there is no specific statutory authority for an exclusion, the conclusion derives from the notion that individuals required to travel and entertain business associates are really at work, and that it is virtually impossible to design a tax law or tax administration that can measure the indirect benefits that one derives from working in pleasant surroundings. On the other hand, for those who have been there, it is equally impossible to measure the implicit costs associated with the many long evenings spent in boring company and away from home, no matter how luxurious the surroundings. On balance, any implicit deductions might be greater than any implicit income that an academic theoretician could identify.

In a practical sense, what these rules should say to the members of the entrepreneurial class is that they ought to give adequate consideration to the tax aspects of alternative ways of doing business combined with pleasure. When the conditions are favorable, it is not terribly difficult to convert a great number of expenditures for personal pleasure into tax deductions. Relative to domestic travel, for example, once the taxpayer can establish that the primary purpose of a trip is business, the cost of the transportation and most related expenses during business days becomes tax deductible. Relative to foreign travel, different rules are applied. The interesting little rules required to get a deduction for foreign travel sometimes make the entire scene look like part of a comic opera, and the substantiation requirements appear to be a chapter from George Orwell's *1984*. In a nutshell, under the current rules, the deduction for travel to a foreign convention is limited to coach air fare; and even that deduction depends on the taxpayer spending more days devoted to business than to pleasure. Moreover, in order to deduct other travel costs, the taxpayer must be able to prove that he or she engaged in at least four out of six hours of scheduled business on any one business day. In this area more than any other, an ounce of prevention is worth a pound of cure, so see your tax adviser and go well prepared. The way can be both rewarding and enjoyable for those who know the rules. For the poorly advised, it is pocked with pitfalls.

Automobiles (and Airplanes?)

The company car has become as much a part of the American scene as the Florida winter convention. For the fortunate employee, the company car is the one that produces no taxable income but whose entire cost is deductible by the employer corporation. The models may vary from four-cylinder compacts to the chauffeur-driven limousines parked two deep around Wall Street and Rockefeller Center at 3:00 P.M. The tax results are the same. Use the car for purely personal purposes, and you suddenly have realized gross income. Use it solely for business purposes, and you just might escape tax-free. Use it for both personal and business purposes, and anticipate an argument with an IRS agent. Business purpose? Personal use? Definitions are a dime a dozen.

Why stop with automobiles? For the jet set, a plane is vastly more effective. After all, if the company plane is scheduled to fly to Acapulco to pick up a business client, there can be little basis for imputing income to the corporate executive (or member of his or her family) who happens to have the day off and flies along just for the fun of it. Or if Air Force One happens to be flying the president or a member of his Cabinet to Hawaii, why shouldn't wives, families, and friends accompany the government official tax-free? And a senator or congressman on a military jet bound for a fact-finding mission in the Orient may just find enough time to stop for Christmas shopping in Hong Kong.

The opportunities for tax saving are obviously as real as the social inequities created by what has to be class legislation. Unfortunately, there are no easy answers. Business travel and business entertainment are as legitimate business expenses as are expenditures for heat, light, water, and rent. The unique social problem created by travel and entertainment, however, is that it is next to impossible to distinguish on any reasonable basis between the legitimate business expense and disguised compensation. What is unfortunate is that so few have an opportunity to avoid taxes in this way. No social order or system of government can change that situation. It is simply unfortunate that the taxpayer who inevitably gets tagged is the salesperson whose spouse has been invited to the Las Vegas convention at company expense. That salesperson knows that in all likelihood he or she will have to report as taxable income at least the marginal cost of the company's sending the spouse, whereas other, more fortunate taxpayers, all too frequently, ride high, wide, and handsome. If the IRS and the SEC get their way, the end of overly generous executive fringe benefits may be in sight. Recent activities of both organizations imply that new enforcement efforts to crack down on abuses have been made. Just how the courts will react to those efforts remains to be seen. Fair answers are especially difficult to determine in this general area.

Employee Discounts

If an employee is given the opportunity of purchasing the employer's ordinary inventory at a small discount, and if this discount is extended to all employees, the employee generally need not report the bargain price element as gross income. On the other hand, if the price discount becomes too great, or if it is not made generally available to all employees, the IRS will be quick to find that the employee must report as taxable income the difference between the fair market value and the lower price actually paid to acquire the employer's property. Initially the opportunity to escape any substantial amount of tax liability in this manner seems to be small and hardly worth investigating.

Conceptually, however, this opportunity presents an entirely new possibility, and for that reason it may be important. Observe that what really happens in the courtesy discount situation is that the corporate employer achieves its potential tax advantage, *not* by gaining a deduction, but by reporting less gross income itself. In other words, the corporate employer cannot deduct the value of the "bargain price" element so long as the employee need not report any income. The net effect to the corporation, however, is the same as the creation of a deduction because the sales to employees simply reduce the employer's gross revenue from sales and thereby reduce taxable income by the amount of the net price reduction. The employee's benefit depends upon the right to exclude the economic benefit received from income. In the case of courtesy discounts this results from an administrative pronouncement, not from a code provision. Probably the reason for the generosity of the IRS is attributable to the administrative difficulty of applying any other standard. Imagine, for example, the practical problem that the IRS would create for itself if it tried to tax the small employee discounts given to literally millions of employees.

In a few industries the same administrative difficulties probably keep the IRS from applying a stricter standard to what have become much more than minor employee discounts. In the airline industry, for example, one of the really significant tax-free economic benefits available to employees is the coveted pass that may allow the employee to circle the world on a grand vacation at little cost. This real economic benefit may be quite significant to young travel-oriented employees, and it may even induce them to accept a lower-than-normal rate of pay. The extra benefit stems from the fact that there is no convenient way that the IRS can tax this economic advantage; measuring the actual value of the pass to any particular employee is next to impossible. Observe, again, that the employer airline gets no additional deduction in this instance; it simply deducts all of the operating expenses incurred in running an airline, and the fact that a particular passenger happens to be flying on a free pass makes little difference in terms of the expense incurred. Economically, what does happen, however, is that the airline's gross revenues do not increase for this passenger and that it has therefore been effectively able to give the employee a tax-free benefit without increasing its own revenue, which in one sense is tantamount to a deduction for the employer and an exclusion for the employee.

Interest-free loans

A short leap of the imagination will quickly lead the reader to other opportunities based on the same fundamental idea as company discounts and airline passes. For example, why shouldn't an employer corporation make an interest-free loan to a very special corporate officer (or to a special star athlete)? The corporate employer will certainly not get a deduction for anything in this instance because it has incurred no real out-of-pocket expense. Very important, however, is the fact that the corporate employer has avoided earning any taxable income on the $50,000 or $100,000 loaned to the employee, and has thereby reduced its taxable income by an equivalent amount. At the present time there is some authority for the recipient employee to receive an interest-free loan tax-free. A quick look at any compound interest table, at market rates of interest, will demonstrate just how important this opportunity could be to the lucky employee. The eventual imputation of interest in this situation seems inevitable if enough taxpayers begin to take advantage of it. To date, the IRS has had relatively little success in the cases it has litigated, but the possibility of legislative action in this area seems probable. In the meantime, the desired tax result may be possible as long as the parties take all necessary precautions that will allow them to prove that the loan is a *bona fide* debt, which the employee will repay, *and* that the loan is based on a *noninterest-bearing demand* note. The courts have imputed interest on term notes and on notes providing any lower than normal rate of interest greater than zero.

Before we proceed to the second-ranked form of compensation, a word of caution seems to be in order. Obviously, the IRS and the courts are not ignorant of what is taking place in the area of disguised compensation. They examine the records of closely held corporations with particular care just because the opportunity for owner-managers to divert corporate funds for purely personal purposes is substantial. In the large publicly owned corporation, even the very top executives may eventually have to answer to a higher authority at the next stockholders' meeting. The most obvious abuses in this area frequently lead to the courtroom and an eventual judicial settlement. The owner-manager must be particularly careful to establish sound business purposes for whatever he or she does. Extra caution in maintaining proper records, to give any transaction the *bona fide* look, is essential. This is not a job for an amateur. Recent activity by the SEC suggests that abuses could result in securities problems as well as tax problems.

Techniques Providing an Immediate Corporate Deduction and a Tax-Deferred Benefit to the Employee

A second class of compensation techniques is characterized by the ability to produce an immediate deduction to the corporate employer and only a deferred (and sometimes preferential form of) gross income to the employee. In terms of the absolute dollar amount of tax-sheltered compensation, there can be little doubt that this class of tax-saving techniques dominates in the aggregate. The most common forms of this second-ranked class are the qualified pension and profit-sharing plans. In the same class of benefits, but of much less common occurrence, is the qualified stock bonus plan. All *qualified* pension, profit-sharing, and stock bonus plans share several common characteristics. On the other hand, two fully qualified plans may differ significantly from each other. In the discussion that follows, we will first examine the common characteristics, then look at some of the more important differences among qualified plans, and finally consider briefly a few of the considerations that should be given careful thought before undertaking the implementation of any of these plans. The technical rules that govern this complex area of taxation are contained in the Employee Retirement Income Security Act of 1974, popularly known by the acronym ERISA.

Common Characteristics of All Qualified Pension, Profit-Sharing, and Stock Bonus Plans

All qualified pension, profit-sharing, and stock bonus plans attain their preferred tax position because of certain unique tax provisions that are applicable to them. They must all meet certain requirements before they can be considered to be qualified plans. And they all trigger tax consequences for the employee under similar circumstances. Before we consider the many requirements applicable to qualified plans, let us look briefly at the available benefits.

The tax opportunities available. The tax benefits available in most qualified pension, profit-sharing, and stock bonus plans can be separated into six distinct considerations.

1. Subject to varying maximum limits, the corporate employer will get an immediate tax deduction for its contribution to the employee trust fund created to administer these assets.
2. The employee trust fund will be treated as a tax-exempt entity, which allows it to accumulate earnings and grow at a substantially faster rate than would otherwise be possible.
3. The employee will not be taxed on either the employer's current contributions or on the growth from prior contributions until he or she either withdraws the funds or until the funds are otherwise made available to the employee.
4. An employee may designate that, in the event of death, his or her interest in an employee trust fund may be paid as an annuity to someone other than the executor of the estate, and can thereby remove from the value of the estate (for estate tax purposes) any interest in the trust fund that is attributable to the employer's contributions.
5. If in one year an employee withdraws all of his or her rights from a qualified employee trust in a lump-sum settlement, several options exist. First, the employee may elect to treat part of the distribution as ordinary income and part as long-term capital gain. The latter portion is equal to that fraction of the total distribution determined by reference to the number of years the employee participated in the plan before 1974 compared to the total num-

ber of years he or she participated in the plan. Second, the ordinary income portion of any lump-sum distribution—assuming that the employee elects to treat part of the distribution as a capital gain—can be taxed either as routine ordinary income or as "ordinary income" subject to special ten-year forward-averaging rules. Third, the employee may elect to treat the entire lump-sum distribution as "ordinary income" subject to ten-year forward averaging. (Nonlump-sum distributions are taxed like any other retirement annuity or pension.) Which of the several alternatives is the best option depends on more considerations than can be explained here. The more critical options will be explained briefly in subsequent chapters.

6. An employee may sometimes be able to contribute additional funds to a pension trust out of his or her own pocket and thereby put those funds to work in a tax-free environment. In rare circumstances, the additional contributions made by an employee may be taken from the employee's salary by the employer on a before-tax basis. In other words, the employee may be able to contribute a large number of dollars to the fund if they can be treated as a salary *reduction* rather than as a salary *deduction*. In most cases, however, the employee's personal contributions must come from aftertax dollars, but to the extent that this is true, the employee will be able to recover those amounts free of any further income tax on separation from service, retirement, or death.

This list of tax benefits available through a qualified pension or profit-sharing plan is truly impressive, and the dollar significance of this opportunity to any employee can hardly be overrated. The magnitude of the tax savings is, of course, directly related to the marginal tax bracket of the employee. For upper-income-bracket individuals, it would require a tremendous increase in cash salaries to purchase an equivalent retirement annuity in a taxable commercial enterprise. The compounding effect of tax-free contributions and tax-free growth is almost phenomenal over the working life of an individual. To grasp better the significance of the difference, consider two taxpayers in the 50 percent marginal tax bracket who each divert $5,000 per year to a retirement plan and earn an annual 8 percent return on their retirement investment for a period of 25 years. The only difference between the two taxpayers is that taxpayer A prepares for retirement in a nontax-sheltered way, whereas taxpayer B prepares for retirement through a qualified pension program. At the end of the 25 years, taxpayer B's retirement fund will amount to approximately $365,000, whereas taxpayer A's fund will have grown to only $104,000. Obviously, these two amounts are not appropriate as a final comparison, since taxpayer B still has to pay an income tax on all retirement income, whereas most of taxpayer A's retirement income will be free of further income tax (that is, all but the additional earnings produced by the remaining assets during the retirement years). Nevertheless, the dollar difference in their retirement pensions will be substantial. The larger size of B's fund will permit much larger payments to be made, and the larger fund will continue to earn larger sums during B's retirement. In addition, B will probably be in a lower marginal tax bracket after retirement, so even an ordinary income tax might not be onerous. And if B elects a lump-sum settlement, the aftertax proceeds would very likely be more than twice the value of A's accumulation. Perhaps in no small measure it is because these benefits are so impressive that requirements for qualification are so demanding.

Qualification of a plan. A pension, profit-sharing, or stock bonus plan will not qualify for the tax shelters listed above unless it satisfies the numerous code requirements of Section 401. Among the conditions required for qualification are the following:

1. That the plan be created for the exclusive benefit of the employees and/or their beneficiaries.
2. That the sole purpose of the plan be either to give the employees or their beneficiaries a share of the employer's profits or to provide them with a retirement income.
3. That the plan be a written, permanent plan and that it be communicated to the employees.
4. That the plan *not* discriminate in favor of corporate officers, stockholder-employees, or supervisory or highly paid employees.

5. That the plan provide for a vesting of full benefits after no more than 15 years of service to the employer.
6. That the plan be "funded"—that is, the employer must make annual contributions, often in significant amounts.

Each of these requirements is stipulated with considerable detail in the code and the related regulations. For anything other than the smallest corporate enterprise—that is, for all but the "one-man" corporation—the two most important requirements are perhaps the one that precludes discrimination among employees and the one that insists on funding. Most owner-operators would be delighted to provide themselves with a tax-sheltered pension or profit-sharing plan, but they are reluctant to do so when this also requires that all other employees share the pot. On the other hand, some employers who might be willing to cover all employees may not have sufficient capital to fund a qualified plan. Although a qualified plan cannot discriminate, because contributions to the plan may be made a percentage of the employee's salary, the real benefits obtained are not equal for every employee by any means.

Taxpayers owning more than one corporation might be tempted to be selective in determining which corporation would institute a generous qualified pension or profit-sharing plan. The corporation with the highest ratio of owner-employees to total employees is the obvious candidate. The effort to discriminate through the careful selection of one of several related corporate entities generally will not succeed. In most instances, multiple businesses under common control must be treated as a single business.

Assuming that a pension or profit-sharing plan meets all code requirements for qualification, the accumulated assets of the employee trust fund must sooner or later be distributed to the employees. When this happens, the employee must recognize taxable income. As noted earlier, that income may be either ordinary income or a capital gain.

Taxation of employee benefits. An employee covered by a qualified pension or profit-sharing plan need not report as taxable income any benefits under that plan until they are paid or otherwise "made available." Usually, benefits are not distributed by employee trust funds until an employee terminates employment, retires, or dies. Very often a qualified plan will allow the employee to select from several options when deciding how to receive any accumulated benefits. He or she may, for example, be given a choice between (1) a lump-sum settlement, (2) a lifetime annuity for one life, or (3) a smaller lifetime annuity for as long as either the employee or the employee's spouse shall live. Another common option is a "refund" feature, which guarantees the employee or the heirs the right to receive a minimum payment, regardless of how long the employee may live. The option selected by the employee significantly determines the tax consequence of any distribution. Once again, the specific rules that determine the exact tax results are too numerous and too complex to justify their inclusion in a book aimed at tax recognition rather than tax solution. Suffice it to observe here that no employee should make any election until he or she has fully investigated the tax results of every option. Generally that will require the assistance of a qualified tax adviser.

If all details are properly arranged in advance, an employee may rarely be able to obtain an earlier benefit from an economic interest in a qualified plan without termination of employment and without triggering the usual tax consequences for all accumulated benefits. For example, some qualified profit-sharing plans provide that employees can make a partial withdrawal of vested rights if they can show need (such as unusual medical costs or college expenses) and if they can gain the approval of either the fund trustee or of an administrative committee created to make such decisions. So long as the employee does not have an absolute right to make such early withdrawals, but only has the right to request withdrawal in appropriate and specified circumstances, the tax deferral privilege may be maintained.

Some Important Differences in Qualified Plans

Although all qualified pension, profit-sharing, and stock bonus plans have many things in common, such plans also differ in many important ways. Some of the important differences have more to do with everyday economics than with taxation. Some of the differences are of primary importance to the employer corporation; others are of greater importance to the employee. Perhaps the most important differences relate to funding and to the tax deduction limitation.

Pension plans. A pension plan has as its primary purpose the provision of a retirement fund for covered employees. Once instituted, a pension plan generally becomes a fixed obligation of the employer corporation. This means, of course, that the employer must make the contractual contribution without regard for the presence or absence of corporate profits. Because of the substantial cash requirement implicit in a pension plan covering any sizable group of employees, new and riskier ventures are typically reluctant to institute such a plan. Employees, especially middle-aged and older employees, on the other hand, strongly prefer the relative security of a fixed contractual arrangement. Because pension plans are intended to provide for retirement income, they seldom make provision for any acceleration of benefits, even in cases of demonstrated need.

Vesting rights were, for many years, a controversial aspect of qualified pension plans. Since 1974, ERISA has provided that an employee's rights to any employer contributions must vest under one of three different schedules. In every case, an employee's rights must be 50 percent vested after 10 years of service and fully vested after 15 years of service. This means, of course, that an employee with at least 15 years of service with a single employer is now guaranteed certain rights under a qualified pension program, whether or not he or she continues employment with the same employer until retirement. Obviously, an employee who leaves the employ of a corporation after a few years will receive a smaller retirement pension than will an employee with many years of service. By the accumulation of two or three small pensions with different employers, however, the more transitory employee can now look forward to a reasonable retirement income, even if not all of it is paid by a single trust fund.

The maximum tax deduction that an employer corporation may claim in any tax year for its contribution to a qualified pension plan depends in part upon the funding method it elects. The actuarially determined cost of the plan fixes the maximum deduction under any method. Pension costs are based upon assumptions about the future, including estimated employee earnings, mortality, turnover, retirement, and vesting rights. Because qualified pension plans include credit for prior service (that is, for services rendered to the employer prior to the institution of a pension plan) as well as for future service, the current year's tax deduction may well exceed the cost that relates only to current employee services rendered to the employer.

Profit-sharing plans. Rights under a profit-sharing plan depend, as the name implies, upon the presence of employer profits. If the corporate employer earns no income in a particular year, it has no obligation to make a contribution to a qualified profit-sharing plan that year. Corporations with highly volatile income find this feature especially appealing. Young, new employees, who look forward to a number of prosperous years, may also find profit sharing a desirable alternative, whereas older employees, with fewer years remaining prior to retirement, generally prefer some other plan.

The maximum deduction for amounts contributed by the employer to a profit-sharing plan is generally equal to 15 percent of the compensation paid to participating employees. If an employer contributes less than the maximum deduction in one year, it obtains a carry-over credit, which allows contribution deductions in subsequent years to exceed the normal maximum by the amount of any carry-forward. In no instance, however, can the deduction in a single year exceed 25 percent of current employee compensation. This carry-over credit is unique to profit-sharing plans (underfunding of pension plans in any year simply goes into the formula calculation for subsequent years). Amounts contributed in excess of the current year's maximum deduction can generally be carried over and deducted in succeeding years to whatever extent the succeeding years' contributions are less than the maximum deduction.

Stock bonus plans. The tax rules for qualified stock bonus plans generally parallel those applicable to profit-sharing plans. The major difference between the two is the fact that stock bonus plans are payable in the stock of the employer corporation rather than in cash. This means, of course, that the employees' rights under the plan depend not only upon the presence of profits but also upon the value of the employer's stock. New corporations, many of which are critically short on cash, may be especially attracted to stock bonus plans because they minimize cash requirements. Young employees may find that the possible increase in benefits is worth the additional risk associated with the future value of their employer's stock. Older employees and majority stockholders may find stock bonus plans less acceptable because of the extra risk and the dilution of equity, respectively.

As noted earlier, it is easy to underestimate the significance of the benefits available through qualified pension, profit-sharing, and stock bonus plans. Implementing the plans and selecting the most desirable options within those plans are much more difficult tasks. Some of the more important considerations will be reviewed very briefly.

Related Considerations

Any taxpayer considering the possibility of implementing a qualified pension, profit-sharing, or stock bonus plan should consult with a team of experts to assist in making a wise decision. Normally the team will consist of representatives of the employer and the employees, as well as an accountant, attorney, and actuary (or life underwriter). The team should carefully estimate the cost of implementing any plan, as well as the benefits expected from it. The costs and benefits are doubly difficult to predict, not only because they are based on many estimates of the future, but also because they may significantly influence that future through changes in employee morale, and thus changes in the corporate performance generally. A good plan is one that helps develop and retain a strong and permanent complement of employees who are anxious to do their part to make the corporation more profitable.

Decisions related to the vesting options are often difficult. Full vesting at too early a stage may unnecessarily encourage employee turnover. Deferred vesting may undercut employee morale and encourage the most capable employees to seek greater security elsewhere. On the other hand, amounts contributed on behalf of any employees who did not stay long enough to acquire a vested interest serve to decrease the employer's cost for those who remain.

Qualified pension plans may provide the retired employee with either a *fixed* or a *variable* annuity. A fixed annuity is one that stipulates in advance the exact number of dollars that the employee may claim at some future date under any given option. A variable annuity is one that provides benefits of varying amount, depending upon the relative success or failure of the trustee's investment of fund assets during the interim years. Many authors describing fixed annuities suggest that they are less risky than variable annuities because the dollar benefits paid to the employee are not subject to the vagaries of the securities markets. However, that statement is at least as misleading as it is accurate. Although it is true that the employee may know how many dollars he or she will receive under a fixed annuity, that fact provides no knowledge about what any number of dollars may buy at some future date. The more rapid the inflation prior to retirement, the greater the risk in a fixed annuity. Unfortunately, the risk in a variable annuity may also be sizable because of wide fluctuations in the price of stocks, such as occurred in 1973–75. Few if any employees contemplating retirement in the period from 1950 to 1970 would have accurately estimated the absolute dollar cost of a minimal retirement living in 1980. Given the importance of the unknowns, it is often very difficult to select wisely between fixed and variable annuities.

Contributions made by an employer to an employee trust fund obviously do not lie idle pending the employee's retirement. These assets might be directly invested by the fund trustee; they might be turned over to some other professional or to a mutual fund for investment; they might be put into government bonds; or they might be lodged directly with an insurance company, which could provide an annuity contract for each covered employee. The eventual financial success of any employee trust fund is directly determined by the investment decisions.

Prior to the passage of ERISA in 1974, a number of employee trust funds seemed to be manipulated more for the benefit of the corporate employer than for the employees. For example, the assets of some trust funds were loaned back to the contributing employer at low rates of interest. Other funds purchased assets from employers and/or the employer's stockholders at apparently inflated values. Still others hired the employer's stockholders at high salaries. All of these and many other questionable practices were made the subject of severe penalty provisions in the 1974 legislation. As a consequence, most self-serving transactions have been ended. In fact, the new rules may be too restrictive. Some trustees are now being overly conservative; they are thereby reducing the earnings of the employees' trust funds and thus the benefits that will eventually be received, at least under variable annuity plans.

Life, health, and accident insurance are sometimes made a part of the qualified pension, profit-sharing, or stock bonus package. Generally, the presence of any of these benefits makes some part of the employee's rights immediately taxable. Other plans combine pension and profit-sharing plans into a single "combined" plan. Such plans may maximize the number of dollars that can be tax-sheltered. Still other plans facilitate the transfer of employees between related employers by providing a single qualified plan for a group of related employers. Affiliated corporate groups can create plans that allow profitable member corporations to make contributions for the benefit of an unprofitable member corporation's employees. Deciding whether or not to include these or many other benefits within the context of a qualified plan complicates the basic decision. Even with the multiple complexities, however, few tax-saving plans create more impressive benefits than do qualified pension, profit-sharing, and stock bonus plans.

The next class of compensation arrangements to be discussed is the class that includes the most common form of employee compensation—that is, the routine wage or salary. The tax planner should always remember that the aggregate compensation paid to an employee must be *reasonable in amount* before it can be deducted by the employer corporation. This reasonableness test encompasses all forms of compensation considered together.

Techniques Providing an Immediate Corporate Deduction and an Immediate Tax to the Employee

In addition to cash wages and salaries, this third class of techniques includes almost all nonqualified compensation arrangements. For example, if a corporate employee is given the right to make a bargain purchase of a corporate asset, the amount of that bargain generally will be included as part of his or her compensation. If a corporation purchases an entertainment facility—say, a resort condominium or a hunting lodge—and makes it available only to corporate executives, the value of their use of such a facility could very easily be treated as additional compensation. If an employee's spouse and family are provided with a "free trip" at company expense in connection with a convention or other business trip, the employee can anticipate having to report the amount expended by the employer for the spouse and the family as additional gross income. In summary, assuming that the aggregate value of all of the items paid by the employer primarily for the employee's benefit is a *reasonable* compensation, it will be immediately deductible by the employer and immediately taxed to the employee, unless it can be fitted into one of the special exceptions discussed earlier in this chapter.

Cash Salary

The regular cash wage or salary is still the most common form of employee compensation. It may be surprising that it qualifies only as a third-ranked class of compensation techniques—that is, as one that produces an immediate deduction for the employer and an immediate gross income for the employee. The reason for its overwhelming popularity is, naturally, the need and desire of every employee to obtain cash and the personal flexibility in spending that goes with it. Even if an expert were able to create a tax-sheltered world in which every employee was adequately provided with a company home, company food, a company car, company entertainment, a company medical plan, and a company pension, the need and desire for additional cash salary would remain. In fact, in such a protected world, the implicit or psychic cost associated with any further tax shelter would almost certainly be greater than the benefit of the additional tax saving under even the most onerous income tax that the human mind could devise.

Nonqualified Stock Options

Stock options have had a long and checkered history in the tax annals of the United States. Because many very restrictive conditions were placed on the qualified forms of the stock option during the past few years, the only viable stock option today is a *nonqualified* option. To understand the economics involved in a stock option, we must review some basic concepts.

A stock option is nothing more than a right to purchase a corporation's stock for a given period at a given price. Even if the price is set equal to the market price on the date the option is granted, the option itself has real economic value only if the period of the option is of any reasonable length. To illustrate, if someone were to offer you the guaranteed right to purchase General Motors common stock at today's market price, wouldn't you be willing to pay something for that option if it ran for, say, a period of five years? Wouldn't you be willing to pay even more if it ran for 10 or 20 years? Under these conditions, the opportunity to make a substantial profit with a minimum investment is very real. An option holder would simply hold the rights unexercised as long as the value of the stock remained constant or decreased. If the market price decreased and remained depressed for the term of the option, the option would finally expire and prove to be worthless. On the other hand, if the value of the stock increased, the option would become as valuable as the spread between the later market price and the option price multiplied by the number of shares authorized in the option.

At one time, the tax laws were interpreted so that an employee was required to report as ordinary income only the initial spread between an option price and the fair market value of the stock on the date the option was granted. Any subsequent increase was capital gain. Today, the rules that control the tax consequence of an employee stock option differ, depending upon whether or not the fair market value of the *option* is readily ascertainable when the option is granted. If it is, the employee must immediately report that value, less anything he or she might have to pay to acquire the option, as ordinary income; the same amount is immediately deductible by the employer corporation. In this situation, any further increment in value will be reportable as a capital gain. If the fair market value of the option is not readily ascertainable when the option is granted, the employee will not realize any taxable income until he or she exercises the option and acquires the property. At that time, the employee reports the entire fair market value of the property received, again less any payment made to acquire the property, as ordinary income; the corporate employer receives a corresponding deduction at that time. The appropriate rules, although difficult to state in words, can be illustrated simply, as shown in Figure 7–1.

FIGURE 7–1

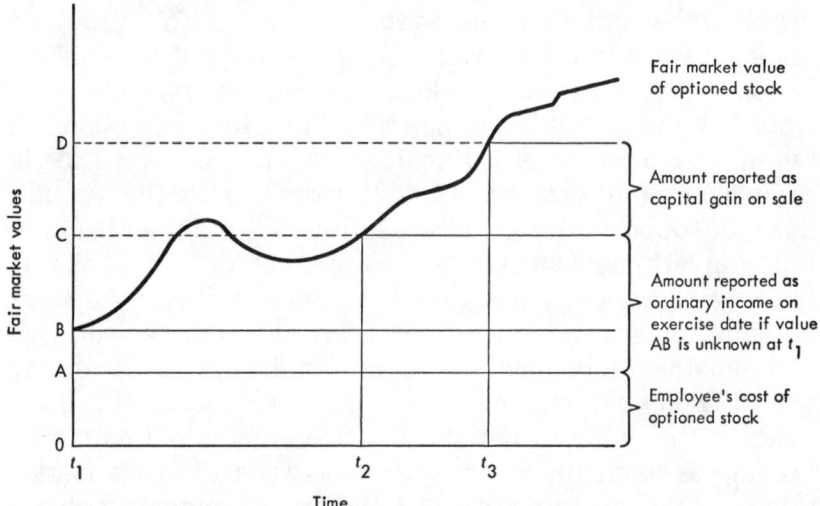

Where: *OA* equals the option price.
  OB equals the fair market value of the stock on the date the stock option was granted.
  OC equals the fair market value of the stock on the date the stock option was exercised.
  OD equals the fair market value of the stock on the date the stock was sold.
  t_1 represents the date the option was granted.
  t_2 represents the date the option was exercised.
  t_3 represents the date the stock was sold.

The distance *OA* represents the amount of capital that the employee must contribute to the corporation to acquire the stock when exercising the option. Distance *AB* represents the spread between the option price and the fair market value of the stock on the date the option was granted. If distance *AB* is known on date t_1, it is immediately taxed to the employee and deducted by the employer. If the distance *AB* is not known on date t_1, than distance AC is taxed to the employee and deducted by the employer on date t_2. In the later case, the only element of capital gain remaining in the employee stock option is the distance CD, the increment in value after the exercise date and before the sale date. If the time lapse between t_2 and t_3 is more than one year, the distance CD will be long-term capital gain and will carry with it the usual advantages associated with such a gain. Stock subject to a restriction—for example, stock that can only be sold to the employer corporation at a fixed price if the employee resigns within a prescribed time period—is subject to special rules.

Given the fact that most of any increment in value in an employee stock option is now taxed as ordinary income, the reader may wonder why an option has any remaining potential compensation value. The answer has to lie in nontax considerations. First, note that the option price (OA) can be set low enough to allow even a nonpropertied junior executive a "piece of the action" with a minimum investment. Second, note that the value of any option eventually depends upon the value of the stock. If the stock becomes very valuable, so does the option. Initially, all stock options were defended on exactly this ground. The proponents of stock options argued that the value of any corporate executive was entirely dependent upon what he or she could do with the company. If he or she could make the company highly profitable, and thus make the stock increase substantially in value for the shareholders, the executive was a very valuable person and should be compensated accordingly. Stock options made a direct relationship between stock prices and compensation arrangements possible. For the third and final advantage, note that a stock option may provide a real economic benefit to an employee with no cash cost to the corporation. In fact, if an option is exercised, the corporation may actually receive an additional cash contribution to its own capital. This cash-free cost assumes that the corporation can issue either (1) previously authorized but unissued shares or (2) treasury stock already owned by the employer. The real economic cost is shifted to the stockholders by dilution of their equity interests. In large corporations, where no one person owns anything but a small fraction of the total stock, this dilution of equity is minimized if an executive can increase the stock dollar value of shareholders' stock, notwithstanding a small dilution of each shareholder's relative interest. In summary, under the appropriate circumstances, a stock option may be a viable form of compensation even though it presents relatively little tax-saving opportunity.

The possible variations on a basic stock option theme are amazing. Some options involve additional restrictions on the property acquired by the employee, which may affect the date and the measurement of taxable income. Other plans involve phantom stock rather than actual shares. Phantom plans are useful whenever the stockholders desire to avoid any dilution of their ownership interests, but still desire to give an employee a compensation based on stock values. Under a phantom plan, the employee acquires an "equivalent unit," based on stock prices and on a stock plan agreement. These units even pay "dividend equivalents," which are accumulated and held on the employee's behalf. On separation from service, the employee claims all vested rights and withdraws all accumulated benefits over an agreed time period. Details of these and other plans could be described at length. The fundamental ideas would not change significantly, however, and thus it seems preferable to move to other techniques utilized in compensation arrangements.

Techniques Providing a Deferred Corporate Deduction and a Deferred Tax to the Employee

In relatively rare instances, an employee may be provided with an unfunded equivalent of a pension plan. These arrangements, commonly known as *deferred compensation plans*, involve an employer's promise to make continued payments to a particular employee following retirement from service. The payments supposedly represent additional compensation for services already rendered by the employee. If the deferred compensation plan is a nonqualified one, no corporate assets are actually set aside to cover the contractual agreement; the employee's rights are forfeitable; the employee will not report any gross income until he or she actually receives payments under the agreement; and the corporate employer will not claim a tax deduction until that same year. If the plan is funded and the employee's rights become vested, the tax consequences may be accelerated for both parties. Typically, the tax benefit of a deferred compensation plan must derive from the deferral of income to a date at which an executive is in a lower marginal tax bracket. Economically speaking, these arrangements place the retired employee in the position of a general creditor of a former employer. If all goes well with the corporation financially, a deferred pay contract is valuable and a comfortable retirement is assured. If the employer gets into financial difficulty, however, the deferred compensation arrangement may be essentially worthless to a former employee. Perhaps for this reason as much as any other, deferred compensation arrangements are often limited to smaller businesses or to a key executive or two.

Techniques Providing No Corporate Deduction but a Tax to the Employee

A reader might question whether any technique that provides no deduction to a corporate employer can really constitute an employee compensation device. It can be argued that, definitionally, such an item cannot exist. Although that conclusion may be justified on definitional grounds, as a practical matter it might pay to examine briefly two situations in which apparent employee compensation is associated with a nondeductible result to an employer corporation.

Disguised Dividends

If a court sustains an IRS contention that payments made to an employee are unreasonable in amount, the court is also likely to find that such payments are in effect a disguised dividend if the recipient is also a corporate stockholder. If a payment is found to constitute a dividend, we know that the corporation will not be entitled to any deduction, even though the recipient shareholder will be required to report the entire amount received as ordinary income. The likelihood of this disastrous tax conclusion is significantly increased in the closely held corporation in which the corporate executives are also the major stockholders and dividend payments are kept to a minimum. Taxpayers in this situation may be able to provide some protection against the initial conclusion if they have an advance, written contractual agreement with their corporate employer that provides that they must return to the corporation any amount finally determined to constitute unreasonable compensation. If successful, such an agreement will remove the initial problem of ordinary income with no deduction, but it may create further problems in the area of the accumulated earnings tax. The need for expert assistance in such a sensitive area is obvious.

The reader should also understand that in making the reasonableness determination, the IRS will look to the entire compensation package, not just to cash salaries. To the extent that fringe benefits increase aggregate compensation, they also increase the likelihood of the reasonableness issue. The successful defense against an unreasonable compensation charge may turn upon such facts as the special skill and ability of the employee, the scope of his or her services, the dividend history of the employer, the relative ownership interests of the employees whose salaries are being questioned, the adequacy of compensation in prior years, and general comparisons with other taxpayers in the same industry. Each case stands on its own facts, and generalization of results is hazardous.

Special Tax Considerations For Self-Employed Taxpayers

Many tax-sheltered compensation techniques are simply not available to the self-employed taxpayer. Those not available to such a person include group-term life insurance, health and accident insurance, meal and lodging opportunities, and any arrangements dependent upon stock for their success. The major exception to the above list is the pension plan. Since 1962, a self-employed proprietor or partner can claim a deduction on his or her own tax return for amounts contributed to a nonemployee retirement plan. As usual, a number of restrictive conditions and related factors must be considered before anyone can determine whether or not this tax shelter is desirable for a particular taxpayer.

Pension plans for a self-employed proprietor or partner are commonly known as *Keogh plans* or as *H.R. 10 plans*, because

Congressman Keogh introduced House Report 10, which first authorized this particular deduction. The most demanding condition for H.R. 10 qualification is that the plan must also include pension coverage for all full-time employees who have worked for the self-employed person or the partnership for three years or longer. Thus, the tax value of the additional deduction for a self-employed taxpayer may be more than lost to the extra cost of covering other employees. The most restrictive condition of a qualified Keogh plan is that the self-employed individual can never deduct more than the lesser of 15 percent of earned income or $7,500 per year. (In contrast the current *maximum* corporate contribution to a qualified plan for any one employee is $36,875. This figure is revised annually to reflect inflation.) In addition, before such a plan will be qualified, the taxpayer must have sufficient income from an unincorporated personal service business; income from passive investments will not qualify for this deduction.

If a self-employed taxpayer succeeds in creating a qualified pension plan, the tax shelter available is much like that available to the corporate employee in a qualified pension plan. In other words, the important tax results arise (1) because the contributions to the plan (to the $7,500 maximum) come from before-tax income and (2) because the accumulated amounts can grow tax-free in a retirement fund. Most self-employed people utilize an extant mutual fund, bank trust fund, or insurance plan to administer the assets during the years of accumulation. The self-employed individual, with an annual earned income of more than $50,000 and a small number of permanent employees is the most likely prospect for a Keogh plan.

Individual Retirement Accounts

The Individual Retirement Account (IRA) was first introduced by ERISA. It provides individuals (employees as well as the self-employed) who are not participants in a qualified pension or profit-sharing plan with the opportunity to obtain some of the tax advantages associated with a qualified retirement plan. The annual deduction for an IRA contribution cannot exceed the *lesser* of 15 percent of the taxpayer's earned income or $1,500 ($1,750 if a joint account for a qualified taxpayer and spouse is created). Generally the opportunity for tax-free growth of IRA funds is very similar to that of other qualified pension plans; the only major limitation of an IRA is the low annual contribution ceiling. Nevertheless, this most recent extension of tax benefits for retirement funds has become an important alternative, especially for the smaller businessperson. It provides a method for setting aside limited funds for retirement under tax-favored circumstances, without the more onerous requirements common to all other pension plans.

Because of the very substantial reporting and funding requirements applicable to all other qualified plans after ERISA, many employers terminated their previous pension plans. The significant reduction in the number of employees covered by a sound pension plan was, of course, exactly the opposite result to that which Congress had hoped to achieve when it passed ERISA in 1974. Consequently, as part of the 1978 Revenue Act, Congress extended the IRA idea to nearly all employers, in what is technically called a *simplified employee pension plan*, or (more commonly) a SEP-IRA. To implement such a plan the employer must include all employees who (1) are 25 years of age or older, and (2) have worked for the employer during any part of the current year and any three of the prior five years. Qualified SEP-IRA plans are eligible for the same contribution deduction limits as H.R. 10 plans—that is, the lesser of $7,500 or 15 percent of the employee's gross income. The limits are, of course, considerably more favorable than those applicable to regular IRA accounts. In addition, unlike all other qualified employee plans, the employee generally can withdraw benefits from a SEP-IRA prior to age 59½ if he or she is willing to pay any previously deferred income tax plus a 10 percent penalty. In every instance, a SEP-IRA must have 100 percent, immediate vesting. Unfortunately, according to recent reports in *The Wall Street Journal*, some employers are discovering that SEP-IRAs are not as simple as they were first professed to be.

Summary

Compensation arrangements more than almost any other common business transaction provide a host of opportunities for major tax savings. The entrepreneur and the corporate business manager would do well to review their own compensation arrangements in light of the broad outlines described in this chapter. Sometimes the need to create a new corporate entity will be obvious, but this is rarely a difficult task today. If suggested improvements appear possible, the reader should discuss his or her particular situation in detail with a competent tax adviser.

Before leaving this topic, however, a final word of caution seems appropriate. Although the ideas in this chapter have been developed along a continuum beginning with the "best" and ending with the "worst" alternative, the reader should clearly understand that the continuum may be viewed more realistically as a circle than a line. In other words, instead of thinking of the five "preference-ranked" alternatives noted on page 145 as a line

1	2	3	4	5
Best				Worst

it might be preferable to conceptualize those same five options as in the diagram.

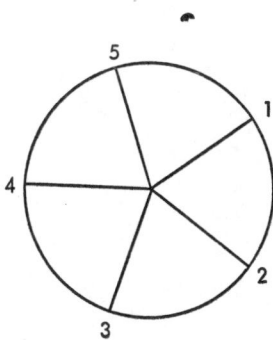

In reality, the "best" alternatives are those most likely to be challenged by the IRS and recharacterized as the "worst" alternatives. It is not unusual for the IRS to contend that a company car, a family vacation, and all other executive perquisites are really disguised dividends, especially if they are identified in a closely held corporation. Thus the person who seeks too much tax advantage is likely to lose under the "pig theory." That theory suggests that one can make money being a bull, or make money being a bear, but will only lose if the IRS perceives his or her actions to be those of a pig. Too much is still too much. Both the IRS and the courts have a special way of dealing with those who are especially greedy in matters of taxation. Careful compliance with all statutory and regulatory requirements is a minimal condition for success. The reader must therefore temper any enthusiasm for the ideas suggested here with a clear appreciation of the need for a tax expert in this important area of federal taxes and management decisions.

CHAPTER 8

Tax Factors in the Acquisition, Use, and Disposition of Fixed Assets

The term *fixed asset* is used to refer to any asset that will benefit more than a single accounting period. Thus, this term usually encompasses such mobile assets as cars, trucks, and airplanes, as well as more "fixed" assets, such as buildings, land, and utility poles. The term also covers both tangible and intangible properties. For tax and financial accounting purposes, income is generally measured in intervals of one year. Because fixed assets benefit more than one year, they present some unique problems in income measurement. One basic problem involves the proper method of allocating the total cost of a fixed asset over its estimated useful life.

The tax rules governing the acquisition, use, and disposition of fixed assets have become increasingly volatile in recent years because Congress has been convinced that changes in those rules have a greater-than-normal impact on the way our economy performs. In years when economic stimulation is deemed necessary, we find that Congress tends to increase the amount of the depreciation that may be deducted and, in some years, to allow an investment tax credit based upon the cost of certain fixed assets purchased during the year. In years when an economic depressant is deemed necessary, we have come to expect the opposite changes; that is, the amount of the depreciation deduction is typically reduced and the investment tax credit is suspended or rescinded. Because change has been so frequent, and because the rules are so diverse, we will concentrate our attention in this chapter on the general planning opportunities associated with investments in fixed assets.

Before we look at more specific details, we might pause to observe the range of alternative treatments available for fixed assets in general. At one extreme, it is possible for the law to authorize as an immediate deduction the entire cost of a fixed asset, notwithstanding the fact that the expenditure will benefit one or more future accounting periods. The consequence of this alternative is, of course, to understate income in the year of purchase and to overstate it in subsequent years. In a limited number of circumstances, the Internal Revenue Code actually authorizes such an immediate deduction. At the other extreme, it is possible for the law to deny a taxpayer the right to claim any deduction for any portion of the cost of a fixed asset until disposition. Generally, this is the tax treatment prescribed for all nonwasting assets, such as investments in stocks and land, which are deemed to be indestructible. The third and intermediate alternative requires the taxpayer to capitalize the cost of a fixed asset initially, but then allows a recovery of this cost over the intended life of the fixed asset, utilizing some predetermined cost allocation technique. This last alternative is the most widely used one, and the cost allocation technique authorized is commonly known as a depreciation method. The several depreciation methods authorized, and some restrictions on their application, will be discussed later in this chapter.

The chapter has been divided into five major sections. The first section explains the fundamental relationships between tax rules, present value concepts, and profit opportunities. The second, third, and fourth sections deal with tax factors related to the acquisition, use, and disposition of fixed assets, respectively. The fifth section provides an illustration demonstrating the potential importance of tax rules on fixed-asset investment decisions. Although this organizational arrangement has certain pedagogic advantages, the reader should understand that he or she may have to examine several sections of this chapter for the "whole story" on one specific form of investment. For example, if a reader really wants to understand the tax factors associated with ownership of an apartment house or an oil well, he or she must sequentially evaluate the tax factors pertinent to the acquisition, use, and disposition of that particular form of fixed asset.

Fundamental Relationships between Tax Laws, the Present Value Concept, and Simple Economics

The reader should observe that acquisition of a fixed asset may provide a tax deduction without an immediate cash disbursement. Suppose, for example, that a taxpayer acquired in one day two identical fixed assets to be used for the same purpose by paying $10,000 cash for asset 1 and signing a $10,000 promissory note, due in five years, for asset 2. In each case the taxpayer's basis in the asset is $10,000. Furthermore, the taxpayer would be entitled to exactly the same tax deductions and credits on each asset. This ability to acquire a tax deduction, and possibly an investment tax credit, with a minimal cash disbursement is a basic reason why high-marginal-bracket taxpayers have a continuing interest in certain fixed assets.

To illustrate the critical interaction between tax rules and fundamental economics, let us begin with a grossly oversimplified illustration. If on January 1, 19x1, taxpayer A acquires a $200,000 fixed asset with a four-year life by signing a $200,000, 10-percent simple-interest note, which will be payable on January 1, 19x5, and if we know with 100 percent certainty that this fixed asset will provide its owner with new assets that can be sold on January 1, 19x5, for exactly $280,000, and that the initial fixed asset will vanish into dust on exactly that same date, the reader might conclude that the taxpayer should not proceed with the investment. If we assume that there is no income tax, the result can be detailed as follows:

Year	Item	Cash inflow	Cash outflow
19x1	No cash transactions	$ —	$ —
19x5	Sale of new assets	280,000	—
19x5	Payment of note	—	200,000
19x5	Payment of interest	—	80,000

Obviously, this investor would have to utilize the entire sales proceeds to pay off the note and would have no profit for the effort expended.

If we want to illustrate the critical interface between tax rules and simple economics, we will have to begin to modify our stated assumptions. This time let us assume that taxpayer A lives in a country that imposes a flat-rate 50 percent tax on all income, that authorizes the amortization of fixed asset costs equally over the life of an asset, that authorizes the deduction of interest expense, and that collects the income tax on January 1 of each year for income earned in the previous year. These extreme assumptions might still lead a reader to conclude that taxpayer A should not proceed with this investment since the inevitable result will be cash-receipt equivalents equal in value to cash disbursements. The revised calculations would be as follows:

Year	Item	Cash inflow or equivalent	Cash outflow
19x1	Tax saving due to new $50,000 depreciation deduction allowed taxpayer	$ 25,000	
19x2	Same as 19x1	25,000	
19x3	Same as 19x1	25,000	
19x4	Same as 19x1	25,000	
19x5	Payment of note—face amount		$200,000
19x5	Payment of note (the deduction for interest provides new tax savings)	40,000	80,000
19x5	Sale of new assets	280,000	
19x5	Income tax on sale of new assets		140,000
	Total over life of investment	$420,000	$420,000

Interestingly, the effect of introducing a 50 percent income tax into our earlier illustration is simply to increase the cash-receipt equivalents and the cash disbursements by 50 percent—that is, from $280,000 to $420,000. The desirability of the investment does not seem to be changed by this fact alone.

The next step in understanding the interface between tax rules and simple economics involves appreciation of the present value concept. Stated in its most elementary terms, this concept suggests that money has a time-preference value. A dollar today is worth more than a dollar that you cannot have until one year from now, and a dollar that you cannot have until one year from now is worth more than a dollar that you cannot have until five years from now. The exact difference in the present value between these dollars depends upon the investor's discount rate. Stated crudely, the discount rate is the rate of income that an investor can earn on capital during an interim period. If we assume that a taxpayer has a discount rate of 5 percent, a dollar deferred for one year is now worth about $0.95238095. In other words, if the taxpayer puts that latter amount to work at 5 percent (after taxes), it will be worth exactly $1 one year later. A dollar that a taxpayer could not have for five years, discounted at 5 percent, would be worth approximately $0.78352617 right now.

Returning to our previous calculations, we can now determine the discounted present value of the investment opportunity, based upon an assumed 5 percent (aftertax) rate of return, as shown.

Year	Item	Present value of inflows	Present value of outflows
19x1	$25,000 tax saving discounted for one period ($25,000 × 0.95238095)	$ 23,810	
19x2	Same tax saving discounted two periods	22,676	
19x3	Same tax saving discounted three periods	21,596	
19x4	Same tax saving discounted four periods	20,568	
19x5	$280,000 sale discounted five periods	219,387	
19x5	$200,000 note discounted five periods		$156,705
19x5	$80,000 interest discounted five periods	31,341	62,682
19x5	$140,000 tax liability discounted five periods		109,694
	Total present value of investment	$339,378	$329,081

In other words, the effect of the tax law is to give this investor dollar-receipt equivalents (in the form of tax savings), which can be invested at 5 percent (after taxes). Assuming that the taxpayer actually makes these investments at this rate of return, the investment opportunity will actually provide a $10,297 profit *solely because of the combined effect of tax laws and the time-preference value of money.*

If we were to make a systematic study of this example to discover the magic of the $10,297 profit and what it has to say about pragmatic investments in fixed assets, we would not have to tarry long to observe that the sooner the tax deduction (and thus the cash-inflow equivalent) can be realized, and the longer the taxable income can be deferred, the greater the opportunity to profit. The tax magic of many fixed assets can be explained this simply: They provide immediate tax deductions with deferred income recognition possibilities. Obviously, it is even possible to create illustrations in which the nondiscounted cash outflows actually exceed the cash-inflow equivalents but which still yield an actual profit on a discounted basis. In the daily financial press, such losses are termed *tax losses* to distinguish them from real economic losses. The longer the time period between the tax deduction and the income realization, and the higher the discount rate, the greater the opportunity to reap a tax loss and an economic gain.

When we further relax the extreme simplifying assumptions made in our initial illustration, we can begin to understand why many high-tax-bracket investors continue to look to fixed-asset investments for tax relief. For example, if a taxpayer is in a high marginal bracket at the time he or she is entitled to claim a deduction (say, during prime years as a corporate executive, a successful athlete, or a surgeon) and anticipating a substantially lower marginal tax bracket at the time income is realized (say, after retirement), the opportunity for profit is increased.

An increasingly rare possibility involves the right to claim a tax deduction against ordinary income and to reap the deferred income as a capital gain. The differential in the marginal tax rates applicable to the early deduction and the deferred income can become significant in very short time periods when this difference in classification can be arranged. Prior to 1969, cattle breeding operations and citrus groves provided exactly this kind of investment. The rules have been restricted in these areas, however, and these forms of investment have lost some of their tax appeal. A few such opportunities remain viable in the mineral industries and in certain housing projects. These and other tax-sheltered investments will be examined in greater detail in Chapter 9.

To demonstrate the double parlay available when capital

gains become involved, let us consider another very simple illustration. This time let us assume that a taxpayer invests $50,000 in an asset that the tax law authorizes as an immediate deduction and that produces a $55,000 investment two years later. Let us also assume that the taxpayer borrows the entire $50,000 on an 8-percent prepaid interest note, payable in 24 months, that the taxpayer is in a 60-percent marginal tax bracket relative to ordinary income, and that the entire gain of $55,000 can be reported as a long-term capital gain and can be taxed at 30 percent (one half the ordinary rate) two years later. Initial calculations, without giving effect to either tax rules or discounted present values, would look like this:

Year	Item	Cash inflow	Cash outflow
19x1	Prepayment of interest		$ 8,000
19x2	Sale of investment	$55,000	
19x2	Payment of note principal		50,000
	Total over life of investment	$55,000	$58,000

In summary, without considering either present values or income tax effects, it seems that the taxpayer will lose $3,000 on this investment.

If we add the tax effect, we observe that the picture changes as follows:

Year	Item	Cash inflow or equivalent	Cash outflow
19x1	Prepayment of interest		$ 8,000
19x1	Deduction of interest expense saves taxes of $8,000 × 0.60	$ 4,800	
19x1	Immediate deduction of basic investment saves taxes of ($50,000 × 0.60)	30,000	
19x2	Payment of note principal		50,000
19x2	Receipt from sale of investment	55,000	
19x2	Capital gain tax on sale		16,500
		$89,800	$74,500

In effect, the tax rules have changed a $3,000 tax loss into a $15,300 real economic profit without giving consideration to the time-preference value of money in this illustration.

If we add time-preference calculations, and presume that the taxpayer can make the investment during the final days of one tax year and defer the income recognition until the first days of the second subsequent tax year (thus holding the investment for just a few days in excess of two years), we can squeeze out a little larger profit even with a low discount rate. A 5-percent aftertax return has been assumed in the following calculations:

Year	Item	Present value of inflows	Present value of outflows
19x1	Prepayment of interest which is immediately deductible	$ 4,800	$ 8,000
19x1	Immediate deduction of investment	30,000	
19x2	Present value of note payment (deferred two periods)		45,351
19x2	Present value of proceeds on sale (deferred two periods)	49,887	
19x3	Present value of capital gain tax (deferred three periods)		14,253
	Total present value of investment	$84,687	$67,604

Finally, then, tax rules plus present values have changed an apparent $3,000 tax loss into a $17,083 real economic profit, assuming the accuracy of all values and a correct interpretation of tax laws.

These illustrations should have demonstrated that the real economic success of an investment in any fixed asset is critically affected by several variables, including: (1) the timing of the tax deduction; (2) the timing of the income recognized; (3) the marginal tax rate applicable to the tax deduction; (4) the marginal tax rate applicable to the income recognized; and (5) the discount rate assumed by the taxpayer. Generally speaking, real economic profits will be increased if (a) the time between the tax deduction and the income recognition is lengthened, and (b) the deductions are claimed in high-marginal-tax-bracket years and the income is recognized in either low-marginal-tax-bracket forms or years. These differences substantially influence investors' decisions relative to the acquisition, use, and disposition of various fixed assets.

Tax Factors Pertinent to the Acquisition of Fixed Assets

When a taxpayer first considers the prospect of acquiring a fixed asset, he or she should give adequate consideration to the form of that acquisition, since each form may produce significantly different tax and financial results. The most obvious and common "form" of acquiring a fixed asset is, naturally, by direct purchase. Even in this simple case, however, we have observed how the tax result may vary significantly depending upon whether the taxpayer pays cash for the asset or borrows the funds required to make the purchase. As an alternative to the direct purchase of an asset, a taxpayer sometimes has the opportunity to acquire a controlling interest in the stock of a corporation that owns the desired asset. In this way a taxpayer can acquire the effective use of a desired asset, even though ownership of the asset is indirect, through the corporate entity. This alternative may create tax problems or opportunities for the unsuspecting investor. As an alternative to either a direct or an indirect purchase, the taxpayer should also consider the possibility of leasing an asset. In this way, he or she acquires the use of an asset without acquiring legal title to the asset. That taxpayer will probably be entitled to a deduction for the lease rents paid. Finally, in some circumstances a taxpayer may be able to construct or develop a desired asset. This method of acquisition may present several new and interesting tax consequences.

Direct Purchases

The most common form of acquiring a fixed asset is the outright purchase of the finished product from an unrelated party. Tax factors in this sort of acquisition are reduced to such fundamental problems as determining the correct amount to capitalize in the fixed-asset account (for example, the cost of freight charges and installation expenses are properly added to the asset account in addition to the initial purchase price), estimating a useful life and eventual salvage value for the asset acquired, and selecting an appropriate depreciation method. Also, the taxpayer must determine whether the asset is one that qualifies for an investment credit. Each of these tax factors will be discussed in remaining portions of this chapter.

Indirect Acquisitions through Stock Ownership

If taxpayer A desires to acquire a certain collection of assets which are owned by XYZ Corporation, essentially two alternatives exist. Taxpayer A can try to negotiate for the direct purchase of these assets with the executives of the XYZ Corporation, or A can negotiate for the purchase of a controlling interest in the stock of XYZ with its stockholders. Significant tax differences attach to each alternative from the standpoint of both the buyer and the seller. The most important differences for the seller were considered in Chapter 6.

To understand the important differences between direct and indirect acquisitions of assets from the standpoint of a buyer, consider the two alternatives which appear in Figure 8–1. In this illustration, taxpayer B owns 100 percent of the

FIGURE 8–1

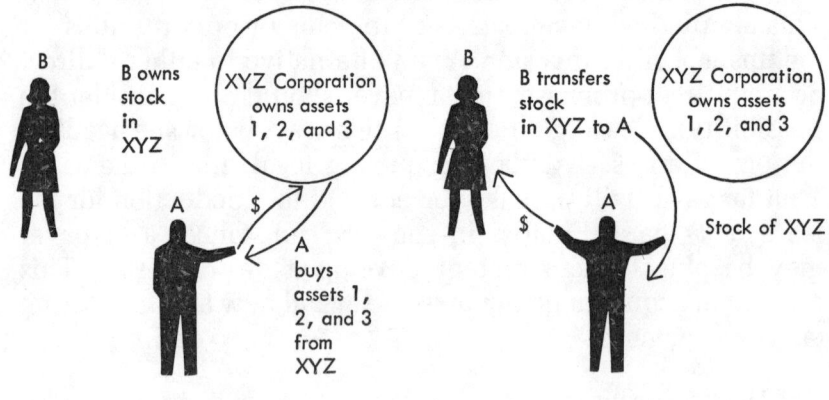

Direct acquisition   Indirect acquisition

stock of XYZ Corporation, and XYZ owns assets 1, 2, and 3. Let us assume that all parties agree that the fair market values of assets 1, 2, and 3 are $10,000, $20,000, and $30,000, respectively. If the only assets owned by XYZ are assets 1, 2, and 3, and if XYZ owes no liabilities, one might conclude that the stock of XYZ ought to be worth $60,000 since the ownership of this stock gives the stockholder the indirect ownership of the same assets. If we assume, however, that XYZ has depreciated these assets so that the remaining tax basis in them is $1,000, $2,000, and $3,000, respectively, a special problem in valuation is presented. If A acquires the assets *directly* for $60,000, A's tax basis in these assets will be $10,000, $20,000, and $30,000, respectively. This means, of course, that A can depreciate the assets and thereby reduce his future taxable income by that same amount.

If A had made an *indirect* acquisition for $60,000, A's tax basis would be *in the stock of XYZ, not in assets 1, 2, and 3*. The assets would still have their low tax basis ($1,000, $2,000, and $3,000), and the taxable income of XYZ would be substantial in the future because it would have only very limited amounts of depreciation left to deduct. Under some questionable judicial authority, taxpayer A *might* be able to liquidate the XYZ Corporation shortly after having acquired control over it and thereby transfer his higher ($60,000) basis from this stock to the assets.

This last opportunity is guaranteed, under prescribed conditions, for corporate taxpayers acquired a second (subsidiary) corporation in Section 334(b)(2). However, if any acquiring taxpayer liquidates XYZ, the XYZ Corporation may have to recognize as taxable income the "paper gain" on assets 1, 2, and 3 in the year of liquidation. This would mean, of course, that XYZ would have to pay a corporate income tax on a $54,000 taxable income in its final year, and the new owner of XYZ would not find this solution of much help.

To summarize, if A understands the tax factors associated with an indirect acquisition of assets 1, 2, and 3, A would not, under the circumstances described here, be willing to pay $60,000 for 100 percent of the stock of XYZ, even though he might be willing to pay that same amount for the assets acquired directly. The appropriate price reduction for an indirect acquisition would depend upon the kind of income—that is, capital gain or ordinary income—that would have to be recognized on the liquidation of XYZ and upon the marginal tax bracket of taxpayer A. Observe also that under the reverse conditions—that is, when the fair market value of assets is less than their tax basis—an indirect acquisition may provide an economic benefit to the purchaser so that he or she may be willing to pay more than the apparent fair market value of the assets to acquire the tax advantage that would go along with an indirect acquisition.

Leasing Fixed Assets

A lease quite obviously provides a taxpayer with an opportunity to acquire the use of a fixed asset without acquiring other risks or benefits of ownership. In many instances the utilization of a lease in preference to other methods of acquisition is predicated upon financial considerations alone. A new company with limited capital, for example, may find the lease to be the only effective way to acquire certain assets. A leasing arrangement will usually prove to be more expensive than direct ownership because it must include a profit for the lessor. Thus, under many circumstances, the lease is less attractive to an established firm with large amounts of capital and adequate credit. However, even under these conditions, the tax consequence of a lease may make it more profitable than ownership.

Perhaps the easiest situation in which to demonstrate the potential tax value of a lease arrangement is in connection with land. If a taxpayer purchases land (for cash or on credit), there will be no tax deduction for that investment until the taxpayer disposes of the land, since land is a nonwasting asset. This means, of course, that a taxpayer may make a substantial real economic investment with no immediate tax benefit. We observed earlier that the chances of obtaining a real economic profit usually increase if we can accelerate the timing of a tax deduction. Thus, for tax reasons, a taxpayer may be inclined to lease land rather than purchase it. The cost of a few hundred feet of ocean frontage in Honolulu, Miami Beach, Southern California, or New England might be prohibitive for any taxpayer but the largest hotel corporation. A lease arrangement, with attendant tax deductions for (land) rents paid, might change this financial requirement substantially.

The temptation for many taxpayers to disguise a purchase as an alleged lease has resulted in a close scrutiny of certain rent deductions by the IRS. If, for example, a legal document were technically written as a lease of land by providing for a series of 30 annual payments of $100,000 and giving the lessee the option, at the end of 30 years, of paying an additional

$50,000 to acquire title to the land, the IRS would have no trouble in getting a court to agree that in reality this contract was a purchase and in taxing it accordingly. On the other hand, if the same lease were written without the final option to purchase, or if that option were stated in realistic financial terms, the acquiring taxpayer would be entitled to immediate tax deductions for each lease payment. The need for expert legal assistance in drafting sale and lease agreements, and thus in obtaining maximum tax deductions, is obvious.

Constructing or Otherwise Creating Fixed Assets

A taxpayer will sometimes construct or otherwise create a fixed asset simply because the desired asset is not already extant and because the taxpayer knows no one else capable of making it. In other cases, a taxpayer will construct or create an asset only because that option is less costly. In many more situations, however, a taxpayer's primary reason for joining in a project to construct or otherwise create a fixed asset must be found in the peculiar tax treatment that will be accorded such a project. The most notable tax rules pertain to (1) the construction of residential housing, (2) locating and developing a natural resource, and (3) land development and certain agricultural growth opportunities.

Constructing buildings. Many taxpayers prefer to join in the construction of a building, rather than buy an extant building, because of a few tax rules. As we will discover in the next section of this chapter, the most rapid depreciation methods authorized are generally restricted (a) to residential housing projects and (b) to initial owners. Once again, because taxpayers generally desire to accelerate tax deductions, there is good reason to prefer an investment in a new apartment project to other investments.

Locating and developing oil and gas wells. The tax law provides that all *intangible* drilling and development costs associated with locating and developing an oil or gas well can be deducted immediately. These costs often represent as much as 80 percent of the cost of a producing well. The obvious benefit of the right to deduct 80 percent of an investment in a fixed asset is one reason these investments are more attractive than many others to certain taxpayers.

It should be equally obvious, however, that the right to an immediate tax deduction is *not* tantamount to the promise of an economic profit. The odds of drilling a dry hole are something like 8.5 to 1. And a dry hole is essentially worthless to everyone. The tax law authorizes the deduction of any remaining costs associated with an attempt to locate and develop an oil or gas well when the drilling venture proves to be worthless. The right to immediately deduct the entire cost of a worthless venture, as well as a majority of the costs of a successful oil or gas venture, helps to make them attractive to high-marginal-bracket taxpayers. If things go badly, the government stands ready to share up to 70 percent of the losses (through tax savings to the investors). On the other hand, if things go well, the government still stands ready to share 70 percent of the initial costs, but to demand, for reasons that will be explained later, a lesser percentage of the final profit in income taxes.

Risks are high in the oil and gas business. The wealthy taxpayer, however, might find those high risks to be preferable to low-risk investments because of the liberal tax treatment of (1) the initial investment, (2) the income produced from a successful investment, and (3) the proceeds received on the disposition of an investment in mineral rights. The windfall profits tax will have the opposite effect.

Land development and agricultural growth. In a series of special provisions, the code has tried to encourage investments in agriculture. Again, the exact limitations of the separate rules are too detailed to justify our investigating them. However, we should note in passing that, under prescribed conditions, the tax rules do authorize the immediate deduction of (a) soil and water conservation expenditures, including "levelling, grading and terracing, contour furrowing, . . . drainage ditches, earthen dams, watercourses, outlets, . . . and the planting of windbreaks"; (b) expenditures for fertilizer and "other materials to enrich, neutralize, or condition land used in farming"; and (c) certain land clearing costs. Until the passage of the Tax Reform Act of 1969, the right to an immediate deduction was usually coupled with the right to claim a capital gain on the deferred disposition of the improved land. The double parlay of the immediate deduction of the expenditure against ordinary income, coupled with the deferred recognition of a long-term capital gain, served to increase the attractiveness of investments in agricultural land. The 1969 Act reduced the popularity of these investments, however, by providing that some or all of the gain might have to be reported as ordinary income if the improved land were sold less than ten years after the tax deduction was claimed. Under this act, taxpayers willing to wait the ten-year period retain many of the former benefits, which, under the proper circumstances, can be very valuable.

A comparable incentive to invest in motion pictures, sound recordings, books, and similar properties existed prior to the passage of the 1976 Tax Reform Act. A large portion of such investments was immediately deductible. Changes in the 1976 Act now require taxpayers to capitalize those costs and to recover them over the period that the investment produces income.

The Investment Credit

An investment tax credit was first introduced into the federal income tax in 1962. It was revised in 1964, suspended in 1966, reinstated in 1967, repealed in 1969, reenacted in 1971, liberalized in 1975, and expanded in 1978. Given this checkered history, one is tempted to ignore the investment credit and to proceed with more stable aspects of our tax system. That temptation should be overcome solely because of the potential dollar significance of the investment tax credit in certain fixed-asset acquisitions.

At present, the code authorizes a taxpayer to claim as a tax credit an amount equal to 10 percent of an investment in qualified property. In other words, if a taxpayer purchases qualified property at a cost of $10,000, the government will authorize the taxpayer to reduce that year's income tax liability by $1,000 just because of the investment. The real economic result of an investment credit is, quite obviously, a better than 10 percent reduction in the cost of a fully qualified asset since the entire cost can be depreciated. The only reason the government is willing to pick up such a large tab—in terms of lost revenues—is that investment spending is deemed to be a key variable in the way our economy performs. The recession in

1975 was responsible for the liberalization of the credit, from 7 percent to 10 percent. When the difference between a projected profit or loss on a fixed-asset investment is small, an immediate 10 percent tipping of the scales in favor of investment may be sufficient to accomplish the intended objective.

Before a taxpayer can claim an investment tax credit, there must be an investment in a qualified property. In general, qualified investments are of three types:

1. Tangible, nonreal property for which a depreciation deduction is authorized.
2. Tangible, real property *other than buildings and building components*—
   a. If the property is used in manufacturing, producing, extracting, or furnishing a good or a utility service.
   b. If the property constitutes a research or storage facility.
3. An elevator or an escalator.

Observe that the first category covers, among many other things, most factory and office equipment, automobiles, trucks, airplanes, hotel and motel furnishings (similar furnishings in a nontransient apartment are usually made ineligible by other provisions of the code), and even livestock used for draft, breeding, or dairy purposes. The second category includes blast furnaces, pipelines, tanks, and similar facilities, but is specifically *excludes* buildings and building components.

After a taxpayer makes a qualified investment, many additional rules must be examined to determine the exact amount of the investment tax credit. All qualified investments must be separated into one of four categories based upon the estimated useful life of the asset purchased. Only assets that are estimated to last seven years or longer are eligible for the full 10 percent credit. The four possible categories are as follows:

Category	Estimated useful life	Fraction of cost deemed to constitute a qualified investment
1	Less than three years	0
2	Three to five years	$\frac{1}{3}$
3	Five to seven years	$\frac{2}{3}$
4	Seven years or longer	All

To illustrate this second step, assume that a taxpayer purchased qualifying property in each estimated life category at a cost of $6,000. The investment tax credit would be computed as follows:

Category	Total investment	Qualified investment
1	$6,000	$ 0
2	6,000	2,000
3	6,000	4,000
4	6,000	6,000
Total qualified investment		$12,000 × 10 percent = $1,200.

Thus the taxpayer in this illustration could actually claim an investment tax credit of $1,200.

Even this cursory examination of the rules applicable to the investment tax credit suggests some planning opportunities. The following ideas are illustrative.

1. When in doubt, extend the estimated useful life to the next appropriate life estimate category. For example, if you think that an asset may last either four or five years, estimate five years and gain the additional tax credit. If a taxpayer initially underestimates the life of a fixed asset, there is no opportunity to go back and claim the larger credit on the asset's longer actual life. (On the other hand, if the taxpayer overestimates the asset's life and disposes of the asset too early, a recapture of the extra credit is mandatory.)

2. Time purchases of qualified assets wisely. A tax credit can only be claimed when the tax return is filed. Given the present value of money, it makes eminent sense to purchase qualifying assets late in one tax year rather than early in the next tax year.

3. Select and install assets carefully. A built-in television set could constitute a building component in a motel and thus be ineligible for an investment credit. A mobile set would constitute a furnishing and qualify.

Other opportunities for tax planning are hidden in more esoteric rules that generally apply only to large taxpayers. There are, for example, rules that set annual limits on the amount of *used* property that can qualify for the investment credit (currently $100,000); there are other rules that set limits on the maximum credit that can be claimed in any single year; and there are still other rules that disqualify property used to furnish lodging rented to nontransients. Every rule creates new pitfalls and new opportunities in slightly different situations.

One esoteric rule that has received a fair amount of attention in the press, but relatively little interest by taxpayers, is the additional 1 to 1½ percentage points in the investment credit that can be claimed by any corporation that agrees to contribute its own stock—equal in value to the tax savings generated by the extra 1 or 1½ percent in the investment credit—to an employee stock ownership plan (ESOP). The idea behind the ESOP is to increase the percentage of corporate ownership held by the employees who work for that corporation. Employees who own a share of their own employer are presumed to be better employees, or at least more interested in matters that might otherwise not be of mutual concern.

In addition to the regular investment credit, the Energy Tax Act of 1978 added two new investment-type credits for taxpayers who purchase certain energy-saving assets. One set of rules applies to items purchased for residential properties—for example, insulation, weather-stripping, and solar and wind energy equipment—whereas the other applies to certain properties used in a trade or business. The latter category includes boilers and burners that use an energy source of anything other than oil or gas, wind and solar energy properties that generate electricity used to heat or cool, equipment used to recycle waste, equipment used to extract oil from shale, and certain other energy-related property. Each of these categories is subject to specific limitations, definitions, and calculational nuances, which are far too extensive to justify examination here. In general, the rate of the energy-investment credit is 10 percent, but, in a few instances, that rate was increased to 15 percent in the 1980 windfall profits tax bill. For properties that qualify, both the regular and the energy investment credit may apply. In a few rare instances, therefore, the government might actually pay for 26½ percent of the cost of a fixed asset—that is, (1) 10 percent as a regular investment credit, (2) 15 percent as an energy credit, and (3) 1½ percent as an ESOP. Furthermore, none of these credits would reduce the basis, subject to depreciation by the taxpayer. Hence, through depreciation plus the various tax credits, taxpayers actually are able to recover more than their initial capital investments. Taxpayers who purchase large amounts of fixed assets must get advice before they act if they want to maximize their investment tax credit each year. In some years, certain dates become all-important.

Tax Factors Pertinent to the Use of Fixed Assets

After a taxpayer acquires a fixed asset, another series of tax considerations is typically encountered. The first major question commonly involves the selection of a cost allocation method. If the fixed asset is a tangible asset other than a natural resource, we refer to this cost allocation as *depreciation;* if it is a natural resource, as *depletion;* if an intangible asset, as *amortization.* Because of the interaction of the tax rules and the present value concept, which was explained earlier in this chapter, a taxpayer typically wants to claim a maximum depreciation, depletion, or amortization deduction as quickly as possible for tax purposes. For financial accounting purposes, however, a taxpayer may prefer just the opposite prescription; that is, for financial accounting purposes it may be preferable to defer deductions as long as possible so that a larger financial income may be reported for the interim period. The need to report a maximum financial income is increased in large, publicly owned corporations and in closely held corporations seeking external credit. Interestingly, a taxpayer is generally free to use one depreciation, depletion, or amortization method for tax purposes and a wholly different method for accounting purposes. The income reported to the government for income taxation is quite obviously, then, often a different and smaller figure than is the income reported to stockholders, which may, in turn, be a different figure than that reported to banks and other credit agencies. In this book we are interested only in the best tax alternatives.

Depreciation Methods

Code Section 167(a) authorizes a deduction for depreciation in broad terms, as follows: "There shall be allowed as a depreciation deduction a reasonable allowance for the exhaustion, wear and tear (including a reasonable allowance for obsolescence)—(1) of property used in the trade or business, or (2) of property held for the production of income." The next subsection of the code legitimates certain specific depreciation methods as "reasonable" methods under varying circumstances. The authorized methods include what are commonly known as the straight-line method, as well as certain rapid depreciation methods. The rapid depreciation methods include all methods that provide a relatively larger depreciation deduction in the earlier years of an asset's life and a relatively smaller deduction in the later years. The most common rapid methods are the sum-of-the-years'-digits method (SYD) and the declining-balance method.

The straight-line method. A straight-line depreciation method is one that allocates the total depreciable cost equally over the estimated life of an asset. Thus, if an asset has a tax basis of $10,000 and an estimated life of ten years, straight-line depreciation would amount to $1,000 per year; that is, tax basis divided by estimated life equals straight-line depreciation. For tax purposes, it is generally acceptable to ignore estimated salvage values unless they are expected to exceed 10 percent of the cost of the fixed asset. Theoretically, estimated lives are a question of fact to be determined in each specific instance by the taxpayer. In order to administer the depreciation provisions more uniformly and to reduce unnecessary conflicts, the IRS, in 1962, published tables that suggest specific lives as being reasonable estimates for thousands of specific properties. These IRS estimated lives are known as guideline lives. The guideline lives first divide all fixed assets into broad groups of properties and then subdivide those groups into industry classes. Finally, the government tables specify an estimated life for each category. Thus, for example, Group 1 includes all assets used by business in general; Group 2 includes assets used in nonmanufacturing activities, excluding transportation, communications, and public utilities; and so forth. Group 1 is next broken down into office furniture, fixtures, machines, and equipment (each of which is assigned an estimated life of ten years); transportation equipment, land improvements, buildings; and so forth. These categories are further broken down into other subclasses. Under transportation equipment, for example, the subclasses include automobiles (with an estimated life of three years) and vessels and other water transportation equipment (with an estimated life of 18 years).

Early in 1971, the existing guideline lives were modified by authorizing a taxpayer, under specified conditions, to increase or decrease the guideline estimates by as much as 20 percent. This last modification, eventually approved by Congress, is properly referred to as the ADR (asset depreciation range) system. Thus, ADR authorizes a taxpayer to utilize an estimated life as short as 8 years, or as long as 12 years, for any asset with an original guideline life of 10 years. A vast majority of the larger taxpayers have elected the shorter life, thus increasing their profit potential still more. The ADR reduction in estimated lives was, of course, another attempt to stimulate the economy through further increases in investment spending.

The sum-of-the-years'-digits method. One of the popular rapid methods of depreciation authorized in the code is the sum-of-the-years'-digits (SYD) method. To determine a depreciation deduction for a particular year using this method, a taxpayer must know (1) the adjusted basis of the asset, (2) the number of years of estimated remaining life of the asset as of the first of the year, and (3) the *sum* of the total years estimated originally. To illustrate this method, let us determine the SYD depreciation for an asset that had an adjusted basis of $10,000 (initially) and an estimated life of five years (initially). Before we can determine the depreciation for any year we must find the sum of $5 + 4 + 3 + 2 + 1$, which is 15. Knowing that sum we can find the depreciation for any year as follows:

Year 1: $5/15 \times \$10,000$, or $3,333
Year 2: $4/15 \times \$10,000$, or $2,667
Year 3: $3/15 \times \$10,000$, and so on.

Obviously the SYD method yields a larger depreciation deduction in the early years of the asset's life than does the straight-line method.

The declining-balance method. Another popular form of rapid depreciation is the declining-balance method. In this method a fixed percent is multiplied by a declining adjusted basis of the asset to determine any year's depreciation deduction. The constant percentage to be used depends upon (1) the estimated life of the asset and (2) the particular variant of the declining-balance method being used. The code authorizes a 200 percent declining-balance method (also called *double-declining balance,* or DDB), a 150 percent declining-balance method, and a 125 percent declining-balance method. To determine the constant percent, the taxpayer must first determine the straight-line *rate* of depreciation for the asset. The straight-line rate is the percentage obtained by dividing the asset's original estimated life into the number 1. Thus the straight-line rate for an asset with an estimated life of 20 years is 5 percent ($1/20$); for a ten-year life, 10 percent ($1/10$); and for a five-year life, 20 percent ($1/5$). Once the straight-line rate has been determined, the taxpayer can readily convert to the desired declining-balance constant by multiplying the stipulated percent by the straight-line rate. In other words, the constant fraction for a 200 percent declining-balance method when applied to an asset with a five-year life is 40 percent—200 percent of 20 percent. The constant fraction for a 150 percent declining-balance method, applied to an asset with a five-year life, is 30 percent—150 percent of 20 percent.

A comparison of results. Table 8–1 compares the depreciation deduction as determined under (1) the straight-line

TABLE 8–1
A Comparison of the Depreciation Deduction Determined under Three Common Depreciation Methods

Year	Straight-line method		Sum-of-the-years'-digits method		200 percent declining-balance method	
	Deduction for year	Adjusted basis on January 1	Deduction for year	Adjusted basis on January 1	Deduction for year	Adjusted basis on January 1
1	$ 1,000	$10,000	$ 1,818	$10,000	$2,000	$10,000
2	1,000	9,000	1,636	8,182	1,600	8,000
3	1,000	8,000	1,454	6,546	1,280	6,400
4	1,000	7,000	1,273	5,092	1,024	5,120
5	1,000	6,000	1,091	3,820	819	4,096
6	1,000	5,000	909	2,730	655	3,277
7	1,000	4,000	727	1,821	524	2,622
8	1,000	3,000	545	1,094	420	2,098
9	1,000	2,000	364	549	326	1,678
10	1,000	1,000	183	186	270	1,352
Total	$10,000		$10,000		$8,918	

method, (2) the sum-of-the-years'-digits method, and (3) the 200 percent declining-balance method. This comparison is based upon an assumed asset costing $10,000, having an estimated life of ten years, and having no salvage value. A brief review of Table 8–1 will reveal that the 200 percent declining-balance method yields the largest depreciation deduction in the first year, but the smallest over a ten-year period. The sum-of-the-years'-digits method provides the second largest deduction in the first year and, like the straight-line method, allocates the total cost over the estimated useful life of the asset. The straight-line method provides the smallest deduction in the first year. If the 150 percent declining-balance method and the 125 percent declining-balance method were added to this table, they would, of course, lie between the straight-line method and the SYD method in terms of the size of the first year's deduction.

Generally speaking, a taxpayer is free to switch from any rapid depreciation method to the straight-line method at any time. The taxpayer cannot, however, switch in the opposite direction without the consent of the IRS. A taxpayer will usually switch to the straight-line method if the change provides a larger deduction than would retention of the old method. In Table 8–1, for example, a taxpayer initially electing the 200 percent declining-balance method would be likely to switch to the straight-line method in the seventh year because that would increase the authorized depreciation deduction from the scheduled $524 to $655; that is, the $2,622 remaining basis is divided by the four years of remaining life. By making this change on a timely basis, the taxpayer would also insure the right to deduct the full $10,000 cost, rather than the $8,918 shown in Table 8–1.

Depreciation Method Restrictions

A taxpayer is not free to apply any depreciation method to any investment in a fixed asset. The current rules provide that, under most circumstances, for assets acquired after July 24, 1969, a taxpayer cannot claim a depreciation deduction that would be larger in amount than one determined according to the method indicated in Table 8–2. The reader who understands the present value notions introduced earlier in this chapter will find it easy to review the restrictions stated in

TABLE 8-2
Depreciation Method Limitations Applicable to Fixed Assets Acquired after July 24, 1969

Type of property	Maximum depreciation method authorized
Depreciable tangible property other than buildings	
If the property is new	200 percent declining balance
If the property is used	150 percent declining balance
Depreciable buildings	
If residential rental property	
Acquired new	200 percent declining balance, or SYD
Acquired used with an estimated remaining life of 20 years or more	125 percent declining balance
Acquired used with an estimated remaining life of less than 20 years	Straightline
If other than residential property	
Acquired new	150 percent declining balance
Acquired used	Straightline
All intangible property	Straightline

Table 8-2 and thus to identify yet another reason for the conclusion that investments in certain assets may be preferred to investments in other assets by high-marginal-bracket taxpayers. For example, the reader should now understand more clearly why many taxpayers continue to look at investments in furnished residential rental units as a preferred form of investment. Very few other opportunities provide for such a large depreciation deduction so quickly.

In the past few years, component depreciation has been recommended by many tax advisers. In a nutshell, the term *component depreciation* refers to the idea that a single asset should, for tax depreciation purposes, be broken down into its component parts. For example, a building might be viewed as a roof, electrical wiring and fixtures, plumbing, heating and air-conditioning equipment, flooring, walls, and so forth. Since nearly all building components have a significantly shorter estimated useful life than the building as a whole, these tax advisers are recommending that separate and shorter depreciable lives should be used for each component. In this manner, only the building shell will be subject to the long estimated life suggested for buildings in the ADR guidelines. To the extent allowed by the IRS, component depreciation obviously can accelerate tax deductions. In addition, items that might otherwise have been considered to be part of a building may become eligible for the investment credit; movable walls are a good example. It should be observed, however, that component depreciation does involve a substantial amount of detailed record keeping and, frequently, expert engineering valuations as well. In very large investments, these extra costs may be justified by the additional tax savings generated; in smaller investments, component depreciation seems to be of questionable value.

Other Special Rules Related to Depreciation

Even though this book makes no pretense of being comprehensive, a brief look at some special depreciation rules seems appropriate. One of these rules authorizes an extra first-year depreciation deduction, which may be of particular interest to small taxpayers. The other rules, commonly known as the rapid amortization provisions, are of greater interest to wealthy investors.

The first-year depreciation deduction. In addition to the regularly authorized depreciation deduction discussed above, every taxpayer can claim an additional first-year depreciation deduction if he or she purchases qualifying property. Any investment in tangible personal property (that is, nonrealty) acquired after 1957, with an estimated life of six years or longer, is eligible for this special 20 percent deduction. The maximum deduction authorized under this special provision is $2,000 per taxpayer per year. In other words, a taxpayer can claim the first-year deduction only on the first $10,000 (cost) of qualifying property purchased in any year—20 percent of $10,000 yields the $2,000 maximum. On the joint return of a married taxpayer, this can be increased to $4,000 because both the husband and the wife are deemed to be taxpayers. If the taxpayer claims the special first-year deduction, the basis utilized in determining the depreciation deduction under the regular provisions must be adjusted downward accordingly. In other words, if a married taxpayer filing a joint return purchased qualifying property at a cost of $20,000 and she utilized the 200 percent declining-balance method of depreciation on a ten-year life, her calculations would be made as follows:

First year	
Special deduction (20% × $20,000)	$4,000
Regular DDB deduction on remaining basis	
(20% × $16,000)	3,200
Total depreciation deduction authorized in	
first year	$7,200
Second year	
Regular DDB deduction (20% × $12,800)	$2,560

The important effect of this special deduction provision is to allow the taxpayer a quicker-than-normal recovery of an investment, which tends to increase the profitability of making an investment.

Rapid amortization provisions. In a limited number of cases, the tax rules authorize the deduction of an investment in a particular fixed asset over a 60-month period without reference to any of the usual rules. Expenditures for certified pollution control devices are a current example. Because the provisions are of restricted application, they will not be investigated further here. The rapid recovery of an investment through a special tax deduction is intended to increase investments in certain assets by making them more profitable to the investors who take advantage of the special provisions. It is hoped that the increased investments will help cure certain social ills.

10:5:3 depreciation. One of several currently popular Washington legislative *proposals* that is intended to increase capital investments in the future is 10:5:3 depreciation. The proposed bill that includes this new idea currently has the bipartisan support of over 270 members of the House and over 40 members of the Senate. If enacted, this bill would authorize the tax depreciation of all buildings over a ten-year life, all equipment over a five-year life, and automobiles and light trucks over a three-year life. The bill places a maximum investment of $100,000 per year on property that could be amortized over a three-year life. Obviously this is but one more extension of the fundamental idea that shortened depreciation lives serve to stimulate business investment in capital assets and, thereby, to increase national income and employment. Because the 10:5:3 proposal would result in a major revenue loss for the government, it is doubtful that it will be passed in its present form; the ten-year write-off of buildings seems particularly vulnerable. Some variation of this idea is, however, a very likely prospect for future tax legislation.

Depletion Methods

As minerals are extracted from the ground and sold, a taxpayer owning an economic interest in the mineral rights is entitled to recover his or her investment through a depletion deduction. Except for the critical difference that an extracted mineral cannot be restored by human action, from an accounting standpoint a depletion deduction provides for replacement capital in the same manner that the depreciation deduction does. In an operational sense, however, depletion and depreciation may be radically different because, in some situations, the code authorizes a method of depletion, called *statutory depletion*, which may continue to provide a tax deduction even though the adjusted basis of the investment has been wholly recovered in prior periods. The alternative method, called *cost depletion*, does *not* provide that same opportunity.

Cost depletion. Cost depletion effectively guarantees the right of a taxpayer to recover an original capital investment in a mineral property, assuming production. To illustrate this cost recovery technique, we will consider the tax factors associated with a $500,000 investment in a mineral venture. If the intangible drilling and development costs approximate 80 percent of the investment, the taxpayer will deduct $400,000 of the initial $500,000 investment in the first year. The remaining $100,000 investment is deducted as production proceeds. If the engineers estimate that the mineral deposit contains 500,000 barrels of oil (or cubic feet of gas), the taxpayer can deduct 20 cents for each barrel of oil extracted and sold. The $100,000 unrecovered tax basis is divided by the 500,000 estimated barrels of oil to determine a cost depletion allowance of 20 cents per barrel. When the well is exhausted, the taxpayer will have deducted an amount equal to the original investment: $400,000 as an immediate deduction for intangible drilling and development costs, and $100,000 as cost depletion over the productive life of the well. If the initial estimates of the mineral deposit prove erroneous, an appropriate adjustment must be made to the cost depletion allowance. Under all circumstances, however, the effect of *cost* depletion is to guarantee the taxpayer's right to deduct only the initial investment, and not a dollar more.

Percentage depletion. The tax magic of the percentage depletion deduction is that it is *not* restricted to the unrecovered cost of an investment in a mineral deposit in terms of the total dollar amounts that can be deducted. Percentage depletion may go on and on, thus providing a lucky taxpayer with a tax deduction that is many multiples of the initial investment if the well continues to produce. This tax distinction of percentage depletion is of major economic significance to potential investors. Prior to the Tax Reform Act of 1976, percentage depletion was equally available to large integrated oil companies, small independent producers, and the landlords who owned the land on which the well was located. Since 1975, however, only *independent* producers and royalty owners have been able to claim percentage depletion. Furthermore, even those taxpayers have been eligible for smaller amounts of percentage depletion each year. Since 1980 the maximum production limit has been 1,000 barrels of oil per day; the statutory rate will decline from 22 percent in 1980 to 15 percent in 1984.

Technically, the percentage depletion deduction is determined by multiplying (1) a statutory rate by (2) the gross income from the mineral property. The statutory rate varies from one mineral to the next. The code currently authorizes a rate of 22 percent for molybdenum, sulfur, and uranium deposits; a rate of 15 percent for gold, silver, iron ore, and copper; a rate of 5 percent for gravel, sand, and certain other minerals; and many other statutory rates for many other minerals. Because we are interested only in the principle of percentage depletion, we will utilize a 22 percent rate in the remaining illustrations, even though the 22 percent historically associated with oil and gas wells will be decreased, beginning in 1980, until it reaches 15 percent in 1984 and thereafter. The "gross income from the property" is usually an estimated value or a posted price of a mineral in its crude state, before transportation and refining have increased its value. Thus, if an oil well produced $50,000 in gross income in a particular year, a taxpayer with the rights to that production might be entitled to claim a percentage depletion deduction of $11,000

(22 percent of $50,000). Incidentally, any taxpayer can always claim cost depletion if it is larger than percentage depletion or if that taxpayer is not eligible for percentage depletion.

Percentage depletion is always limited, however, in that it can never exceed 50 percent of the *net* income from the property in any particular year. This rule effectively sets a ceiling on statutory depletion, which comes into play in high-cost operations. If, for example, the $50,000 gross income produced for the taxpayer in the previous illustration required a $40,000 expense to obtain it, percentage depletion would be reduced from the apparent $11,000 determined earlier to $5,000—that is, to 50 percent of ($50,000 − $40,000). For years after 1975, percentage depletion is further limited in that it cannot exceed 65 percent of any taxpayer's net taxable income from all sources, computed without a depletion or net operating loss deduction.

Because of the 50 percent net income limitation, a complex series of rules is brought into consideration in some circumstances. Note that both percentage depletion and the net income limitation are based upon the gross or net income *from the property*. Exactly what are the definitional bounds of "the property"? Is each well a "separate property"? Are all wells on a single lease "a property"? Must all wells on one lease be combined, or can they be treated separately? If contiguous leases are obtained at the same time, can wells on different leases be combined? Must they be combined? Is the date of the lease significant? The answers to these and many related questions are much too complex to state here. The reader should simply observe that, when allowed, certain combinations may prove to be very valuable with regard to taxes. The two illustrations in Tables 8–3 and 8–4 amply demonstrate this conclu-

TABLE 8–3
Two Wells That Should Be Combined and Treated as One Property if Possible

Well no.	Gross income	Net income	Percentage depletion	
			If separate	If combined
1	$100,000	$10,000	$ 5,000	
2	100,000	80,000	22,000	
1 + 2	$200,000	$90,000	$27,000	$44,000

TABLE 8-4
Two Wells That Should Not Be Combined and Treated as One Property, if Possible

Well no.	Gross income	Net income (loss)	Percentage depletion	
			If separate	If combined
1	$100,000	($20,000)	$ 0	
2	100,000	30,000	15,000	
	$200,000	$10,000	$15,000	$5,000

sion, which, like so many other tax opportunities, turns on definitional considerations.

In summary, the tax advantages associated with the use of an investment in mineral properties (that is, during the production period) stem from the fact that the taxpayer may be able to claim percentage depletion in excess of the unrecovered tax basis. Before this opportunity is meaningful, however, the taxpayer must (1) have invested in a producing well, (2) operate it commercially at a reasonable cost so that the net income limitation does not come into play, and (3) be eligible for statutory depletion—that is, be either an independent producer or a royalty owner. The final tax factors pertinent to such an investment involve disposition considerations. Before we turn to these considerations, we must examine briefly one remaining tax problem associated with the use of fixed assets.

Expenditures During Use—Repair or Improvement?

Typically, after a taxpayer begins to use a fixed asset, a number of expenditures that present additional tax difficulties will be incurred. Expenditures for routine repairs are quite properly deducted immediately; expenditures for capital improvements are added to an asset account and recovered through subsequent cost allocation provisions. At the extreme, the difference between such expenditures is easy to illustrate for an individual taxpayer. For example, the gasoline used in an automobile on a business trip is, quite obviously, a deductible expense. A major overhaul of a "business" automobile is an equally obvious capital expenditure. The problem, of course, lies with intermediate expenditures, such as new tires, paint jobs, and minor overhauls. Are these expenditures immediately deductible, or must they be capitalized and recovered through depreciation? The classification problem is greater with buildings than with automobiles because of the major differences in estimated lives, potential changes in use, dollar amounts involved, and related values. Yet the need to distinguish between an expense and a capital expenditure is common to the use of all fixed assets.

In this problem area, as in the area of depreciation, the taxpayer may want to make one election for tax purposes and another for financial accounting purposes. The usual answer, naturally, is to expense as much as possible for tax purposes, but to capitalize as much as possible for accounting purposes. To a limited extent, a different treatment is possible, although the right of the taxpayer to differentiate here is not as clear-cut as it is in the case of depreciation.

The reader should simply be aware that one of the tax benefits that attaches to an election to report depreciation deductions under the new ADR (asset depreciation range) system is the right to use new percentage repair allowances. Stated very crudely, what the new rules do is provide the taxpayer with a dollar range—determined by administratively stated percentages and the taxpayer's total dollar investment in certain fixed assets—within which the IRS agent cannot challenge the taxpayer's treatment of repair expenditures. In other words, as long as the expenditure was not for a specifically excluded addition, an IRS agent cannot challenge a taxpayer's decision to expense a certain item, rather than capitalize it, as long as that expenditure does not exceed prescribed dollar limitations.

Tax Factors Pertinent to the Disposition of Fixed Assets

The tax factors associated with the disposition of a fixed asset can be classified into three basic areas. The first and most important factor is classification of the gain or loss realized on disposition as a capital gain or loss or as an ordinary gain or loss. The second factor involves the potential recapture of an earlier investment tax credit. The third factor relates to each of the first two in that it considers alternative ways of disposing of a fixed asset so that the taxpayer might influence the character of the gain or loss or the need to recapture the investment credit. Fortunately we have considered each of these problems earlier in this book; only a brief review is necessary here.

Capital Gain or Ordinary Income?

Chapter 5 includes a discussion of the definitional problems associated with capital gains and losses. Table 5–1 adequately summarizes the most probable tax treatment of the gains and losses typically realized on the sale or exchange of a fixed asset used in a trade or business. As demonstrated in the first section of this chapter, the distinction between capital gain and ordinary income has a major impact on the profitability of many fixed-asset investments. What the taxpayer usually seeks, of course, is a long-term capital gain on disposition. The likelihood of a capital gain is common to the following assets.

1. All "pure" capital assets according to the statutory definition.
2. Any depreciable *real* properties used in a trade or business *if*—
   a. The gain can be attributed to the land.
   b. The gain can be attributed to a building or building component *and* that building was depreciated on a straight-line method.
   c. The gain can be attributed to certain low-income residential rental property *and* the property was owned for more than 16 years and 8 months. (*Note:* If the low-income rental property was held for more than 10 years and less than 16 years and 8 months, some portion of the gain will be ordinary income and some portion will be capital gain.)
3. Part of the gain associated with a mineral right, *if* the disposition is complete, the transaction is worded properly, and the gain is greater than the amount of any intangible drilling cost that is recaptured on a pro rata basis with the recovery of the minerals.

Most other dispositions of fixed assets will produce ordinary income rather than capital gain.

Investment Credit Recapture

If a taxpayer originally estimates that a fixed asset will be used for a longer time period than it is actually used, part or all of the investment credit claimed in an earlier year may be recaptured at the time of disposition. On page 192 we noted the critical importance of the estimated life of an asset to the amount of the investment tax credit that could be claimed. If a taxpayer originally estimates a longer life and disposes of the asset in a shorter time, the correct investment credit based upon the actual holding period must be determined and the government must be repaid any difference between the original amount claimed and the revised amount.

To illustrate, assume that a taxpayer purchased qualified assets costing $600,000 and estimated the life of these assets at seven years. Based on the initial estimate, the taxpayer would claim an investment tax credit of $60,000. If, after five years of use, the taxpayer disposed of those assets, a corrected amount of the investment credit of $40,000 would be known. In the year in which the taxpayer makes this disposition, the tax liability must be increased by $20,000 to recapture the investment credit erroneously claimed in the earlier year. Incidentally, a taxpayer need not pay interest or penalty on this additional tax liability; thus, the taxpayer's erroneous claim may effectively create an interest-free loan from the government in the interim.

In a few instances, a taxpayer might be able to delay a disposition for a very brief period and thereby avoid the need to recapture any investment credit. The need for detailed records is obvious. Finally, the reader should observe that the term *disposition* covers many events in addition to the obvious sale or exchange.

Form of Disposition

Just as a taxpayer can change the tax consequences associated with the acquisition of a fixed asset by changing the form of the acquisition, so too the tax consequences associated with a disposition can be changed. In Chapter 6 we noted how a taxpayer might convert a potential ordinary income into capital gain by (a) transferring assets into a corporation and then selling the corporate stock or (b) converting a property from business to personal use on a timely basis. Unintended dispositions, through casualty or theft, initially create the usual tax problems associated with all other dispositions. However, special rules often apply to alleviate the tax burdens that might attach to an unintended disposition if the taxpayer makes certain elections on a timely basis. Some of these options will be considered in Chapter 10. Finally, the reader should observe that it may be desirable to modify intended disposition plans at least temporarily to achieve certain desirable tax consequences. For example, instead of selling a fixed asset, a taxpayer may be able to modify it to another use and thereby modify the holding period or change the year of reporting so that a tax benefit can be maximized. The number of alternatives is almost unlimited, and a good imagination combined with some knowledge of the tax rules (directly or through an adviser) can occasionally pay handsome dividends.

An Illustrative Comparison of Tax Effects on Investment Decisions

The multiple interrelationships among tax rules and economic benefits make understanding even a relatively simple illustration difficult. Nevertheless, if a reader is to understand the potential impact of the several tax rules studied in this chapter, it seems necessary to attempt a meaningful comparison. To do this, let us assume that a taxpayer invests $200,000 cash in an unincorporated venture and that this venture produces nothing the first year, but that for the next five years it generates a cash flow of $40,000 and requires the payment of additional cash expenses of $20,000. This leaves the venture with $20,000 excess cash, which is returned to the investor each year. Finally, let us assume that, at the end of the six-year period, the investor sells all rights in the venture for $160,000. *If we exclude all tax considerations,* the initial projections might look something like this:

Year	Item	Cash in	Cash out
1	Initial investment..................................		$200,000
2	Excess cash generated by new investment.........	$ 20,000	
3	Same as year 2	20,000	
4	Same as year 2	20,000	
5	Same as year 2	20,000	
6	Same as year 2	20,000	
6	Sale of investment	160,000	
	Totals	$260,000	$200,000
	Net before-tax profit..........................	$60,000	

If a person were totally unaware of the interface between tax rules and the profit concept, he or she might conclude that the investor in this situation could simply multiply the before-tax profit by the marginal tax rate to determine the tax effect and then, by simple subtraction, determine the net aftertax profit. In other words, if this were an investor in the 60-percent marginal tax bracket, a reader might conclude that the income tax on the $60,000 profit would total $36,000, and that the aftertax profit would be $24,000. Whether or not the taxpayer should proceed with the investment would then depend upon whether or not he or she would be satisfied with that minimal aftertax return on an investment of $200,000 for six years. An application of the actual tax rules and the present value calculations would provide a more correct analysis and permit the investor to make a better decision.

The tables at the end of this chapter contain three projections based on the facts mentioned in the two previous paragraphs. The only additional fact assumed is that the taxpayer pays a marginal tax rate of 30 percent on all long-term capital gains. In Table 8A–1 the investment is made in used industrial equipment; in Table 8A–2 it is made in a new apartment house; in Table 8A–3 it is made in a successful oil venture. A comparison of the net results on a nondiscounted basis, but giving full consideration to all income tax rules, is as follows.

	Equipment	Apartment	Oil well
Nondiscounted aftertax profit	$30,667	$3,073	$45,600

The modification in the solution for equipment is largely attributable to the investment tax credit. The major difference in the oil well investment in this illustration is attributable to the partial capital gain treatment on the sale—percentage depletion has only minimal effect on these results because the total depletion recovered exceeds the tax basis by only $4,000 in five years.

If we finally assume that this investor would demand no less than a 5 percent aftertax rate of return on his or her capital before making an investment, the comparisons on a discounted basis become much more meaningful. The discounted present value comparisons are as follows.

	Equipment	Apartment	Oil well
Discounted present value of aftertax profit (or loss)	($7,405)	($35,185)	$18,784

These comparisons suggest that, based on the prospectus of profits and giving full consideration to all tax laws, the investor should *not* proceed with plans to invest in either the equipment or the apartment house, *if* the investor really demands a 5 percent aftertax return on investments. The oil well investment quite obviously will more than satisfy this investor's demands if the profit prospectus proves to be accurate.

Although these calculations do reflect the major federal income tax rules, the reader should understand that the illustration is by no means intended as a realistic comparison of investments in equipment, apartment houses, and oil wells. There was no attempt to incorporate into these figures the typical amount of expense that must be incurred to generate a given amount of revenue in any investment or in any industry. Thus, for example, the personal property tax on business equipment is totally ignored and simply assumed to be part of the annual $20,000 in expenses. Similarly, the real property tax ordinarily imposed on apartment houses is deemed to be part of the $20,000 annual expense. And the windfall profits tax, recently imposed on oil and gas properties, is likewise treated as part of the same annual expense figure. The assumed tax on capital gains is equally unrealistic; no one pays a 30 percent rate on those gains today. In other words, this comparison would be valid only if a ceteris paribus (all other things being equal) assumption were valid. In the real world, obviously, all other things are *not* equal. Hence, the sole purpose of this illustration is to demonstrate the major impact of the federal income tax rules in an unreal world.

In summary, this comparison should have demonstrated to the reader that the federal income tax rules must be given careful consideration in making investment decisions. The three illustrative cases used in this comparison are unrealistic. One cannot generalize from this single comparison because the results will vary substantially depending upon how we slant the illustration in terms of absolute gains and losses, as well as on how we distribute the proceeds from an investment between interim income and final disposition gain. The time factor can also modify the results significantly. In this comparison, for example, the benefit of the rapid depreciation implicit in the apartment project was not sufficient to override the benefit of the investment credit in the machine. The results are also biased by the fact that the illustration demands an immediate cash outlay of $200,000; most investment projects in equipment and in real estate do not require such a large initial cash outlay because of unique leverage opportunities. The importance of this comparison lies *solely* in its ability to demonstrate the critical nature of federal income tax rules with regard to investment decisions.

Appendix

TABLE 8A–1
Investment in Used Machinery ($170,000 purchase price, $30,000 rehabilitation costs)

Year	Item	Nondiscounted cash inflow or equivalent	Nondiscounted cash outflow	Discounted cash inflow or equivalent	Discounted cash outflow
1	Initial investment		$200,000		$200,000
1	Investment credit ($100,000 maximum for used property)	$ 10,000		$ 10,000	
2	Excess cash generated by new investment	20,000		19,048	
2	Taxes saved on loss reported (after depreciation)	6,000		5,714	
3	Excess cash generated by new investment	20,000		18,141	
3	Taxes saved on loss reported	3,300		2,993	
4	Excess cash generated by new investment	20,000		17,276	
4	Taxes saved on loss reported	1,005		868	
5	Excess cash generated by new investment	20,000		16,454	
5	Taxes paid on gain reported		946		779
6	Excess cash generated by new investment	20,000		15,670	
6	Taxes paid on gain reported		2,604		2,040
6	Sale of investment	160,000		125,360	
6	Taxes paid on sale of investment		42,755		33,499
6	Recapture of investment tax credit		3,333		2,611
	Totals	$280,305	$256,927	$231,524	$238,929
	Net profit or (loss) after taxes nondiscounted	$30,667		Discounted @ 5% ($7,405)	

Major tax rules applicable in this illustration:

a. Investment credit is available but only to maximum amount because of used property; partial recapture required.
b. Maximum depreciation that can be claimed is 150 percent declining balance because property is used; estimated life used here is ten years.
c. Entire gain on sale of investment will be ordinary income by operation of Section 1245.

TABLE 8A-2
Investment in New Apartment Dwelling

Year	Item	Nondiscounted cash inflow or equivalent	Nondiscounted cash outflow	Discounted cash inflow or equivalent	Discounted cash outflow
1	Initial investment		$200,000		$200,000
2	Excess cash generated by new investment	$ 20,000		$ 19,048	
2	Taxes paid on gain reported (after depreciation)		6,000		5,714
3	Excess cash generated by new investment	20,000		18,140	
3	Taxes paid on gain reported		6,300		5,714
4	Excess cash generated by new investment	20,000		17,276	
4	Taxes paid on gain reported		6,585		5,688
5	Excess cash generated by new investment	20,000		16,454	
5	Taxes paid on gain reported		6,856		5,640
6	Excess cash generated by new investment	20,000		15,670	
6	Taxes paid on gain reported		7,113		5,573
6	Sale of investment	160,000		125,360	
6	Taxes paid on sale of investment		24,073		18,804
	Totals	$260,000	$256,927	$211,948	$247,133
	Net profit or (loss) after taxes, nondiscounted		$3,073	Discounted @ 5%	($35,185)

Major tax rules applicable in this illustration:

a. Maximum depreciation that can be claimed is 200 percent declining balance because property is *new, residential* property; estimated life, 40 years.
b. Gain of $20,244 (equal to "excess" depreciation) on sale of apartment will be ordinary income due to Section 1250. (Assumed post-1975 rules were fully applicable.)
c. No portion of the investment is eligible for the investment credit.

TABLE 8A-3
Investment in Oil Well

Year	Item	Nondiscounted cash inflow or equivalent	Nondiscounted cash outflow	Discounted cash inflow or equivalent	Discounted cash outflow
1	Initial investment		$200,000		$200,000
1	Taxes saved on immediate deduction of intangible drilling and development costs	$ 96,000		$ 96,000	
2	Excess cash generated by new investment	20,000		19,048	
2	Taxes paid on gain reported (after depletion)		6,720		6,400
3	Excess cash generated by new investment	20,000		18,140	
3	Taxes paid on gain reported		6,720		6,096
4	Excess cash generated by new investment	20,000		17,276	
4	Taxes paid on gain reported		6,720		5,804
5	Excess cash generated by new investment	20,000		16,554	
5	Taxes paid on gain reported		6,720		5,528
6	Excess cash generated by new investment	20,000		15,670	
6	Taxes paid on gain reported		6,720		5,266
6	Sale of investment	160,000		125,364	
6	Taxes paid on sale of investment		76,800		60,174
	Totals	$356,000	$310,400	$308,052	$289,268
	Net profit or (loss) after taxes, nondiscounted	$45,600		Discounted @ 5%	$18,784

Major tax rules applicable in this illustration:

a. Assumed that $80,000 of initial $100,000 investment could be deducted in first tax period as intangible drilling and development cost.
b. Percentage depletion is allowed and claimed in each year—22 percent statutory rate assumed applicable. (This would be less for years after 1980.)
c. No portion of the investment is eligible for the investment credit. (This assumption is questionable.)
d. Assumed that 60 percent of gain on sale of investment will be recaptured as ordinary income due to Section 1254.

CHAPTER 9

Tax Shelters

Investing in tax shelters is widely believed to be a legal alternative to paying federal income taxes. Relatively few people, however, really understand exactly why or how tax shelters work (or fail to work). The primary reasons for the apparent widespread confusion are easily identified. First, most tax shelters are sold by people who do not themselves understand the many intricacies of the tax law, but who do understand the dramatic tax savings that can be achieved legally by the mere purchase of a given investment. Second, most of the taxpayers who buy tax shelters are equally confused by the intricacies of the tax law, but they do understand that if they do nothing special very soon, they most certainly must pay a very substantial income tax bill. Third, being uncertain, conservative taxpayers turn to their professional counselors—attorneys, accountants, bankers, brokers, investment counselors, and others—for assistance and advice. What they typically receive in return is a lot of carefully hedged statements about possible long-run adverse consequences—and, in some cases, a brief lecture on financial risks—but almost always a clear endorsement of the short-term tax magic originally promised by the tax shelter salesperson. Realizing that the future is necessarily very uncertain for everyone, knowing that no one ever became wealthy without taking a risk, but being assured that immediate relief from a large tax liability is not only legal, but almost guaranteed, the final action is predictable: The tax shelter is purchased and the tax liability is dramatically reduced. The only question is: What really happens in the long run?

This chapter is an attempt to explain both the short- and long-run tax implications of investing in those assets that are typically sold as tax shelters. To understand this chapter, it is absolutely essential that you understand the basic message in Chapters 2, 3, 4, 5, and 8, plus a few additional tax provisions to be explained here.

Before we turn our attention to those details, a final commentary on the setting in which tax shelters thrive seems appropriate. The vast majority of Americans probably do not truly appreciate how much of their income is devoted to the payment of the federal income tax. Most wage and salary earners are mesmerized into complacency by what is known as a withholding system. Their employer withholds from their paycheck an estimated amount, the total of which (in most cases) will be sufficient to pay nearly all their federal income tax liability on April 15. Although these people are aware of the significant amount withheld, they focus only once each year on how large the total really is, and, at that time of the year, they are more concerned with getting the necessary tax return correctly filed on time than they are with esoteric issues about the distribution of the tax burden.

There are, however, a growing number of people to whom the withholding system applies only partially or not at all. They are the taxpayers who are either part-time employees or wholly self-employed. Many of those individuals are earning surprisingly large incomes, in monetary if not in real terms. Since, in these cases, there is no convenient employer to do the withholding for the government, the law requires that the taxpayers pay an estimated tax four times each year. Specifically, for calendar-year taxpayers, estimated payments must be made on April 15, June 15, September 15, and January 15. Having part of your pay withheld from every paycheck, and facing a quarterly payment of $1,000, $10,000, $50,000, or more, are two dramatically different phenomena. Although the typical, well-compensated, self-employed person fully comprehends that a large quarterly estimated tax payment will soon be due, actually writing that check to the government is something of a heartrending experience. The people writing those large checks are, in most instances, aggressive, intelligent, hardworking, self-made, busy individuals. Very often they are engaged in such learned professions as medicine, dentistry, engineering, or law, or they are successful athletes, artists, contractors, or authors, with limited knowledge of business. It is totally understandable, therefore, that they could be equally mesmerized by a salesperson—whose basic message is endorsed by all professional advisers—offering a potentially viable business *investment* as a legal alternative to paying taxes. That very real alternative is what we will investigate here.

This chapter is divided into three major parts. The first explains three additional federal income tax rules that may play an important role in correctly evaluating a tax-sheltered investment. The second part attempts two things: (1) to identify the common ingredients of the investments that historically have been sold as shelters and (2) to explain some of the tax rules that have recently been added to the law to reduce the effectiveness of shelters. The final part examines in detail a specific example of a tax-shelter investment under two alternative economic projections.

Three Additional Tax Provisions

Before we can fully understand the tax implications of certain investments, we must examine the general outline of a few additional details found in three Internal Revenue Code provisions. One provision involves the imposition of a tax on tax preferences, called a "minimum tax." The second concerns an interaction between this minimum tax on tax preferences and the maximum tax on personal service income. The third provision is the alternative minimum tax, which is a mandatory federal income tax computation that is an alternative to everything explained thus far in this book.

The Minimum Tax

In addition to the "regular" federal income tax, Section 56 imposes an additional tax—known as the minimum tax on tax preferences—on selected taxpayers. The taxpayers selected for this dubious honor are those who have taken a greater-than-average advantage of 11 specific tax provisions identified in Section 57 as tax preferences. The precise rules differ for individuals, fiduciaries, corporations, Subchapter S corporations, personal holding companies, and certain financial institutions. In general, however, the five most important tax preferences identified in Section 57 can be summarized as follows:

1. The excess of accelerated depreciation over straight-line depreciation on real property.
2. The excess of accelerated depreciation over straight-line depreciation on *leased* personal property.
3. The excess of percentage depletion over the adjusted basis of oil and gas properties, coal, iron, ore, other minerals, and timber.
4. The excess of intangible drilling costs incurred on productive wells over any income the taxpayer may have from oil and gas properties.
5. The excess of any 60-month amortization deductions over the straight-line depreciation of those same properties.

Most of the remaining six tax preferences identified in Section 57 are for specific taxpayers only. For example, corporate taxpayers must include a percentage of any net capital gain realized as one of their tax preferences. Individuals must include the bargain element in any qualified stock option exercised during the year. (Although the 1976 Act generally terminated the issuance of new options, individuals continue to exercise qualified options granted before this Act became law.) As you may already have observed, the five major tax preferences are among the more important special rules related to fixed assets considered in the prior chapter. As you are about to discover, these same rules are generally of special importance to tax shelters.

To continue, however, the minimum tax on tax preferences is determined by adding together the taxpayer's total tax preferences for the year and subtracting a *de minimis* amount. In the case of individual and fiduciary taxpayers, the *de minimis* amount is the *larger* of (1) half the regular income tax or (2) $10,000. In the case of corporate taxpayers, it is the *larger* of (1) the regular income tax or (2) $10,000. After making this subtraction, any positive difference remaining is multiplied by 15 percent. The product of that multiplication is the minimum tax on tax preferences, which must be added to the taxpayer's regular federal income tax, determined in the normal manner. The sum of these two amounts is the *tentative* gross tax liability of the taxpayer for the year; it is tentative for reasons to be explained momentarily. Before we consider the *alternative* minimum tax, however, we should observe one other important aspect of tax preferences.

Interaction between Tax Preferences and the Maximum Tax

In Chapter 4 we noted that the marginal tax rate applicable to the personal service taxable income of any individual will never exceed 50 percent because of the maximum tax provision. But exactly what is *personal service taxable income?* Until now, we have assumed that personal service taxable income was equal to anything earned by an individual—a sweat-of-the-brow concept, albeit air-conditioned sweat in many cases. That assumption, unfortunately, is less than complete. Section 1348 requires both that (1) itemized deductions be allocated between the taxpayer's earned and unearned income and (2) the amount of earned income otherwise eligible for the 50 percent maximum rate be reduced by any tax preferences reported by the taxpayer. The tax preferences of concern here are exactly the same as those subject to the minimum tax on tax preferences, which was discussed above. In other words, taxpayers must give up a dollar's worth of personal service income (taxed at no more than 50 percent) for every dollar's worth of tax preference reported on their return.

As a practical matter, this means that many of the very people who will be tempted to invest in a tax shelter may unwittingly be transferring a portion of their apparent 50-percent income into a 70-percent income bracket. Because of this danger, people with a large amount of *earned* (or personal service) income should examine very carefully any investment in a tax shelter that will produce any tax preference. In the worst case, a tax preference can increase the taxpayer's federal income tax by 37½ percent. In this case, instead of gaining a deduction worth 50 cents on each dollar invested—as usually promised by the shelter sales representative—the taxpayer may really gain only 12½ cents on the dollar.

The Alternative Minimum Tax

Finally, to be complete, we should note that, in a small number of cases, an individual taxpayer will not determine his or her tax liability as suggested thus far in this book. After computing his or her federal income tax in the normal manner—including the addition for the minimum tax on tax preferences—every individual theoretically must make an alternative tax computation. If the alternative computation produces a larger tax than the normal computation, the alternative tax is the tax that must be paid. But exactly how do you compute the alternative minimum tax?

Once again, in the interest of achieving other objectives, we will sidestep some of the details associated with the calculation of the alternative minimum tax. We should note, however, that the base for this alternative tax consists of the sum of three elements:

1. The individual's *taxable income*, computed in the normal way, except for possible NOL adjustments.
2. A quantity called "excess itemized deductions."[1]
3. The amount claimed as a long-term capital gain deduction.

---

[1] In general, excess itemized deductions is defined as:

Total itemized deductions	$xxx
Less deductions for (1) medical expenses, (2) casualty losses, and (3) state and local taxes	xxx
Remainder	$xxx
Less amount determined as follows:	
AGI .... $ xxx	
Less deductions for (1) medical expenses, (2) casualty losses, and (3) state and local taxes xxx	
Remainder .... $ xxx	
Times 60 percent .... ×0.60	
Product of above multiplication	xxx
Equals excess itemized deductions	$xxx

This sum is reduced by an arbitrary $20,000, and the remainder, if any, is multiplied by the following tax rates:

1. 10 percent on the first $40,000.
2. 20 percent on the next $40,000.
3. 25 percent on any remaining amount.

As noted above, if the product of this multiplication is greater than the individual's federal income tax determined in the normal way, then this amount is the correct federal income tax liability for the year.

Although the alternative minimum tax was added to the code primarily to catch people who report large amounts of net capital gain and very little other income, in a few circumstances it can also catch those with no net capital gain or itemized deductions but with large amounts of investment credit. In other words, for a few individuals, the federal income tax computed in the normal way will amount to little or nothing because of a relatively large amount of investment credit (or some other credit). Once again, these individuals are likely to invest in tax shelters. Thus, before determining exactly how much or how little a tax-sheltered investment will really reduce taxes, a taxpayer must always consider the possibility of the alternative minimum tax.

With these additional tax provisions explained, we are ready to identify the common ingredients of most tax shelters. At the same time that each of these ingredients is explained, we will note in passing some of the provisions that have been enacted to minimize the continued effectiveness of the common ingredients to future tax planning.

The Essential Ingredients of a Tax Shelter

There simply is no single, generally accepted definition of *tax shelter*. Some authors would include within their definition such items as investments in state or local bonds and qualified pension and profit-sharing plans. Certainly those items may save federal income taxes, and we would not quarrel with their inclusion within the definition of tax-sheltered investments. In order to give this chapter a more manageable scope, however, we will consider here only the fixed-asset type of investments that have commonly been marketed as tax shelters. These include investments in developed realty, oil and gas ventures, equipment leasing, citrus and almond groves, cattle feeding and breeding operations, timber, motion pictures, videotapes, master records, and books. If you study this list of diverse investments carefully, you will discover that they typically have in common one or more of the following characteristics: (1) an opportunity for leveraging the investment; (2) a mismatching of revenues and expenses, at least in the classical accounting sense; (3) an opportunity for major preferential income tax treatment; and (4) avoidance of the corporate entity. Let us consider the importance of each of these essential ingredients in greater detail.

Leveraging

A taxpayer's basis in a fixed asset is determined not by the amount of cash expended immediately to acquire the asset, but by the total cost of the fixed asset, regardless of the taxpayer's method of accounting. To illustrate, assume that a taxpayer acquired a fixed asset by paying $10,000 down and signing a $90,000, ten-year, 12-percent note for the balance. That taxpayer's right to claim depreciation or any other tax benefit would be based on the $100,000 purchase price, not on the $10,000 down payment. This opportunity to use a limited cash investment to acquire a much larger benefit is known as *leveraging*.

Many tax shelters are ideally suited to leveraging precisely because they involve fixed assets. Lenders are willing to loan money if they can obtain, as security for their loan, a first mortgage against the property that the loan is made to acquire. Oil drilling ventures are an obvious exception to this rule since few creditors would be willing to loan money, with little security, to someone who may well end up owning nothing more than a dry hole. (Loans for trips to Las Vegas are equally difficult to arrange for exactly the same reason.) With that major exception, however, most tax shelters involve a property that can be used as security for a sizable loan. Thus, the first basic ingredient of a tax shelter is present. Assuming that the asset in question is one that qualifies for depreciation, leverage may allow the salesperson to promise tax savings in the first year that will exceed the cash expenditure required. Who can resist an offer like that: make a $30,000 *investment* and save, say, $45,000 in tax expense! Everyone knows that any investment *might* prove to be surprisingly successful, whereas an expense can never provide anything in the future. And what if the investment does prove to be worth little or nothing—what is there to lose? Hasn't the taxpayer already saved more in taxes than the amount invested? The answer, of course, seems to be the debt. What about that other $90,000 that the taxpayer promised to pay, with 12 percent interest, sometime during the next ten years?

Prior to the Tax Reform Act of 1976, and to a lesser extent the Revenue Act of 1978, the tax shelter salesperson had an answer for that, too. The debt might be arranged as a *nonrecourse* debt. A nonrecourse debt is one that does not require the borrower to repay anything from his or her own funds should something go wrong. To put it in other words, a nonrecourse debt is one in which the creditor cannot look beyond the pledged property for security. If the mortgaged property cannot produce enough in income or sales proceeds to pay the creditor in full, it is the creditor's bad luck—not the debtor's. Many tax shelters sold prior to 1976 were sold on exactly those terms; the buyer was legally promised that it would be impossible to lose more than the amount invested. The tax laws of 1976 and 1978 changed all that, however, by providing that tax benefits generally could be obtained only to the extent that the taxpayer was "at risk." One major exception to the new rules was carved out for investments in real property. This means that today an investor in any tax shelter other than real property will not get any tax benefits beyond those based on the total of the amount invested immediately, *plus* the amount that the borrower *might have to pay* on a debt if worse comes to worst; that is, if the creditor calls the loan, and the proceeds received from the sale of the secured property do not provide sufficient funds to pay any remaining debt. This conclusion suggests that every investor/taxpayer must be very careful in assessing the dependability of all economic projections associated with any nonrealty tax shelter.

But what about current investments in real estate or in other tax shelters prior to 1976 or 1978? That leaves us with the very interesting question, suggested earlier: Why shouldn't a taxpayer make, for instance, a $30,000 investment in real estate if that investment can guarantee an immediate tax savings of $45,000 and no risk of additional debt? How can the taxpayer lose anything? The answer this time is more difficult to understand.

To begin to understand it, you must revert to the problem of defining income, as discussed in Chapter 2. Recall that any increase in net worth, combined with an external transaction, is generally sufficient to trigger the recognition of income for federal income tax purposes. Furthermore, a cancellation of debt is tantamount to an increase in net worth. Even if a taxpayer's assets do not increase, if debts decrease, there is an increase in net worth. Getting rid of a leaky tax shelter inevitably involves a transaction of some sort. The foreclosure of a mortgage, a gift to charity, a gift to one's loved or not-so-loved ones, or even abandonment all change the form or substance of a taxpayer's property or property right, and all involve another taxpayer, at least indirectly. Thus, any and all of these methods of disposition typically have been held to create taxable income any time a taxpayer is relieved of debt related to a tax shelter, even if it is a nonrecourse debt! The financial press generally refers to this income as "phantom income." In one sense, it is phantom income because the taxpayer who receives nothing at a foreclosure sale clearly feels no richer than he or she did before the sale. For federal income tax purposes, however, there is no way to escape the conclusion that any disposition of a worthless shelter—short of the death of the investor/taxpayer—will create taxable income at least equal in amount to the debt canceled. Furthermore, the reader should note in passing that this income is no more of a phantom than the basis on which the tax benefit was claimed in the first place. In fact, the tax laws very carefully work out a parity between the two. In spite of these facts, we will continue to use the term *phantom income* in this chapter since it is so commonly understood.

Although the specter of phantom income based on the principle of leverage may be unnerving, it does not lead directly to the conclusion that tax-sheltered investments—with or without nonrecourse debts—are necessarily unprofitable. Rather it means only that the investor-taxpayer must examine carefully exactly how much he or she could lose in the investment, the marginal tax rate to be applied to the income initially removed through the purchase of the tax shelter versus the marginal rate to be applied to the phantom income realized later, and any income that will be earned on the tax saving in the interim. In a very real sense, the amount of tax saved because of the investment can be viewed as an interest-free loan from the government. *If* the taxpayer invests the tax savings wisely, and if sufficient time elapses between the time the tax would otherwise have been due and the time it is due, a sufficient income may be produced to pay the tax on the phantom income after all. The real danger occurs when the taxpayer consumes the apparent tax savings achieved through the investment and makes no provision for its later payment. Only slightly less risky is the investment of the tax savings in a nonliquid investment. Tax liabilities on phantom income all too often have a way of coming due just when a taxpayer is least able to pay them.

Let us next consider the characteristic of mismatched revenues and expenses.

Theoretical Mismatching of Revenues and Expenses

In classical financial accounting, net income is defined as the difference between the revenues realized in a given period and all expenses incurred to produce those revenues. Observe that revenues are measured first; only then are expenses *matched* against the revenue they produce. The practical application of this financial accounting principle necessarily defers the time when many immediate (cash) expenditures can be deducted; it also necessitates the estimation and immediate deduction of other expenditures, which may not be incurred for some time to come. Because of purely pragmatic considerations, income tax law provides nothing truly equivalent to the matching concept of financial accounting in various circumstances. After all, tax laws must be administered in a manner satisfactory to most of the people most of the time if they are to be effective. This often means that theoretical constructs must give way to pragmatic considerations where matters of income taxation are concerned. Specifically, it often means that taxes will be collected whenever the taxpayer receives the revenue (whether or not earned); and, as a corollary proposition, deductions sometimes may be allowed whenever the taxpayer pays them, without regard for the period in which the correspondent revenue is recognized. The problem lies in striking a reasonable balance between the practical administration of an imperfect tax law and opening the door for widespread tax avoidance, especially commercialized tax avoidance.

In agriculture. Many traditional tax shelters are directly dependent upon the theoretical mismatching of revenues and expenses. Agribusiness has been particularly amenable to manipulation. Seeds must be purchased and crops planted now; harvesting will come later, perhaps in another year. Breeding herds must be purchased, fed, and nurtured for several years before they develop into a final product. Citrus groves and almond trees must be planted and carefully cultivated for several years before they produce their first crop. As long as any opportunity to minimize taxes from this kind of mismatching of agricultural investments was restricted to "real" farmers or ranchers, no one was particularly concerned. When those same agricultural ventures began to be packaged by Wall Street brokers and were sold as tax shelters to high-tax-bracket individuals who never ventured outside the city limits, however, the tax authorities decided to give the matter another look. Eventually this led to the adoption of provisions such as Section 278, which states that expenditures incurred in planting and developing citrus and almond groves must generally be capitalized for the first five years. After that, the capitalized costs may be amortized over the estimated useful life of the grove. In other words, none of the planting and developing costs can be deducted until the grove has a reasonable chance to produce some revenue, a period deemed to be five years. Section 464 places similar limitations on the deduction of other expenses common to agricultural and horticultural businesses. This section is applicable only to *farming syndicates;* it provides that amounts paid for feed, seed, fertilizer, and many other farm types of supplies can be deducted only in the taxable year that they are actually used or consumed.

In oil and gas. A theoretical mismatching of revenues and expenses is by no means restricted to agribusiness industries. It is also the common ingredient on which tax-sheltered investments in the oil and gas industry thrive. In this instance, however, there are at least two basic problems: (1) the technical accounting problem related to the unit of account and (2) the social and economic problems of inadequate oil and gas reserves.

Relative to the first problem, the question concerns the proper income tax treatment of the intangible drilling and development costs incurred in oil and gas exploration. Should each well be treated as a separate property, or should all or some part of the exploration and development activities of a given entity be combined? If so, how? In other words, should the cost of drilling each hole be treated separately—which would allow the cost of at least all dry holes to be immediately deductible—or should the cost of several holes be combined and treated as the necessary aggregate capital investment required to get a productive well (or field of wells)? Industry statistics suggest that only one in ten wildcat wells is productive, and even many of those are not commercially successful because of the limited reserves discovered. Only one in 200 wildcat wells results in the discovery of a medium-sized field; one in 1,000, a large field. Requiring the capitalization of all exploration, drilling, and development costs under these conditions would, of course, be very discouraging to the development of new reserves because it defers the tax deduction.

Whatever theoretical arguments might favor capitalization, there is little popular support for such a move because of serious oil and gas shortages. Instead of discouraging the development of new reserves, most people are interested in encouraging those activities. For these and several other valid reasons, it appears safe to say that the right to claim an immediate deduction for all intangible drilling and development costs is secure for years to come. Thus, investments in oil and gas exploration ventures will remain a viable shelter. Their tax shelter characteristic derives directly from the fact that most or all of the amount invested can be immediately deducted for federal income tax purposes, regardless of when (or if) those investments produce revenues.

Because leverage is not a factor in oil and gas investments, they can be used most easily to demonstrate the axiom that a bad economic investment is always a bad tax investment. Suppose, for example, that a person in the 70-percent marginal tax bracket invested $50,000 in an oil venture that drilled nothing but dry holes. That investor would most certainly get a sizable tax deduction—70 percent of 70 percent of the amount invested is common, and 70 percent of 100 percent of the investment is possible—but the value of the tax saving will never equal the amount invested. If we take the best possible case and assume that the investor is allowed to deduct the entire $50,000 invested, he or she will save no more than $35,000 in federal income taxes. In the end, therefore, as long as the drilling venture provides the investor with nothing but dry holes, he or she necessarily will lose $15,000 or more. Although additional consideration for state and local taxes might improve this financial picture slightly, unless the taxpayer is subject to marginal tax rates in excess of 100 percent, any *cash* investment in an economically unproductive investment will always be greater than the tax savings from that investment.

In real estate. The theoretical mismatching of revenues and expenses takes a slightly different twist in the real estate industry. Originally it involved at least two different issues: (1) the tax treatment of the interest and property tax expenses incurred during the construction period (i.e., the period prior to occupancy) and (2) the depreciation deduction claimed after occupancy.

Real estate investments frequently involve major construction projects, which require several years to complete. Under these circumstances, the interest expense incurred during the construction period, as well as the property taxes that accrued during that same period, amount to thousands of dollars. Historically, a taxpayer had an option to either deduct these expenses immediately or capitalize them and write them off as they would any other cost of the property. This option contributed significantly to their use as a tax shelter investment for many years. The 1976 Revenue Act deleted the old option; the code now requires that those same costs be capitalized and amortized over a ten-year period. The code sets forth a series of effective dates and phase-in provisions, which make it considerably more complex than the simple rule suggested above. *After* 1981, this rule will, however, be fully operative for investments in nonresidential real estate; *after* 1983, for investments in residential real estate; and *after* 1987, for investments in low-income housing. Hence, one of the traditional ingredients of a real estate shelter has been reduced.

Nevertheless, real estate remains a viable tax shelter. As explained earlier, it is the only remaining tax shelter that can utilize nonrecourse debt. In addition, at least to the extent detailed in the preceding chapter, real estate investments remain eligible for rapid depreciation. In effect, therefore, rapid depreciation amounts to yet another example of theoretically mismatched revenues and expenses. The depreciation deductions allowed during the early years of a real estate project typically are considerably larger than the decline in the economic value of the related asset. Thus, the right to claim the larger deductions—and through them obtain an interest-free loan from the government—remains an important ingredient in any real estate investment.

In other ventures. Investments in research and development projects, prepublication (book and magazine) ventures, movies, videotapes, master records, and other ventures have also been packaged and sold using the concept of accelerated deductions. That is, because each of these activities typically involves a substantial expenditure of funds prior to the recognition of any related revenues, they have been packaged and sold as tax shelters. A few years ago, some of these were sold with nonrecourse financing, some with conventional financing, and some demanding immediate investments of cash. In every instance, their value as a tax shelter was closely related to their value as an economic investment—those that had little or no economic substance proved to have little or no value as a tax shelter, much to the dismay of many investors.

Preferential Income Tax Provisions

A third ingredient common to many tax shelters involves some special or preferential income tax provisions. To some extent, the right to claim rapid depreciation, to deduct immediately any intangible drilling and development costs, to deduct immediately any research and development costs, to deduct immediately any prepublication costs, or to deduct immediately the cost of seedlings, feed, fertilizer, and many other things might all be viewed as preferential tax provisions. Those provisions have, however, already been considered as mismatched revenues and expenses. There remain other preferential income tax provisions, which largely explain other tax shelters.

The opportunity to claim an investment tax credit and the right to report certain amounts of income as a net capital gain are two of the more important tax incentives in the law. Because they are so important, they too have become a common ingredient in many tax shelters. These two ingredients are especially powerful when they can be combined with one or more of the other ingredients already discussed.

The investment tax credit. As explained in Chapter 8, a taxpayer may be allowed to claim an investment tax credit equal to 10 percent (or more) of the cost of qualifying property purchased. Not every taxpayer, however, will be equally able to use the investment credit. For example, some taxpayers have such large net operating loss carry-forwards that they owe little or no taxes in the current year anyway. Others have sufficiently large foreign tax, energy, job, and other credits to reduce their federal income taxes significantly. For these taxpayers, the investment credit adds little incentive to purchase anything. Nevertheless, they may need additional capital equipment that qualifies for the investment credit.

Enter equipment leasing. This setting was exactly the one that gave rise to the equipment leasing tax shelter. People who could put the investment tax credit to good advantage were encouraged to purchase equipment and lease it to those who needed it but could not benefit from the credit. Because it could so easily be combined with ample financing opportunities—either on a conventional or nonrecourse basis—the leased airplane, railroad rolling stock, truck tractor, and other heavy equipment made an ideal tax shelter. Because of the combined effect of the investment credit and rapid depreciation on heavily leveraged equipment, investors were nearly always guaranteed an immediate tax savings greatly in excess of their capital investment. The heyday of equipment leasing ended for many *individual* taxpayers when Congress (1) limited tax loss deductions to the amount "at risk," (2) classified much of the depreciation as a tax preference item, (3) eliminated the investment credit for most noncorporate lessors, and (4) classified the interest payments as investment interest (which is subject to a maximum $10,000 annual deduction). Although equipment leasing remains a viable possibility for corporate taxpayers, it has lost much of its original appeal for individuals.

Noncorporate lessors can currently claim the investment credit on leased equipment only if (1) they personally produce the equipment, or (2) it is leased for less than half the estimated life of the equipment *and* the ordinary expenses—other than depreciation, interest, taxes, and a few others—exceed 15 percent of the rental income from the property during the first 12 months of the lease. The latter alternative effectively increases the real economic risk that the lessor has in the property. In short, if the individual lessor is truly willing to assume the financial risks of owning leased property, then and only then is he or she authorized to claim the investment credit on that property. Corporate lessors are in a much better position. Generally they still can use nonrecourse notes; they can claim the investment credit; they are less concerned with tax preferences; and they are not subject to the excess investment interest limitations.

The net capital gain. The opportunity to convert ordinary income into capital gain has been a prime objective of many taxpayers for years. Tax-sheltered investments very frequently provided that opportunity in prior years. More recently this advantage, too, has been increasingly rare.

In the traditional tax shelter, an investor would depreciate the investment asset acquired using the most rapid depreciation method possible. The depreciation deductions would, of course, directly offset equal amounts of ordinary income. Although the amount of depreciation claimed for tax purposes would also reduce the adjusted basis of the investment property, this decrease was of little concern so long as the taxpayer could report any gain on the sale or exchange of the investment property as a long-term capital gain. The opportunity to convert ordinary income into capital gain through depreciation deductions was largely terminated for years after 1962 by Section 1245, at least with regard to investments in personalty (i.e., nonrealty). Since 1962, the taxpayer has had to report as ordinary income the lesser of (1) the gain recognized or (2) the post-1961 depreciation claimed on the personalty sold. Only the portion of the gain exceeding the post-1961 depreciation could be reported as Section 1231 gain, and thus have a chance of becoming long-term capital gain. Thus, Section 1245 was the first of the depreciation recapture sections.

The rules applicable to the recapture of depreciation from real property are not as strict as those for personal property. In general, a taxpayer can still convert ordinary income into capital gain through the deduction of depreciation on real estate, *so long as the realty is depreciated on a straight-line basis*. Note also that straight-line depreciation on realty avoids the creation of a tax preference, thus avoiding the potential 15 percent penalty tax and not disturbing the amount of income that the taxpayer might otherwise report as personal service taxable income. The combined force of these factors has been a major impetus behind the idea of component depreciation, which was explained in Chapter 8. By using straight-line depreciation of components, a taxpayer can often obtain depreciation deductions in the early years of a building's life that are roughly comparable to those that otherwise could be obtained only through the use of rapid depreciation methods. For tax shelters, the technical difference between the two methods of getting to those large numbers may be a big difference.

Investments in land—raw land, as well as developed land—have also been favored because of the possibility of reporting long-term capital gains at the time of a sale or exchange. This same major tax provision explains much of the interest in syndicated cattle operations, citrus groves, timber, Christmas trees, and oil and gas ventures. Although the technical details of each prospect are too numerous to investigate here, suffice it to say that each of these investments can produce substantial amounts of long-term capital gain, and, for that reason, they are often highly touted as tax shelters.

The percentage depletion allowance. The opportunity to claim a percentage depletion allowance far in excess of the amount invested continues to make investments in various mineral ventures of special interest to some taxpayers. For reasons explained in Chapter 8, percentage depletion is, at present, of less importance in the oil and gas industry than it was a few years ago. Nevertheless, under the right circumstances, percentage depletion can still be important in evaluating a tax shelter proposal in oil and gas or many other mineral operations. The chance of making a major discovery is what keeps mineral exploration ventures interesting; the risks are high, but so are the potential rewards.

Avoiding the Corporate Entity

Nearly all tax-sheltered investments must be sold without use of a corporate entity. Tax shelters provide tax savings only if the tax attributes of the investment can be passed to, and mixed with, the other items of gross income and deduction reported on the investor's federal income tax return. In order for this to happen, the tax shelter activity cannot take place within a corporate entity. If it did, the law would recognize the corporation as a separate taxpayer and "bottle up" within that entity any favorable tax attributes, such as the "extra" deductions attributable to leverage, deductible expenses incurred prior to the recognition of the related income, the investment credit, a net capital gain, an intangible drilling and development deduction, or any other tax consequence that commonly forms the foundation for the tax shelter in the first place.

The inability to use a corporate entity for a tax shelter activity has sometimes proved troublesome for those who package and sell tax shelter investments. The capital requirements of most tax shelters are generally greater than the amount of capital that a single investor cares to risk in a venture, even if he or she is financially capable of doing so. This need to raise large sums of capital outside the corporate entity is further complicated by the unlimited liability that accompanies the status of general partner in an ordinary partnership. Few investors are willing to become general partners with strangers in a largely unknown business venture because of the risk of liability. In most tax shelters, therefore, the investment vehicle finally settled upon is the limited partnership. This form of business allows the tax shelter salesperson to sell participation units to numerous individuals, each of whom receives the financial protection afforded by his or her status as a limited partner. Furthermore, the selling price of the participation units can be set at an amount that is likely to encourage only those investors who are properly thinking about an investment of that general nature and risk. Minimum participation units of $5,000, $10,000, and $20,000 are common.

Someone must, of course, play the role of the general partner and assume the liability that attends that position. Very often the general partner in a limited partnership is a corporate entity owned by the promoters and developers of the shelter. Being a corporate entity, the corporate general partner has achieved a certain amount of protection for its own stockholders. In recognition of the natural urge of the promoter-developer to create a straw, or dummy, corporation to play the role of general partner, the IRS has published guidelines to explain which limited partnerships it will recognize as viable partnerships and which it is likely to challenge as associations to be taxed as corporations. Thus, the investor in a tax shelter is given one last item of concern: Either the investor is willing to purchase and directly own a complete and specific independent unit of investment property (such as a specific railroad tank car, an apartment house, or ten head of cattle) or he or she must have competent legal assurance that the unit in the investment vehicle will withstand any IRS challenge that might suggest treating the vehicle as a corporation for federal income tax purposes. After all, if an investor wishes to offset the loss from a tax-sheltered investment against income from salaries, business profits, interest, rents, dividends, or any other source, it is absolutely essential that the tax shelter not be treated as a separate tax entity.

Several years ago it was common for limited partnerships to offer a full year's share of partnership losses to investors who purchased their interest on one of the last days of the taxable year. This ability to "buy" large tax deductions on the last days of the year led to many hastily arranged transactions with grossly inadequate investigations on the part of investors.

To make their packages even more attractive, some limited partnerships provided investors with strangely contorted allocations of various items of income and deduction. In most cases, of course, those allocations were fashioned to maximize the tax value of each allocated item to each investor. Eventually Section 704(b) and Section 706(c) were enacted to limit special allocations to those with real economic substance, and to disallow retroactive allocations to year-end partners.

The recent history of tax shelters is obviously fraught with a kind of hucksterism more commonly associated with the development of capitalistic countries 60 to 100 years ago. The Professor Harold Hill (à la "The Music Man") of modern times gains credibility by knowing just a little more about federal income taxation than does the reluctant taxpayer in search of relief. The modern-day checks and balances commonly associated with professional advisers has failed in the area of tax shelters for at least two reasons. First, the inherent complexity of the tax provisions makes it virtually impossible for even the most conscientious tax adviser to explain all the critical variables to the investor in a manner that the layperson would understand. Second, there are critical economic uncertainties implicit in virtually every legitimate tax shelter. Absolutely no one can predict the future course of economic events. A possible third and most unfortunate factor complicating professional advising on tax shelters is that professional advisers are often given "a piece of the action." The author, for example, frequently receives unsolicited proposals from "investment bankers" introducing possible tax shelters that might be brought to the attention of qualified clients, who are, of course, the very same people seeking qualified advice. A "consulting fee" of 10 percent of any investment sold to a client through presentation of a "detailed private placement memorandum" is commonplace. Thus the attorney, accountant, banker, broker, and other counselors have special reason not to be unduly harsh in their evaluation of certain tax shelters.

All this is not meant to suggest, however, that investments in tax shelters are necessarily bad. Nothing could be farther from the truth. Whether a tax-sheltered investment is good or bad depends most importantly on:

1. The real economic success or failure of the investment activity.
2. The specifics of the investor's tax situation in the year that the investment is made.
3. The specifics of the investor's tax situation in each of the years the investment will remain "active."
4. The specific tax characteristics of the investment.
5. The ability of the taxpayer to save and invest any tax savings at a projected rate of return.

Even a cursory review of these five variables reveals how tentative any conclusions related to tax shelters must be. Since no one can clearly see into the future, the best that any taxpayer can expect from an adviser is a carefully constructed "with the investment" and "without the investment" projection of results under several reasonable alternative assumptions about future economic events. A good tax adviser with national connections should also be able to detect the fraudulent proposals that might be presented to an innocent taxpayer. The cost of making an investigation and projecting possible future results is likely to be substantial. Nevertheless, without such careful consideration, any investment in a tax shelter is tantamount to a roll of the dice.

In the remaining pages of this chapter, we will examine very briefly a simplified tax shelter illustration to demonstrate the kind of considerations that must go into making an intelligent investment decision.

An Illustration of a Tax-Sheltered Investment under Two Alternative Assumptions Regarding Return

To illustrate the kind of "with" and "without" tax-shelter projection that should be made by (or for) anyone seriously considering such an investment, consider the consequences of a single investment made under the following assumptions:

Details concerning the investor:
Married, filing joint return, claiming two personal exemptions in every year.

No itemized deductions in excess of zero bracket amount.

Annual income of $300,000, exclusive of any income from tax-shelter investment, all of which is personal service income.

Details concerning the tax-shelter investment:
Cost—$110,000.
Terms—$10,000 down, balance in five equal payments due at end of each year, with 10 percent simple interest on unpaid balance.
Estimated life—five years.
Depreciation method—sum-of-the-years' digits.
Eligible for the investment credit (at two-thirds cost).

Projected cash revenues and expenses:
Anticipated revenues—$40,000 per year plus $10,000 salvage value (which would be ordinary income).
Anticipated expenses—year 1, $30,000; thereafter, $10,000 per year.

Depreciation schedule:
Year 1: $36,667
Year 2: 29,333
Year 3: 22,000
Year 4: 14,667
Year 5: 7,333

Note repayment schedule:

	Principal	Interest	Total
Year 1	$20,000	$10,000	$30,000
Year 2	20,000	8,000	28,000
Year 3	20,000	6,000	26,000
Year 4	20,000	4,000	24,000
Year 5	20,000	2,000	22,000

Alternative 1

An honest salesperson marketing a proposal based on the facts assumed above would very likely make a presentation based on projections that looked something like the following:

Year 1: Cash required:
- Down payment $10,000
- Note payment (end of year) 20,000
- Interest on note (end of year) ... 10,000
- First-year expenses 30,000

Total cash required in first year $70,000

Cash provided by investment:
- First-year revenue $40,000

Tax savings on additional deductions
- First-year expenses $30,000
- Interest on note 10,000
- Depreciation 36,667

Total additional deductions $76,667
Less additional income 40,000

Net decrease in taxable income anticipated $36,667
Times marginal tax rate 0.50

Tax savings anticipated 18,334
Investment tax credit 7,333

Total cash provided in first year 65,667

"Real" cash-cost of investment in first year .... $ 4,333

Year 2: Cash required:
- Note payment (end of year) $20,000
- Interest on note (end of year) ... 8,000
- Second-year expenses 10,000

Total cash required in second year $38,000

Cash provided by investment:
- Second-year revenue $40,000

Tax savings on additional deductions:
- Second-year expenses $10,000
- Interest on note 8,000
- Depreciation 29,333

Total additional deductions $47,333
Less additional income 40,000

Net decrease in taxable income anticipated .... $ 7,333
Times marginal tax rate 0.50

Tax savings anticipated 3,667

Total cash provided in second year 43,667

Extra cash generated for investor in second year ...... $ 5,667

Net increase in investor's cash by end of second year $1,334

After making such a detailed projection of cash flow for two years, some salespeople might simply note that, for all years after the second year, the investment would provide $40,000 or more each year in revenues and require only $10,000 each year in expenses, leaving the investor with at least $30,000 to pay any income taxes. The more honest ones would make cash projections for all five years. Nevertheless, the taxpayer is left with the impression that $30,000 should be adequate to pay any taxes that might be generated on a $40,000 annual revenue. These projections appear to look pretty good; investing in a productive property certainly seems preferable to paying taxes! Although the hypothetical investor in this illustration is required to "invest" $70,000 in year 1, his or her cash receipts were directly increased by $40,000, *and*, most important from a psychic point of view, the federal income tax bill did fall from $138,678 to $115,946! That $22,732 decrease is what tax shelters are all about—genuine investments that decrease tax bills.

Unfortunately, as good as the two-year projections appear to be, they fail to tell an accurate story. A better, but still incomplete, projection, might look something like that illustrated in Table A–1. In order to facilitate comparisons, the taxpayer's present situation is depicted as year 19x0; it is an accurate projection of the tax liability for the assumed facts *without* making the tax-sheltered investment. At present, this taxpayer's entire taxable income would be personal service taxable income, and the gross tax payable would be $138,678. If the taxpayer were to make the proposed investment, the correct first-year results would be comparable to those depicted for year 19x1. The taxpayer's gross tax liability would have decreased from $138,678 to $115,946, but not to $113,013 as anticipated. Why the slightly disappointing results? What is misleading about the cash-flow projections for year 1?

In this particular illustration, the disappointment stems from the fact that the proposed investment would produce a $14,667 tax preference for the investor. Although this taxpayer's remaining "regular" tax liability is sufficiently large to negate any danger of a (15 percent) minimum tax on tax preferences, that will not negate the fact that $14,667 of the taxpayer's personal service income has now been converted (by law) into "passive" income to be taxed at the 70 percent marginal rate. This amounts to an indirect penalty of $2,933 (or 20 percent of $14,667). Incidentally, this same tax rule creates an overstatement in the expected cash in the second year in the amount of $1,467 (i.e., 20 percent of the $7,333 tax preference).

Table A–1 also highlights the fact that year 3 is the "turnaround" year for this investment; that is, instead of providing the investor with additional tax deductions in years 3 through 5, this investment actually increases the taxpayer's taxable income by $2,000, $11,333, and $30,667, respectively. It also highlights another interesting problem for year 4. In that year, even though there are no tax preference items, the portion of the taxpayer's taxable income subject to the maximum tax is still reduced (and a 20 percent penalty paid on $11,260) because of the deduction allocation required by the formula used to compute personal service taxable income.

In summary, there simply is no satisfactory alternative to a complete "with" and "without" projection to determine the economic viability of any tax-shelter investment. Even the rather lengthy example of Table 9A–1 (on page 245) is incomplete because (1) it totally ignores the time preference value of money, and (2) it assumes that the taxpayer earns nothing on the taxes saved in years 1 and 2. These inaccuracies will not be corrected in this illustration because, even though they very likely would change the apparent $5,817 cash loss into a very small profit, they would add nothing beyond the concepts already introduced in the prior chapter. Any reader interested in making the additional calculations could easily do so with the assistance of a present-value table and a few more assumptions about when various amounts of cash were paid and received.

Rather than belabor any inaccuracies due to the time value of money, let us consider another possibility. In examining a proposal such as this, an astute investor might observe that either (or both) the projected revenues were unrealistically large or the anticipated expenses were unrealistically small. This absolutely essential analysis is what was suggested earlier as a realistic appraisal of the economic or financial projections presented in a prospectus. For example, the proposal suggested here might be one that would apply to a five-year lease. As noted, on page 233, an individual taxpayer is not entitled to an investment credit for leased property unless one of two conditions is satisfied. Assuming this investor did not manufacture the property, the fact that the investor was given the investment credit necessarily means that the initial lease could not extend beyond two-and-one-half years. What are the prospects for renewing the lease at the same favorable rate at the expiration of the first lease? Is this a property—a computer, for example—in which obsolescence is a major factor? If so, how must the economic projections be revised to be made realistic?

Alternative 2

Suppose, for example, that a careful review of industry statistics suggests that more realistic projections of cash revenues and expenses might look something like this:

	Year 1	Year 2	Year 3	Year 4	Year 5
Revenues					
Original	$40,000	$40,000	$40,000	$40,000	$50,000*
Revised	40,000	40,000	30,000	20,000	20,000†
Expenses					
Original	$30,000	$10,000	$10,000	$10,000	$10,000
Revised	30,000	15,000	20,000	20,000	20,000

* Assumes salvage value of $10,000.
† Assumes no salvage value.

How seriously would the economic viability of this investment be affected by these revised projections? The only good way to make that decision would be to make another "with" and "without" calculation, as illustrated in Table 9A–2 (on page 246). However, in this case, even some rough calculations would suggest the answer. Any investment that generates only $150,000 in cash receipts and requires $245,000 in cash expenses cannot be an economically viable investment, even if it does produce tax losses.

As illustrated in Table 9A–2, the revised five-year aggregate decrease in tax liability is $61,897 (i.e., from $693,390 without the investment to $631,493 with the tax shelter). At the same time, however, there is also a real aftertax cash loss of $53,103. At the end of five years, this taxpayer would have been far better off never to have purchased this tax shelter.

Even with realistic present-value calculations and an assumed interest on the taxes saved, the revised estimates suggest that this investment does not make good economic sense.

But who is to say which projection is correct? Maybe things will be even better than originally anticipated. Probably no projection can ever reflect the actual facts that one knows looking back, five years later. The assumptions built into this and every projection can never be entirely realistic. Very few taxpayers can predict their change in salary or business profits over a five-year period; very few taxpayers earning nearly $300,000 per year can correctly estimate their itemized deductions for the next five years; and very few wealthy taxpayers will make only one investment in a five-year period. Those are reasons that explain why taxpayers get nothing but carefully guarded statements when they seek competent tax advice. No one can predict the future with certainty; hence, all predictions—especially those that might carry financial liability for any gross inaccuracy—will be nothing more than hedged statements. Nevertheless, this is the best that anyone can do. In making investment decisions, estimate as best you can. But always remember that tax laws can never convert real economic losses into profits.

TABLE 9A–1
Alternative 1

	19x0	19x1	19x2	19x3	19x4	19x5	Five-year total Without	With
Gross income								
Salary	$300,000	$300,000	$300,000	$300,000	$300,000	$300,000		
Investment income	0	40,000	40,000	40,000	40,000	40,000		
Gain on disposition of investment	0	0	0	0	0	10,000		
Deductions								
Interest on note	0	10,000	8,000	6,000	4,000	2,000		
Investment expenses (cash)	0	30,000	10,000	10,000	10,000	10,000		
Depreciation	0	36,667	29,333	22,000	14,667	7,333		
Personal exemption deduction	2,000	2,000	2,000	2,000	2,000	2,000		
AGI	300,000	263,333	292,667	302,000	311,333	330,667		
Taxable income	298,000	261,333	290,667	300,000	309,333	328,667		
Tax preferences	0	14,667	7,333	0	0	0		
Personal service taxable income	298,000	246,666	283,334	298,000	298,073	298,186		
Excess investment interest	0	0	0	0	0	0		
Regular tax liability	138,678	123,279	136,478	140,078	146,597	160,108		
Minimum tax (on preferences)	0	0	0	0	0	0		
Total regular tax before credits	138,678	123,279	136,478	140,078	146,597	160,108		
Investment credit	0	7,333	0	0	0	0		
Total regular tax after credits	138,678	115,946	136,478	140,078	146,597	160,108	$693,390	$699,207
Alternative minimum tax	0	0	0	0	0	0		
Cash receipts	300,000	340,000	340,000	340,000	340,000	350,000		
Cash disbursements	138,678	185,946	174,478	176,078	180,597	192,108		
Aftertax cash	161,322	154,054	165,522	163,922	159,403	157,892	806,610	800,793

TABLE 9A-2
Alternative 2

	19x0	19x1	19x2	19x3	19x4	19x5	Five-year total Without	With
Gross income								
Salary	$300,000	$300,000	$300,000	$300,000	$300,000	$300,000		
Investment income	40,000	40,000	30,000	20,000	20,000	20,000		
Gain on disposition of investment	0	0	0	0	0	0		
Deductions								
Interest on note	0	10,000	8,000	6,000	4,000	2,000		
Investment expenses (cash)	0	30,000	15,000	20,000	20,000	20,000		
Depreciation	0	36,667	29,333	22,000	14,667	7,333		
Personal exemption deduction	2,000	2,000	2,000	2,000	2,000	2,000		
AGI	300,000	263,333	277,667	272,000	281,333	290,667		
Taxable income	298,000	261,333	275,667	270,000	279,333	288,667		
Tax preferences	0	14,667	7,333	0	0	0		
Personal service taxable income	298,000	246,666	275,667	270,000	279,333	288,667		
Excess investment interest	0	0	0	0	0	0		
Regular tax liability	138,678	123,279	127,512	124,678	129,345	134,012		
Minimum tax (on preferences)	0	0	0	0	0	0		
Total regular tax before credits	138,678	123,279	127,512	124,678	129,345	134,012		
Investment credit	0	7,333	0	0	0	0		
Total regular tax after credits	138,678	115,946	127,512	124,678	129,345	134,012	$693,390	$631,493
Alternative minimum tax	0	0	0	0	0	0		
Cash receipts	300,000	340,000	330,000	320,000	320,000	320,000		
Cash disbursements	138,678	185,946	170,512	170,678	173,345	176,012		
Aftertax cash	161,322	154,054	159,488	149,322	146,655	143,988	806,610	753,507

CHAPTER **10**

The Nontaxable Transactions

In Chapter 2, we noted that realization is a necessary condition to the recognition of a profit for income tax purposes. In addition, we observed that virtually any change in the form or the substance of a property or property right may be sufficient to constitute realization as far as the tax laws are concerned. This chapter examines a number of special statutory exceptions to the general rule that income must be recognized for tax purposes as soon as it has been realized. These special exceptions are commonly referred to as the nontaxable transactions.

The importance of the nontaxable transaction to business management derives from the fact that postponement of the date on which a tax is due allows a taxpayer to keep a larger amount of capital at work for a longer period of time. Other things being equal, this increases the absolute amount of capital that an entrepreneur can accumulate and manage over a lifetime. For example, if a taxpayer invested in a particular property that has substantially increased in value, the taxpayer may be reluctant to dispose of that investment, even if its present financial performance is unsatisfactory, and even if several better investment opportunities can be identified right now. If this taxpayer were to dispose of the initial investment, an immediate income tax would be payable on the entire unrealized gain, and only the aftertax proceeds would be available for reinvestment in the new opportunity.

To illustrate the importance of the tax factors to an investment decision, consider the situation in which an investor has a tax basis of $10,000 in an asset worth $110,000 at present and generating an annual $6,600 income (that is, a 6 percent return based on present worth). If the taxpayer is in a 60 percent marginal tax bracket, an income tax of approximately $60,000 would be payable if this asset were to create ordinary income on sale. (If the asset were a capital asset held for more than one year, the tax would be approximately $24,000.) After paying an ordinary income tax, the investor would have only $50,000 to reinvest in a new property. Accordingly, the new investment would have to provide an annual return of more than 13.2 percent before it could be considered preferable to the initial investment (that is, $6,600 divided by $50,000 equals 0.132). Investment opportunities that would yield a return of 8, 10, or even 12 percent would have to be rejected in favor of the extant 6 percent return simply because of the tax consequences. The increase required in the new return depends importantly on: (1) the absolute amount of the unrealized (or "paper") gain; (2) the marginal tax rate that would be applied to that gain; and (3) the present return on the investment. In general, the larger the amount of the paper gain, the higher the marginal tax rate, and the higher the present return, the greater the increase that will be required to make the change.

If one understands how important these tax factors are to investment decisions, it is easy to see why knowledgeable business managers and investors are most interested in the nontaxable exchange provisions of the Internal Revenue Code. Before we begin to examine any of the specifics of the several statutory provisions, however, we need to consider a few characteristics common to all of the nontaxable transactions.

Common Characteristics of Nontaxable Transactions

The detailed requirements of each of the several statutory provisions that authorize a nontaxable transaction vary substantially. Some of the provisions are mandatory if the prescribed conditions are met, whereas others are elective under all circumstances. Some apply to gains only; others apply equally to gains and losses. Some demand a direct exchange—that is, a barter transaction involving no cash—whereas others allow a taxpayer to pass through a temporary cash position, provided that reinvestment is completed within a prescribed period. In spite of the many differences, all nontaxable transactions commonly share a "boot" requirement, a transfer of tax basis, and a time constraint. In this first section of Chapter 10, we will consider these common characteristics so that the subsequent discussions of specific provisions can proceed with minimal attention to the general characteristics.

The Potential Need to Recognize Some Gain

The term *nontaxable transaction* is commonly used to refer both to partially taxable transactions and to transactions that are wholly free from any immediate income tax. To be entirely free of any income tax, a taxpayer involved in a nontaxable transaction generally cannot *receive* anything except *qualified property*. Observe that a taxpayer *may* be able to *give* nonqualifying property and still not be subject to tax; he or she simply cannot receive such property. Exactly which property will pass as a qualifying property varies from one nontaxable exchange to the next; in all nontaxable exchanges, however, it is common to refer to any nonqualified property as boot. Cash is, of course, the most frequently encountered form of boot. Finally, observe that the tax consequences to one party to a transaction need not be determined by the tax consequences to the other party to that transaction. In other words, a single transaction may create wholly taxable ordinary income for one party and be a wholly nontaxable transaction for the other party.

The fundamental concepts common to nontaxable exchanges that have been stated thus far can be illustrated by use of a simple diagram, as in Figure 10–1. Knowing nothing further about the transaction than what is shown in that illustration, we can safely make the following tax conclusions:

1. The transaction generally *cannot* be wholly tax-free to B because she received boot.
2. The transaction *may be* wholly tax-free to A, even though he gave boot.

FIGURE 10-1

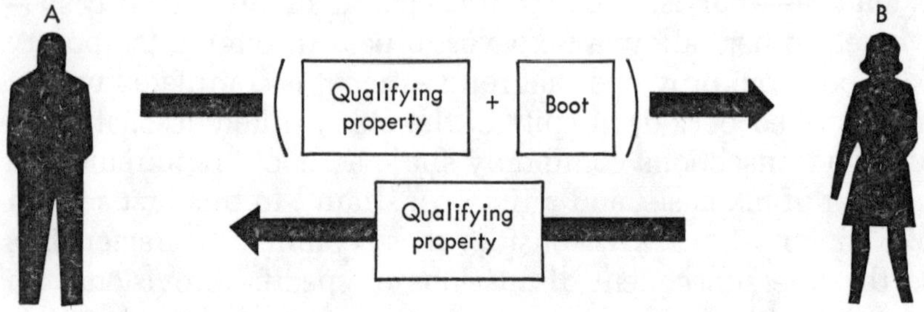

[Figure 10-1: A transfers Qualifying property + Boot to B; B transfers Qualifying property to A.]

3. A's tax consequences are not necessarily affected by B's.
4. B's tax consequences are not necessarily affected by A's.

The need to recognize taxable income in any transaction is always dependent upon the presence of a gain. To determine whether or not a gain is present, we must apply the tax rules stated beginning on page 106. Although the rules stated there were worded in terms of capital assets, they are equally applicable to all assets. A taxable profit is simply the difference between (a) the fair market value (FMV) of everything received in a transaction and (b) the adjusted tax basis of everything given up in that same transaction. No taxpayer ever needs to recognize for income tax purposes more gain than that realized. To give meaning to these sentences, let us return to our simple diagram and add some assumed values to that illustration, as shown in Figure 10-2. In this modified illustration, A's gain realized is $6,000; that is, $20,000 in value was received (we call this the "amount realized") and $14,000 in tax basis was given up ($10,000 in qualifying property and

FIGURE 10-2

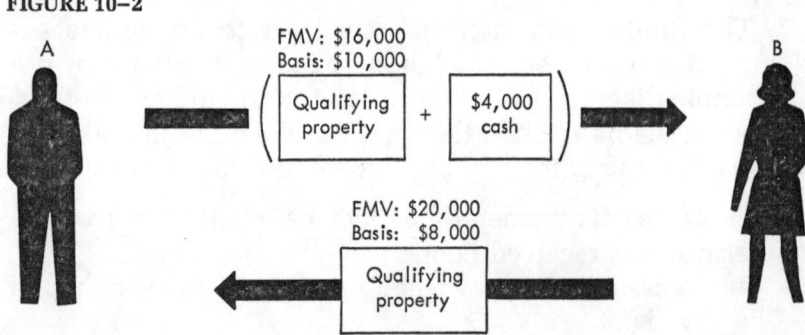

$4,000 in cash); hence, $20,000 − $14,000 = $6,000. By applying the same determination method, we find that B's realized gain is $12,000 (that is, $20,000 − $8,000). If this particular transaction qualifies under one of the special statutory provisions that will be examined later in this chapter, it means that A would *not have to recognize any of the $6,000 gain that he had realized*. If the same transaction also qualifies as a nontaxable exchange for B, it means that B *must recognize $4,000 of the $12,000 gain that she realized* because she received the boot.

Observe again, however, that a taxpayer need never recognize more gain than that realized. In other words, if, in this transaction, B's adjusted tax basis in the property given to A had been $18,000 instead of $8,000, then B's realized and recognized gain is reduced to $2,000 notwithstanding the fact that B received $4,000 cash. Although this rule is often confusing to the uninitiated taxpayer first encountering the nontaxable exchange rules, the problem is really one of being caught up in words rather than in complexity. Note what would have happened if B had simply sold her qualifying property to someone for $20,000 cash. If her basis were $18,000, she would report only a $2,000 taxable income. Why, then, should the tax answer be different if, instead of selling the property for cash, a taxpayer trades it for another property plus cash? Obviously it should not be different—and that is what the rule stated accomplishes. The fact that more cash than gain may be realized in an exchange simply means that the taxpayer is getting a partial return of capital as well as realizing a profit on the exchange.

Transfer of Basis

The apparent intent of the law in all nontaxable exchanges is to provide for only a postponement of an income tax rather than a permanent forgiveness of that tax. The postponement is accomplished through related provisions, which require that a taxpayer assume a "carry-over" tax basis in any property acquired in a nontaxable exchange. The law assumes that sooner or later the taxpayer will dispose of any property in a taxable transaction and will, at that time, report as taxable income the difference between the value received and the basis carried over from the prior property. In the case of an individual taxpayer, this may be an invalid assumption since individuals often die with appreciated property, and neither they nor their heirs would have to recognize the deferred gain. Thus, if a taxpayer can exchange properties in only qualified nontaxable exchanges until the time of death, everyone will effectively escape income taxation on predeath appreciation in value. The fresh-start basis rules for inherited property cause the "old" gain to disappear if the property is sold by the deceased taxpayer's heir or devisee immediately after the decedant's death. If a taxable disposition is made before the taxpayer's death, the carry-over basis rule of the nontaxable exchange ensures the recognition of the "correct" amount of gain or loss on the several transactions combined.

To demonstrate the effect of the carryover basis rules, let us return to the facts assumed in connection with Figure 10–1. If this transaction qualifies under one of the nontaxable exchange provisions of the code for both A and B, we can determine that A's tax basis in the property received would be $14,000. That is, A would take as his tax basis the basis he had in the property given up in this nontaxable transaction. Because he had $10,000 adjusted basis in the qualifying property given to B, and because he gave B an additional $4,000 in cash (and cash always has a tax basis equal to its face value), A's adjusted basis in the property received is deemed to be $14,000. B's tax basis is somewhat more difficult to determine.

Remember that, as the problem was originally worded, B was required to recognize $4,000 of the $12,000 gain realized in this exchange. This means that B must report on her next tax return an additional taxable income of $4,000 and that she must pay an income tax on that amount. Because B has to recognize that income and pay that tax, she also obtains the right to increase her tax basis in the property received by that same amount. In other words, B can increase her tax basis from $8,000 to $12,000. However, B must also divide the new and larger tax basis between the boot (cash) and the qualifying asset received in the transaction. The law always assumes that cash has a basis equal to its face value; hence B must allocate $4,000 in basis to the cash, leaving her with a continuing $8,000 basis in the new property acquired in the exchange.

The reasonableness of the carry-over basis rules can be demonstrated by further assuming that each taxpayer sold the newly acquired property shortly after completing the exchange. If there were no further change in the value of any properties, this would mean that A could sell his property for $20,000. Since A's carry-over basis is $14,000, he would have to recognize income of $6,000 at the time of the sale. Because A did not recognize any of the $6,000 gain realized at the time of the initial exchange, this carry-over of basis yields a correct result, considering the two transactions together. If there were no further changes in value, B would have to recognize $8,000 on any subsequent sale. This again is a correct solution, considering both exchanges, since B initially recognized $4,000 of the $12,000 gain realized at the time of the first exchange and no further change in values transpired before the second sale.

In some circumstances, it becomes rather difficult to determine the adjusted basis of property acquired in a nontaxable exchange, especially if a single exchange involves both qualified and nonqualified property and the nonqualified property is something other than cash. In general, however, a taxpayer can most easily determine a correct adjusted tax basis for property acquired in a nontaxable transaction by use of the following formula:

> Fair market value of noncash property received minus gain realized but *not* recognized on the exchange equals the adjusted basis of the property received.

Returning to our earlier illustration and applying the above formula to each taxpayer, we can confirm our prior calculations as follows:

	Taxpayer A	Taxpayer B
Fair market value of noncash property received	$20,000	$16,000
Less gain not recognized on the exchange	6,000	8,000
Adjusted basis of property received	$14,000	$ 8,000

These results are consistent with the determinations made earlier.

If the property involved in a nontaxable transaction is a capital asset, it is sometimes important to determine a date basis as well as a cost basis because holding period requirements may determine how a gain is taxed. For all capital assets acquired in a nontaxable exchange, the law usually provides that the taxpayer can "tack" together the holding periods. Thus, for two assets, if a taxpayer held the original capital asset for 4 months and 10 days and the subsequent capital asset for 6 months and 8 days, and the second asset was acquired in a nontaxable transaction, the taxpayer would be assumed to have held the second asset for a total of 10 months and 18 days at the time of the taxable disposition.

Time Constraints

Most of the nontaxable exchange provisions require that a taxpayer go directly from one investment into a second investment in a barter transaction. A few nontaxable exchange provisions, however, allow a taxpayer to move indirectly from one investment, through a temporary cash state, into a second investment, and still avoid the recognition of gain in the interim. In these provisions, the code stipulates a maximum period for the reinvestment. If the taxpayer does not meet the time requirements, the gain or loss following the traditional rules must then be recognized. The exact time requirements stipulated for each provision will be noted, along with other details, in the next section of this chapter.

Specific Nontaxable Exchange Provisions

The most important nontaxable exchange provisions in the code, in terms of their impact on business behavior, are those dealing with transactions between corporations and corporate shareholders. These are among the most complex provisions in the entire tax law. Consequently, the discussion that follows must be superficial in coverage. Hopefully, this brief discussion will permit the reader to appreciate the general constraints that are operative, as well as the golden opportunities that are available. In addition to examining several corporation–corporate shareholder transactions, we will examine the nontaxable exchange provisions covering productive-use and investment properties; involuntary conversions from condemnation proceedings, fire, storm, shipwreck, and other casualties; sales of the taxpayer's primary residence; and investments in low-income housing.

Exchange of Productive-Use or Investment Properties

Code Section 1031 provides that a taxpayer will not recognize taxable gain or loss on the exchange of "property held for productive use or investment in trade or business or for investment (not including stock in trade or other property held primarily for sale, nor stocks, bonds, notes, choses in action, certificates of trust or beneficial interest, or other securities or evidence of indebtedness or interest) . . . solely for property of a like kind to be held either for productive use in trade or business or for investment." The reader should observe that this provision (1) requires a direct exchange before it is operative, (2) applies equally to gains and losses, and (3) is mandatory, not elective. In other words, if a taxpayer trades one qualifying property for another, the tax law provides that he or she cannot simply recognize gain or loss by means of the usual rules and that the carry-over basis rules will automatically apply. This observation is often important in loss situations: If a taxpayer desires to recognize a tax-deductible ("paper") loss on a productive-use or investment property, it is imperative that he or she sell the property in one transaction and purchase the desired property in a second transaction. If the taxpayer directly trades for the second property, any loss will go unrecognized and the higher tax basis of the old property will be carried forward in the new property.

Words and phrases such as *productive use, investment, trade or business, held primarily for sale, solely,* and *like kind* create obvious definitional problems in applying this code section. Perhaps our first critical observation should be to note that, even though the section purports to deal with investment properties, the most common forms of investment properties are specifically ruled out of consideration by the parenthetic restrictions. That is, stocks, bonds, notes, and securities cannot be treated as investment properties for purposes of this section. If an investor were to directly exchange 100 shares of General Motors common stock for shares with an equivalent value in another corporation, Section 1031 would *not* be authority to defer the income tax recognition of any paper gain or loss that had accumulated between the date of purchase and the date of the exchange. Indeed, under these circumstances, the taxpayer would have to report the gain or loss realized just as if the GMC shares had been sold for cash and the other corporation's stock was subsequently purchased for cash.

Section 1031 does apply to almost all real and depreciable properties used in a trade or business, as well as to other investments. It applies, for example, to such assets as machinery and equipment, factory buildings, warehouses, and parking lots used in a trade or business, as well as to farmlands and speculative investments in apartment houses, oil wells, and art objects. The section would not be applicable to an exchange of a personal residence or a private automobile because these are neither investment nor productive-use properties. Even though the portion of the code provision quoted earlier would seem to require that there be no boot in a qualifying Section 1031 exchange—that is, the quoted portion requires that the exchange be *solely* for property of a like kind—other sections of the code modify the apparent stringency of this rule and provide that the recipient of boot must report as taxable income the lesser of the gain realized or the boot received.

The most troublesome qualification in Section 1031 has proved to be the like-kind requirement. At present, a taxpayer can exchange almost any form of productive-use or investment property for any other form of productive-use or investment property and still qualify the exchange as a nontaxable transaction so long as either both properties are real properties or both are personal (nonreal) properties. It does not seem to change the tax consequences if one property is developed real estate and the other is undeveloped, or if one property is used in a business and the other is held as an investment. Thus, the exchange of undeveloped ranchland for a midtown apartment building would qualify as a nontaxable transaction (realty for realty), whereas the exchange of an airplane for an apartment building would not qualify (personalty for realty). The exchange of an airplane for apartment furnishings (personalty for personalty) could qualify so long as both were either used in a trade or business or held as an investment. One major exception to the general rule just stated was codified in the 1969 Tax

Reform Act. That statutory change specifically disallows the exchange of livestock of different sexes from like-kind treatment under Section 1031.

In many Section 1031 exchanges, only one party to the exchange is affected by the existence of the nontaxable exchange rules. For example, if a car used entirely for business is traded for a new model through an automobile dealer, only the taxpayer giving up the old car and acquiring a new one is affected by the nontaxable exchange provisions. Both the used and the new car would constitute inventory (or "stock-in-trade") for the auto dealer, and therefore the exchange could not be even partially nontaxable for the dealer. On the other hand, if a dentist and a farmer were to exchange a city duplex (which the dentist had owned as an investment) for some farmland (which the farmer had been tilling), the nontaxable exchange provisions would apply to both taxpayers involved in the exchange. Incidentally, this provision is equally applicable to individual, corporate, and fiduciary taxpayers.

To illustrate how this section might apply to an actual situation, let us review the tax results that would accompany an exchange of 100 acres of mountainous timberland owned by ABC Corporation for a large corner lot in Silver City owned as an investment by Tom Jones, a local attorney. Assume that both ABC and Jones agree that the fair market value of the timber tract is $200 per acre and that the city lot is worth $30,000. To complicate matters a little more, let us also assume that Jones has an outstanding mortgage of $18,000 on his lot and that ABC Corporation agrees to assume that mortgage. Under these assumptions, Jones's interest in the city lot is currently worth only $12,000, whereas the timberland is worth the full $20,000; thus, Jones would be expected to give ABC Corporation $8,000 boot. Before we can proceed to determine the tax results, we must know what adjusted basis each taxpayer has in the property traded. Let us assume that Jones's basis in the city lot is $21,000 and that ABC Corporation's basis in the timberland is $3,000.

The determination of the tax consequences in nontaxable exchanges is often facilitated by a simple visual presentation of all critical facts. In order to restate the facts of this illustration, let us utilize Figure 10–3, a diagram similar to the one intro-

FIGURE 10-3

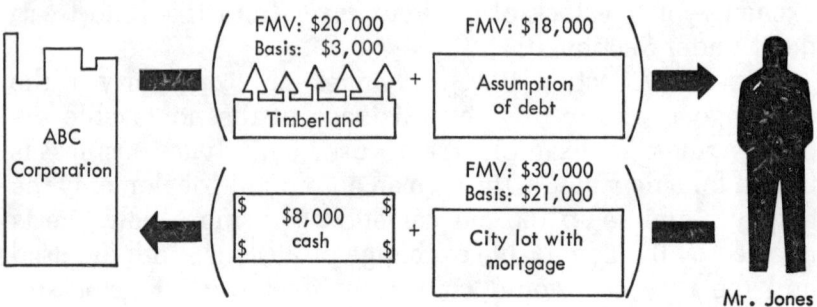

duced earlier in this chapter. The introduction of a mortgage is the only new addition to the former diagram. For purposes of a like-kind exchange, the assumption of a mortgage is tantamount to giving the debt-relieved taxpayer an equivalent sum of cash. In this illustration, therefore, ABC's assumption of Jones's $18,000 mortgage will be treated just as if ABC Corporation had paid Jones $18,000 cash.

The pertinent tax results are summarized in the accompanying table. Because the transfer of the $18,000 mortgage from Jones to ABC is treated just like an equivalent amount of cash, Jones must recognize his entire $9,000 gain in the period he makes this exchange. Since Jones must recognize his entire gain realized, his basis in the property received becomes its fair market value, or $20,000.

For ABC Corporation
Amount realized ($30,000 lot plus $8,000 cash) $38,000
    Less adjusted basis given ($3,000 in land plus $18,000 in debt) 21,000
    Gain realized on the exchange $17,000
    Less gain recognized (due to receipt of $8,000 cash boot) 8,000
    Gain realized but not recognized .... $ 9,000

Fair market value of noncash property received $30,000
    Less gain realized but not recognized 9,000
    Adjusted tax basis in city lot received $21,000

For Tom Jones
Amount realized ($20,000 land plus $18,000 debt transferred) $38,000
    Less adjusted basis given ($21,000 lot plus $8,000 cash) 29,000
    Gain realized on the exchange .... $ 9,000

Even though the reader may feel uncertain of several of the calculations, he or she should understand the few really basic tax results demonstrated in this illustration: first, that the transfer of a mortgage or other debt is treated as if the debtor had received an equivalent sum of cash in the exchange and used that sum to pay any prior obligation; second, that even though both taxpayers in this transaction exchanged qualifying property, the effect of Section 1031 applied to only one party because the amount of boot received by the other party was larger than the gain realized; third, that a taxpayer receiving a partial tax deferral because of a nontaxable exchange provision has a substitute (or carry-over) basis in the property received. In this illustration, ABC's tax basis in the city lot becomes $21,000, which represents a carry-over of the former basis ABC had in the timberland plus an additional $18,000 in basis, which it obtained by assuming the mortgage against the city lot. As this illustration demonstrates, the economic importance of the right to engage in a nontaxable exchange varies from one situation to the next. Other things being equal, the greater the amount of the unrealized gain, the more important it is for a taxpayer to arrange a nontaxable transaction.

Although this issue is by no means settled as we go to press, the Ninth Circuit Court of Appeals in 1979 held, in *Starker*, that a Section 1031 exchange need *not* be a simultaneous exchange. In that case, a taxpayer transferred appreciated timberland to another taxpayer but deferred receipt of the like-kind property because it had not yet been identified. In fact, the taxpayer took three years to locate all the desired properties needed to complete this exchange. Most important, the taxpayer transferring the timberland had only the *unsecured* promise of the other party to the transaction until all details of the transfers were completed some three years later. No segregation of funds was made to assure that the transferee would be able to honor the "exchange value credit account" established in the interim period. Although this recent decision is contrary to the traditional wisdom about Section 1031, it does make economic sense and does have a counterpart in tax-free mergers and other corporate acquisitions. In the latter transactions, it is commonplace for the final exchange ratio to be settled nearly five years after the initial stock exchange takes place.

Nontaxable Transactions between a Corporation and Its Shareholders

Transactions between a closely held corporation and its stockholders are often of more significance in terms of legal form than they are in terms of economic substance. For example, when a taxpayer incorporates a business that has been operated for a number of years as a sole proprietorship, the act of incorporation is of very little economic importance to anyone so long as all of the new corporation's stock is issued to the former proprietor. Under these circumstances, it seems entirely reasonable to suspend the usual rules requiring that any unrealized gains or losses be recognized for income tax purposes on the date of incorporation. The rationale for extending nontaxable exchange benefits to transactions between giant corporations and minority shareholders is much more difficult to explain. Nevertheless, under the proper circumstances, both classes of transactions can be brought within the purview of the nontaxable transaction rules.

Forming a corporation. Code Section 351 provides that no gain or loss shall be recognized for income tax purposes if one or more persons transfer property to a corporation solely in exchange for the stock or securities of that corporation *and* the person or persons transferring the property own 80 percent or more of the voting control of the corporation after the transfer. The importance of this provision is that it allows taxpayers to create new corporations without immediate tax consequences as long as those who transfer property to the new corporation own 80 percent of the corporation's stock after the transfer and receive no boot. Once again, if all the conditions are satisfied, this tax result will follow whether the taxpayer wants it to or not. If a taxpayer desires to engage in a taxable transaction, there are three options: (1) the taxpayer can make certain that the transaction is arranged as a sale rather than as an exchange of property for stock and/or securities; (2) the taxpayer can make certain that sufficient boot is distributed to guarantee the right to recognize a gain that he or she desires to recognize; or (3) the taxpayer can make certain that the transferors of property own less than 80 percent of the transferee corporation's stock.

In any exchange to which Section 351 applies, the usual carry-over basis rules also apply. Observe, however, that the effect of a nontaxable transfer to a corporation is to double the aggregate tax basis without incurring any tax. The transferors of property in a wholly nontaxable Section 351 transaction will transfer their former tax basis in the property transferred to the new stock or securities received; at the same time, the corporate transferee also acquires that same tax basis in the properties that it receives. This doubling of basis can be illustrated simply, as in Figure 10–4, in a before-and-after comparison.

FIGURE 10–4

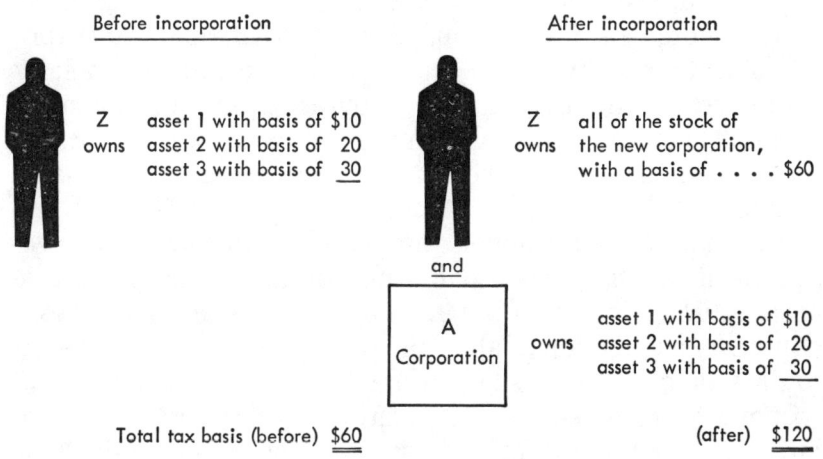

Under some circumstances, a taxpayer is well advised to attempt a nontaxable incorporation; under other circumstances, a taxable one might be preferred. In the previous illustration, for example, taxpayer Z might prefer to purchase stock in corporation A for cash if asset 1 were a plot of undeveloped land with a tax basis of $10,000 and a fair market value of $310,000. After taxpayer Z purchases the stock for cash, corporation A might subsequently purchase taxpayer Z's land for $310,000. If the form of these two transactions can be sustained, taxpayer Z may assure the right to report a $300,000 capital gain on the sale of the land (unless such a gain is precluded by a related-party sale rule, such as that contained in Section 1239, discussed on page 134. If taxpayer Z had transferred the low-basis land into the corporation and the corporation had proceeded to develop that land, the entire profit recognized by corporation A—including the $300,000 pretransfer appreciation in value—would have to be reported as ordinary income. As suggested in Chapter 6, the desirable tax result can usually be achieved, but only if the taxpayer makes each move very carefully.

Reorganizing a corporation. The officers of an extant corporation sometimes decide that the corporation can achieve its objectives better if it can be reorganized in some way. For example, the corporate officers may decide to divide one corporation into two or more corporate entities in order to allow each to pursue a different business. Alternatively, the corporate officers may try to add economic strength to a financially distressed corporate organization by arranging a reorganization that would decrease the amount of outstanding debt and increase the amount of the stockholders' equity by the same amount. Under still other circumstances, the officers of one corporation may desire to acquire another corporate organization or all of its assets. Such a corporate acquisition can be accomplished in any of several ways—by merger, by consolidation, by acquisition of all of the second corporation's operating assets, or by acquisition of sufficient stock of the second corporation to make that corporation a subsidiary of the acquiring corporation. Each of these corporate reorganizations can be accomplished as a nontaxable transaction if all parties to the transaction fully comply with the intricate rules of Subchapter C of the Internal Revenue Code.

The general requirements of the corporate reorganization provisions follow the characteristics common to all nontaxable exchanges described earlier in this chapter, except for the fact that the corporate reorganization provisions usually apply to both parties to the transaction if they apply to either one. If the reorganization is to be accomplished wholly tax-free, the parties to the reorganization usually can exchange only qualifying property. A limited amount of boot is allowed in certain corporate reorganizations, but not in all of them. In the nontaxable reorganizations, the only form of qualifying property is stock or securities in corporations that are party to the reorganization.

To demonstrate the importance of the corporate reorganization provisions, let us consider the case of an assumed Adam Smith, who owns 100 percent of the stock of Smith Industries, Incorporated. Smith, who is approaching retirement age, has decided to dispose of his interest in Smith Industries. Initially, Smith thought that he might sell his entire interest to a local investor group, which had expressed an interest in his company. Smith discovered, however, that such a sale would be almost prohibitively expensive in terms of the income tax. He had formed his corporation many years ago with invested capital of $100,000. During the intervening years, this small corporation had grown, until today it is worth in excess of $5 million. If Smith were to sell his stock, he would trigger an immediate income tax of something like $1.4 million, leaving him with $3.6 million to reinvest. Instead of selling, therefore, Smith agrees to exchange all of his stock in Smith Industries for stock in Giant Conglomerate Corporation of America. If everything is properly arranged, this means that the exchange will proceed without tax consequences to Adam Smith, Smith Industries, or Giant Conglomerate Corporation. This result will be possible even if Smith ends up owning only, say, 1 or 2 percent of the outstanding stock of Giant, and even if Smith Industries constitutes only a small part of Giant Conglomerate Corporation. In this situation, the economic transformation achieved by Adam Smith is much more than one of legal form alone. Before the nontaxable exchange, Smith owned and operated his own business; after the exchange, he owns a small interest in a giant enterprise engaged in a multitude of diverse economic endeavors. Even though the realization of economic gain in this illustration is as complete as it can ever possibly be, the tax laws authorize the total deferral of any income tax if all of the code requirements are met. In this area even the tax experts fear to tread alone. Before a corporate reorganization is finalized, most tax experts and corporate officers will insist upon an advance ruling on all tax consequences by the Internal Revenue Service. If the IRS issues an adverse ruling, or if it will issue no ruling, the original reorganization plans are almost invariably called back and modified or dropped. The tax consequences are often so substantial for so many people that no corporate officers or tax advisers are willing to risk the potential liability of proceeding in the face of an adverse ruling, even if they are of the opinion that the ruling is incorrect and would not be upheld by a court.

The fact that corporate reorganizations can proceed as nontaxable exchanges has had a tremendous impact on our economy. In the 1960s, in particular, corporate stocks and securities almost became a second form of money. Stocks and securities were as good as money only because they could, under the right circumstances, be exchanged tax-free. Empires were built, and often lost, through corporate mergers and acquisitions alone. Very little of this merger activity would have been possible had the tax laws not provided nontaxable exchange opportunities. If a corporation or its shareholders had to recognize all prior appreciation in value for income tax purposes before proceeding with a corporate reorganization, reorganizations would be economically impractical.

The reader should now be in a position to understand why, on previous occasions, the author could state that the double tax often was not a major consideration in the life cycle of the closely held corporation. In most closely held corporations, the owners currently extract (with only a personal income tax) whatever amount of income they need for personal consumption in the form of salaries, interest, and rents during their years of active interest in corporate affairs. All corporate income in excess of the owners' personal needs may be accumulated within the corporate shell, where it is expanded through new and larger business investments. If the owner does not die sooner, and if he or she does not desire the control of the corporation to pass to another member of the family, the owner typically allows the firm to be reorganized as part of a larger venture in a nontaxable transaction. Finally, then, the stock of either the original company or of the merged organization is passed to heirs or devisees who inherit the property with a basis equal to the stock's value on the date of the decedent's death. Thus the accumulated corporate income is never "realized" by the family; instead, the personal income tax has been permanently deferred. Because corporate (business) reorganizations are of major importance, the next chapter will consider the pertinent tax factors in detail.

Liquidating a corporation. The liquidation of a corporation typically can be accomplished almost tax-free as far as the corporate entity is concerned, but under most circumstances a liquidation necessitates the recognition of taxable gain or loss on the part of the recipient shareholders. The need of the shareholder to recognize some gain on the liquidation of a corporation means, quite obviously, that it is often much more expensive with regard to taxes to get out of a corporate form of business organization than it is to get into it. For this reason, a taxpayer should never take lightly a decision to incorporate. The inconsistency of the tax rules can be demonstrated simply, as in Figure 10–5. The gain or loss realized by the stockholders

FIGURE 10–5

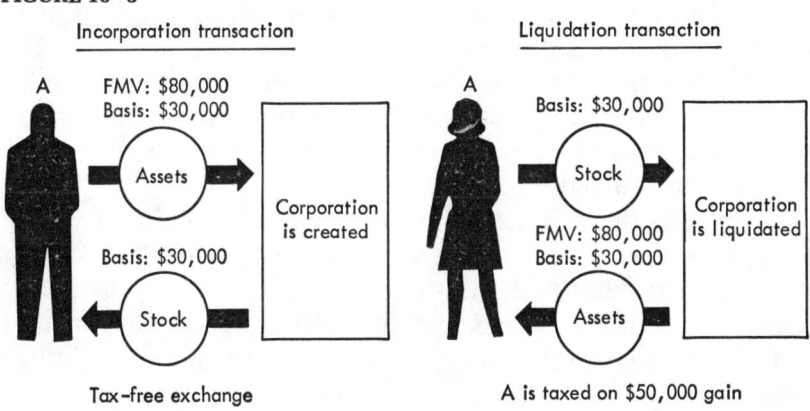

on the liquidation of the corporation can be classified either as ordinary income or capital gain. If the corporation is not a collapsible corporation, the gain realized by the shareholders will generally be classified as a capital gain. Incidentally, the corporation being liquidated may have to recapture depreciation it previously claimed when it is liquidated; that is, it must recognize as ordinary income the amount of ordinary income that it would have recognized had it sold the depreciable assets in an arm's-length transaction.

Involuntary Conversions

If a taxpayer's property is involuntarily converted into cash or other property by action of a condemnation proceeding, a casualty, or a theft, the taxpayer is usually free to treat the involuntary conversion as a nontaxable transaction as long as it resulted in a gain *and* the taxpayer reinvests the proceeds received in a similar property within a prescribed period. The proceeds received in an involuntary conversion are typically either a condemnation award or insurance proceeds, both of which are commonly paid in cash. Section 1033 gives the taxpayer an option: He or she is free to report the gain realized on an involuntary conversion under the usual tax rules if it is desirable to do so; if not, the gain may be treated as the gain realized on a nontaxable exchange if the destroyed property is replaced with a similar property within two years after the end of the year in which the gain was realized. If the taxpayer does not reinvest the entire proceeds in a similar property, the amount retained is treated as boot. Interestingly, the option of treating an involuntary conversion as a nontaxable transaction does not extend to losses; these must be reported and deducted in the year realized.

To illustrate the tax rules applicable to involuntary conversions, assume that a taxpayer had the four assets, listed in the accompanying table, destroyed by fire, that the insurance company made reimbursements in the amounts indicated, and that the taxpayer reinvested the amounts shown in a similar property within the prescribed period.

Asset	Adjusted basis	Insurance proceeds	Amount reinvested
1	$10,000	$15,000	$17,000
2	20,000	26,000	24,000
3	30,000	37,000	28,000
4	40,000	30,000	n.a.

The gain realized on asset 1 is, of course, $5,000 ($15,000 − $10,000). If the taxpayer elects, however, there is no need to recognize any of the $5,000 gain realized because all of the insurance proceeds, and more, were reinvested in a similar property. Assuming that the taxpayer elects not to recognize the gain realized, the basis in the replacement property will be $12,000—that is, a carryover basis of $10,000 from old asset 1 plus the extra $2,000 cash ($17,000 reinvested minus $15,000 insurance proceeds) invested in the similar property.

The gain realized on asset 2 is $6,000 ($26,000 − $20,000). Because the taxpayer retained $2,000 of the insurance proceeds ($26,000 received − $24,000 reinvested), $2,000 of the $6,000 gain realized must be recognized. The taxpayer may, however, elect to defer recognition of the remaining $4,000 gain realized. Assuming that the taxpayer does elect to defer recognition of that $4,000, the basis in the replacement property will be $20,000 ($24,000 fair market value of the new property less $4,000 gain not recognized).

The gain realized on asset 3 is $7,000 ($37,000 − $30,000). Because the taxpayer invested only $28,000 in the replacement property—that is, $9,000 in cash was retained—the entire gain of $7,000 must be recognized. The basis of the new property then becomes its cost, $28,000.

The involuntary conversion of asset 4 resulted in a $10,000 loss. The taxpayer has no option but to report that loss in the year of the involuntary conversion. It is immaterial whether the taxpayer reinvests any or all of the insurance proceeds from asset 4; the loss must be recognized immediately. If replacement is made, the basis of any new property will be its cost.

Surprisingly, perhaps, a most difficult aspect of applying Section 1033 has been in the determination of what constitutes a qualifying replacement property. The code requires only that it be "similar or related in service or use" to the property destroyed. The IRS and the courts have interpreted the statutory requirement rather narrowly. If the taxpayer desires to exercise the right to treat any gain from an involuntary conversion as a deferred gain, great caution must be taken in selecting replacement properties. Because the law is constantly changing in this regard, no attempt will be made to summarize the kinds of replacements that will satisfy each of the many courts in the various jurisdictions. The need for expert assistance in making replacement investments is obvious.

Residence Sales

If a taxpayer sells his or her primary residence at a gain, the usual rules would require that the gain realized be reported immediately as a capital gain. If a taxpayer sells his or her primary residence at a loss, the usual rules deny the right to any deduction since the residence is a purely personal property. Section 1034 of the code provides the taxpayer with some relief from the usual rules, but only if he or she sells a primary residence at a gain.

Section 1034 in effect allows a taxpayer 18 months (before or after a sale) during which he or she must replace a former primary residence with another one if the recognition of any gain realized on the sale of a former home is to be deferred. If a taxpayer builds a new home, the replacement period is extended to 24 months. Within these prescribed periods, a taxpayer may replace any form of primary residence with any other form and still avoid recognition of gain. For example, if both were in fact the taxpayer's primary residence, he or she could move from a ketch-rigged sailboat to a mobile home, or from a condominium to a country estate, and avoid the recognition of any gain on the sale of the former home. This provision is also worded to be mandatory if the conditions are satisfied. If a taxpayer desires to recognize the gain realized on the sale of a former home, he or she must either reinvest a sufficiently small amount in the new home or remain without a purchased home for longer than the prescribed time period.

If the taxpayer does not reinvest the entire cash proceeds from the sale of the former residence in a new home, any excess cash retained is again treated like boot. In this regard, the rules applicable to involuntary conversions are very much like the rules applicable to sales of a primary residence. To demonstrate their comparability, let us assume numbers with residence sales that are identical to the numbers assumed earlier for involuntary conversions, and then compare the tax results of the two situations. (Obviously, these dollar amounts are not realistic, but the principle would not change just because larger numbers were used.)

Case	Adjusted basis of old home	Amount realized on sale of old home	Cost of new residence
1	$10,000	$15,000	$17,000
2	20,000	26,000	24,000
3	30,000	37,000	28,000
4	40,000	30,000	n.a.

Because the analysis of the tax results is so similar to that of the earlier discussion, it will not be repeated here. In summary form, the critical tax results of each of the above "cases," assuming that all time requirements are satisfied, are shown in the table below.

Case	Gain (or loss) realized on sale of old home	Gain (or loss) recognized on sale of old home	Adjusted tax basis of new home
1	$ 5,000	$ 0	$12,000
2	6,000	2,000	20,000
3	7,000	7,000	28,000
4	(10,000)	0	n.a.

The only difference between the tax results for involuntary conversions and for residence sales concerns case 4. There, because the loss realized on the sale of a personal asset is not deductible, the tax result differs from the case of the involuntary conversion—in which instance a tax deduction is always authorized.

Special rules are applicable to residence sales made by taxpayers who are 55 years of age or older. The special rules grant the senior citizen the right to *exclude* the first $100,000 of gain realized on the sale of a primary residence, in addition to the more general right to treat the sale of a residence, as a nontaxable transaction if gain is realized and a replacement is made on a timely basis. For tax-planning purposes, it is important that every taxpayer realize that he or she may be entitled to a special $100,000 *exclusion* if the primary residence is not sold until after the taxpayer's 55th birthday. It would be especially unfortunate if a taxpayer sold a primary residence at a sizable gain shortly before becoming eligible for that special exclusion. Because it is of limited applicability, however, we will not discuss the details of that special provision here. Readers who are approaching 55 years of age, and who own homes that have appreciated in value, should be especially careful in timing their home sales wisely.

Low-Income Housing

Another special provision is contained in Section 1039, which allows a taxpayer one year in which to reinvest proceeds from the sale of certain low-income housing, and thereby avoid the recognition of gain. Before the recognition of the entire gain can be postponed, the sale must be made to a qualified party (generally an occupant or tenant), the sale must be approved by the secretary of housing and urban development, and the entire proceeds from the sale must be reinvested in another qualified housing project. Retention of any portion of the sales proceeds will be treated as boot and cause the recognition of some portion of the gain realized.

In Chapter 8, we noted the special 60-month amortization provision, which can also be applied to investments in certain low-income housing. The opportunity to obtain a quick recovery of an initial investment, plus the right to obtain a tax-free rollover of the proceeds realized on the sale of such an investment, may increase investments in low-income housing. Obviously, that was the hope and intent of Congress. The only major tax stumbling block that remains for the investor is the fact that the gain realized on a disposition that cannot be treated as a nontaxable transaction is likely to be classified as ordinary income under Section 1250, at least to the extent of any excess of rapid depreciation claimed over the "would-be" straight-line depreciation on the same property. The only way the investor can convert the entire gain into long-term capital gain is through retention of an investment in low-income housing for a period of 16 years and 8 months or longer or by claiming straight-line depreciation. Retention of such an investment for more than ten years guarantees some capital gain, assuming that the final sale results in a gain rather than a loss. The greater the time period beyond ten years, the larger the ratio of capital gain to ordinary income that can be reported. If the taxpayer utilizes the tax-free rollover of Section 1039, the holding period for the initial investment will add to each subsequent reinvestment, but only for the initial amount invested. If a taxpayer is willing to be committed to a long-range program of investments in low-income housing, the tax laws may serve to increase the probabilities that such investments will be profitable.

Other Nontaxable Exchanges

This discussion does not exhaust all of the nontaxable exchange provisions in the code. Section 1035, for example, authorizes a tax-free exchange of insurance policies under prescribed conditions. Section 1036 authorizes a nontaxable exchange of stock for other stock in the same corporation (which guarantees the tax-free character of any stock split). And Section 1037 authorizes the reacquisition of real property on a tax-free basis under certain circumstances. These and other nontaxable exchange provisions will not be discussed here, either because they are of limited applicability or because they are of minimal importance to most tax-planning opportunities. In the few remaining pages of this chapter, we will consider briefly several planning considerations of more general importance.

Planning Considerations in Nontaxable Transactions

Many taxpayers seem to be remotely aware of the nontaxable exchange provisions, and yet they seem to take inadequate advantage of them. Perhaps their reluctance is attributable to some misunderstanding of the more practical aspects of completing a nontaxable exchange successfully. For example, the taxpayer may believe that he or she must personally locate another investor who is willing to trade properties before it is possible to successfully engage in a tax-free rollover of a productive use or investment property. If that belief were factually correct, there would indeed be few meaningful tax opportunities available. Fortunately, many tax-free exchanges can be arranged through the use of a property broker in what is known as a three-cornered exchange.

Three-Cornered Exchanges

A taxpayer who owns a substantially appreciated productive-use of investment property should generally spend more time and effort locating a desirable replacement property, and less time and effort locating a potential buyer for the property to be exchanged, if he or she wants to maximize the tax opportunity available. After the taxpayer has located an appropriate replacement property, the taxpayer should proceed to contact a property broker to play the necessary intermediary role in a tax-free exchange. That is, the taxpayer requests the broker to purchase the property that the taxpayer wants to acquire, and following such a purchase by the broker, the taxpayer and the broker exchange properties. This, of course, leaves the broker with the appreciated property that the taxpayer wanted to sell. Because selling such properties constitutes their business, brokers are quite willing to make such arrangements if they can see a reasonable profit in the deal for themselves. The seller may be quite willing to pass along to the broker a small portion of any profit because this allows the seller to achieve investment objectives at a minimal tax cost. The sequential steps of the three-cornered exchange can be diagramed as in Figure 10–6. If all parties take suffi-

FIGURE 10–6

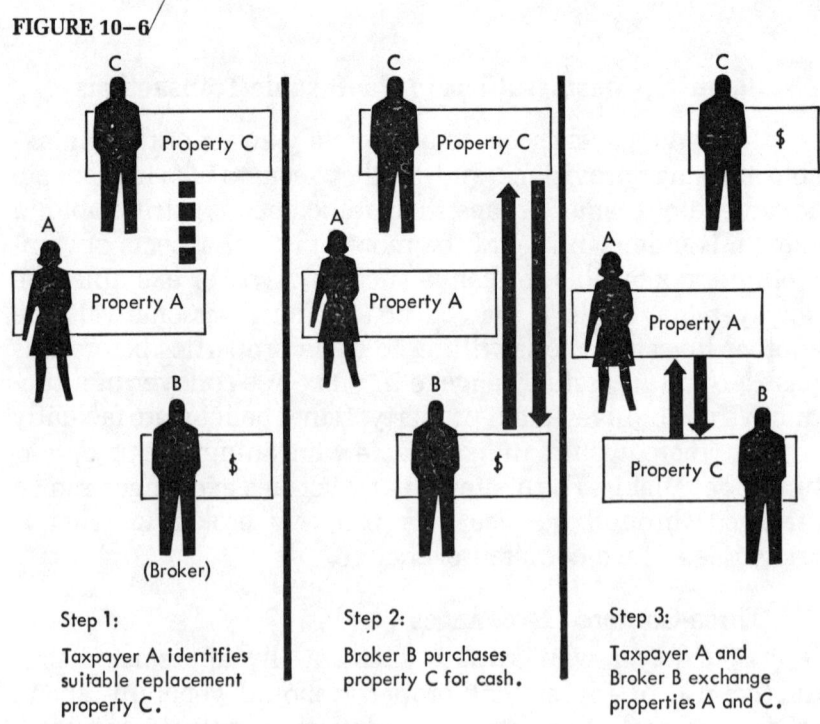

Step 1: Taxpayer A identifies suitable replacement property C.

Step 2: Broker B purchases property C for cash.

Step 3: Taxpayer A and Broker B exchange properties A and C.

cient care in arranging the details of these separate transactions, taxpayer A can achieve her investment objectives tax-free. The arrangements between A and B are especially critical. If the tax authorities can determine that B only acted as an agent of A, the plan will fail and A will be treated as if she personally purchased property C for cash. Taxpayer A also must be careful in her dealings with C. If A proceeds too far into the negotiations with C, so that the sale is all but finalized before the broker is introduced into the deal, some courts will conclude that A actually purchased property C, even though the legal papers show that technically the sale by party C was made to B rather than to A. For those who know the rules and who document their way carefully, however, the three-cornered exchange can be a useful technique in minimizing the tax consequences of semiroutine business transactions.

Mortgaged Properties

Taxpayers sometimes reject the use of a tax-free exchange, believing that the existence of a mortgage on a property will in effect be treated as boot and therefore, for all practical purposes, convert an apparently tax-free transaction into a wholly taxable one. This danger was adequately demonstrated in the illustration on page 258. What was not explained there, however, is that the tax authorities will not treat the transfer of a mortgage as an equivalent of cash to the extent that two mortgages offset each other.

If the two taxpayers in the illustration on pages 257 and 258 understood the tax rules, they would have arranged a slightly different transaction from the one proposed there. Specifically, ABC Corporation might first arrange to borrow $18,000 against 150 acres of its timberland. This would, of course, give ABC $18,000 cash tax-free since borrowing money is not deemed to constitute realization, even if property is mortgaged in the process. Then ABC Corporation and Attorney Jones might proceed to exchange the city lot, with its $18,000 mortgage, for the 150 acres of timberland, which also carries an $18,000 mortgage. Under these revised conditions, neither party would have to recognize any taxable income on the exchange because the two mortgages exactly cancel each other out. Thus, Mr. Jones ends up with 150 acres of timberland (rather than 100 acres) and an $18,000 mortgage, but he need not pay any income tax on the $9,000 gain, which now remains entirely unrecognized. Jones's tax basis in the 150 acres would be $21,000—a carry-over basis from his old city lot. ABC Corporation, under the revised circumstances, ends up with $10,000 more cash than it had before, 50 acres less timberland,

and the right to ignore $8,000 in taxable income that had to be recognized in the previous arrangement. ABC Corporation's basis in the city lot would be $4,500, a carry-over basis from the 150 acres of timberland. (Since ABC's tax basis in 100 acres was $3,000, it is assumed that its basis in 50 contiguous acres would be another $1,500.)

The Role of Intent

Each of the nontaxable exchange provisions contains potential tax traps for the unwary taxpayer. For example, before a taxpayer can properly defer the recognition of a gain realized on the sale of his or her home, the taxpayer must be able to establish that the home sold was in fact his or her *primary residence*. If the taxpayer were to try to apply that provision to the gain realized on the sale of a summer cottage on the coast, this would probably not be sustained. If a taxpayer has more than one home, determining which home constitutes the primary residence turns largely upon the role of intent. The number of days spent at each location may be indicative of intent, but such a simplistic criterion need not control in any particular disposition. The point is that a taxpayer must sometimes take great care in documenting intent if he or she wishes to retain the right to claim that a particular transaction is a nontaxable one.

One case history in this regard seems especially instructive. A California taxpayer decided to dispose of a particular investment property. At the moment he could not identify a satisfactory replacement property, but a buyer was anxious to purchase the property that he wished to sell. In order not to lose the sale, the taxpayer agreed to make an exchange with a broker that would allow the anxious buyer to acquire his property. The property accepted in return was not what the California taxpayer really wanted, and this fact was adequately documented in correspondence between the taxpayer and the broker. Everyone wanted it well understood that, as soon as an appropriate property could be located, the broker was to acquire that property and trade for the one temporarily accepted by the California taxpayer. Before long, the taxpayer found his desired investment property and the second exchange was promptly completed. Much to everyone's surprise, however, the tax authorities found that the series of exchanges did not satisfy the requirements of Section 1031. The IRS argued that the California taxpayer never intended to hold the intermediate property as either a productive-use or an investment property. It was held only as an expedient to attain certain tax results. The taxpayer's own letters proved his intent, and the IRS position was sustained by the courts. As this case demonstrates, a nontaxable transaction can very easily be converted into a taxable transaction by taxpayers who proceed without giving sufficient attention to every detail.

CHAPTER 11

Corporate Reorganizations

For reasons explained in Chapter 10, the tax rules authorizing a tax-free corporate reorganization are among the more important provisions in the Internal Revenue Code. They are also, unfortunately, among the most complex provisions in the tax law. What follows in this chapter is an introduction to this important and fascinating aspect of the American way of taxation. Just enough information is provided here to enable the typical business executive to begin to understand the major tax opportunities and problems that must be given detailed attention in the actual acquisition or disposition of any corporate business venture. Related problems of securities regulations and financial accounting requirements must remain outside the scope of this book.

This chapter is divided into three major sections. The first section is devoted to definitional distinctions among the several forms or types of corporate reorganizations. The second section investigates the most important code sections that come into operation whenever any type of corporate reorganization is found to exist. The third section includes a brief discussion of five of the more common problem areas often associated with corporate reorganizations.

Basic Definitions

Section 368(a)(1) of the Internal Revenue Code defines six different types of corporate reorganization. Other sections provide the operative consequences. If any particular business rearrangement cannot be fitted into one of these six definitions, the reshuffling of corporate ownership and/or corporate properties will generally be treated like any other transaction and thus be subject to the usual tax rules explained in Chapter 2.

In the financial press, the six types of corporate reorganization are commonly known as types A, B, C, D, E, and F—a derivation of their tax heritage. Subparagraph A of Section 368(a)(1) defines the type A reorganization; Section 368(a)(1)(B) defines the type B reorganization; and so on. Because this terminology has been generally accepted, and because it facilitates reference to some otherwise cumbersome descriptive phrases, we shall utilize it throughout the chapter.

The Type A Reorganization

The type A reorganization involves the merger or consolidation of two or more corporate entities under state law. If one of the old entities survives the reorganization, it is known as a merger; if neither of the old entities survives and a new entity is born, the reorganization is referred to as a consolidation. In skeletal form, the typical merger can be depicted as in Figure 11–1. The specific merger transaction involves the exchange by Group II of all their B stock for A stock or other property, the transfer of all assets from corporation B to corporation A, and the dissolution of corporation B.

The type A reorganization is popular in part because the code imposes no restrictions on the form or amount of compensation that can be used by corporation A to effect the merger. The acquiring corporation can, for example, purchase for cash the shares of B owned by dissident stockholders, or it can issue its own bonds or preferred stocks rather than its own common stock to certain former shareholders of corporation B. Only judicial doctrines of uncertain scope are applied to distinguish between a routine sale and a type A reorganization in borderline cases.

FIGURE 11–1
Type A Reorganization

BEFORE

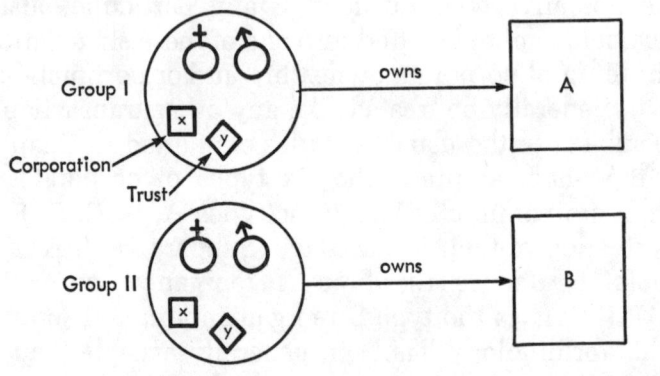

TRANSACTIONS

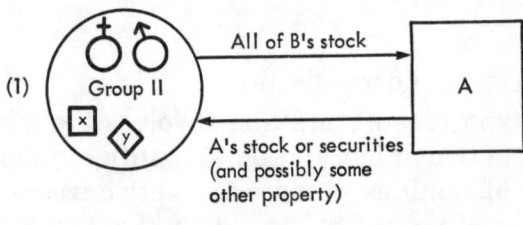

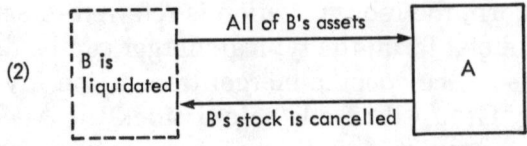

AFTER

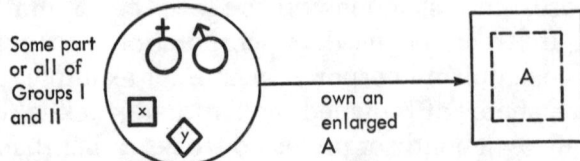

Although the type A reorganization has minimal restrictions on the amount and form of consideration that can be utilized, it is sometimes rendered ineffective by the fact that it generally requires the approval of a stipulated majority of both corporations' shareholders before it can be accomplished. In addition, the acquiring corporation generally inherits all of the acquired corporation's potential problems as well as its possible benefits. Consequently, if contingent liabilities, for example, are of major significance in a given situation, a type A reorganization may be quickly ruled out of contention for wholly nontax reasons.

The Type B Reorganization

The type B reorganization is defined as the acquisition of control (meaning 80 percent of the voting power and value of the stock) by one corporation over another corporation, with acquisition achieved *solely* by the exchange of voting stock for voting stock. A reorganization in which any consideration other than voting stock is used to effect the transfer cannot be a type B reorganization. Nevertheless, a "creeping" type B acquisition—that is, one spread over a reasonable period and involving *unrelated* transactions, some of which may have included cash—is possible under the proper circumstances. In other words, it is not mandatory that the 80 percent control be achieved in a single stock-for-stock transaction, but if the control is not achieved by the exchange of voting stock, the classification of the final acquisition as a tax-free reorganization may be open to challenge. If the acquiring corporation obtains less than an 80 percent control over the acquired corporation, the transaction cannot be a type B reorganization under any circumstances. The net result of a type B reorganization is the acquisition of a subsidiary corporation by a parent corporation. In skeletal form, the acquisition can be diagramed as in Figure 11–2. The specific transaction in a type B reorganization involves only the exchange of B stock for A stock by part or all of Group II.

A comparison of Figures 11–1 and 11–2 emphasizes one very important difference between type A and type B reorganizations. In the latter, both corporations are kept alive. This

FIGURE 11-2
Type B Reorganization

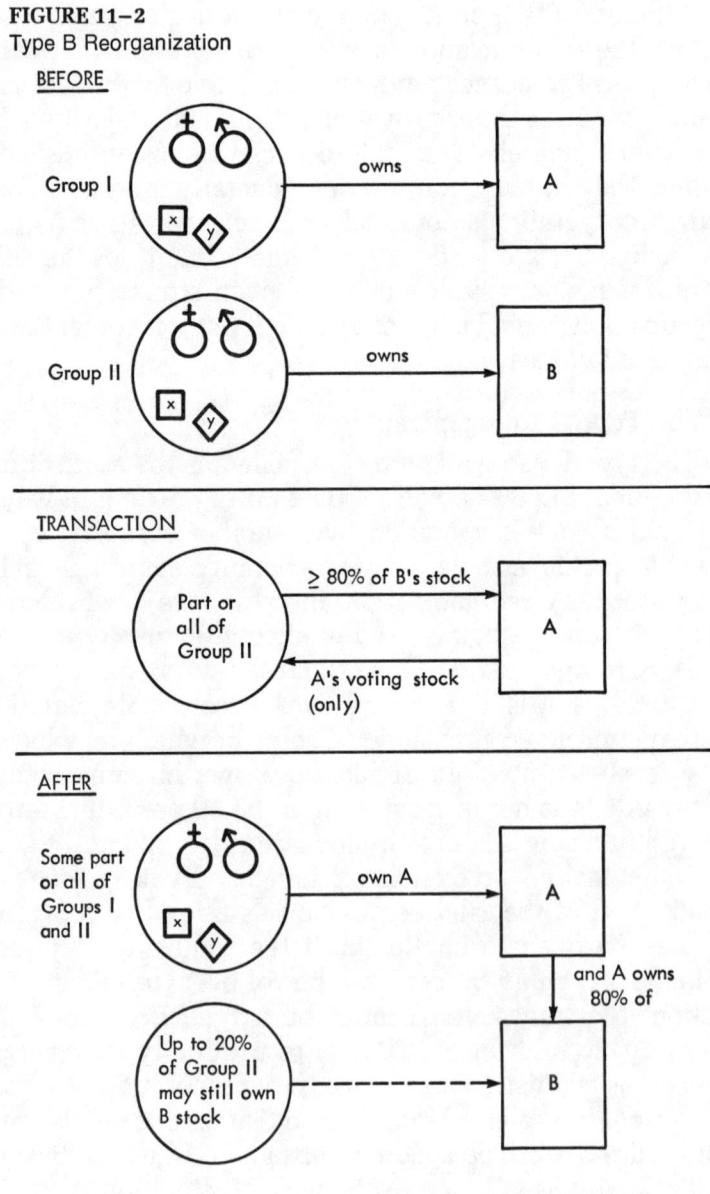

means, of course, that any liabilities of corporation B generally do not extend to the assets of corporation A. It also means that any unique value that corporation B may have—such as a well-known name, customer goodwill, a scarce franchise, or any other privilege—can be permanently retained by corporation A through its control over corporation B. Type B reorganizations may also be preferred over other types because of lesser appraisal rights given dissenting shareholders, or because the shareholders of the acquiring corporation may not have to be consulted before such reorganizations can be effected. These specific rules are part of our securities laws.

The major restricting condition of the type B reorganization is the voting-stock–for–voting-stock requirement. Even apparently routine concomitants of a normal reorganization—such as fractional shareholders' rights, reorganization legal and accounting expenses, debt assumptions, and contingent exchanges—have sometimes raised havoc with this one requirement. In general, the IRS and the courts have taken a narrow interpretation of the restricting code provision, and all tax planners must exercise extreme caution in this area.

Finally, the reader should note that it is entirely possible for the acquiring corporation to liquidate its new subsidiary shortly after a type B reorganization. In that event, the economic effect is, for all practical purposes, the same as a statutory merger. The form and the sequence of the events that transpire, however, will determine which (if any) form of reorganization has occurred. A type B reorganization will always create a parent subsidiary relationship, at least temporarily. If an acquisition fails to satisfy at least one of the definitions contained in Section 368(a), the transaction generally becomes wholly taxable.

The Type C Reorganization

The type C reorganization is one in which the acquiring corporation obtains *substantially all* of the properties of another corporation in exchange for its own, or its parent corporation's, voting stock and possibly a limited amount (not more than 20 percent in value) of other consideration. In skeletal form, the assets-for-stock merger contemplated in a type C reorganization can be depicted as shown in Figure 11–3. The specific transaction in this situation involves the transfer of assets, and very often of liabilities as well, from corporation B to corporation A in exchange for corporation A's voting stock and, possibly, a limited amount of cash or other property.

FIGURE 11–3
Type C Reorganization

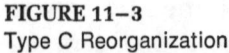
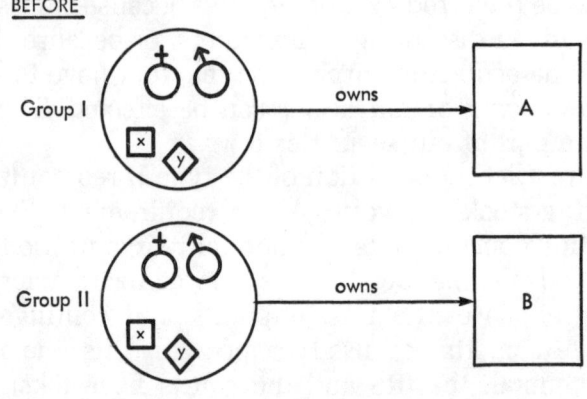
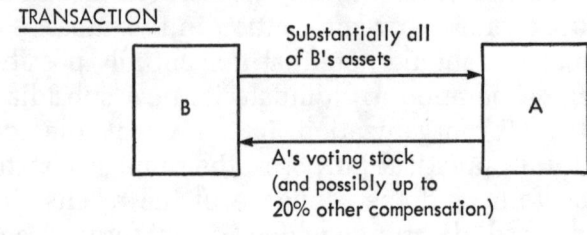
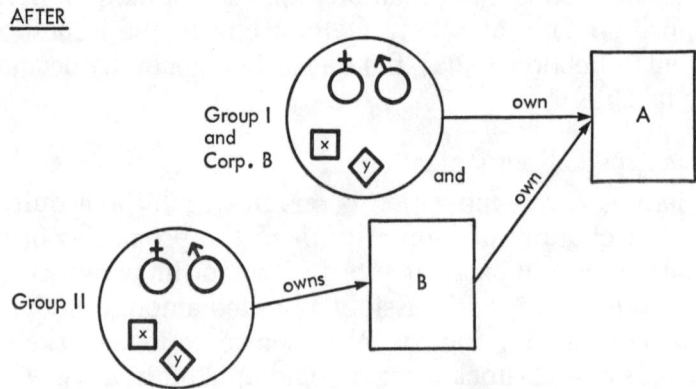

The most troublesome requirement of the type C reorganization has proved to be the "substantially all" requirement. If corporation B initially owns some assets that corporation A does not wish to acquire, great care must be taken in the manner and the timing of the disposition of the unwanted assets if the subsequent asset-for-stock exchange is to withstand an IRS challenge as a valid type C reorganization. If a corporation is nearly insolvent, a type C reorganization may also prove difficult to arrange because the acquired corporation has few assets that can be acquired. In this situation, most of the assets belong to the corporation's creditors, and therefore the acquiring corporation will find it nearly impossible to acquire "substantially all" of the insolvent corporation's properties.

The boot relaxation rule—that is, the provision authorizing up to 20 percent of the consideration in some form other than voting stock of the acquiring corporation or its parent corporation—can also be troublesome in certain circumstances. If any consideration other than voting stock is utilized in a type C reorganization, then the liabilities assumed by the acquiring corporation must also be treated as part of the boot. Because such liabilities often exceed 20 percent of the value of the assets in a reorganization exchange, the opportunity to utilize any consideration other than voting stock may be severely limited. An error in the valuation of properties might also prove fatal to a type C reorganization that attempted to take advantage of the boot relaxation rule. If the original valuation of the properties transferred for voting stock proved to be in excess of their real fair market value, and the value of the properties transferred for other consideration proved to be greater than that originally estimated, then the 20 percent limitation might be exceeded and the exchange fail to qualify under the type C requirements.

As is emphasized in the skeletal diagram of the classic type C reorganization (Figure 11–3), one important result of this type of business rearrangement is the creation of a holding company (corporation B in the diagram). Note that because corporation B was required to transfer substantially all of its assets to corporation A, it is left with little or nothing but A stock. Under these circumstances, it is not surprising to discover that, following a type C reorganization, Group II will sometimes liquidate corporation B and distribute the A stock to its shareholders. When this happens, the economic result is again tantamount to a type A merger, but the form of the transaction and the sequence of the events are distinct, and failure to comply with all of the requirements of one or the other will again normally result in a fully taxable transaction rather than in a nontaxable corporate reorganization.

The Type D Reorganization

The type D reorganization encompasses two essentially dissimilar business rearrangements. It can apply to the transfer of substantially all of the assets of a corporation to *its own* subsidiary corporation if this transfer is followed by the liquidation of the transferor (parent) corporation. The net effect of this form of the type D reorganization is to put a new corporate shell around an old corporate body, which is essentially the equivalent of a type E or type F arrangement. Alternatively, a type D reorganization may apply to the division of an existing corporation into two or more corporations. Because the latter alternative is by far the more important and common variety, we will restrict our attention to the divisive form. In skeletal form, the simplest divisive type D reorganization can be illustrated as in Figure 11–4. The specific transactions in this divisive type D reorganization involve the transfer of some part of corporation A's assets to a new or existing corporation B in exchange for B's stock and the distribution of this stock by corporation A to all or some portion of its shareholders (that is, to Group I, but not necessarily pro rata to the members of that group). If the distribution of the B stock is made to only some part of Group I, and if this distribution is made in exchange for all of that part's shares in corporation A, the "after" diagram would have to be modified to look like that in Figure 11–5.

Before a corporate division can be effected as a tax-free type D reorganization, other code requirements must also be satisfied. Among the most important collateral requirements is the one in Section 355, which stipulates that both surviving corporations must be engaged in an active trade or business that had been conducted by the now-divided corporation (or corporation A in our diagram) for no less than five years preceding the division. Suffice it to say here that both the meaning of the phrase *trade or business* and the outer boundaries of the "five-year rule" have been the source of many disputes between taxpayers and the IRS. Litigation in this area is commonplace, and only the bravest or most foolish entrepreneur

FIGURE 11-4
Type D Reorganization (spin-off form)

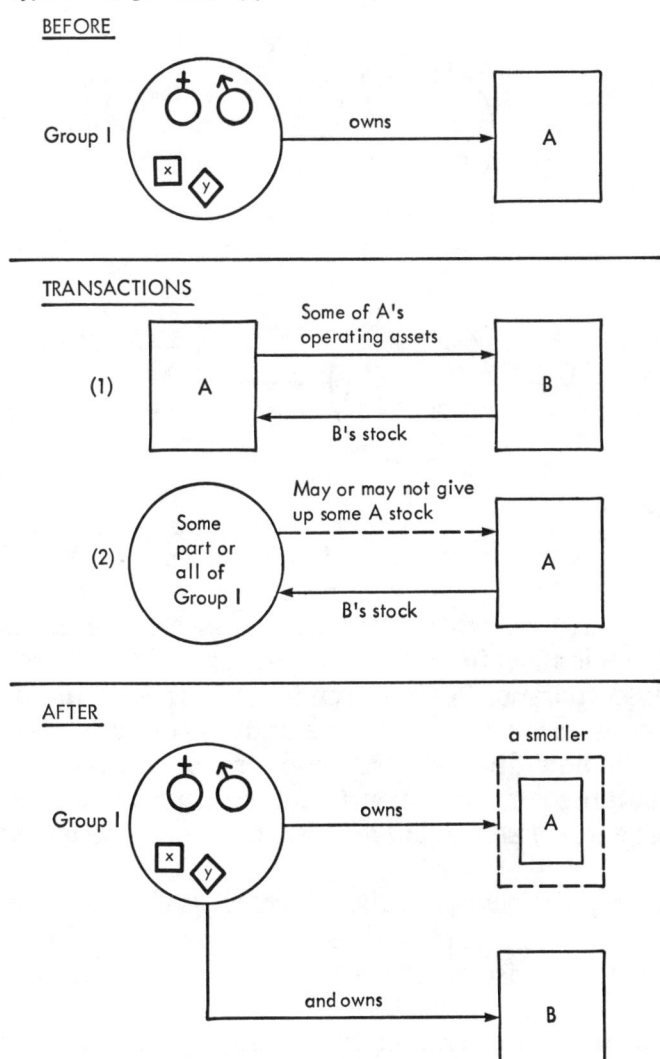

would attempt to draw his or her own conclusions as to the meaning of the requirements without competent advice.

The requirement that the shares of the second entity be distributed in a divisive type D reorganization can be satisfied

FIGURE 11-5
A Split-off

AFTER

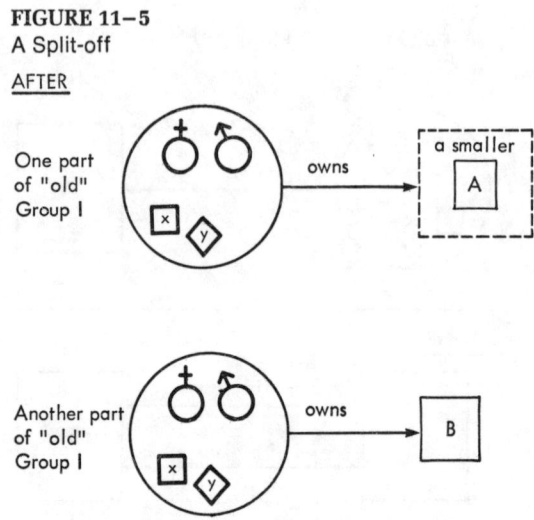

in one of three ways. Returning to our earlier diagram (Figure 11–4), if the old Group I shareholders surrender no stock in corporation A when they receive the B shares, the division is properly called a *spin-off*. If some part or all of some owners' shares in corporation A are surrendered on the receipt of the B stock, the division is known as a *split-off* (Figure 11–5). Finally, if the now-divided corporation transfers all of its assets to two or more corporations (say, for example, to corporations B and C) and is itself liquidated, the division is called a *split-up*.

The type D reorganization is very useful in separating warring factions of stockholders of a single enterprise. It may also be useful in isolating the riskier trades or businesses in separate corporate shells. This can also be accomplished, of course, by the easier creation of a subsidiary corporation under Section 351 if the stock of the riskier entity is not to be distributed. Historically, the divisive type D reorganization was also of importance in dividing what was essentially one business into two or more corporations to gain the added advantage of another corporate surtax exemption. As explained on pages 55 and 56, that possibility may once again be increasing in popularity under more closely controlled conditions.

The Type E Reorganization

The type E reorganization encompasses the recapitalization of an existing corporation. The precise definitional boundaries of a "recapitalization" are admittedly elusive. In general, the expression refers to a reshuffling of the outstanding stocks and bonds of a single corporation in terms of their amounts, priorities, maturity dates, or other features. The exact transactions involved in a type E reorganization may involve the exchange of (1) "old" stocks for "new" stocks, (2) "old" bonds for "new" bonds, (3) "old" bonds for "new" stocks, or (4) "old" stocks for "new" bonds. Each of these alternatives presents slightly different tax possibilities. In general, only the movement *from* an equity (or stock) interest *to* a creditor (or bond) interest creates major tax problems. The stock-for-bonds exchange may be treated as essentially equivalent to a dividend and taxed accordingly.

The type E reorganization is commonly associated with a corporate insolvency. Corporations in financial difficulties are often reorganized in a way that it is hoped will shore up their financial structure and stave off bankruptcy. In terms of tax-planning opportunities, the type E reorganization is of limited importance.

The Type F Reorganization

A mere change in identity, form, or place of organization is a type F reorganization. Like the type E reorganization, it has little tax-planning importance. To say that a code provision is not of much importance for tax-planning purposes is certainly not to suggest that the provision is void of tax importance. Note, for example, that, if it were not for the type F reorganization, a stockholder could be taxed on the difference between the present fair market value and the tax basis in shares of stock in a corporation that decided for good business reasons to reincorporate in another state.

As noted earlier, if a particular business reorganization satisfies any one of the six definitions of Section 368(a)(1), the usual tax result is a nontaxable transaction and a carry-over tax basis. The seller of a business that has increased significantly in value over the years generally has a strong preference for a nontaxable disposition. The buyer, on the other hand, often prefers to make a business acquisition in a taxable manner. Tender offers and prices paid, therefore, may vary substantially, depending on how the details of the transaction are arranged.

Tax Consequences

Code Sections 354 and 361 are the provisions that guarantee nontax treatment to the various parties to a corporate reorganization. Sections 356 and 357 make an otherwise nontaxable transaction partially or wholly taxable in the event that boot is involved in the transaction. Finally, Sections 358 and 362 demand a carry-over tax basis in the event of a nontaxable reorganization. In general, the effect of these several separate code sections is comparable to those detailed in Chapter 10 for less complex nontaxable transactions.

The Recognition of Gain or Loss

Stockholders and security holders are granted immunity from the usual tax rules by Section 354 only to the extent that they exchange stock and securities of a corporation that is a party to a reorganization for stock and securities of another corporation that is a party to that same reorganization. (For purpose of this section, the word *securities* refers to long-term debt.) If a stockholder receives shares in a corporation that is not party to that reorganization, he or she will be treated as receiving boot in an amount equal to the fair market value of those shares. Furthermore, the dollar value of securities that can be received tax-free is usually limited to the dollar value of securities surrendered. In other words, even in a corporate reorganization, a taxpayer typically cannot move upstream from an equity interest to a creditor interest without imposition of an income tax. A few years ago, the hybrid securities issued in some of the more glamorous corporate acquisitions caused major problems with tax definitions. Because of the combined forces of a depressed market and tighter security laws and accounting rules, as well as some changes in the tax laws, the era of extremes in equity-flavored investment units has already passed.

Corporations frequently transfer operating assets and other properties in types A, C, and D reorganization transactions. Such corporate transferors are protected by Section 361 from the need to recognize any gain in the transaction so long as those assets are transferred pursuant to a plan of reorganization and to another corporation that is a party to the reorganization, and so long as the transferor receives in return only the stock or securities of the other corporation. If property other than qualifying stock or securities is received, the transferring corporation may generally avoid paying a corporate income tax on such boot if, in pursuance of the plan of reorganization, it distributes such boot to its shareholders. Incidentally, Section 361 also denies the transferring corporation the right to recognize (that is, to deduct) any loss realized in a reorganization-related transfer of properties.

The treatment of liabilities. Corporate reorganizations frequently include the transfer of liabilities as well as assets. Generally Section 357 provides that the assumption of a liability will not be treated as boot or money received by the party being relieved of the debt if the transaction would otherwise be tax-free. Two exceptions to this general rule should, however, be noted. In the event of (1) a transfer of liabilities created either to avoid the federal income tax or to accomplish nonbusiness objectives, or (2) an assumption of liabilities in excess of the tax basis of properties transferred, the debt-relieved corporation must treat the assumed liabilities as the equivalent of cash boot. No ready operational definition of the several critical words and phrases can be stated briefly. Suffice it to say that this is one aspect of a planned business acquisition or disposition that a qualified tax adviser will investigate carefully before recommending action to a client.

The treatment of boot. If any party to a corporate reorganization receives additional consideration—that is, if the transaction involves any property other than that authorized to be received tax-free by Section 354 or Section 355—the recipient taxpayer must recognize taxable income equal in amount to the lesser of (a) the boot received or (b) the gain realized. For a review of the meaning of the phrase *gain realized*, the reader should return to Chapter 5; in broad terms, gain realized is the difference in amount between the "amount realized" and the "adjusted basis" of the assets surrendered. If taxable income must be recognized, it can be classified as either ordinary income or capital gain, depending upon all the facts and circumstances surrounding the transaction. Loss cannot be recognized even if boot is received.

Basis Rules

Taxpayers involved in wholly nontaxable corporate reorganizations usually take a carry-over tax basis in any assets received by operation of Section 358 or Section 362. Returning to our earlier diagram of a type A statutory merger (Figure 11-1), for example, the Group II stockholders would simply transfer whatever tax basis they had in their "old" corporation B stock to their "new" corporation A stock. In the type C reorganization diagram (Figure 11-3), corporation A would simply assume whatever tax basis corporation B had previously had in the assets transferred and corporation B would take that same tax basis in the corporation A stock it received.

As noted in Chapter 10, the idea of the carry-over basis is to achieve a temporary postponement rather than a permanent forgiveness of the pending income tax. The temporarily deferred gains and losses will be realized *and recognized* whenever the newly acquired properties are later disposed of in a more "normal" (taxable) transaction.

If boot is received and gain must be recognized in an otherwise nontaxable transaction, the parties to the reorganization may be able to increase their tax basis by the amount of the gain recognized. The taxpayer receiving boot, however, must also decrease the tax basis by the amount of boot received. Because the amount of gain recognized is often equal to the amount of boot received, the increase authorized by the gain recognized is often exactly offset by the amount of boot received, and the net effect of the two rules just stated is (for the recipient of boot) a return to the prior basis. For the party giving the boot, however, an increase in basis usually results. Fortunately, business managers can let their tax advisers worry about the many details associated with the actual application of these tax basis rules. The good manager should always remember that a proper allocation of tax basis among the assets received may spell the difference between a profitable and an unprofitable exchange. In most circumstances, the selling taxpayer wants to allocate so as to maximize capital gains, whereas the buying taxpayer wants to allocate so as to maximize future tax deductions in as short a period as possible.

Special Problems

Corporate reorganizations often involve hundreds of taxpayers and millions of dollars' worth of properties. It is little wonder, therefore, that the tax rules in this area are complex and the problems legendary. To close this brief review of reorganizations, we will examine just five of the more common special problems briefly.

Unwanted Assets

An acquisition-minded corporation may desire to obtain something less than all of the assets of a business being offered for sale. As a consequence, the overly anxious seller may be tempted to make a hasty disposition of unwanted assets. Any seller must exercise great care to make such a disposition at a minimal tax cost. If, for example, the officers of the selling corporation were to distribute the unwanted assets to the corporation's shareholders to facilitate a subsequent merger, the likely result would be an ordinary dividend taxed at ordinary rates for the recipient stockholders. If a stock redemption were involved, the distributing corporation might also discover that it too had to recognize a taxable income because of the distribution of property to the shareholders. A sale of unwanted assets to a third party could be equally costly if not prearranged properly. Under some circumstances, a corporation may be able to separate "wanted" and "unwanted" properties in two or more corporations via a tax-free type D reorganization before consummating a merger of the wanted-property corporation. In this event, however, a type C reorganization probably could not be arranged, even for the desired-asset corporation, because of the "substantially all" requirement. A type A or type B reorganization, however, might be successfully arranged under these circumstances. Both competent advice and an advance ruling from the Internal Revenue Service would be warranted under these conditions.

Net Operating Losses

Profitable corporations at one time actively sought to acquire essentially worthless corporate shells solely because, by acquiring such corporate shells, they could also acquire the right to claim the acquired corporations' accumulated net operating loss deductions against their own taxable income. Interestingly, the most worthless corporate shells—that is, the ones with the greatest accumulation of losses—brought the highest prices. The tax rules have been substantially modified during the past 20 years to preclude much success in this way today. Generally, the net operating loss deductions carried forward will be allowed as a tax deduction in a consolidated tax return, after a type B acquisition, if and only to the extent that the old (or acquired) business produces profits after its purchase. Whether or not the net operating loss deduction of a business acquired in a type A or C reorganization can be carried forward depends upon the rules stated briefly on page 40. The rules that determine exactly how much and in what manner an acquired business can be modified without destroying a loss carry-forward deduction are legion. In addition, the accounting conventions that allocate revenues and expenses among several divisions of a single enterprise are at best rough approximations. Consequently, trading in corporate shells with accumulated net operating losses is not impossible; it is simply not an amateur's game.

Contingent Acquisitions

Buy-sell agreements are sometimes drawn up as conditional contracts. For example, the number of shares of stock to be issued to the selling corporation or to its stockholders may be made contingent upon the profit performance of the acquired business for the next several years. Contingencies commonly raise numerous and difficult tax problems. For one, contingent consideration may create the possibility of boot. If the only additional consideration that can be received is more shares of qualifying stock, if the portion of the shares held in reserve is reasonable in relation to the total number of shares to be transferred, and if the entire transaction must be finalized within a reasonable number of years, then such a contingency usually will not constitute boot. Determining a tax basis for any shares disposed of during the period of the contingency, however, is less easily resolved. If the acquiring corporation retains the right to back out of an acquisition, or if it retains the right to rescind the transaction under specified circumstances, the tax problems multiply rapidly. Fortunately, the tax stakes in such arrangements are typically so great that they are usually given proper attention before it is too late to correct any problems inherent in the arrangements.

Liquidation-Reincorporation

A reincorporation that follows closely on the heels of a corporate liquidation can easily be converted into a *taxable* reorganization by the IRS and the courts. If this result were not possible, a taxpayer might be tempted to accumulate all temporarily "excess" income within a corporate shell without any payment of dividends. Then, when the owner had need of the accumulated assets, he or she could liquidate the corporate entity and receive the funds at the cost of a capital gains tax rather than pay an ordinary income tax on any dividends. If the owner wished to continue the essential business, he or she could immediately transfer the necessary operating assets back into a new corporation and begin the accumulation process all over again. The accumulated earnings and profits account of the old corporation would have been wiped clean in the liquidation, and the new corporation could open with a clean slate. Does this sound too good to be true? Usually it is! Unless the owners of the reincorporated business are a significantly different group from the old owners, or unless the new corporation is engaged in a significantly different business from that of the prior corporation, the courts are likely to sustain an IRS contention that the liquidating distribution was really an ordinary dividend distribution and that the new corporation has inherited all attributes of the predecessor corporation.

Certainly a bailout of accumulated corporate income at the price of only a capital gains tax to the shareholders remains a viable alternative. The wise business manager will simply make certain that he or she does not inadvertently take actions that not only destroy this possibility, but also serve to convert what could have been capital gains into ordinary income.

Debt-Financed Acquisitions

Many business managers have sold their corporations for the long-term debt of an acquiring corporation. Because such a sale is ordinarily a taxable transaction, the seller may be able to negotiate a better price for any of several reasons. One factor increasing the price in a debt-financed acquisition is that the buyer can often deduct part of the purchase price as interest during years of payment for the new property. In addition, the buyer frequently gets a new and higher basis in the assets purchased, and thus a larger tax deduction in the future years than would have occurred had the sale been arranged in a nontaxable manner. Such a sale is often tolerable for the seller because the tax recognition of any gain realized may be deferred by virtue of the installment sale provisions of the code. (See Chapter 13 for a discussion of the installment sale.) In many cases, the tax recognition can be deferred for 20 years or longer by the terms of the debt. If the seller discovers a need for additional funds in the interim years, he or she is always free to sell some portion of the acquiring corporation's debt and to pay tax on only the portion of the bonds sold.

In 1969, Congress reduced the popularity of the debt-financed acquisition by enacting two important provisions. First, the installment sale provisions of Section 453 were modified so as to preclude the deferral of the recognition of gain if the seller receives demand notes, coupon bonds, or any other security that is readily tradable in an established market. Second, the acquiring corporation may be denied the right to deduct interest on debt obligations issued after October 9, 1969, to acquire another business directly or indirectly. The latter revision, Section 279, is applicable only for interest in excess of $5 million, and then only under specified circumstances. Needless to say, the few readers of this book who engage in such hefty acquisitions can also obtain ready reference to the other pertinent details. For smaller acquisitions dealing with unlisted securities, debt-financed acquisitions remain one of the several options available.

CHAPTER 12

Family Tax Planning

Family tax planning centers on the taxation of gifts and estates. Although many states also impose inheritance taxes, the federal estate and gift taxes are dominant. Historically, the federal gift and estate taxes were two entirely separate taxes; since 1976, however, they technically are both a part of one tax—the donative transfers tax. Nevertheless, for pedagogical reasons, we will generally treat them as two separate taxes. The two were first enacted many years ago (a) to raise federal government revenues, and (b) to achieve at least a limited amount of wealth redistribution in the United States. For all practical purposes, the two generally failed to achieve either objective. In 1979, federal gift and estate tax collections were estimated to be approximately $5.4 billion, about 1.7 percent of total tax revenues. All empirical studies attempting to determine the effect of the two taxes on wealth redistribution conclude that they have had a very limited impact. Although neither tax was a real success in terms of the original objectives, the effect of many years of inflation was to make the old provisions, which had not been modified in a significant manner since 1942, even less satisfactory than they had been when they were originally adopted. In 1969, estate tax returns were required in only 7 percent of all deaths; by 1972 this had increased to 9 percent; and by 1976 it was estimated at 11 percent. Most of the increase was, of course, attributable to smaller estates—that is, to estates valued at just over $60,000, the minimum point at which the estate tax could take effect under pre-1977 rules. Consequently, when, in 1972, Senator George McGovern called for sharply increased estate taxes, his proposal received little support. On the other hand, when President Ford, in 1976, called for a substantial increase in the basic estate tax exemption (from $60,000 to $150,000), his proposal received widespread support. Once Congress began to tamper with the estate tax provisions, however, it did not stop with an increase in the basic exemption. Instead, Congress proceeded to enact massive changes in the area of gift and estate taxation, which will be important to family tax planning for years to come.

In this chapter, we will review in a general way the current provisions that determine the tax liability imposed by the federal gift and estate tax, as well as possible methods of minimizing that tax. The chapter is divided into three sections. The first section deals with the tax on gifts; the second deals with the tax on estates; the final section attempts to integrate a few ideas on income, estate, and gift taxes into relatively simple family tax planning.

Federal Taxation of Gifts

The federal gift tax is an excise tax imposed on certain gratuitous transfers of property. The tax is a liability of the donor, the person making the gift, not of the donee, the person receiving the gift. The tax applies equally to all forms of property: real and personal property; business, nonbusiness, and purely personal-use property; tangible and intangible property; and to both present and future interests in property. In other words, if a taxpayer today makes an irrevocable transfer of a future interest in a property to a person not yet born, the transfer is immediately subject to the gift tax, even though the full economic impact of the transfer of property rights may not be realized for many years. The problems encountered in valuing a future interest in property are sometimes substantial. Suffice it to note here that valuation may involve the need to determine a discounted present value of an estimated earnings stream based on the life expectancy of several parties to a gift.

Note also that a transfer must be irrevocable before the gift tax will apply. If a person prepares a last will and testament, or names a beneficiary to a life insurance policy, such action does not constitute a gift so long as the taxpayer retains the right to modify a present intention at any time in the future. Finally, the reader should understand clearly that the gift tax has essentially nothing to do with the income tax. For example, the interest on state and local government bonds is exempt from the federal income tax. A gift of either a state bond or the interest from such a bond, however, would be wholly subject to the federal gift tax. Similarly, a gift paid from a salary already reduced by the income tax may be further reduced by the gift tax.

Basic Provisions

A determination of the gift tax liability proceeds conceptually in a manner very similar to that used to determine an income tax liability. The broad outline of the gift tax calculation can be stated as follows:

Gross value of all *gifts* made minus *exempt gifts* and *deductions* equals *taxable gifts*.

Taxable gifts multiplied by *tax rate* equals *gross tax liability*.

Gross tax liability minus *tax credits* equals *net tax payable*.

Translating real-world events into such a simplistic formula is subject to the usual number of definitional and calculational problems. We shall examine only a few of the more common problems and opportunities.

Gross gifts. The determination of a dollar value to represent the "gross value of all gifts made" typically involves two major kinds of problems. One set of problems involves the specification of exactly which transfers will be deemed to constitute gifts (as opposed to nongratuitous transfers); the second set of problems involves the determination of the fair market value of those transfers found to be gratuitous. The former problem is generally resolved by the intent of the taxpayer.

The Internal Revenue Code provides that any transfer of property for less than an adequate and full consideration in money or money's worth shall be included in computing the amount of gifts made. The intent of this provision is apparent, but its application is sometimes difficult. If a person makes a foolish deal—if the person, for instance, unwittingly sells a property worth $500,000 for $300,000—the code would seem to require that a gift tax be paid on the miscalculation (in this instance, on $200,000). In practice, the IRS is not that cruel. Instead of trying to apply the code literally, the IRS usually tries to determine the intent of the taxpayer. If he or she entered into an arm's-length transaction in the ordinary course of business, the transaction will not be subject to a gift tax. If the transaction is one between related parties, or if the IRS has any other reason to suspect that the transaction is not a *bona fide* sale or exchange, it may attempt to tax as a gift the difference between the fair market value given and the consideration received.

In unusual circumstances, a gift tax may also become payable through the inadvertent or unintended action of a taxpayer. In these circumstances, a taxpayer may not have given any conscious thought to making a gift, but the taxpayer's actions may in fact accomplish such a result. Suppose, for example, that a father and his adult son began raising a herd of cattle in a joint venture. Under these circumstances, it would not be unusual for the father to create, solely from his personal funds, a joint bank account for the use by both his son and himself in the cattle venture. Without formalizing their agreement, the two men may generally understand that the proceeds of the venture will be split equally and that both are free to draw upon the bank account for personal as well as business needs. The potential gift element in such an arrangement is easiest to see if we will assume that (1) both men contribute an equal amount of effort to the operation, (2) after ten years of operation, the business breaks exactly even, (3) neither party ever used the bank account for personal needs, and (4) the two finally split the balance in the account when they terminated their joint venture. Under these extreme assumptions, it is clear that the father effectively made a gift to his son of one half of the amount he initially placed in the joint bank account.

When the simplifying assumptions are removed and the venture is allowed to make a profit or a loss in various years, when the relative contributions of the two men are unequal in terms of personal effort as well as capital, and when the account is used for both personal and business needs, the determination of the amount of any gratuitous transfer is much more difficult to establish. Theoretically, however, it is necessary that the gratuitous transfer be separated from any nongratuitous transfer in this arrangement and that the former quantity be made subject to the federal gift tax. The latter quantity might also be subject to the income tax.

After a taxpayer has identified a gratuitous transfer, it is necessary to determine its fair market value on the date of the gift. If the transfer is one of a total present interest—that is, the donee receives an immediate rather than a deferred value of an entire property—only the normal problems of valuation are present. Even "normal" problems of valuation are substantial for all properties not regularly traded on an open market, and occasionally they are substantial, even for widely traded properties. In settling disputed values, the courts commonly refer to such ephemeral criteria as a willing buyer, a willing seller, a free market, and full knowledge—assumed conditions that do not exist even in the most active markets of an economic world more accurately characterized by substantial ignorance than by full knowledge. Nevertheless, the valuation process must go on, and when taxpayers and government authorities cannot agree, the parties can only turn to the judicial system for an arbitrated settlement of their differences.

If a taxpayer transfers less than a total interest in a property, new and even more difficult problems of valuation are encountered. For example, a taxpayer may make a gift of the income from a property to person A for her lifetime, a gift of the same income stream to person B for his lifetime, but to take effect only after the life of person A, and finally a gift of the remainder interest in the property to person C. Before the gift tax consequences can be determined, we must know the value of the gifts made to persons A, B, and C. Obviously, such valuations can only be made with certain presumptions about the size of the income stream over a period of years, a discount rate, and a mortality table of expected human lives. In these instances, the code specifies the use of designated actuarial tables. Any attempt to investigate problems of valuation would lead us far afield of the objectives of this book. We will therefore assume that such valuation problems can somehow be solved, and proceed with the more direct tax consequences.

Exempt gifts and deductions. The taxpayer may subtract "exempt gifts and deductions" from the gross value of all gifts to determine taxable gifts. Exempt gifts and deductions fall into three categories: (1) a $3,000 exclusion per donee each year; (2) all gifts to nonprofit religious, charitable, literary, scientific, or educational organizations, and to the U.S. government and its political subdivisions; and (3) a marital deduction for property given the taxpayer's spouse.

The $3,000 individual exclusion is an annual exclusion that makes the vast majority of gifts nontaxable events. Note that any individual can give an unlimited amount of property away without a gift tax if he or she is willing to give it to enough different people. Also note that, over a lifetime, a rather large sum can be given tax-free to any one individual if the donor will begin early to take advantage of the annual exclusion. Over 50 years, for example, a person could transfer $150,000 to one child without incurring a gift tax, if the taxpayer would but make the maximum $3,000 tax-free gift each year. If a husband and wife each make gifts in that amount, the total that can be transferred tax-free is doubled. Gifts of future interests are not eligible for the annual exclusion.

Although gifts to religious, charitable, literary, scientific, and educational institutions are generally exempt from the gift tax, such gifts must be reported and then deducted on the gift tax return if they exceed $3,000 to any one donee in any one year. A taxpayer may desire to retain a property for as long as he or she lives, but wish to guarantee the passing of the property to a charity at death (or the death of a spouse). In these circumstances, the taxpayer can either make an appropriate provision in a will or make an immediate and irrevocable gift of the remainder interest to charity. The tax treatment of a charitable remainder interest is dependent upon special rules that will not be considered here.

Any taxpayer can give his or her spouse up to $100,000 without incurring a gift tax because of the gift tax marital deduction. For gifts to a spouse in excess of $100,000 but less than $200,000 the law provides no gift tax marital deduction. For gifts in excess of $200,000, there is a deduction equal to 50 percent of the value of the gift. Although gifts to a spouse of up to $100,000 in value seem to have a real tax advantage, this advantage is more apparent than real because any taxpayer making such a gift must reduce his or her estate tax marital deduction by the difference between the gift tax marital deduction allowed and one half of the fair market value of any gift to a spouse up to $200,000. Thus, for example, if a taxpayer gave a spouse a gift of $100,000 cash, that taxpayer's estate tax marital deduction would be reduced by $50,000 (that is, by the $100,000 gift tax marital deduction allowed minus 50 percent of the $100,000 given). A gift of $150,000 to one's spouse would reduce a taxpayer's estate tax marital deduction by $25,000 (i.e., by $100,000 minus 50 percent of $150,000). Finally, all taxable gifts must be added back to determine the total taxable estate, as well as the gross estate tax liability, of a deceased taxpayer. Because of these two adjustments, there may or may not be an advantage to making gifts to a spouse. At this juncture it is sufficient to note that a taxpayer will not necessarily reduce the aggregate gift and estate taxes by making such gifts. A more detailed explanation of this apparent conundrum, however, must await further explanation of the estate tax provisions.

Tax rates. The tax rate applied to all taxable gifts is determined according to a progressive rate schedule specified in the code. The present gift tax rates are stated in Table 12–1. The reader should observe that this one progressive rate schedule is applicable to the total taxable gifts made during a person's lifetime. Thus, the gift tax liability for gifts made during any one year depends upon the aggregate value of all taxable gifts made during the taxpayer's life, not just upon the gifts made in one year. The difference between the gift tax and the income tax is striking in this regard. Regarding the income tax, every taxpayer starts over at the lowest possible marginal rate each year, therefore, spreading taxable income equally over time serves to minimize the aggregate income tax liability. Except for the annual $3,000 exclusion provision, spreading gifts over time is of no benefit for gift tax purposes.

TABLE 12-1
Unified Estate and Gift Tax Rates

(1) Taxable transfer equal to or more than	(2) Taxable transfer less than	(3) Tax on amount in column (1)	(4) Rate of tax on excess over amount in column (1) (percent)
$ 0	$ 10,000	—	18
10,000	20,000	$ 1,800	20
20,000	40,000	3,800	22
40,000	60,000	8,200	24
60,000	80,000	13,000	26
80,000	100,000	18,200	28
100,000	150,000	23,800	30
150,000	250,000	38,800	32
250,000	500,000	70,800	34
500,000	750,000	155,800	37
750,000	1,000,000	248,300	39
1,000,000	1,250,000	345,800	41
1,250,000	1,500,000	448,300	43
1,500,000	2,000,000	555,800	45
2,000,000	2,500,000	780,800	49
2,500,000	3,000,000	1,025,800	53
3,000,000	3,500,000	1,290,800	57
3,500,000	4,000,000	1,575,800	61
4,000,000	4,500,000	1,880,800	65
4,500,000	5,000,000	2,205,800	69
5,000,000		2,550,800	70

Tax credits. In order to determine the net gift tax liability for any single reporting period, a taxpayer must first determine a gross tax liability on all taxable gifts made during the taxpayer's life (as explained above), and then subtract from that gross tax liability the sum of all gift taxes paid in prior periods. (For gifts made prior to 1977, this tax credit is calculated using the current tax rate schedule, and that amount, rather than the amount actually paid, is utilized in determining the aggregate credit for prior taxes.) The prior gift tax payments constitute a tax credit for the current period. Only by utilizing this tax credit arrangement can a progressive tax over a lifetime be achieved with more frequent reporting periods.

In addition to the cumulative credit for all gift taxes paid in prior years, the new law also provides a unified gift and estate tax credit. The amount of the unified credit is $47,000 for all persons dying after December 31, 1980. The effect of the unified credit is to allow a minimum amount, in addition to the annual $3,000 per donee exclusion, to wholly escape the federal gift and estate tax. The current $47,000 credit is equivalent to a $175,625 exclusion.

An Illustration

In order to illustrate the progressive nature of the federal gift tax, let us determine, *ignoring the unified credit* explained above, the gift tax liability for an imaginary single taxpayer who makes the gifts detailed below.

Year	Gifts to daughter	Gifts to son	Gifts to charity	Current taxable gifts
19x1	$10,000	$ 3,000	$ 5,000	$ 7,000
19x2	10,000	17,000	10,000	21,000
19x3	20,000	20,000	10,000	34,000
19x4	10,000	10,000	30,000	14,000

The illustration assumes that the taxpayer had made no prior taxable gifts, and that all gifts are of present interests. If there were no unified credit, the taxpayer in this illustration would have to file a gift tax return and pay a gift tax in each of the years 19x1 through 19x4, because gifts in each year exceed the $3,000 annual exclusion per donee.

In terms of the general formula suggested earlier, this taxpayer's gift tax computation might be summarized as follows:

Year	Gross gifts, current year	Current exemptions and deductions	Current taxable gifts	Aggregate taxable gifts	Gross tax liability*	Aggregate tax credit*	Current net tax liability*
19x1	$18,000	$11,000	$ 7,000	$ 7,000	$ 1,260	$ 0	$1,260
19x2	37,000	16,000	21,000	28,000	5,560	1,260	4,300
19x3	50,000	16,000	34,000	62,000	13,520	5,560	7,960
19x4	50,000	36,000	14,000	76,000	17,160	13,520	3,640

* Ignoring the unified gift and estate tax credit.

Aggregate taxable gifts are, of course, the sum of all taxable gifts in the current and prior years. The gross tax liability for any year is calculated on this base (aggregate taxable gifts), but a credit is granted for all gift taxes paid in prior years. For example, in the above illustration, the taxpayer in 19x4 would determine the gross tax liability based on aggregate gifts of $76,000 (even though in that year the taxpayer actually made taxable gifts totaling only $14,000). Based on gifts of $76,000, the gross tax liability is $17,160, but this taxpayer would claim a credit of $13,520 for all of the gift taxes paid in 19x1–x3. Thus the actual tax liability for 19x4 would be only $3,640, ignoring the unified credit. Obviously a taxpayer must maintain a record of all gifts made throughout a lifetime if he or she is to complete the gift tax return correctly.

Planning Considerations

The gift tax is exceedingly easy to avoid. If a taxpayer does not want to incur this tax, all that he or she has to do is refrain from making any gifts. In practice, therefore, tax planning relative to the gift tax usually relates to the determination of the lesser of two evils. The taxpayer will accept the need to pay a gift tax whenever doing so reduces some other tax by an amount greater than the gift tax incurred. The general constraints to be considered in making such a determination will be considered in the final section of this chapter.

Systematic giving. Taxpayers with substantial amounts of property should begin a systematic pattern of living as early in life as possible if they want to minimize the aggregate tax they or their heirs must pay. In some situations, a taxpayer may believe that nontax considerations are more important than tax savings, and the actions of such a taxpayer should be guided accordingly. A taxpayer who believes that childhood wealth leads to laziness, unhappiness, or family strife, for example, would be well advised to forgo any tax savings in the interest of a better quality of human existence. For those who do not believe that early wealth contributes to a less meaningful existence, however, systematic giving can be beneficial.

Only systematic pattern of giving can assure a taxpayer that he or she has taken maximum advantage of the $3,000 annual exclusion. Observe that this tax-minimizing provision is applicable to every taxpayer. Thus, if a husband and wife want to maximize their gift tax opportunities, they should make all gifts jointly. If both parties consent to this special treatment, even if the property given belongs entirely to one spouse, the annual exclusion for the couple increases from $3,000 to $6,000 per donee. A consent to make gifts jointly must be in writing and filed on a timely basis with the IRS.

To demonstrate the importance of systematic giving, observe that if a couple has two married children, and if each child has two children, that couple can transfer nearly half a million dollars tax-free to members of their family in just 20 years. That is, if each parent gives each child, child's spouse, and grandchild $3,000 per year, the total—$6,000 × 8 × 20—amounts to $480,000 in 20 years!

Charitable gifts. A taxpayer may have many good reasons for making a gift to charity. Most important, charitable gifts allow an individual to support personally those eleemosynary institutions and activities he or she believes to be the most deserving. There are also at least four important tax reasons for making charitable gifts. Two tax reasons are related to the income tax, and a third is associated with the estate tax. Further aspects of these tax consequences will be discussed in the next two sections of this chapter. For the moment we need only note that a charitable gift can be made without incurring a gift tax.

Cross gifts. Several years ago one imaginative taxpayer tried to avoid the gift tax provisions in a unique way. He arranged an agreement with close friends whereby each of them would make gifts of $3,000 to designated persons. By pooling their individual rights to a $3,000 annual exclusion per donee, the taxpayer hoped to be able to increase effectively his own ability to give more to a limited number of people without a gift tax. The basic idea of cross gifts is illustrated simply in Figure 12–1. Under this plan, taxpayers A, B, and C would each designate three individuals to whom they wish to make tax-free gifts each year; in this illustration, the donees are designated a1, a2, a3, b1, b2, and so on. Each of the three donors would make the maximum tax-free gift to each of the nine donees. The effect of a three-person agreement is obviously to triple the maximum tax-free gift from $3,000 per donee to $9,000 per donee. If successful, the idea could be expanded with larger numbers of participants to the agreement. In this

FIGURE 12-1

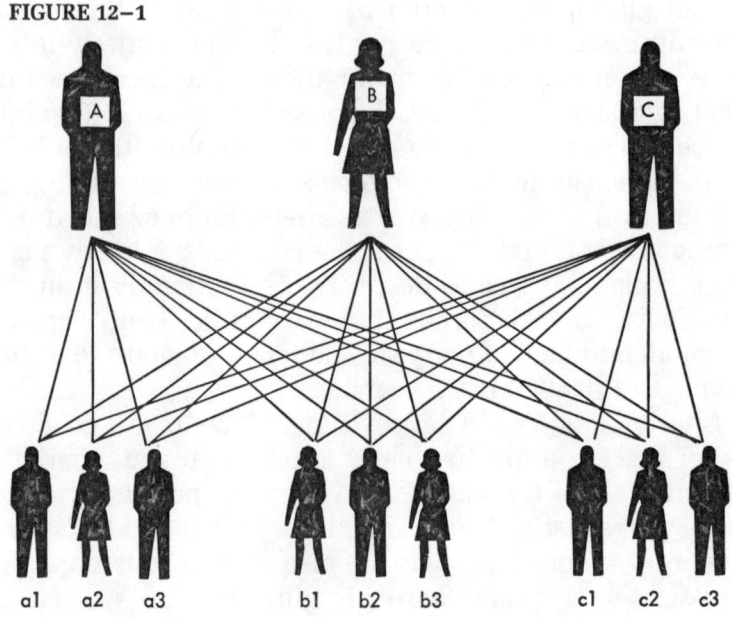

case, the court found, however, that the transfers were not gifts, since there was consideration exchanged by each party to the agreement—that is, the promise of the other parties to make a reciprocal transfer. Although the rationale for the tax result is confusing, the court apparently decided that the extra amounts would not be eligible for the annual exclusion because they were *not* gifts, and that the same extra amounts would be subject to the gift tax because they were gifts! The theory of substance over form seems to be a more adequate explanation of the conclusion than does the definitional nuance suggested by the court.

Serial gifts. Under certain circumstances, a taxpayer may desire to transfer a particular property to a donee, but the transfer of the entire property at one time may be made expensive because of the gift tax rules. Suppose, for example, that, after exhausting their unified credit, a couple jointly desired to transfer a specific property worth $120,000 to their daughter. If they made the complete transfer in a single year, the transfer would be subject to a gift tax on $114,000. Instead of arranging the transfer as a gift, the couple might consider selling the property to the daughter, with the initial payment to be made in the form of 20 interest-free $6,000 promissory notes, with one note maturing in each of the next 20 years. Each year, the couple might forgive the daughter the $6,000 note due that year and thus avoid any gift tax on the transfer. This possibility raises several interesting tax questions for both the parents and the daughter. For example, the form of the initial transfer might be disregarded and the transfer treated as a gift rather than a sale under the substance-over-form rule. If the form of the transaction is sustained, it could create taxable income for the parents, even though they receive no cash and attempt to report the alleged sale on an installment basis. The tax basis of the property to the daughter, for income tax purposes, would depend upon how she is deemed to have acquired it; one set of basis rules applies to property acquired by gift and another set to purchased property. (See Chapter 5 for a statement of the different basis rules.) Although this serial gift notion creates several interesting tax problems, it has been used successfully in the minimization of gift taxes.

Federal Taxation of Estates

The federal estate tax is an excise tax that is imposed when an individual transfers property rights at death. The estate tax is *not* a tax on property as such, but a tax on the right to transfer property at death. In other words, the estate tax is a tax on *the transfer of ownership* occasioned by the death of a property owner. Note also that the estate tax is not an inheritance tax on the right to receive property. Although the estate tax may reduce the net size of an inheritance received, it is a tax liability paid by the executor of the deceased taxpayer, not a tax on the recipients' rights to receive. Because the federal estate tax is a tax on the transfer of property at death, the initial determination essentially must be an inventory process. That is, in order to determine the estate tax it is first necessary to determine exactly what properties a person owns at the time of his or her death.

Basic Provisions

The final determination of an estate tax liability proceeds conceptually as follows:

    Gross value of the estate
  − Exemptions and deductions
  = Unadjusted taxable estate
  + Adjusted taxable gifts
  = Total taxable estate
  × Tax rate
  = Gross tax liability
  − Tax credits
  = Net tax payable.

Once again, it is the translation of real-world phenomena into a simple formula that creates both problems of compliance and opportunities for tax avoidance. The estate and gift taxes share the major common problem of valuation; both taxes demand that an explicit dollar value be specified for certain property rights, whether or not the properties are ever sold or exchanged. If the tax collector and a taxpayer cannot agree on valuation, the courts must resolve all differences of opinion. We shall again assume that all necessary valuations can be made, in one way or another, so that we may concentrate our attention on the related estate tax problems and opportunities that may be subject to deliberate intervention.

Gross estate. If we ignore the problems of valuation, the major problems remaining in the determination of the estate tax liability are those of discovery and identification. All property owned by a decedent at the moment of death must be included in the estate. This includes real and personal property, tangible and intangible property, and business as well as purely personal-use property. Code Section 2033 states it this way: "The value of the gross estate shall include the value of all property to the extent of the interest therein of the decedent at the time of his death."

One of the common definitional problems encountered in determining an estate tax involves property that is jointly owned. The law recognizes several different forms of joint ownership, including joint tenancy, tenancy in common, tenancy by the entirety, and community property. Under some forms of joint ownership, the value of the entire property must be included in a deceased taxpayer's estate; under other forms of ownership, only a fractional share is included. The dower and curtesy rights of a wife or husband can also be factors in the determination of a taxpayer's gross estate. And under yet other circumstances, a person may have to determine whether or not the value of a gross estate must include property over which the deceased person held certain "powers of appointment." These and many other problems can only be noted in passing. Solution of them in any specific circumstance may require many hours of work by a qualified attorney.

More generally, we can observe safely that a gross estate typically does not include property that a taxpayer gave away prior to death. The major exception to this conclusion involves transfers made within three years of death. Since December 31, 1976, the gross estate must automatically include the value of any gifts made in the three years prior to a decedent's death; in addition, if such a gift resulted in the payment of a gift tax, the value of the gift tax must also be added back and treated as part of the decedent's estate.

The automatic inclusion under the law is important for two reasons. First, it puts an end to many administrative complexities associated with the prior "contemplation-of-death rule." (That rule provided for the inclusion of predeath gifts in an estate only if the gifts had been made in contemplation of death; naturally, it was often very difficult to prove such an intention.) Second, by requiring the gross-up of gifts—that is, by requiring the inclusion in the estate of both the value of the gifts and the gift tax—the new rule eliminates many benefits previously associated with deathbed giving.

If a gift is made with the intent of reducing the size of an estate, the would-be donor must take care to complete the gift in every respect. For example, a taxpayer, as explained earlier, does not make a gift simply by naming a beneficiary for an insurance policy; since the insured may change a designated beneficiary up to the moment of death, there is no gift and the value of the policy must be included in the deceased taxpayer's estate. It is possible, of course, for a person to make a gift of an insurance policy or of any other property prior to death, but this act requires more than good intentions.

Sometimes a donor will try to make a gift of less than a complete property in order to reduce the estate tax. Although a partial gift is always a possibility, special care must be exercised in these circumstances. For example, prior to the 1976 Tax Reform Act, the Supreme Court ruled that the retention of voting rights of stocks otherwise transferred to another in trust was not sufficient to justify the inclusion of the value of those shares in the deceased donor's estate. The new law expressly repeals that decision of the Supreme Court and demands the full inclusion of value under those circumstances. Thus, in making partial gifts, extreme caution is warranted.

A taxpayer's rights in an annuity, pension, or profit-sharing plan may also present unusual problems in estate tax determinations. Whether or not such rights must be included in the gross estate depends upon how the rights were acquired (by purchase or through employment), how the plan is worded, who the employer was, and what options were exercised prior to death. The number of possible alternatives is too large to permit a restatement of all possible results here. One major rule, however, should be noted: Retirement plans that can *only* be satisfied by a lump-sum payment on the death of the insured must be included in a decedent's estate; those providing for a nonlump-sum distribution may be excluded. Taxpayers with substantial estates should make certain long before their death that such contracts are arranged in the most favorable way.

After the executor or administrator of an estate has determined which properties must be included in a deceased taxpayer's gross estate, attention turns to problems of valuation. In the case of the federal estate tax, the executor can generally elect to value all properties at either the date of the decedent's death or six months afterward. Usually, the executor will select the value on the date that will yield the lower aggregate valuation and therefore the lower estate tax. Unless a special exception applies, the fair market value of any property is the selling price that would obtain in a free market, with a willing buyer, a willing seller, and full knowledge, assuming that the property will be put to its highest and best use. In the absence of an actual sale, of course, this theoretical value may be nearly impossible to determine. Furthermore, the general valuation rules may not apply to real estate used in a family farm or other closely held business.

In an attempt to minimize concern over the fact that an estate tax liability could force the disposition of a family farm or business, Congress wrote several special provisions into the law. Among those special provisions is one that allows an executor to reduce the value of land used in a family farm or other closely held business by as much as $500,000 if certain conditions are satisfied. Among those conditions are the following: (1) a family member must have been actively involved in the farm or business for at least five of the eight years immediately preceding the decedent's death; (2) the real estate must represent at least 25 percent of the adjusted value of the decedent's estate; (3) the value of all property used in the family farm or business must represent at least 50 percent of the adjusted value of the decedent's estate; (4) the real estate must pass to a qualified heir (generally a family member or a close relative); and (5) a family member must continue to operate the farm or business for 15 years after the decedent's death. If all of the conditions are fully satisfied, the executor may value qualifying real estate at its "special use value" rather than its "highest and best use value." For example, if a farm were located near a growing city's limits, the fair market value of the land as residential or commercial property might be considerably in excess of its value as farmland. Nevertheless, if the stipulated conditions were satisfied, the land could be valued as farmland and the estate tax determined on that lesser value. Other privileges—such as a deferred payment of the estate tax with a minimal interest rate—might also apply in this situation.

Exemptions and deductions. The estate tax, like every other tax, has a list of exemptions and deductions that serve to reduce the size of the tax base. The most important deductions and exemptions for estate tax purposes are (1) a deduction of all debts against the estate or against the deceased taxpayer, (2) all funeral expenses and the administrative expenses of settling the estate, (3) a marital deduction, generally equal to the greater of $250,000 or 50 percent of the adjusted gross estate, for property that passes to the surviving spouse, and (4) most contributions to charitable organizations. Each of these deductions is in turn subject to special interpretations and applications in particular circumstances. We can only note in passing the broad outlines of each item.

The authorized deduction of all debts against the gross estate in the determination of the taxable estate means, of course, that the federal estate tax is imposed on the *net* value of the taxpayer's property, not on its gross value. A taxpayer who purchases a $300,000 property on a contract requiring a $50,000 down payment and assumption of a $250,000 mortgage shortly before death would not be increasing the size of the taxable estate by making such an acquisition. This result is in direct contrast with the usual property tax based on gross values. As noted earlier, the estate tax is not a property tax, even though valuation of property owned is the first step in the tax determination process.

The deduction authorized for administrative expenses includes the executor's commission, attorneys' fees, court costs, and all costs associated with selling property and otherwise managing the estate after the taxpayer's death and prior to the property distribution. An executor cannot, however, get both an income tax deduction (on the decedent's final return) and an estate tax deduction for a single expenditure. For example, the cost of selling a property can only be deducted once, either in the income or the estate tax calculation. The right to deduct funeral expenses serves similarly to reduce the estate tax base to the net value of property that a deceased person could actually pass to family or other heirs.

As noted above, the current law provides an estate tax marital deduction equal to the larger of $250,000 or 50 percent of the adjusted gross estate for any property passed from a decedent to a spouse. This is the unadjusted estate tax marital deduction. Remember also that, as explained on page 301, the otherwise allowable estate tax marital deduction must be decreased by the difference between the *gift tax* marital deduction allowed and one half of the fair market value of any gifts made to a spouse (up to $200,000). The significance of this adjustment will be clarified momentarily. Suffice it to note here that the estate tax marital deduction serves two important purposes. First, it serves to remove most small estates from the federal estate tax so long as there is a surviving spouse. Second, it tends to equate the tax results of persons living in community property states with the tax results of persons living in common-law states. Community property laws generally provide that one half of everything accumulated during a marriage belongs equally to each partner to the marriage. This presumption serves, of course, to reduce the size of the estate that passes at the time of a primary wage earner's death in a community property state. Thus the estate tax marital deduction tends to correct the potential inequity that would otherwise apply in favor of residents living in community property states.

Finally, the law authorizes a deduction for property transferred to a nonprofit religious, charitable, scientific, literary, or educational organization, or to the U.S. government or one of its political subdivisions. In general this deduction is limited to present interests in property. A remainder interest—that is, an interest that will mature on the death of a designated person at some time in the future—may be deductible, however, if the charitable remainder is in a farm or personal residence. Special rules apply to the deduction of charitable gifts made in trust.

The addition of taxable gifts. The fact that gifts and estates are really subject to a single, unified tax is implicit in the general formula stated on page 308. Observe in that formula that adjusted taxable gifts are added back to the taxable estate to determine the total taxable estate. The same rate schedule is currently applied both to taxable gifts made during life and to assets transferred at death. Because the tax base for the estate tax includes predeath gifts that were already taxed, it must also allow a tax credit for any gift tax paid by the deceased prior to death.

At this point, we are in a position to understand just why it may make little difference whether or not a taxpayer takes full advantage of the gift tax marital deduction. That observation, without a full explanation, was first noted on page 301. To better illustrate that important conclusion, let us now compare the results in two pairs of cases. Assume that taxpayers A and Y have each accumulated assets worth $600,000, that taxpayers B and Z have each accumulated $1 million, and that all four taxpayers will pass their entire accumulation of assets to their spouses. Furthermore, assume that taxpayers A and B make no gifts to their spouses before death, but that taxpayers Y and Z make gifts of $100,000 and $300,000, respectively. Calculation of the estate tax base would proceed as shown in the accompanying table.

	Taxpayer A	Taxpayer Y	Taxpayer B	Taxpayer Z
Accumulated assets	$600,000	$600,000	$1,000,000	$1,000,000
Less gifts to spouse	0	100,000	0	300,000
Remaining gross estate	$600,000	$500,000	$1,000,000	$ 700,000
Less marital deduction	300,000	200,000*	500,000	350,000†
Unadjusted taxable estate	$300,000	$300,000	$ 500,000	$ 350,000
Plus taxable gifts	0	0	0	150,000‡
Total taxable estate	$300,000	$300,000	$ 500,000	$ 500,000

* Unadjusted maximum of $250,000 − ($100,000 nontaxable gifts to spouse − 0.5 × $100,000 value of gifts), or $250,000 − ($100,000 −1/2 × $100,000), which equals $200,000.

† Unadjusted maximum of $350,000 − ($150,000 nontaxable gifts to spouse − 0.5 × $300,000 value of gifts), or $350,000 − ($150,000 − 1/2 × $300,000), which equals $350,000.

‡ Remember, gifts to a spouse are taxed as follows: first $100,000, fully deductible; next $100,000, no deduction; anything over $200,000, a 50 percent deduction. Consequently, if Z gave his or her spouse $300,000, $150,000 (or $100,000 + 0.5 × $100,000) would have been subject to the gift tax.

As illustrated in the table, the combined effect of (1) the adjustment to the estate tax marital deduction (due to any gift tax marital deduction allowed) plus (2) the inclusion of all taxable gifts in the value of the taxable estate, serves to emasculate the gift tax marital deduction of much value. Alternatively, the required adjustments serve to create greater equity between the person who appears to be generous to his or her spouse before death and the person who may seem to husband assets unduly.

Tax rates. The progressive tax rates applied to the total taxable estate to determine the gross estate tax liability are, as noted above, exactly the same tax rates as those applied to taxable gifts. Thus, as is evident in the heading, Table 12–1 is equally applicable to gifts and estates. The adjustment mechanism that keeps lifetime gifts from being taxed twice—that is, once when given and again at death, because of the inclusion of taxable gifts in the estate tax base—is the tax credit.

Tax credits. The federal estate tax authorizes tax credits for (1) any federal gift tax paid on values also included in the total taxable estate, (2) state inheritance taxes, subject to certain limits and adjustments, (3) prior federal estate taxes paid on properties included in more than one estate within a ten-year period, and (4) a new unified gift and estate tax credit. Each of the first three tax credits, as well as a possible foreign death tax credit, is intended to reduce the multiple taxation of a single tax base. We noted earlier the need to include all taxable gifts within the value of the taxable estate. This means, of course, that a single property transfer could be subject to both the federal gift tax and the federal estate tax. In order to avoid the multiple taxation of a single property transfer, the estate tax authorizes a tax credit for any gift tax paid (or payable).

The tax credit allowed against the federal estate tax for taxes paid as state inheritance taxes serves to provide all states with a minimum revenue from inheritance taxes. If an individual state did not impose such a tax, its residents would obtain no personal benefit since the federal estate tax would be increased accordingly. On the other hand, if an individual state attempted to increase its own state inheritance tax substantially above the maximum federal tax credit, it would stand a real chance of losing its wealthier citizens to another state. The few states that have attempted to impose significantly higher inheritance taxes have found that state residency is often a mobile condition, especially for the wealthiest taxpayers.

The tax credit allowed for successive federal estate taxes on specific properties included as part of more than one taxable estate within a single ten-year period is intended to reduce the potential cumulative effect of the estate tax. The amount of this credit is directly related to the time interval that has elapsed between the deaths of the various owners. If two years or less have elapsed since the property was last passed through a taxable estate, the tax credit is 100 percent of the previous estate tax; if two to four years have elapsed, the credit is equal to 80 percent of the prior tax; if four to six years, it is 60 percent; if six to eight years, 40 percent; and if eight to ten years, 20 percent. No tax credit is allowed if the property last passed through a taxable estate more than ten years earlier. As a practical matter, this tax credit is of limited importance because most people with substantial property try to arrange their personal affairs to ensure that property will not pass through a taxable estate in such a short period under ordinary circumstances.

The $47,000 unified gift and estate tax credit was explained on pages 302 and 303. As noted there, the effect of this credit is to exempt $175,625 of otherwise taxable gifts and/or estates from federal tax. If a taxpayer desires to maximize the amount of property to be left to a surviving spouse, without any consideration for the possible additional tax cost when the property passes to other survivors on the death of the surviving spouse, it is possible to leave a spouse $601,250 completely free of any federal gift and/or estate tax. This is possible because of the combined effect of the gift tax marital deduction, the $250,000 estate tax marital deduction, and the $47,000 unified credit.

An Illustration

To illustrate how the net estate tax payable is determined, let us review the estate tax calculation for each of two taxpayers, M and N, who accumulate assets of $1,500,000 during their lifetimes and provide in their wills a maximum formula estate tax marital deduction.

Assume further that taxpayer M makes no gifts, but that taxpayer N gives his or her spouse $675,625 during life (more than three years prior to death). Assume that no other gifts are made and ignore the $3,000 annual exclusion. Under these assumptions, we can summarize the general outline of the federal gift and estate taxes in the table below.

Perhaps the most important generalization implicit in this illustration is that if we ignore the $3,000 annual exclusion, the reduction of an estate due to the payment of a gift tax, and the time value of money, making substantial gifts during the life is not an effective way to reduce an estate.

Planning Considerations

Since death is a certainty for everyone, the federal estate tax cannot be permanently avoided unless a taxpayer is willing to renounce U.S. citizenship and become a citizen and resident of a non-estate-taxing country. If a taxpayer dies intestate (that is, without a will), the laws of the state of residency

	Taxpayer M	Taxpayer N
Accumulated assets	$1,500,000	$1,500,000
Less gifts to spouse	0	675,625*
Remaining gross estate	$1,500,000	$ 824,375†
Less maximum marital deduction	750,000	412,187
Unadjusted taxable estate	$ 750,000	$ 412,188
Plus taxable gifts	0	337,812
Total taxable estate	$ 750,000	$ 750,000‡
Gross estate tax liability	$ 248,300	$ 248,300
Less tax credits:		
Unified credit	(47,000)	(47,000)§
Gift tax paid	0	(53,656)
Net estate tax payable	$ 201,300	$ 147,644
Total taxes paid:		
Gift tax	$ 0	$ 53,656
Estate tax	201,300	147,644
Lifetime total	$ 201,300	$ 201,300

* Against the $675,625 given to a spouse, taxpayer N would be entitled to a gift tax marital deduction of $337,812. Against the gift tax of $100,656, payable on the remaining gifts of $337,813, taxpayer N would claim a $47,000 unified tax credit. Hence the gift tax payable would be $53,656.

† For purposes of this illustration, ignore the fact that the gift tax of $53,656 would serve to reduce the remaining estate. However illogical, this assumption better illustrates the cumulative lifetime effect of the unified gift and estate tax.

‡ Note that, under the rules, the taxable estate is the same (if we ignore the reduction of the estate due to the gift tax payment) whether or not a taxpayer makes lifetime gifts. This result is very different from that which obtained under the law in existence prior to 1977.

§ At first blush it may seem that taxpayer N is getting double credit for a single $47,000 unified credit. That conclusion is *not* justified. Observe that all *taxable* gifts were "added back" to determine the taxable estate. In other words, only the gift tax marital deduction was not added back (because that subtraction was made *to determine taxable gifts*—which must be contrasted with a reduction of the gross gift tax, attributable to the unified credit). The failure to add back the gift tax marital deduction in taxpayer N's estate is offset by the larger estate tax marital deduction in taxpayer M's estate.

will determine how property is divided among potential heirs. In general, a person's property will be divided between a surviving spouse and children, if any. If no child or spouse survives the taxpayer, the property will usually pass to any grandchildren. If there is no surviving spouse, child, or grandchild, the property will typically be divided among siblings. The exact rules are commonly referred to as the *laws of descent and distribution,* and they vary from one state to the next. If a taxpayer prepares a valid will prior to death, he or she may, within certain limits, distribute properties in any manner deemed appropriate. Prior to the Tax Reform Act of 1976, much of the sting of the federal estate tax could be avoided for many years by the simple expedient of a trust that skipped several generations. In other words, in arranging the disposition of his or her property, a taxpayer could create a testamentary trust giving a successive life interest (and possibly a limited right to invade corpus under specified conditions) to a surviving spouse or any children, grandchildren, and even great-grandchildren. A *life interest* is just what the words imply: A person receiving a life interest has only the right to income from certain property for so long as he or she lives. A life interest does not grant the recipient any right to decide who shall receive the trust corpus at the time of his or her death. Under prior law, when a person with a life interest died, there was nothing to be included in the decedent's estate for estate tax purposes. That was the tax beauty of a generation-skipping trust; a wealthy individual could "take care of" several successive generations without the imposition of the estate taxes. Only the recipient of the remainder interest—that is, the person who finally received the right to dispose of whatever was left when the intervening life interests had all been satisfied—received anything that could be subject to another round of estate taxation. And only the legal rule against perpetuities required the designation of a remainder interest somewhere down the line. The current rules are by no means as generous.

Generation skipping. A generation-skipping tax will apply to any "taxable distribution" and/or "taxable termination" occurring after April 30, 1976, unless such distribution or termination is attributable to an irrevocable trust in existence on that date, which was not modified after that date, and whose grantor dies before January 1, 1982. Although it is tempting to investigate the many nuances of the new generation-skipping tax, such an excursion would do little to accomplish the objectives of this book. Consequently we will satisfy ourselves with the broad outlines of current provisions.

In general terms, the 1976 act put an end to generation-skipping transfers. It achieved this result by (1) the definition of generations and (2) an operative provision that provides that any trust with two or more generations of beneficiaries who belong to a generation younger than that of the grantor will be a generation-skipping trust. Under current law, therefore, if a trust were created with a life interest for a spouse (deemed to be of the same generation as the grantor), with subsequent life interest for any children (deemed to be of the next younger generation), and with a remainder interest for any grandchildren (considered to be two generations younger than the grantor), it would be a generation-skipping trust. (There is a limited special exception for trusts created for the benefit of the children of a grantor's children. The maximum permissible under this special rule is $250,000 per child of the grantor. Hence a grantor with three children, each with one or more children, could exempt $750,000 under the special exception.) On the other hand, a trust with only a life interest for a surviving spouse and a remainder distribution to any great-grandchildren would *not* be a generation-skipping trust because it provides for only one generation of beneficiaries who belong to a generation younger than that of the grantor.

The new generation-skipping tax is, for all practical purposes, equivalent to the gift or estate tax that would be payable if the property were transferred from the estate of a "deemed transferor" to a "younger generation beneficiary." The new tax will be payable either because of the death of one younger generation beneficiary, who held only a life interest, or because of a distribution of trust property, to a younger generation beneficiary, from a trust that also benefited another younger generation beneficiary who is (was) a member of a generation older than that of the distributee. The new tax, however, is ordinarily payable from the assets of the trust, not from the assets of the deemed transferor. In order to determine the amount of tax payable, it is necessary for the trustee to determine (1) who is the deemed transferor and (2) the gift or estate tax that would have been payable had that person made the property distribution directly. Needless to say, we cannot allow ourselves to be sidetracked by the many problems implicit in the above general rules. We might, however, note a few important conclusions implicit in those rules.

If an individual is *not* concerned with the financial well-being of intermediate generations, aggregate estate taxes can be minimized, other things being equal, by passing any property to the youngest possible generation. Tax minimization will result so long as the designated beneficiary does not predecease a beneficiary of an intervening generation. In other words, so long as a designated great-grandchild does not die before his or her parents or grandparents, the aggregate estate tax will be minimized if property is left by a decedent to the great-grandchild, because only that sequence of distribution will necessarily avoid any estate tax on the intervening estates of any children and grandchildren (who include the affected grandparent and parent of the designated recipient). Most people are not likely to prefer such a strangely contorted distribution of assets. In all probability, most people will prefer to ensure the financial welfare of their children and grandchildren, even if that decision results in fewer assets being passed along to great-grandchildren or to beneficiaries of a still younger generation. In families with large accumulations of assets, however, an advantageous arrangement is still possible. First, a husband and wife should divide their properties so that each will leave an estate of equal size. Then the first parent to die might leave a will that creates trusts for the benefit of their children. The second parent to die might leave a will that leaves nothing to their children but that bequeaths his or her property to any grandchildren. By dividing the parents' estate equally, and by passing one half of the accumulated assets to each of two successive generations, a larger accumulation can be moved to younger generations than would be possible under alternatives that provide for more generous distributions to the spouse and/or the couple's children.

The potential impact of the new generation-skipping tax can be illustrated as in Figure 12–2. Although that illustration ignores several possible modifications, which would be commonplace in most real-world circumstances—for example, it ignores all possible marital deductions, as well as the special $250,000 exclusion for the grandchildren of a grantor—it serves to indicate the potential impact of the new provisions. In summary, it shows how a great-grandson might have received $1,247,000 under prior law, whereas he would receive only $522,000 under the new law, given otherwise comparable circumstances. The figure is based on the assumption that a mother put $2 million in trust, with respective life interests for her son, her granddaughter, and her great-grandson. Under the

FIGURE 12-2

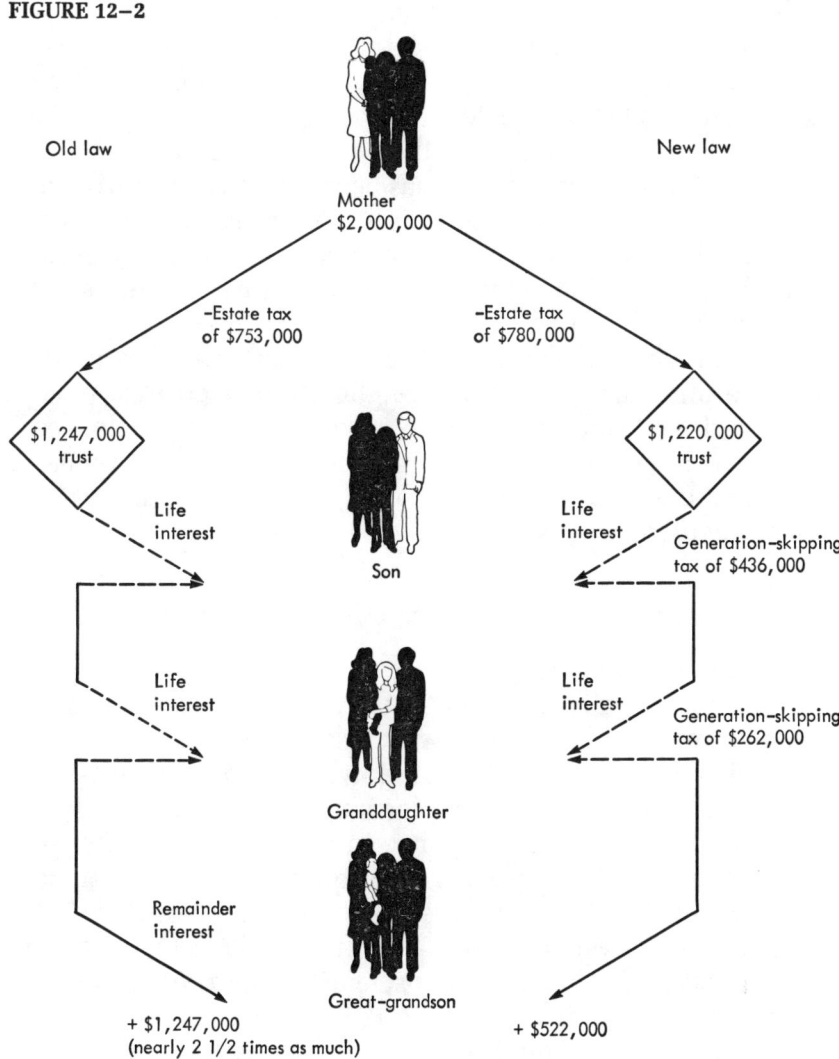

old law, the only estate tax was that incurred at the death of the mother. Current law would impose a generation-skipping tax at the deaths of the son and the granddaughter. Both taxes would, of course, reduce the amount passing to the great-grandson.

A time to give. If a taxpayer desires to minimize both the gift and the estate tax, a careful selection of property and good predictive ability (possibly good luck) is now required. Note that the tax base for both the gift and the estate tax is the value of the property transferred on the date it is transferred. Any appreciation in value that takes place after a gift has been completed, and before the death of the donor, escapes both the gift and the estate tax so far as the donor is concerned. Thus a new tax minimization strategy has been created: The early gift of a property that will subsequently appreciate in value will minimize the federal gift and estate tax of the donor. Because of the basis rules for inherited property, however, that same gift may increase income taxes.

A full consideration of the possible tax impact of family tax planning must give further weight to the disposition plans of the recipient, the marginal tax rate of all possible donees, and the time-preference value of money. These and related considerations will be examined briefly in the remaining pages of this chapter.

Integrating the Income, Gift, and Estate Taxes

In the final analysis, there are only two things that a person can do with any property that is not consumed: it can be retained, or it can be given away. For tax purposes, the first alternative can be further broken down into three choices: (1) hold the property in its present form until death; (2) exchange the property for another property, in a nontaxable exchange, prior to death; or (3) dispose of the property in a taxable transaction before death and reinvest the proceeds. The second alternative can be broken down into two choices: (1) give the property to a charitable/literary/scientific/educational organization, or (2) give it to a "nonqualifying recipient" (e.g., a relative or friend). In summary, a propertied taxpayer seems to be faced with two basic questions: a "how much" question and a "what" question. That is, the taxpayer must decide (1) how much to give and how much to retain, and (2) what to give and what to retain. Even if the only decision criteria to be considered were tax factors, a decision model would be difficult to implement because there are so many unknown future variables in this model. In the real world, of course, nontax factors often govern these decisions. The taxpayer simply should be aware of the tax considerations before making a final decision.

The previous illustrations in this chapter imply that there is relatively little *tax incentive* to give property away to nonqualifying recipients prior to death. That conclusion is only valid, however, if you ignore both (1) predeath changes in value and (2) the fact that any gift tax paid more than three years prior to the decedent's death will reduce the remaining estate by the amount of the tax. (That gift tax, however, will be fully credited against the gross estate tax.) For very large estates, these two additional considerations create a major bias in favor of giving property away, rather than retaining it. In other words, if the objective is to maximize the wealth passed to subsequent generations, the model will ordinarily favor gifts over retention, other things being equal. Unfortunately for the maximizing taxpayer, however, other things generally are not equal. One of the most important unequal factors has to do with the marginal tax rates that are pertinent to the various potential recipients.

The Importance of the Marginal Tax Rate

The importance of the marginal tax rate to successful tax planning cannot be overemphasized. This conclusion is equally valid for any progressive tax, which includes the federal income and the federal donative transfers tax. In terms of successful family tax planning, this means that property ownership may have to be rearranged among family members before it is sold or exchanged outside the confines of the family unit. In Chapter 3 we observed how special entities, such as the trust and the corporation, might be used to help minimize the federal income tax. Let us now consider still other possibilities of minimizing the income tax by rearranging affairs within the family.

Income tax considerations. The aggregate income tax on a family unit will be minimized when the family income is divided equally among all family members. For example, instead of having one (married) individual report an annual family income of $200,000, it *may* be possible to divide that income equally among eight family members and thereby reduce the annual income tax liability from approximately $110,000 to something like $45,000, a saving of over 50 percent! As explained earlier, it is very difficult (if not impossible) to redirect the tax on earned income—for example, the income tax on a wage or salary—from anyone other than the person who earned it. With income from property, however, there are several opportunities to do just that. One possibility, already mentioned, is to transfer the income-producing property in trust and to instruct the trustee to distribute the trust's income to other family members. A second possibility is to give the entire property to another family member so that the donee, rather than the donor, will report any subsequent income earned. A third possibility involves the tax associated with the disposition of an appreciated asset. If a taxpayer decides to make a taxable disposition of any property that has significantly increased in value, that taxpayer should at least consider giving the property to another family member before completing the disposition. Obviously the taxable sale of an appreciated property might best be made by the family member in the lowest marginal income tax bracket. Typically this tax plan involves a gift of the appreciated property (about to be sold) from an older, high-marginal-bracket taxpayer to a younger, low-marginal-bracket taxpayer. Giving the property does, of course, create an immediate gift tax, but that creates no additional gift or estate tax liability (except for the time-preference value of money) in the long run. Since most older family members intend to transfer their accumulated wealth to a younger generation at some time or other, they should always consider the possibility of making part of that transfer whenever they make a decision to dispose of any highly appreciated asset. To make such a gift on a timely basis will clearly add to the total asset values that can be passed to the younger generations.

On the other hand, observe that the tax plan just explained will not work with depreciated properties. A highly depreciated property—that is, a property with a tax basis that is substantially greater than its fair market value—cannot be transferred by gift to a taxpayer in the highest marginal tax bracket to obtain a greater tax savings. Because of the basis rules for property received as a gift, which were explained in Chapter 5, only the original owner can get the tax benefit of any predisposition decrease in the value of property. Also, a depreciated property should always be sold prior to death. If a taxpayer does not sell that property in a taxable transaction prior to death, the potential income tax deduction implicit in the decline in value will be lost forever because of the basis rules for inherited property.

Maximum tax considerations. The 50 percent maximum tax on personal service income adds several new and relatively complex aspects to family tax planning. The details of the "max tax," as it is popularly called, were explained in Chapter 4. Suffice it to recall here that a 50 percent maximum marginal tax rate applies to personal service taxable income. Any income other than personal service (or earned) income will be subject to ordinary tax rates—that is, to rates of up to 70 percent. Furthermore, as explained in Chapter 9, income from property often reduces the amount of income eligible for the max tax because it often creates tax-preference items. For all practical purposes this means that the taxpayer who is highly compensated for services—for example, the actor, athlete, business executive, or successful professional—should generally not also be the family member who receives any passive income, such as interest, rents, or dividends. From a family standpoint it would be much better to rearrange ownership of the assets that produce the passive income so that that income is rechanneled from the highly compensated, service-rendering individual to his or her parents, children, or grandchildren, or to a family trust. In this way, the marginal tax rate applicable to both the personal service income and the passive income can be kept as low as possible.

Estate tax considerations. The importance of giving full consideration to the marginal tax rate is just as applicable to estate planning as it is to income tax planning. The cost of an alternative solution can be demonstrated by an example involving the estate tax marital deduction. Suppose that a husband, H, had an accumulated taxable estate of $6 million and that his wife, W, had an accumulated taxable estate (of separate property) of $2 million. If H were to leave a will providing for a maximum, formula estate tax deduction, and if H were to die before W, H's taxable estate would be reduced, by the maximum marital deduction, from $6 million to $3 million, and H's executor would pay an estate tax of approximately $1,243,800. Although that might serve to minimize H's estate tax, W's tax would be unnecessarily increased. A tax-minimizing plan would have H leave a will with an "equalization clause." That is, H's will would provide for a marital deduction equal to one half of the difference between his and W's adjusted gross estates; or, here, ½ ($6 million − $2 million). Thus H would claim a marital deduction of only $2 million so that both he and W would eventually die with taxable estates of $4 million. By creating two equal estates, and thereby reducing the marginal estate tax rate to the lowest common denominator, the couple would save $80,000 in estate taxes. The details of this conclusion are apparent in the accompanying tabular summary.

	Ignoring marginal rates		Considering marginal rates	
	H	W	H	W
Gross estate (original)	$6,000,000	$2,000,000	$6,000,000	$2,000,000
Marital deduction	−3,000,000	+3,000,000	−2,000,000	+2,000,000
Taxable estate	$3,000,000	$5,000,000	$4,000,000	$4,000,000
Gross estate tax	$1,290,800	$2,550,800	$1,880,800	$1,880,800
Less unified credit	47,000	47,000	47,000	47,000
Net tax payable	$1,243,800 +	$2,503,800	$1,833,800 +	$1,833,800
Total tax paid by H and W	$3,747,600		$3,667,600	
Tax saved by considering marginal rates		$80,000		

The tax savings in this example are not very dramatic. Although the example suggests that this couple can save $80,000 by the careful planning of H's marital deduction (to give consideration to the marginal rates applicable to two estates of different sizes), economic realities suggest that the costlier solution is really a preferable solution in this instance. Note that the apparently "better" plan calls for the earlier payment of $590,000 in estate taxes by H's executor; that is, the apparently "better" plan calls for a payment of $1,833,800 in estate taxes at the time of H's death, whereas the "lesser" plan requires a payment of only $1,243,800. The difference of $590,000 carries with it an implicit interest expense. Assuming that W lives for several years longer than H, the time-preference value of money associated with an $80,000 tax savings would very likely make the interest cost on the extra $590,000 at the time of H's death greater than the tax saved by this plan.

If we ignore the time-preference value of money, we can conclude this portion of the chapter by observing that a maximum marital deduction formula bequest generally provides for the minimum federal estate tax for a married couple only if the second spouse to die has little or no property. If the second spouse to die has substantial property, the federal estate tax will generally be minimized by the "equalization formula clause" explained above.

The Importance of the Basis Rules

As explained in Chapter 5, inherited property ordinarily takes a basis equal to the fair market value of the property on the date of the decedent's death (or, possibly, six months after death). This rule is very important to family tax planning. If a taxpayer owns a property that has substantially increased in value since it was acquired, and if it is likely that the next recipient of that property will dispose of it before his or her death, there is a strong tax incentive to retain that property and allow it to pass through the taxpayer's estate. At the moment of death, the income tax potential implicit in the increase in value is permanently removed for the next owner. Theoretically, the heir or devisee could sell the property immediately after the decedent's death and recognize no taxable income because of this basis rule.

As previously explained in both this chapter and Chapter 5, the basis rules for property acquired by gift make depreciated properties—that is, those properties that have decreased in value since their acquisition—inappropriate for gifts to family members or friends. The ideal gift property for those donees is characterized by a fair market value that is approximately equal to basis. The exception to this rule, already noted in this chapter, is found in a situation in which (for economic reasons) a taxpayer desires to sell an appreciated property prior to death. In that case, a gift of the appreciated property to a family member in a low marginal tax bracket can make good tax sense.

In very large estates it is common to find that a majority of the decedent's assets have values greater than basis. Because of the dominant position of these assets, plus the apparently normal tendency for most people to want to keep much of their estate until death, a simple table can be prepared to give rule-of-thumb answers to the "what to keep" and "what to give" questions. That table appears as follows:

Recommended action	FMV > basis	FMV ≈ basis	FMV < basis
Sell or exchange in taxable transaction prior to death	No	OK	Always
Exchange only in nontaxable transactions	Yes	OK	No
Retain in present form	Yes	OK	No
Give to family or friends before death	No	Yes	No
Give to charity	Yes	OK	No

The tax reasons for selecting only certain properties for gifts to charity will be explained shortly. The reader should understand, however, that the word *charity* is used here to mean any organization that would qualify the gift as a tax deduction—for federal income tax purposes, for federal gift and estate tax purposes, or for both. In general, this can be any charitable, literary, scientific, or educational organization qualified under Section 501(c)(3).

Charitable Gifts

The combined effect of several tax rules is to allow a wealthy taxpayer to support favorite eleemosynary institutions and activities at a minimum economic cost. Before we can determine the actual cost of charitable giving, it is necessary to introduce the income tax provisions pertinent to the charitable contribution deduction. In general, the code authorizes an individual taxpayer to deduct, for income tax purposes, contributions made to charitable organizations up to a maximum of either 50 percent or 30 percent of the taxpayer's adjusted gross income. The 50 percent limit applies to contributions of cash made to public charities; the 30 percent limit applies to contributions of capital gain properties to public charities. Contributions made in excess of these limits in any one year can be carried forward and deducted in subsequent years. Contributions made to private charitable foundations have been subject to more stringent rules since 1969. Because private charitable foundations are no longer of primary importance to tax planning, none of those rules will be discussed here.

The act of making a gift is *not* deemed to constitute realization for income tax purposes, except in the case of tax shelters. This means that a taxpayer with an appreciated property can avoid any income tax by giving away the property. If the gift is made to a charitable organization, the charity can sell the property and avoid any recognition of gain because of its general exemption from the income tax. A charitable gift thus serves to avoid for everyone concerned the income tax implicit in an appreciated property. As noted earlier in this chapter, charitable gifts are also authorized deductions in the computation of the gift and estate tax. Thus the act of making a charitable gift of an appreciated property serves to reduce a taxpayer's income tax and the estate tax without increasing the gift tax.

The measure of a charitable contribution deduction depends upon the class of property given. Contributions made in cash are simply measured by the amount of cash given. Contributions of property that, if sold, would produce a long-term capital gain are measured by the fair market value of the property on the date of the contribution. Contributions of property that if sold, would produce ordinary income (including short-term capital gains) are measured by the basis of the property given unless the fair market value is lower than basis, in which case the fair market value becomes the measure of the deduction.

Translating the many related tax rules that apply to charitable contributions into practical advice, a taxpayer should consider giving *only* appreciated capital gain properties to favorite charities. The correctness of this conclusion can be demonstrated by a comparative analysis. The comparison on the next two pages is based on the assumptions that the contributing taxpayer (1) is in a 70-percent marginal tax bracket as far as ordinary income is concerned, (2) is in a 28-percent marginal tax bracket as far as long-term capital gains are concerned, (3) does not exceed the annual limits for the charitable contribution deduction, (4) makes all gifts to public charities, and (5) would have sold the same properties in a taxable transaction had he or she not given them to the charities. Because of the assumptions implicit in these calculations—that is, the assumptions that the taxpayer is in the highest possible marginal tax bracket for both ordinary income and long-term capital gains, and that the donated property was a very highly appreciated property—we can determine that, under some extreme conditions, a taxpayer is almost as well off giving long-term capital gain property to charity as selling in the open market. In this illustration, the taxpayer would be able to keep only $82,000 of the proceeds if he or she had sold the capital gain property on the open market. That is, the $110,000 realized on the sale minus the $28,000 long-term capital gains tax would leave the taxpayer with $82,000. If the taxpayer gave the same property to a charity, the income tax liability would be reduced by $77,000, that is 70 percent of $110,000. Thus the real economic cost of this generous gift is really only $5,000.

Form of gift	Amount to be given (FMV)	Tax basis of property given	Income tax saved due to contribution deduction	Income tax saved due to nonrecognition of gain	Net real economic cost
Cash	$110,000	$110,000	$77,000	$ 0	$33,000
LTCG property	110,000	10,000	77,000	28,000	5,000
Ordinary income property	110,000	10,000	7,000	70,000	33,000

For the vast majority of the taxpayers, the extreme assumptions made here are unrealistic. Nevertheless, the tax effect on the cost of giving may be substantial. To illustrate a more likely result, let us make the same calculations for a taxpayer (1) in a 50 percent marginal tax bracket as far as ordinary income is concerned, (2) in a 20 percent marginal tax bracket as far as long-term capital gains are concerned, (3) whose charitable contributions do not exceed the annual limitations, and (4) who would have sold the same properties in a taxable transaction had he or she not given them to charity.

The real economic cost of a charitable contribution is determined by the marginal tax bracket of the donor and the amount of the unrealized gain in the donated property. The higher the marginal tax bracket and the greater the unrealized gain, the lower the economic cost of making a charitable gift. In this illustration, we can see how the tax effect has allowed a taxpayer to make a $10,000 contribution to a favorite charity at a real economic cost of only $3,800.

Form of gift	Amount to be given (FMV)	Tax basis of property given	Income tax saved due to contribution deduction	Income tax saved due to nonrecognition of gain	Net real economic cost
Cash	$10,000	$10,000	$5,000	$ 0	$5,000
LTCG property	10,000	4,000	5,000	1,200	3,800
Ordinary income property	10,000	4,000	2,000	3,000	5,000

Both of the last two illustrations actually overstate the real economic cost of making a charitable contribution because the act of making the gift also serves to reduce the size of the donor's taxable estate and thus the estate tax. In some states it also reduces the state income tax. Any refinement of the illustrations to include a measure of this additional tax saving would have to be based upon too many assumptions to have much practical value. The important conclusion, however, is that a substantial charitable gift may sometimes be made at a relatively low real aftertax cost to the donor. Whether or not a large gift to charity is possible, nearly all taxpayers give some thought to their retirement income.

Retirement Income Funds

The proper disposition of assets accumulated over a lifetime of work to provide a possible source of retirement funds presents one of the most complex of all problems in family tax planning. As explained very briefly in Chapter 7, the assets accumulated in a qualified pension, profit-sharing, or stock bonus plan may be taxed under any one of several options at the time those funds are distributed from the employee trust fund to the primary beneficiary and/or the primary beneficiary's heirs. Lump-sum distributions create the most problems and present the most opportunities. Generally speaking, a taxpayer can elect to tax a lump-sum distribution as partially ordinary income and partially capital gain, as wholly "ordinary income," or as a special kind of ordinary income subject to a ten-year-forward income-averaging calculation. If a taxpayer does not make an election and receive the funds before death, the entire amount accumulated will be subject to the estate tax unless the contract provides for a distribution other than a lump-sum distribution to named beneficiaries. If paid as an annuity to the beneficiaries, any receipts will represent ordinary income, subject to no special provisions.

The many special rules necessary to make a wise decision concerning the preferred method of disposing of assets accumulated in a qualified pension, profit-sharing, or stock bonus plan must remain beyond the confines of this short book. Unfortunately, the rules are so complex that any attempt to describe them briefly would probably lead to more misinformation than information.

Successful family tax planning obviously involves the careful consideration of personal objectives as well as income, gift, and estate tax provisions. Most successful tax plans involve a substantial lead time if they are to be implemented properly. The use of life estates, placed in trust prior to a taxpayer's death, may in some instances still serve to decrease the family income tax liability as well as the donor's gift and estate tax liabilities. The careful integration of the many pertinent considerations involves full cooperation on the part of all parties. Any individual who has accumulated over $250,000 worth of property should give serious consideration to discussing his or her personal situation with a qualified tax adviser. The author's personal experience suggests that first-generation wealth is typically least interested in tax consequences. In other words, "the man or woman who made it" is least concerned about what taxes might do to an accumulated estate. Possessors of second-, third-, and fourth-generation wealth are often much more willing to modify personal fortunes to minimize the tax cost for everyone.

CHAPTER 13

Accounting Method Options

Code Section 446 provides the general accounting method requirements that must be satisfied by every taxpayer. This code section is subdivided into five subsections. Subsection (a) states that a taxpayer must compute taxable income on the same method of accounting as is used in keeping the regular books. Subsection (b) gives the Secretary of the Treasury authority to designate a particular accounting method if either the taxpayer has no regular method or the method used does not clearly reflect income. Subsection (c) lists several methods that may be used, including a cash method, an accrual method, and a modified cash method prescribed by Treasury regulations. Subsection (d) allows a taxpayer to use more than one method of accounting if he or she is engaged in more than one trade or business. And Subsection (e) requires the prior consent of the commissioner if a taxpayer desires to change the method of accounting. Collectively, these requirements are sufficiently flexible to permit every taxpayer a maximum opportunity to select the most favorable method of accounting. Except for an occasional refusal to authorize a change in accounting methods, the statutory requirements have been interpreted rather liberally. Thus, it is doubly important for every taxpayer to make the initial selection wisely.

In addition to selecting one general method of accounting for each trade or business, a taxpayer must select many specific accounting procedures and conventions to be utilized in implementing a single method of accounting. The number of alternative accounting procedures and conventions is substantially larger than the number of generally accepted accounting methods. Each election can have a significant impact on the tax liability ultimately reported for any taxpayer. In this chapter, we shall consider some of the more important planning aspects of the various accounting methods and conventions. The first portion of the chapter will be concerned with general methods of accounting; the second portion, with more specific accounting procedures and conventions. The code contains over 50 elections that must be made within the first tax year of any taxable entity and several hundred additional elections that can be made in any year in which they are applicable to a taxpayer. A number of these elections are essentially equivalent to an alternative accounting procedure. We shall consider a few of the more important tax accounting elections.

General Methods of Accounting

The most commonly known methods of accounting are the cash receipts and disbursements method, usually called the *cash method*, the accrual method, and the completed contract method. For tax purposes, a fourth method of accounting, called the *installment method*, has been accepted both for general use and for reporting specific transactions. The income reported by a taxpayer in any single year will differ importantly under each of these accounting methods. Although the aggregate net differences tend to be reduced over a long period of time, they are still important for tax purposes because of the time-preference value of money. The longer a taxpayer can defer a tax liability, other things being equal, the smaller the real economic cost of the tax.

The Cash Method

The vast majority of individual taxpayers report their taxable income on a cash method of accounting. This means, of course, that they report their items of gross income in the year in which they receive cash or other property and that they report deductions in the year in which they pay a deductible expense. The only financial records typically maintained by such taxpayers are a checkbook and an odd collection of canceled checks, "paid" vouchers, sales receipts, and some miscellaneous notes and diary type records. These documents, along with the Form W–2 (the "Wage and Tax Statement" prepared by the taxpayer's employer) and the Forms 1099 (the "U.S. Information Returns" prepared by banks, savings and loan associations, dividend-paying corporations, and other payers of miscellaneous earnings), are somehow combined to provide the necessary information required to complete an individual tax return (Form 1040 or 1040A) by April 15 each year.

Most service-oriented businesses, including the professions of medicine, dentistry, law, and accountancy, also report their taxable income on a cash method. In these instances, however, it is common to find a more complete and accurate set of financial records. Farms, restaurants, gasoline stations, and other businesses that combine a service orientation with sometimes large capital investments typically report on a modified cash basis of accounting. Most of their modifications are attributable to capital investments in fixed assets that can only be capitalized and depreciated over a useful life.

Specific limitations. The only general restrictions historically placed on the cash method of accounting have been those for capital improvements and for businesses in which the sale of merchandise is a material income-producing factor. The prescribed treatment of capital investments was explained in Chapter 8. In businesses in which merchandise is important, the law usually requires an adjustment to the cash method of accounting for changes in year-end inventories. If this adjustment were not mandatory a taxpayer could very easily reduce reported net income by increasing the stock of inventory and could increase reported net income by depleting the normal inventory. The effect of the required adjustment is to change only the computation of the income from gross sales and the tax deduction for the cost of merchandise sold from a strict cash basis to an accrual basis of accounting. The deduction for the cost of merchandise sold must be made as follows:

Cost of merchandise on hand at first of year
+ Cost of merchandise purchased during the year
= Cost of merchandise available for sale
− Cost of merchandise on hand at end of year
= The tax-deductible cost of merchandise sold

In other words, a cash-basis taxpayer can deduct only the amount shown on the last line of the above formula, not the amount shown on the second line of that formula, as the cost of goods sold. Except for the "sales" and "cost of goods sold" figures, the elements of taxable income can generally be reported on a cash receipts and disbursements basis. This is what the Treasury regulations refer to as a *modified cash basis of accounting*.

In addition to the general restrictions for capital expenditures and for the cost of goods sold, a number of special restrictions on the cash method of accounting have been imposed by the IRS and the courts in particular instances. For example, we noted in Chapter 2 that a constructive receipt rule may often modify a strictly cash-basis result. And in Chapter 6, we observed that a cash-basis taxpayer must report capital *losses*, but not capital gains, in the year a sale is made, even though the proceeds of sale are not received until the following accounting period. The rationale for this special administrative interpretation is unknown.

For more obvious reasons, the IRS and the courts require that a cash-basis taxpayer report extraordinary transactions on a cash-equivalent basis rather than on a literal cash basis. If they had not made this interpretation, all barter-type transactions would remain tax-free for all cash-basis taxpayers. Quite obviously, that temptation would be too great to resist. Given our present tax rates, the nation could be turned into a semibarter economy overnight by any contrary interpretation of a cash basis of accounting. This means that even if a taxpayer reports recurring salary, dividends, interest, professional fees, rents, royalties, and other items of routine income on a cash basis, the sale of an investment or "capital-type" asset cannot be reported on that basis unless it involves either a cash or an installment sale. In all barter transactions, the authorities will require that the taxpayer determine the fair market value of any assets received and that taxable income be reported on a cash-equivalent basis. If a cash-basis taxpayer desires to defer the recognition of income from an extraordinary transaction until actually receiving cash, it is necessary either to arrange an installment sale or to fall within the nontaxable exchange provisions of Chapter 10. The installment sale provisions are discussed later in this chapter.

The advantage of the cash method. Except for the specific limitations just observed, a taxpayer reporting taxable income on a cash receipts and disbursements basis has a tremendous ability to control the timing of many tax-critical events. The importance of proper timing has been noted throughout this book. In Chapter 6, for example, we noted how the proper timing of year-end security transactions can critically change the amount of tax payable on particular capital gains and losses. In Chapter 3, we noted how a taxpayer might maximize use of the standard deduction implicit in the zero bracket amount by the careful timing of personal or "other itemized" deductions.

There are literally hundreds of other ways a cash-basis taxpayer can change a tax liability by changing the date on which certain things are done. A taxpayer who has earned an unusually large income in a particular year can help to reduce the marginal tax rate that would be applied to that income by either deferring additional income or by accelerating the payment of all tax-deductible items. A professional person may, for example, defer the mailing of all bills to clients during the last month of a high-income year and thereby discourage many clients from paying until early in the next accounting period. Alternatively or concurrently, a taxpayer might lay in an unusually large stock of expendible supplies in a high-income year and deduct them by making a timely payment. A farmer, for example, could purchase extra feed, fertilizer, or seed near the year-end. Another taxpayer might prepay property taxes, or make early charitable contributions, if more tax deductions are needed in the current year. If an extraordinary sale is made at a large profit near the year-end, the sale may be arranged as an installment sale and the first payment deferred until the next year. These general ideas apply equally well to any taxpayer who has some basis for predicting a substantially smaller taxable income in a subsequent accounting period. Just the opposite kind of action would be recommended for any taxpayer anticipating a substantial increase in taxable income.

In a limited number of extreme circumstances, the IRS and the courts may disallow an otherwise authorized tax deduction claimed by a cash-basis taxpayer on the ground that the item seriously distorts the reported income of the taxpayer. In the case of "investment interest," the Treasury Department persuaded Congress to pass restrictive legislation. The effect of the new statutory provision is to disallow a deduction for interest expense incurred on a loan made to finance investments that do not produce much in the way of ordinary taxable income. This statutory disallowance of investment interest will not apply until the interest expense exceeds $10,000 plus the net ordinary income produced by the investments. Taxpayers borrowing such large sums of money undoubtedly have sufficient expert assistance to alert them to the potential tax problem. Taxpayers with more limited ambitions and opportunities should simply remember that the IRS *may* be able to deny an otherwise legitimate cash-basis tax deduction if that deduction seriously distorts taxable income in a given year. The potential hazard of disallowance notwithstanding, the taxpayer reporting income on a cash method of accounting retains a maximum opportunity for successful tax planning.

The Accrual Method

The accrual method of accounting is utilized by virtually all large corporate businesses. Most professional accountants would insist that only an accrual method of accounting can determine a meaningful income figure, at least for purposes of financial reporting. The essence of the accrual method of accounting is the belief that revenues (or gross income) should be recognized when *earned*, regardless of when cash is received, and that expenses should be matched against the revenues they produce and thereby be deducted in the year the correspondent revenue is recognized, not in the year the expenses happen to be paid. Professional accountants admittedly have problems in deciding exactly when some revenues have been earned and in determining the causal relationship between certain expenditures and the corresponding revenues. They have other problems in measurement relative to both revenues and expenses. Nevertheless, most practicing accountants agree on the general procedures utilized in measuring income on an accrual basis. In recent years, the Financial Accounting Standards Board has attempted to reduce the number of acceptable alternative procedures that can be applied in common situations. Although accrual accounting for tax purposes is occasionally at variance with accrual accounting for financial purposes, there is more similarity than difference between the two concepts.

Required usage. We noted in the introduction to this chapter that Section 446(a) requires a taxpayer to compute taxable income on the same method of accounting as is used in keeping the regular books. This means that, for all practical purposes, most large corporations have no realistic option but to report taxable income on an accrual method of accounting. A few medium-sized businesses have managed to convince the courts that they are satisfying the code requirements by keeping a set of reconciling adjustments between accrual basis books and cash-basis tax returns. A few other institutions, most notably banks, have managed to continue to report their taxable incomes on a cash basis. With these exceptions, however, most taxpayers will find that it is preferable to keep their routine books on a cash basis if they desire to report income for tax purposes on a cash basis. If cash-basis books are adequately maintained, it is relatively easy for an accountant to convert a cash-basis income determination to an accrual basis income determination anytime the need arises. If, for example, a bank or other credit institution demands an accrual basis income statement from a cash-basis taxpayer, a certified public accountant can usually prepare such a statement at a minimum cost so long as a good set of cash-basis records has been maintained. Arranging affairs in this way minimizes the risk that an accrual basis method of tax reporting may be demanded by the IRS under the requirements of Section 446(a).

Special limitations. Even if a taxpayer maintains regular books and files a tax return on an accrual method of accounting, typically there will be a number of differences between specific items as reported on the financial statements and the tax return. Most of the significant differences can be traced to code provisions that were enacted to achieve particular economic or social objectives. The rapid amortization and percentage depletion provisions are just two examples of such differences. Other differences can be attributed to administrative considerations peculiar to taxation. The code, for example, generally does not authorize the deduction of estimated future expenses that are reported currently for financial accounting. Even though the traditional explanation for this difference is made in terms of the large revenue losses for the government, another explanation is the fear that acceptance of such estimated amounts as an authorized tax deduction would lead to widespread disagreement between the taxpayer and the tax collector. To the maximum extent possible, the trend over the past several years has been to reduce the areas of potential disagreement even if that has meant a revenue loss for the government. Two recent cases in point are the acceptance of accelerated guideline lives for depreciation purposes and the acceptance of the repair allowance concept as part of the asset depreciation range system. (For further discussion of these topics, see pages 197 and 207.) In yet other situations, the differences between accrual method accounting figures for tax and financial accounting purposes can be explained on a wherewithal-to-pay concept. The nontaxable exchanges, explained in Chapter 10, have no counterpart in financial accounting. The apparent difference is in no small measure related to the fact that, even if there is a substantial realized gain, a taxpayer has no dollars with which to pay a tax when a nontaxable transaction has been completed. In select situations, Congress has found this sufficient reason to permit the deferral of the tax liability. In financial accounting there is no comparable reason for deferring the recognition of income, and therefore financial accounting typically recognizes all gains and losses as soon as they have been realized.

In addition to these general differences between the use of the accrual method of accounting for financial purposes and for tax purposes, the code provides some very special limitations in unusual situations. A subsection of Section 267, for example, disallows any tax deduction for the loss realized on a sale or exchange of property between certain related taxpayers. The disallowance is applicable for tax purposes, no matter how real the transaction might be in legal or economic terms, if the stipulated code conditions are satisfied. Another subsection of Section 267 disallows the deduction of certain expenses *accrued* by a taxpayer for the benefit of a related cash-basis taxpayer if the accrued liability is not paid within two and one half months after the close of the accrual basis taxpayer's year. The reason for this special provision is most easily understood in the context of a closely held corporation that reports its taxable income on an accrual method of accounting. If the statutory prohibition did not exist, the owner of the corporation could declare a salary payable to himself or herself and thus obtain an immediate tax deduction for the accrual basis corporation. As a cash-basis taxpayer, the owner would not have to report any taxable income from such a salary until the corporation made a payment on the accrued salary. The owner-operator could obviously defer any recognition of taxable income until a most convenient year and still have the benefit of the immediate tax deduction in the corporate entity. The practical effect of the requirement that payment be made within 2½ months is to allow the taxpayer no more than a one-year lag between any deduction by the accrual basis taxpayer and the recognition of income by the related cash-basis taxpayer. And even that one-year deferral requires that the tax year of the accrual basis employer end not more than 2½ months prior to the end of the employee's tax year. Even though the rule limits the potential advantage of this idea, it does not preclude the possibility of a substantial tax saving under the proper circumstances.

Considerations in electing the accrual method. The large incorporated business has little alternative but to keep both its tax and financial records on an accrual basis. The smaller business, on the other hand, has a viable option. Perhaps the greatest disadvantages associated with the accrual method of accounting for tax purposes are (1) the reduction in the taxpayer's control over the timing of both gross income and tax deductions, (2) the extra cost and complexity commonly associated with a complete accrual accounting system, and (3) the potential need to recognize taxable income prior to the receipt of cash with which a taxpayer can pay the tax liability. Most of the advantages associated with an accrual method of accounting are financial rather than tax-related. The greatest advantage is probably the increase in the accuracy of the income measurement, which, it is hoped, permits the manager to operate a business more effectively. The lesser advantages of the accrual method for tax purposes are (1) the relative ease of taxpayer compliance once an accrual accounting system is maintained, and (2) the ability it gives the taxpayer to make a one-time accelerated tax deduction for debts owed to a related taxpayer reporting on the cash basis.

The Completed Contract Method

Construction projects that require longer than a single accounting period for completion can usually be reported under one of two alternative methods of accounting, namely, the percentage-of-completion method and the completed-contract method. The latter method is the more widely utilized. Under the completed-contract method of accounting, no item of gross income or tax deduction is authorized until the entire contract has been completed. Prior to completion, the taxpayer effectively records all advance receipts and disbursements in a suspense account, which is finally cleared when each project is finished.

A major reason for electing the completed-contract method of accounting for tax purposes is the obvious fact that it defers any tax liability on a profitable contract until the last possible moment. A second and equally pragmatic reason for preferring a completed-contract method of accounting for long-term projects is that it minimizes the number of estimates that have to be made. This, in turn, minimizes the number of potential disputes between the taxpayer and the IRS. Finally, the completed-contract method defers the tax liability until a time when the taxpayer has the greatest financial capacity to pay the tax due. Each of these reasons contributes significantly to the popularity of this accounting method in industries characterized by protracted building, installation, and construction projects.

The most serious disadvantage of the completed-contract method of accounting is its tendency to bunch income and losses into years on an irregular basis. This bunching is especially disadvantageous when a progressive tax rate schedule is applied to taxable income. Although income averaging serves to reduce the severity of the tax distortion for individual taxpayers, it is a less-than-perfect solution and it is wholly ineffective in loss years. Typically a corporate taxpayer will be less affected than an individual taxpayer by the bunching of income, both because of the relative absence of progression in the corporate tax rate schedule and because of the more limited number of adjustments that have to be made to convert a negative taxable income into a deductible net operating loss. Large corporations may also be less affected by bunching because of the greater number of contracts negotiated. If an approximately equal number of equally profitable projects are completed each year, bunching tends to disappear. A final reason for rejecting the completed-contract method of accounting is that it defers a deduction for any loss incurred until the last possible year.

The Installment Method

The installment method of accounting may be either a general accounting method used by dealers in personal property or a special tax provision that recently has been made automatically applicable to nearly all *profitable* deferred-payment sales made by a cash-basis taxpayer. Under both circumstances, the fundamental idea is to defer the recognition of taxable income until the receipt of cash. The taxpayer must determine a gross profit ratio for an authorized installment sale and then apply this ratio to each cash collection to determine the amount of gross income that must be recognized. For example, if a taxpayer sold a property with an $80,000 adjusted tax basis for $100,000, a $20,000 gross profit would have been realized on the sale. Thus, the taxpayer's gross profit ratio would be 20 percent ($20,000 gross profit divided by $100,000 sales price), and the taxpayer would recognize only 20 percent of any collections on this sale as taxable income in each year.

Dealer sales. Dealers in personal property may elect to report their taxable income on an installment basis. The dealer's gross profit ratio is generally computed as a single percentage for an entire year. Collections are separated by the year of sale, and the appropriate percentages are applied to collections to determine the gross income to report in any one year. Special provisions are made for repossessions, transfers of debt, imputed interest, and so on.

Casual sales by nondealers. Since October 19, 1980, any gain realized by a nondealer on most deferred-payment sales of both real and personal properties can also be deferred until the cash is received. Instead of determining one gross profit ratio for the entire year—as the law requires of dealers electing the installment method—the casual seller simply computes a gross profit percent for each separate deferred-payment sale and multiplies that percent times the amount of cash received in each year to determine the amount of gross profit to report that year. Observe that the new rules for installment sales are automatically applicable to most sales made at a gain and that they never apply to sales made at a loss. In addition, most of the tax traps historically associated with installment sales by nondealers have now disappeared. For once Congress actually did simplify the law!

Planning considerations. The major advantage of the installment method of accounting for the dealer is that it defers the payment of the income tax as long as possible. For the individual taxpayer concerned with the casual sale of property, the installment sale has additional possible advantages. If a taxpayer anticipates a reduction in the marginal tax rate in the future, perhaps because of retirement, it is especially important to arrange a deferred-payment sale. In this instance the tax is both deferred as long as possible and taxed at the lowest possible marginal rate. On the other hand, a taxpayer looking forward to a substantially increased taxable income in the future should probably avoid an installment sale, even if this means an earlier payment of the tax. The increase in the marginal tax rate could very easily offset any time-preference value of a tax deferral.

Prior to the 1980 tax revision, good tax planning frequently involved the making of an installment sale to a related party who promptly resold the same property for cash (or on an accelerated cash-payment schedule). The double sale allowed the family unit to get more cash immediately and to defer the tax liability until later. The current provisions put an end to this old tax planning technique by requiring an acceleration of recognition by the first seller if the property is resold by the related party purchaser within two years from the date of the original sale. If the property being sold is a marketable security, even the two-year limit is not applicable. Other special rules apply to related party sales if the property can be depreciated for tax purposes by the related buyer.

Finally, recall that a deferred payment sale of a capital asset can convert ordinary income into capital gain if the sales contract provides for a minimum interest and a correspondingly higher sales price. This idea was explained on pages 126–27. In summary, the installment sale must be remembered both as a potential general method of accounting and as a specific tax provision that may apply to the casual sale of most any property.

Accounting Procedures and Conventions

The number of alternative accounting procedures and conventions is substantially greater than the number of alternative general methods of accounting. We noted in Chapter 8, for example, that the code authorizes a number of accounting procedures to determine the cost allocations common to depreciation. The acceptable depreciation procedures include the straight line, the sum of the years' digits, and the 125 percent, 150 percent, and 200 percent declining-balance alternatives. Earlier in this chapter, we also observed the need to determine the deduction for the cost of goods sold on an accrual basis, without regard for the taxpayer's usual method of accounting. We did not note there, however, that the cost-of-goods-sold determination can be made under any of several alternative inventory costing conventions, including Fifo (first-in, first-out), Lifo (last-in, first-out), weighted average, moving average, retail sales, and specific identification. Each of these accounting conventions or procedures will yield a different taxable income in anything other than a perfectly static economy.

Inventory Costing Conventions

Time and space constraints preclude any detailed examination of each of the inventory costing conventions just noted. The reader should be aware, however, that the selection of an inventory costing convention may have a substantial impact on the amount of taxable income that must be recognized. During a period of rising prices, it is generally to the taxpayer's advantage to utilize the Lifo costing technique because, as the name implies, the assumption under that costing convention is that the very last goods to be purchased during a year were the first to be sold! During a period of rising prices, the last goods to be purchased are the most costly. If we assume that the most costly goods were the first to be sold, we are in effect charging the highest priced goods to the tax-deductible cost of goods sold and charging the least expensive goods to the ending inventory, a nondeductible asset. During a period of falling prices, the Fifo costing technique would yield the largest tax deduction and the lowest inventory valuation. The other inventory costing techniques tend to yield an intermediate measure of both the cost of goods sold and the ending inventory. If a taxpayer desires to use the Lifo method of inventory costing for tax purposes, it must also be used for financial accounting purposes. And if a taxpayer desires to change from one inventory costing convention to another, the consent of the commissioner must be obtained and an appropriate adjustment made to the reported taxable income in the year of change.

The Unit of Account

The basic unit of account selected for any single element of a larger accounting system may have a substantial impact on the income reported by that system in a given year. The phrase *unit of account* refers to the lowest common denominator in any accounting classification. Relative to an automobile, for example, the unit of account may be each specific car, some portion of a car (say, the motor), or an entire fleet of cars. Relative to a building, the unit of account may vary from the building as a single physical structure to literally thousands of component parts (such as wiring, plumbing, roofing, elevators and escalators, carpeting, furnishings) or, alternatively, to a cluster of buildings that share a common purpose. The selection of the most desirable unit of account for tax purposes may be especially important because that selection may affect the eligibility of an item for the investment credit, the maximum amount of depreciation that may be applied to the item, the selection of an estimated useful life, and the classification of related expenditures as immediately deductible repairs or as nondeductible capital investments. The general problem of the unit of account is essentially equivalent to the problem relative to percentage depletion considered on pages 205 and 206. We noted there that it is sometimes desirable to combine more than one depletable property and to treat the combination as a single property. We also observed that, under other circumstances, it is desirable to separate two or more properties and to treat them individually for tax purposes. Generally, the broader we make the unit of account, the more likely we are to increase the estimated useful life. On the other hand, the broader the unit of account, the more likely it is that we can treat a particular related expenditure as an immediately deductible repair and the less likely it is that we will need to recognize a gain on the disposition of some small element within the larger unit. The selection of the most tax-advantageous unit of account can only proceed on an item-by-item investigation.

Other Convenient Tax Assumptions

In addition to selecting a most appropriate unit of account, a taxpayer may make certain other assumptions to further simplify the tax accounting system. For example, no taxpayer of any substantial size can calculate depreciation on a daily basis. Fixed assets are bought, sold, and traded throughout the year, and a taxpayer usually cannot afford to make separate depreciation determinations for each of these many transactions. Therefore, in addition to granting the right to group similar fixed assets into a single unit of account, the code authorizes a taxpayer to make certain standard assumptions about the timing of all acquisitions and dispositions during a year. For example, a taxpayer may assume either (a) that all acquisitions occurred in the middle of the year or (b) that all acquisitions during the first six months of the year occurred on the first day of the year and that all acquisitions made during the last six months of the year occurred on the first day of the following year. The IRS will usually accept either assumption if the taxpayer follows it consistently. Once a convention is established, the taxpayer can time acquisitions and dispositions in a most favorable manner.

The Fiscal Year

A year is the period commonly used to measure income for tax purposes. That year can be a fiscal year or a calendar year. Many taxpayers who own and manage their own business attempt to arrange a fiscal year for the business that is slightly different from the tax year they use as individuals. If a business is placed on a fiscal year ending January 31, for example, and the owner-operator is on a calendar year, the business can adjust its salary payments to the owner-operator in January with no tax consequences to the individual for an entire year. This ability to defer the tax liability for the income from a business for an entire year is tantamount to permanently excusing one year's income from taxation.

If a taxpayer wishes to modify the taxable year of any taxable entity, he or she must generally get the consent of the commissioner before making the change. It is sometimes easier to make an initial election wisely than to obtain the commissioner's permission to change. If a taxpayer obtains permission to modify a tax year, a short-period return must generally be filed. In some situations, the adjustment procedure required in preparing a short-period return may result in an unusually large tax liability, which can be corrected only if the taxpayer first pays the tax and then, at the end of the regular accounting period (prior to the change), files a claim for refund based on actual results for the previous 12 months. A failure to file the refund claim on a timely basis may result in the permanent loss of the right to do so.

Records: Good and Bad

Every taxpayer should remember that, in tax matters, the usual presumption of the court is that the IRS is correct until proved wrong. This presumption for the government argues for a good accounting system. At one time in our history, a taxpayer could rely on the mercy of the court to grant a reasonable allowance for any tax item that could not be proved. That doctrine was known popularly as the "Cohan rule" because of a court case between the IRS and the famous entertainer

George M. Cohan over certain entertainment expenses. In the recent past, the courts have exhibited an increasing reluctance to follow the Cohan rule, and taxpayers are well advised to keep the best possible records if they wish to obtain the most favorable tax result.

Small taxpayers in particular may be surprised to discover the reluctance of the IRS to accept what appear to them to be perfectly reasonable validation records. In the case of the charitable contribution deduction, for example, the IRS has sometimes refused to accept a canceled check as sufficient evidence of the fact that a contribution has in fact been made. The reason for its hesitancy in this instance stems from a case in which a taxpayer cashed a check each Sunday with the church treasurer for the alleged purpose of obtaining sufficient change to open an office on Monday morning. The taxpayer in fact used the check as evidence of an apparent charitable contribution. The ruse was discovered, and the canceled check suddenly lost much of its potential value as evidence of a valid tax deduction under some circumstances.

The need for good records is evident in many aspects of successful tax planning. As one final illustration, however, we might return to the world of the capital gain. Taxpayers who have purchased more than a single block of stock in a particular corporation and have allowed their stock certificates to remain in the custody of the brokerage house have occasionally been surprised to discover that their intended long-term capital gain turned into a short-term capital gain because of a failure in communication. This has happened when an investor has simply instructed a broker to sell 100 shares of ABC Corporation common stock without designating which block of shares the broker is to sell. If the broker inadvertently utilizes a certificate purchased within one year of the sale, and if the IRS discovers which block of stock was actually used to complete the sale, the IRS will follow a specific identification inventory method and insist that the asset sold had been held for less than one year, notwithstanding the fact that the taxpayer intended the broker to use an earlier acquisition to complete the sale.

Although it is almost impossible to overestimate the value of a truly good set of accounting records in income tax matters, it is very easy to underestimate the potential value of other records. In some situations, an IRS agent or a court will accept a purely personal (and often sloppily prepared) diary as evidence of certain tax-deductible expenditures. Although such personal records may be worthless in suspicious cases, they tend to corroborate other evidence of good faith, and sometimes spell the difference between getting administrative agreement and going to court. The taxpayer should not destroy charge slips, guest lists, convention programs, and other evidence that may support a questionable tax deduction for travel, entertainment, or other business expenses. Guest logs are necessary to support some tax deductions for club memberships and the use of entertainment facilities. Even a good color photograph may help to sustain a claim for a casualty loss deduction. A taxpayer sensitized to the many tax opportunities and pitfalls should also begin to comprehend the need for validation records, good or bad.

One-Time Elections

The code contains more than 50 elections that pertain to newly organized businesses. A few of these provisions are worded in such a way that the taxpayer has a minimal opportunity to correct an initial "bad" decision. Code Section 248, for example, authorizes a corporation to amortize organization expenses over a period of 60 months or longer. If the corporate officers fail to make the election on a timely basis, however, none of the organization expenses can be deducted until the corporation is dissolved.

In Chapter 8, we noted that a taxpayer can never extend an original estimated life to obtain a larger investment credit if a fixed asset is used for a period longer than originally estimated. For this reason, a taxpayer may be inclined initially to estimate a useful life of at least seven years for all investment purchases that qualify for the investment credit. The taxpayer will discover, however, that the same estimated life must be used for both investment credit and depreciation purposes. Generally speaking, the shortest possible life estimate is preferred for depreciation purposes. Thus the taxpayer must make an important decision at the time of acquiring any property eligible for an investment credit: Should an estimated life be extended to obtain the potential benefit of the larger investment credit even though part or all of that investment credit may be recaptured if earlier disposition is made, or should the estimated life be minimized to obtain the potential benefit of a larger depreciation deduction?

These are just two examples of important one-time elections. The details of each election are sufficiently intricate, and the methods of compliance sufficiently peculiar, that further discussion of each is best left to the books written for those concerned with tax compliance rather than with tax recognition. The good business manager need understand only the importance of obtaining qualified help on a timely basis.

Income Averaging

Individual taxpayers with an erratic income pattern will pay a larger income tax than will other taxpayers earning the same aggregate taxable income in equal amounts over several years. The reason for the difference is, of course, attributable to the progressive rate schedule used by individual taxpayers. In an attempt to minimize the extra tax due to an unusually large income in any single year, the code authorizes an annual income averaging option for individual taxpayers. This option allows the taxpayer to compute the tax liability in a special way, and if that tax is less than the tax computed in the ordi-

Taxable income recognized in the current year................................	xxxx
Less 120 percent of the average taxable income recognized by the taxpayer in the four prior years (this four-prior-year average is called the average base period income)	xxxx
The difference is "averageable income" (income averaging can be elected only if averageable income is more than $3,000)	xxxx
Determine, in the usual way, the tax liability on a taxable income equal to the sum of (a) 120 percent of the taxpayer's average base period income plus (b) 20 percent of the taxpayer's averageable income	xxxx
Deduct the tax, determined in the usual way, on a taxable income equal to 120 percent of the taxpayer's average base period income	xxxx
The difference is the ordinary tax on 20 percent of the taxpayer's averageable income	xxxx
Multiply this difference by five	×5
The product is the tax on averageable income	xxxx
Add the tax, determined in the usual way, on a taxable income equal to 120 percent of the taxpayer's average base period income	xxxx
The sum equals the alternative tax under income averaging	xxxx

nary way, to pay the lower amount. The general formula is utilized in the accompanying special tax computation.

Special rules apply to taxpayers who have not been married throughout the base period years, to income from foreign sources, and to distributions from pension and other retirement funds. Taxpayers who did not furnish at least one half of their support in the four base period years are not eligible for income averaging unless their support was furnished by their spouses. Furthermore, a taxpayer electing income averaging cannot also elect the maximum tax on earned income. These and other special rules can modify the general income averaging formula. Even in situations in which income averaging may be elected, this statutory solution to the problem of bunched income is much less than perfect. Perhaps its greatest deficiency is its failure to authorize income averaging in years of unusually low income, as well as in high-income years. The amount of tax saved by income averaging proves, on close examination, to be rather capricious, because it depends upon a unique interaction among no less than four distinct variables. Even though a detailed analysis of those variables must remain beyond the confines of this book, every taxpayer should be aware of the possibility of tax savings through income averaging in any year in which he or she recognizes an unusually large taxable income.

CHAPTER **14**

Common Tax Traps

Tax traps are often as ruinous to tax planning as sand traps are to shooting par. In the game of golf, the traps are equally visible to all players. In the tax game, unfortunately, the traps may be hidden from the view of all but the most erudite players. These tax traps can be of economic, judicial, or statutory origin.

Economic traps are not unique to transactions characterized by unusual tax consequences. Nevertheless, transactions embodying special tax advantages seem to be especially prone to chicanery. One expert, whose only business is the investigation of potential tax-sheltered investments, reported that, prior to the 1976 Tax Reform Act, no more than 5 percent of the proposals he investigated were economically sound. Obviously, more than 5 percent of such investments were being sold to unwary customers. A possible thesis that might explain the apparent attraction of tax-sheltered investments is that prospective buyers get so involved in trying to understand the tax impact of the proposals that they fail to scrutinize the more mundane economic projections associated with them. These economic dangers were discussed in some detail in Chapter 9.

In this chapter, we will investigate some of the major tax traps that are of judicial or statutory origin. Any result that does not prove to be the most desirable possible result because of a special tax rule may be classified as a tax trap. For example, offsetting short-term capital losses with long-term capital gains in a year when potential short-term capital gains are available may be considered a tax trap—so can claiming straight-line depreciation when rapid depreciation is authorized. However, such a broad definition of tax traps proves to be unwieldy; it is, in fact, bounded only by the generous limits of human ignorance. In order to make our task more manageable, we shall define tax traps to include only those judicial doctrines and statutory provisions that have been designed to limit, defeat, or destroy tax-planning ideas that would otherwise be viable.

Judicial Tax Traps

Judicial tax traps may best be described as the few scattered black clouds dotting the generally clear horizon on a perfect summer day. Even the most experienced tax practitioner cannot predict with 100 percent certainty just when and where those black clouds will wreak disaster on an unsuspecting taxpayer. Although it leaves much to be desired in terms of academic precision, perhaps the safest generalization in tax planning can be expressed in the terms of the *pig theory*. As explained earlier, that theory suggests that you can make money being a bull and that you can make money being a bear, but that you can never make money being a pig. Judicial tax traps have an uncanny way of striking the "tax pig." The most common judicial tax traps have been conveniently labeled the "substance-over-form," the "business purpose," and the "step transaction" doctrines.

Substance over Form

The judicial notion that legal consequences should depend upon the substance of a transaction rather than upon its form is not unique to problems of income taxation. In tax matters, however, the consequences are very often critically different, depending upon what one assumes to constitute the substance of the transaction. Furthermore, the form of a transaction is usually deemed to be indicative of its intended substance. In a closely held corporation, we know that the owner has good tax reasons for preferring to make all corporate distributions to owners as salaries, rather than as dividends. What, then, is to prevent the owner-operating stockholder from declaring a particular corporate distribution to be the more tax-favored one? In other words, can the owner-manager transform a potential corporate dividend into a salary simply by declaring that intention and recording it properly in the corporate records? One court decision seems to suggest that a portion of any assets distributed by a closely held corporation to the owner-manager may be considered to constitute a dividend, *even if the aggregate payment to the owner-manager does not exceed a reasonable compensation for the services rendered to the corporation.* This conclusion of the Court of Claims has been restricted to the case where the corporation has substantial earnings but a very poor dividend record. In a way, this decision constitutes a radical extension of the substance-over-form concept. Previously the danger that tax-deductible salaries might be converted into nondeductible dividends existed only after salaries were found to be unreasonably large. Any time a profitable corporation fails to pay minimal dividends, there is now some danger that a court may find that parts of some other distributions actually constitute dividends, at least in the case of closely held corporations. Certainly there is no statutory basis for this decision; if there is authority, it derives from judicial doctrines such as substance over form.

In Chapter 12, we noted that parents might make a loan on a noninterest-bearing demand note to their child and still avoid both the gift tax and the income tax on any interest that was (or might have been) earned on the funds between the date of the loan and the date the note was called. So far, at least, that is the conclusion of the courts in those cases that the IRS has discovered and litigated. There is no reason to believe, however, that another court might not, in some future decision, find (1) that there is a gift from the parents to the child, in the amount of an arm's-length interest that would ordinarily accrue on such a debt, and (2) that the demand note is a sham and that any interest earned by the child on the loan proceeds must be imputed to (and reported by) the parents making the loan. The doctrine of substance over form certainly is strong enough to support such a conclusion should some court care to apply it.

We have considered here only two specific illustrations of the judicial substance-over-form doctrine. The doctrine can, however, appear in relation to almost any tax problem. The more a taxpayer stretches the boundaries of reasonableness in applying tax rules, the more likely he or she is to encounter this judicial tax trap. On rare occasions, taxpayers may attempt to utilize this judicial doctrine as an equity argument in their own interest. If, for example, a taxpayer clearly intended to do something, but failed to complete each and every technical detail required by the statute to achieve the intended objective, he or she may try to convince the court that the substance of the actions should prevail over any minor oversight in form. Although there is nothing to preclude such an argument, the business manager ought to be aware that most judicial tax doctrines seem to be the exclusive property of the IRS. In other words, as they are actually applied in tax cases, the judicial doctrines we are reviewing here seem to constitute a one-way street leading into a tax trap, not a two-way street that also provides a convenient way for the taxpayer to correct an unfortunate error.

Business Purpose

The judicial doctrine of business purpose says that a transaction will not be given any effect for tax purposes unless it also achieves a valid business purpose. Incidentally, saving taxes alone is not deemed to constitute a valid business purpose. This doctrine stems from the case of *Gregory v. Helvering*, which was first tried in 1932. In that case, the taxpayer, Mrs. Gregory, fully complied with the letter of the tax law. Within a few days' time, she arranged a spin-off of some portion of her corporation's assets into a new, second corporation, a dissolution of this new corporation, a distribution of the assets held by the new corporation to her as sole owner, and a sale of the same assets to a third party. According to the law then in effect, the Revenue Act of 1924, the spin-off should have been a nontaxable transaction; the liquidation plus distribution of assets, a taxable transaction that would produce a capital gain for Mrs. Gregory; and the sale of assets, a taxable transaction, but one that would produce no taxable income. The absence of any taxable income in the final transaction could be attributed to the fact that the assets had received a tax basis equal to their fair market value in the liquidating distribution (which had just been taxed as a capital gain) a day or two prior to their sale. The trial court, the Board of Tax Appeals in this case, agreed with the taxpayer's conclusion, saying, in effect, that it had no authority to do anything but interpret literally the tax laws Congress had passed. The Circuit Court of Appeals for the Second Circuit and the Supreme Court disagreed with the trial court and thereby created the business purpose doctrine. Translated freely, their decisions said that literal compliance with the tax law may not be sufficient; if a transaction has no valid business purpose other than saving taxes, it does not satisfy the intent of Congress, and therefore should be given no effect. The critical result for Mrs. Gregory was that the court found that there had been a dividend distribution by the original corporation, to be taxed as ordinary income, rather than a liquidating distribution by the new corporation, to be taxed as a capital gain. The overlap between the judicial doctrines of substance over form and business purpose is apparent in this case.

Perhaps one of the most intriguing aspects of all judicial tax traps is that one is never certain just when the courts will elect to apply them. In 1956, the Circuit Court of Appeals for the Tenth Circuit, in the case of *Diamond A. Cattle Company* v. *Commissioner*, reached a decision in which it said: "when Congress passes an act in language that is clear and unambiguous, and construed and read in itself can mean but one thing, the act must be judged by what Congress did and not by what it intended to do." Here the taxpayer was allowed to claim a tax privilege that Congress did not intend, notwithstanding the potential application of contrary judicial doctrines that were already well established.

Step Transactions

A third judicial concept sometimes utilized by the courts to destroy what would otherwise be effective tax-saving schemes concocted by taxpayers and their advisers is known as the step transaction doctrine. The effect of this judicial tax trap is to collapse a series of carefully arranged intermediate transactions into a single transaction and to look only at the substance of the net result to determine tax consequences. Although this judicial concept was not specifically mentioned in the Gregory decision, it could have been applied there as effectively as was the business purpose test. Any tax-planning idea that relies upon the recognition of each and every step of a complicated scheme that could be carried out in a much more direct manner, and that involves a minimal time span for its completion, runs a high risk of judicial intervention under one doctrine or another. The step transaction doctrine has been applied most frequently in corporate reorganizations. Again, however, it has not been applied consistently. On some occasions, the courts have given full recognition to each carefully arranged movement in a grand tax minuet; on other occasions, the courts have refused to see the beauty of it all. Even the seasoned opinion of the best legal counsel available may be uncertain of the outer boundaries of any judicial tax trap. In a social sense, the elusive quality of the traps may be their most redeeming feature.

Statutory Tax Traps

The life cycle of most unintended tax loopholes is characterized by four phases of development: (1) discovery, (2) successful application, (3) administrative, and sometimes judicial, intervention, and (4) legislative elimination. For the purposes of this book, we will define statutory tax traps to include only those code provisions that have been enacted as the fourth and final phase of this life cycle. One might think of this collection of code sections as the long fingers of Congress plugging the many holes in a dike that is intended to redirect resources from the private to the public sector. Among the sections we shall consider are the following:

Sec. 532. Corporations Subject to Accumulated Earnings Tax.
Sec. 542. Definition of Personal Holding Company.
Sec. 341. Collapsible Corporations.
Sec. 306. Disposition of Certain Stock.

Sec. 318. Constructive Ownership of Stock.

Sec. 482. Allocation of Income and Deductions among Taxpayers.

The code contains numerous other provisions that could properly be included within our limited definition of statutory tax traps. The above, however, are some of the more important sections for tax planning generally, as well as illustrative of the other sections. Tax practitioners are well acquainted with the details of most of these statutory tax traps. We will consider only their broad outlines for the benefit of the general manager.

The Accumulated Earnings Tax

Because the corporate tax rate historically has been significantly lower than the personal tax rate on equivalent incomes for most wealthy individuals, the corporation has been used as a primary tax shelter by many taxpayers. This tradition was explained in Chapter 4. Congress was aware of the potential abuse of the corporate rate shelter when it passed the initial income tax act in 1913, and therefore included provisions for an accumulated earnings tax in that act. The original idea was to ignore the corporate entity and tax the shareholder on a ratable share of the corporate income, whether distributed or not, if there was evidence of an accumulation of earnings beyond the reasonable needs of the business. That initial idea was dropped in 1921, when Congress enacted the present rules, which provide a wholly separate penalty tax imposed directly on the corporate entity under circumstances similar to those identified in the original bill.

Basic provisions. The major features of the present provisions, contained in Sections 531 through 537, are the imposition of a special tax at the rate of either 27.5 percent or 38.5 percent on unreasonably accumulated taxable income. The latter quantity is an adjusted version of the corporation's taxable income. The code does include an accumulated earnings tax credit of $150,000, but this is an adjusted credit that must be reduced for accumulations of earnings in prior years. The 27.5 percent rate is applicable to the first $100,000 of unreasonably accumulated taxable income in any year; thereafter the rate is 38.5 percent. Because the personal marginal tax rates never exceed 70 percent, the use of a corporate entity to accumulate income is seldom advisable if the accumulated earnings tax will be applied, because the total tax of 73.5 percent (46 percent ordinary corporate tax plus a 27.5 percent accumulated earnings tax) will be greater than the worst possible tax that would be applicable if the income were received directly by the owners without the imposition of an intermediate corporate entity.

Before the IRS can impose the accumulated earnings tax, the court must find that the corporation has been formed or availed of for the purpose of avoiding the personal income tax of the shareholders. As a practical matter, this means that the business manager should give primary consideration to recognizing those bits of evidence that lead a court to find that the forbidden purpose exists, rather than worry about the details of the actual tax calculation.

Unreasonable accumulations of earnings. Most authorities will find that there is no unreasonable accumulation of earnings within a corporation unless one or more of the following factors are present:

1. Substantial loans from the corporation to major stockholders.
2. Corporate ownership of personal-benefit assets used exclusively by major stockholders.
3. An unusually high current ratio—that is, a ratio of current assets to current liabilities much higher than that common to the industry—and either large cash balances or large investments in relatively risk-free assets.
4. A minimal record of dividend payments.
5. Closely held corporate stock.

The reader should understand that these are general observations, not hard-and-fast rules. The imposition of the accumulated earnings tax turns largely on the facts of each individual case. The best defense in such situations is usually a good offense.

Planning considerations. If a taxpayer can prove by the preponderance of evidence that the accumulation of earnings is attributable to a valid business reason, other than tax avoidance, this penalty tax can be avoided. Courts have found that the following constitute valid reasons for accumulating corporate earnings: the intent to expand a business or a plant without the dilution of the present owners' interest and without borrowing; the need to acquire a new business, especially if that business is directly related to the existing business of the accumulating corporation; the need to increase inventories; the intent to retire outstanding debt; the need to provide loans to suppliers or customers; the need to fund pension plans; and the desire to substitute a self-insurance reserve for commercial coverage. Each of these needs and intentions must be adequately documented in the corporate records if it is to be given much weight by an examining agent or the court. If a taxpayer anticipates a potentially dangerous accumulated earnings tax problem in sufficient time, it is usually not terribly difficult to find and document some valid reason for the accumulations made. The greater danger of this statutory tax trap seems to be its application in situations that should have been adequately diagnosed and prevented by anticipatory actions.

The Personal Holding Company Tax

The accumulated earnings tax proved to be an inadequate weapon for the IRS against the use of the corporate rate shelter by wealthy individuals. In 1934, therefore, Congress enacted a second penalty tax in a further attempt to eliminate the use of this tax shelter. The new provisions were worded to provide somewhat more objective standards than the "unreasonable accumulation" criterion of prior law. Specific provisions were included to snare "incorporated pocketbooks" (that is, corporations whose only business consisted of buying, selling, and holding other stocks and securities), "incorporated talents" (that is, corporations whose only business consisted of the disposition of the owner's peculiar talent as an actor, athlete, or other star performer), and "incorporated pleasure facilities" (that is, corporations whose only business consisted of the leasing of a hunting lodge, island estate, or yacht to their owners). In each of these situations, the owner was trying to achieve through the corporate entity tax savings that the owner could not achieve directly as an individual. The incorporated pocketbooks provided the major advantage of the corporate dividend-received deduction plus the lower corporate tax rate. The incorporated talent provided an opportunity to accumulate and reinvest personal compensation beyond consumption needs at a minimum tax cost. The incorporated pleasure facility provided a way to convert a nondeductible personal (pleasure) expenditure into a tax-deductible business.

Basic provisions. The present statutory provisions, contained in Sections 541 through 547, impose a special 70 percent penalty tax on any personal holding company that has undistributed personal holding company income at the end of a year. Thus, this penalty tax may be avoided in either of two ways. First, a corporation can make certain that it is not classified as a personal holding company. Second, the corporation can make certain that it does not retain personal holding company income at the end of the year. The objective of this penalty tax is to force distributions and to make the retention of certain kinds of income in a corporate entity an impractical alternative, not to collect revenues for the government. Thus, the code authorizes a taxpayer to make a retroactive dividend distribution any time that the personal holding company tax would otherwise apply. If such a distribution is made, the tax base automatically disappears. Since the penalty tax rate is so high (70 percent), the individual owner will virtually always prefer a dividend distribution, even if it is taxed at the highest marginal rate for individual taxpayers, to a retention coupled with this penalty tax.

Before a corporation is deemed to be a personal holding company, it must "fail" two tests. They are (1) a stock ownership test and (2) an income test. A corporation will not be considered a personal holding company if the five largest stockholders own less than 50 percent of the value of the corporation's outstanding stock. This means that any corporation with ten or fewer owners automatically fails the ownership test, since some five of those owners would have to own no less than 50 percent of the stock. On the other hand, 11 or more unrelated and *equal* owners would automatically avoid any danger of this statutory tax trap.

If less than 60 percent of any corporation's adjusted ordinary gross income is personal holding company income, that corporation will not be deemed to be a personal holding company. For purposes of this book, we can define personal holding company income as either (1) passive income or (2) income from personal talent. Passive income includes income from dividends, interest, rents (under specified conditions), royalties, annuities, and payments by shareholders for their use of corporate properties. In general, "passive" income is distinguished from "active" income—that is, income collected automatically through ownership is distinguished from income earned by entrepreneurial effort.

Planning considerations. The shrewd manager will realize that the use of the corporate rate shelter has not been eliminated by either the accumulated earnings tax or the personal holding company tax. The task is to combine active and passive income streams in such a way as to avoid the personal holding company tax and then to prepare a record that will substantiate a finding that all accumulations of earnings are reasonable. To illustrate this possibility, let us assume that a taxpayer commands an annual income stream of $100,000 from an active business venture and another $50,000 from dividends. If this taxpayer requires an annual income of about $50,000 before taxes for personal consumption needs, $100,000 (before taxes) remains available for reinvestment. If the taxpayer did not incorporate the two income streams in a single business, the tax liability would be in the vicinity of $75,000 per year. With incorporation and an annual salary of $50,000, the taxpayer's annual tax liability would drop to something like $27,000, determined as follows:

Corporate income tax		
Gross corporate income	$150,000	
Less salary paid to owner	(50,000)	
Less dividend-received deduction	(42,500)	
Corporate taxable income	$ 57,500	
Corporate income tax on $57,500		$11,500
Individual income tax on salary (approximate)		15,000
Total annual tax liability		$26,500

The mixing of dividend-producing stocks with an active business serves to avoid the danger of a personal holding company tax as long as the income from the active business exceeds 40 percent of the total corporate income. The problem of unreasonable accumulations of earnings can best be handled by well-documented plans for corporate expansion, debt retirement, pension plans, and similar programs.

Individuals with nothing but passive income sources might consider the creation of a personal holding company owned equally by 11 taxpayers. The group can enjoy the major benefits of the corporate rate shelter and the corporate dividend-received deduction, even though the owners cannot achieve the same tax advantage individually, because such a corporation would pass the ownership test and thus be ineligible for the personal holding company tax.

Collapsible Corporations

Code Section 341 was enacted in 1950 to stop the wholesale conversion of ordinary income into capital gain through an unintended tax loophole in the corporate liquidation provisions. The basic scheme, which the courts seemed unwilling to end by judicial authority alone, usually involved three steps: (1) the creation of a property within a corporate shell; (2) either the sale of that corporation's stock or the liquidation of the corporation after the completion of the property but before the increase in the property's value had been realized by the corporate entity (a liquidation would involve the distribution of the newly created property to the corporate stockholders); and (3) the subsequent sale of the appreciated property to a third party. The collapsible corporation notion was most suited to such ventures as the production of a movie, a copyright, a building or other construction object, or an aged whiskey.

The tax law generally provides that any assets received by a stockholder in a corporate liquidation are to be taxed as a capital gain. The measure of the gain is equal to the difference between the fair market value of the property received and the basis of the stock surrendered in the liquidation. In the collapsible corporation, this difference is usually equal to the value of the service rendered by the stockholder in the creation of the property prior to the collapse of the corporation. In other words, this difference in value represents the value of the service rendered by the actor and/or the producer in the making of a movie, the value of the author or the composer in the preparation of a copyright, the value of the construction engineer or the builder in the erection of a building, or the value of the distiller in the preparation of an aged whiskey. By starting the operation in a corporate shell, the owner could withdraw any profit as a capital gain so long as he or she could defer the realization of any increment in value until after the corporation's liquidation.

The net effect of Section 341 is to require that the stockholder recognize ordinary income, rather than capital gain, on the sale or the liquidation of a collapsible corporation's stock. The technical definition of a collapsible corporation is much too involved for our consideration. Suffice it to say that any corporation that does not realize a "substantial part" of the income on any property that it produces runs the risk of being classified as a collapsible corporation. More important, perhaps, the statutory presumption of collapsibility will not apply either if the shareholder owns less than a 5 percent interest in the corporation's stock or if more than 30 percent of the gain can be attributed to noncollapsible property. As noted in Chapter 6, a taxpayer with sufficient nerve and a good adviser might still convert some ordinary income into capital gain if the owner will allow the corporation to realize a substantial part of the income (say, 40 percent or more) before the stock is sold or redeemed. If the taxpayer does not cut the objectives too thinly, the tax-saving opportunities that initially seemed to be closed by statutory measures may in fact be made somewhat safer by statutory, judicial, and/or administrative presumptions. While sailing these somewhat hazardous seas, a taxpayer should always keep one eye on the judicial clouds that can spell havoc in even the best-charted waters.

The Preferred Stock Bailout

Taxpayers' attempts to convert ordinary income into capital gain have not been restricted to any single device, such as the collapsible corporation. During the early 1950s, preferred stock bailouts were used rather successfully to this same end. The idea was simple. The corporation would declare a preferred stock dividend that, under the existing tax rules, could be received tax-free by the shareholders. The shareholders would sell the preferred stock received as a stock dividend to a third party in an arm's-length transaction taxed as a capital gain. Shortly thereafter, the corporation would redeem all of its outstanding preferred stock at a small premium. The net economic effect of the several transactions was equivalent to the distribution of a dividend by the corporation. The tax effect, however, was quite different: The transactions produced a capital gain for the stockholders, rather than an ordinary dividend. Incidentally, the reason for using preferred stock in this plan was to minimize any risk of dilution of voting control for the old stockholders. If the third party who purchased the dividend shares had refused to allow the corporation to redeem the newly acquired stock, the former owners' problems were minimized because the new owners held only nonvoting preferred shares.

IRS attempts to fight this tax plan with only judicial authority were unsuccessful. Congress therefore included Section 306 in the Internal Revenue Code of 1954. That section in effect stipulates that any gain realized on the sale of preferred stock received as a tax-free stock dividend will be taxed as ordinary income rather than as capital gain. This statutory provision has a few remaining loopholes that may be useful in planning the disposition of a large estate consisting primarily of stock of a single corporation, and in making a bootstrap sale of a corporation to a new owner. On balance, however, the remaining tax-saving potential is limited, and the greater danger may be the inadvertent disposition of "tainted" Section 306 stock and the need to recognize ordinary income. This statutory tax trap is well understood by most tax advisers, and business managers would be wise to consult them before disposing of any preferred stock that was not purchased directly in an open market.

Constructive Ownership of Stock

Many tax consequences can be determined only after one knows what percentage of a corporation's outstanding stock is owned by the shareholder who is involved in a particular transaction. For some purposes, it is desirable for the owner to reach as large a percentage ownership as possible; in other circumstances, the taxpayer may desire to minimize the percentage of his or her interest. A taxpayer, for example, must own more than 80 percent of a corporation's stock if an individual transfer of property to a corporation is to pass as a nontaxable transaction under Section 351. On the other hand, it was noted above why a taxpayer might desire to be deemed to own as little stock as possible when the personal holding company tax or a collapsible corporation's stock is in question.

In order to achieve a smaller percentage ownership, a taxpayer may be tempted to give or sell some shares to a related person. As a practical matter, such evasive tactics are seldom of any use because of the constructive ownership rules. The code contains several slightly different sets of constructive ownership rules for different purposes. For example, Section 318 contains one set of rules for use in most questions arising under Subchapter C of the code; Section 544 contains another set of constructive ownership rules for use in connection with personal holding company problems; and Section 1563(e), yet another set for use in defining a controlled group of corporations. Although there are important differences in each of the several sets of constructive ownership rules, we need only observe that their common result when determining tax consequences is to find that a taxpayer is deemed to own many shares in addition to those he or she owns personally and directly. Usually, a stockholder must include as his or her own shares any shares owned by a spouse, parents, children, and grandchildren, as well as shares owned by partnerships, corporations, and trusts in which the stockholder has a beneficial interest. Finally, the stockholder must also include as shares owned any shares that he or she has an option to acquire. The net result of these imputations is, of course, to give many taxpayers a larger interest than they would prefer to have for many tax determinations.

Allocation of Income and Deductions

The explicit rules of the statutory tax traps that we have examined thus far tend to be aimed at specific abuses, which were revealed by prior practical experience. The only exception is that relating to the accumulated earnings tax, and in that instance Congress needed no prior experience to predict accurately what would happen in the absence of a statutory prohibition. Although Section 482 has a specific history similar to that of the other statutory tax traps, this provision has been applied in several ways never contemplated when Congress first enacted it. For this reason it is more difficult to determine the limits of this potential statutory tax trap.

In general, Section 482 gives the IRS the authority to distribute, apportion, or allocate any item of gross income, any deduction, or any tax credit between or among two or more controlled businesses if it determines that such an adjustment is necessary to prevent the evasion of income taxes or to reflect income clearly. It is this code section that the IRS has cited as authority for its enforcement of more realistic pricing policies in sales transactions between related persons, especially between domestic parent corporations and their foreign subsidiaries. The same section has been cited as the authority for requiring interest on loans made between related taxpayers and for charging out managerial services rendered by one corporation's employees for a related corporation.

Although we do not know the limits of the commissioner's authority under this statutory provision, we do know that business managers must give more careful consideration in the future than they have in the past to the tax consequences that might attach to transactions between related taxpayers. If a taxpayer desires to keep all of these transactions free of any tax consequences, that usually can be done satisfactorily, either by merging the two businesses or by filing consolidated corporate tax returns. If these alternatives are not satisfactory, the business manager should become aware of the potential tax implications of Section 482. The danger of this tax trap is that it may trigger the recognition of taxable income at an undesirable time and that it may allocate that income to the least desirable entity.

In summary, a taxpayer should always be aware of the fact that the commissioner of the Internal Revenue Service has an arsenal of weapons to defeat a taxpayer's desire to capitalize on a questionable tax privilege. Tax-saving provisions deliberately written into the code by Congress are not at issue here. For example, the tax advantages that attach to routine capital gains, to rapid depreciation allowances, to viable corporate business ventures, and to percentage depletion are well established and beyond question by the IRS. When the taxpayer or a tax adviser extends these special provisions to a new or unusual case, however, he or she may discover that an objective will be challenged by the IRS on the authority of an elusive judicial doctrine or on the basis of prior statutory action of Congress in somewhat analogous situations. In taxation as in love, however, it is often better to try and to fail than never to have tried at all.

CHAPTER **15**

The Taxing Process

Actual participation in the taxing process is quite different from reading about the myriad existing tax rules. Books on taxation usually describe it as a series of apparently sterile rules of the "if A, then B" variety. The reader is tempted to conclude that taxation consists only of learning and impartially applying all of the many rules. Any reasonable exposure to the real process of taxation will quickly dispel that notion. Taxation is in fact a very dynamic process of interaction among people. *Tax rules are made, interpreted, and administered in minutely different situations by unique humans who work with a very imprecise language.* Because the taxing process is an entirely human one, distinct opportunities and problems are created. First, this means that the tax rules are in a constant state of flux and that, under the proper circumstances, they can actually be rewritten or reinterpreted to the distinct advantage (or disadvantage) of one or a few taxpayers. Second, it means that a knowledgeable taxpayer can often prearrange events so that only the most favorable tax result will actually be applicable to a situation. Third, it means that even when a taxpayer fails to exercise any preliminary caution, he or she may be able to argue successfully that a particular situation is (or is not) within the meaning of certain statutory words and that, therefore, rule A rather than rule B ought to apply.

Our income, estate, and gift taxes are all self-compliance taxes. Theoretically, the individual determines the tax liability to argue successfully that a particular situation is (or is not) and reports that determination with the proper remittance to the government on a timely basis. As a practical matter, the tax rules have become so complex that a majority of the taxpayers believe that they are individually incapable of self-compliance, and therefore they turn to ostensible tax experts for assistance. Although an expert can help a taxpayer meet an obligation, the taxpayer alone bears the brunt of the liability for complying with the law.

In practice, the taxing process seems to take place at three different levels: first, at the legislative level, where the initial rules are hammered out in a political process called government; second, at the planning and compliance levels, where the taxpayer works with an adviser and the two attempt to satisfy the legal and financial requirements placed upon the taxpayer; and third, at the level where disagreements are resolved between the government and the taxpayer. At the last level especially, the taxpayer tends to stand on the sidelines watching the experts spar over his or her fate. The taxpayer plays the role of an innocent bystander who must ultimately pay the consequence of battle.

In this chapter, we shall consider only the second and third levels of the taxing process. The first level can be dismissed because so few taxpayers ever attempt to influence tax legislation directly for their individual benefit. Those few who take this narrow route to legal tax avoidance usually have a sophistication far beyond that envisioned for the readers of this book. Virtually every taxpayer, on the other hand, is faced with problems of planning and compliance. A lesser but still significant number face the problems of resolving disagreements with the IRS. The chapter is divided into three major sections. The first section contains a description of tax compliance procedure from the filing of a tax return through the litigation of potential differences of opinion. The second section consists of a brief discussion of the tax experts who offer their assistance on a commercial basis to taxpayers seeking help. The third section consists of a very brief forecast of what may lie ahead in the area of federal taxation.

Compliance Considerations

The first official step in the compliance process generally consists of the filing of a tax return on a timely basis. Long before the reporting date arrives, of course, the taxpayer may have made an investigation into the available alternatives and so arranged matters that a given result is almost certain. This preparation for the filing of a return may even have included a request for an advance ruling on a technical point by the IRS. Whether or not preliminary tax planning has taken place, every taxpayer must eventually report to the IRS the tax result of the events that have actually transpired. The date on which any tax return is due will depend upon many different considerations, including the tax involved (for example, the income, estate, or gift tax) and the kind of taxpayer involved (for example, an individual, a corporation, or a fiduciary). Several hundred forms and instructional booklets have been prepared and distributed by the IRS to facilitate this reporting process. In unusual circumstances, the IRS may accept as satisfactory the taxpayer's computer tapes and individual computer programs in lieu of the more typical forms. However it may be accomplished, the act of reporting is generally the first step in the taxing process.

Filing Tax Returns

In a recent year, approximately 100 million income tax returns were filed with the IRS by individual, corporate, and fiduciary taxpayers. An additional 25 million employment tax returns and 1 million estate and gift tax returns were also filed in that year. On the whole, the income, estate, and gift tax returns represent the greatest challenge in terms of compliance considerations. At present, most tax returns are filed with one of the ten IRS service centers located in various sections of the country. These service centers are largely information processing facilities. They do perform a check of the arithmetic accuracy of virtually all returns received, and a very limited review of obvious errors, but this check should not be confused with an actual audit, which will be discussed shortly. Having confirmed the arithmetic, and determined the general correctness of a return, a service center clerk will prepare a computer record of the documents received. The computer record is forwarded to Martinsburg, West Virginia, for storage and further reference. If the return indicates that a refund is due the taxpayer, the service center personnel will also initiate the action required for the preparation of a refund check. If a remittance is included with a return, service center personnel will separate the check from the tax return and deposit the tax paid to the government's account.

Many taxpayers place unjustified significance upon the fact that they receive a refund check from the government or that the government cashed their check as submitted. As just explained, this means little more than that their return has passed a simple check of arithmetic accuracy and that it has been logged into the government computer for possible retrieval at a later date. It does not mean the tax return has been accepted as filed. For most purposes, the IRS has at least three years during which it may raise questions concerning the accuracy of any return. If a return contains a material error—for example, an omission of more than 25 percent of the gross income—the assessment period is extended to six years. If fraud is involved, the assessment period remains open indefinitely. As a practical matter, much of the routine work being done by IRS agents involves tax returns that are two to three years old. Thus every taxpayer should keep all supporting records for at least three years; certain records are best retained for a lifetime.

Returns Selected for Audit

Several years ago, the actual audit selection process was a special task assigned to some of the most experienced employees of the IRS. Since then, that task has been largely delegated to the computer. Based upon a highly classified discriminate function analysis, the computer scores each tax return received by the IRS. The return with the highest score is supposedly the one most deserving of an audit; the return with the second highest score, the next most deserving of an audit; and so on. Although the computer program utilized by the IRS must remain secret for obvious reasons, it seems reasonable to speculate that it gives special attention to, among other things, deductions that are larger than normal for a taxpayer in any given income bracket, deductions that are especially prone to abuse (travel and entertainment expenses, for example), returns reporting a substantial gross income but little or no taxable income, and returns reporting very large incomes from any source. Some returns are also selected for audit each year on a purely random basis to determine the general compliance standards of taxpayers as a whole.

The audit of a tax return is conducted by IRS personnel assigned to a district office, not by service-center personnel. At present there are 58 district offices scattered throughout the United States. To facilitate compliance the IRS maintains resident audit personnel in each major city, whether or not there is a district office in the city. The audit staff is generally divided between revenue agents and special agents, who perform rather different functions. The revenue agent conducts more or less routine investigations into the adequacy of the returns selected for audit; the special agent is assigned to more investigatory work in cases where fraud is suspected. Routine audits may be conducted either at an IRS office (which audit is classified as an "office audit") or at the taxpayer's place of business (which audit is referred to as a "field audit"). The decision on where the audit should take place is largely a matter of logistics. If a large number of bulky records must be examined, the IRS agents usually will agree to a field audit; otherwise, the taxpayer can expect to report to an IRS facility for completion of an audit.

Settling Disputes

A taxpayer receiving a first notice of an IRS examination may panic unnecessarily. However, unless the taxpayer has reason to suspect that an audit is something more than a routine investigation, he or she usually has nothing to fear. The agent will request that substantiating records be produced for examination. If the taxpayer has maintained good records and the information was reported correctly, the audit may be closed promptly with little or no adjustment. If the records are questionable, or if the agent disagrees with the taxpayer's interpretation of the tax rules, a more detailed administrative review procedure is set into motion. In order to make the contest one between equals, a taxpayer would generally be well advised to be represented in any administrative hearing by a knowledgeable tax expert if the proceeding involves anything other than a simple and direct verification of fact. In other words, it would not be necessary or helpful for a taxpayer to engage a tax expert if all that is asked is proof of ten dependent children or of a charitable deduction *and* if the taxpayer has adequate proof of the facts in question. On the other hand, if the taxpayer is trying to substantiate the conclusion that an aged grandmother really is a dependent, or if a taxpayer is trying to prove weekly cash contributions to an open church offering, an adviser may be most helpful. In more complicated business situations (such as situations involving corporate formations, pension plans, and similar circumstances), a tax adviser is virtually mandatory. Generally speaking, the taxpayer should contact an adviser as soon as he or she receives a notice of examination, not after meeting with the IRS representative. The way a case is initially presented may have something to do with its ultimate resolution.

Administrative reviews. If the original auditor, an IRS supervisor, and the taxpayer cannot agree upon the correct resolution of a particular issue, the code authorizes an additional administrative consultation before the taxpayer needs to consider the possibility of litigating the dispute in a court of law. The administrative review procedure authorizes a conference with a specially trained agent, called a conferee, who is assigned to the regional commissioner's office and is entirely independent of the agent who conducted the original audit. The seven regional offices operate as intermediaries between the district offices and the national office of the IRS in Washington, D.C. Whether or not a taxpayer should utilize the possible administrative review procedure depends largely upon the question under consideration and the professional opinion of the expert handling the case. A visual presentation of the audit procedure is contained in Figure 15–1.

Judicial reviews. If the taxpayer and the representatives of the IRS simply cannot settle their differences of opinion in any administrative proceeding, the debate can proceed to trial.

FIGURE 15–1
Income Tax Audit Procedure—Internal Revenue Service

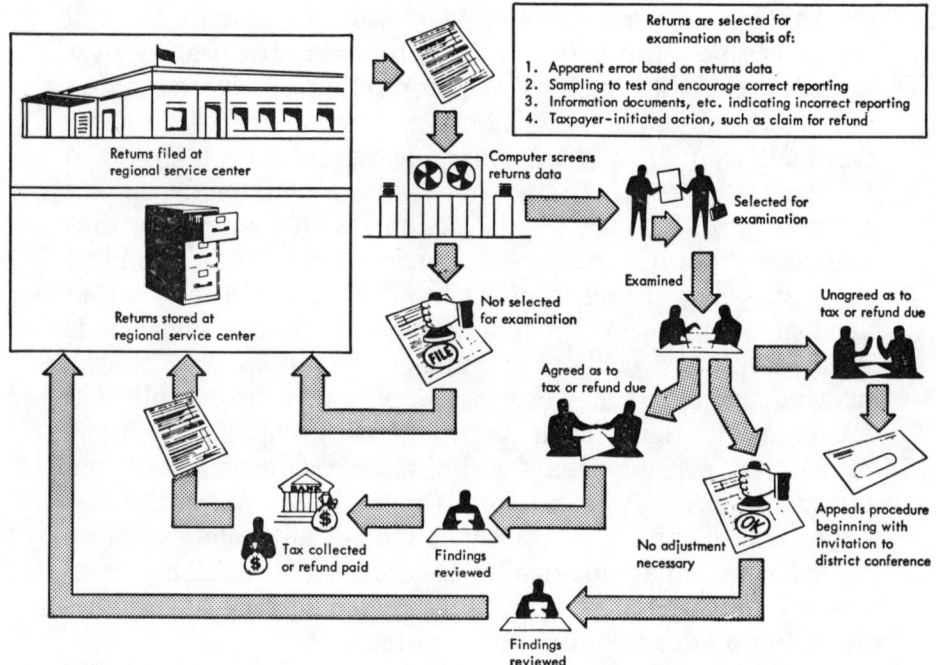

In tax matters, any one of three courts may have initial jurisdiction. A taxpayer will end up in the Tax Court if he or she refuses to pay a tax deficiency assessed by the IRS and the dispute is then litigated. If the taxpayer pays the deficiency assessed by the IRS, that taxpayer may then turn around and sue the government in either a federal district court or the Court of Claims for a recovery of money believed to be wrongfully collected. The selection of the most appropriate judicial forum should, quite naturally, be heavily influenced by the taxpayer's legal counsel. Each of the courts is quite different in its methods of operation, and each may be preferred under particular circumstances. Generally, the Tax Court has the better grasp of technical issues because it is a court whose jurisdiction is restricted to tax controversy. The federal district court is expected to try cases in all aspects of the law, and therefore its judges cannot be equally expert in every technical detail of the tax law. On the other hand, there is no provision for a jury trial in the Tax Court. If the question to be established is one of fact rather than law, counsel may prefer the district court route, believing that a jury may be more sympathetic to a taxpayer's point of view. If, for example, a taxpayer is trying to establish the fair market value of a painting donated to an art museum, there may be good reason to prefer a federal district court to the Tax Court. On the other hand, if the taxpayer is trying to prove that a $500,000 salary is reasonable, there may be good reason to avoid a jury. An appeal from either of these two courts must go to the circuit court of appeals for the taxpayer's place of residence.

An appellate court will generally not review findings of fact. The appellate courts tend to accept the lower court's determination of fact and to consider only errors in the application of the law. The losing party can usually force a disagreement before a circuit court of appeals. Once that body has rendered an opinion, however, the only remaining appeal is to the U.S. Supreme Court. During an average year, the Supreme Court will agree to hear no more than five to eight tax cases. These cases are selected either because the court believes that they contain some important tax principle requiring clarification or because two or more circuit courts of appeal are in disagreement about how essentially identical questions should be answered. Appeals from the Court of Claims can go only to the Supreme Court. A visual presentation of the income tax appeal procedure, including both administrative and judicial elements, is contained in Figure 15–2.

A Summary Observation

In evaluating the IRS procedures, the reader should understand that any individual taxpayer's chance of having his or her tax return selected for audit is statistically about 1 in 50. The reason for this low probability of an audit is that the IRS does not have sufficient personnel to do more, not that all of the unaudited returns are deemed to be correct as filed. In one recent year, the IRS audited about 2.3 million tax returns. Of the returns audited, the vast majority were either accepted as filed or all differences were settled by agreement between the agent and the taxpayer. Only 50,000 cases went beyond the initial auditor to a conference procedure. Nearly two thirds of

FIGURE 15-2

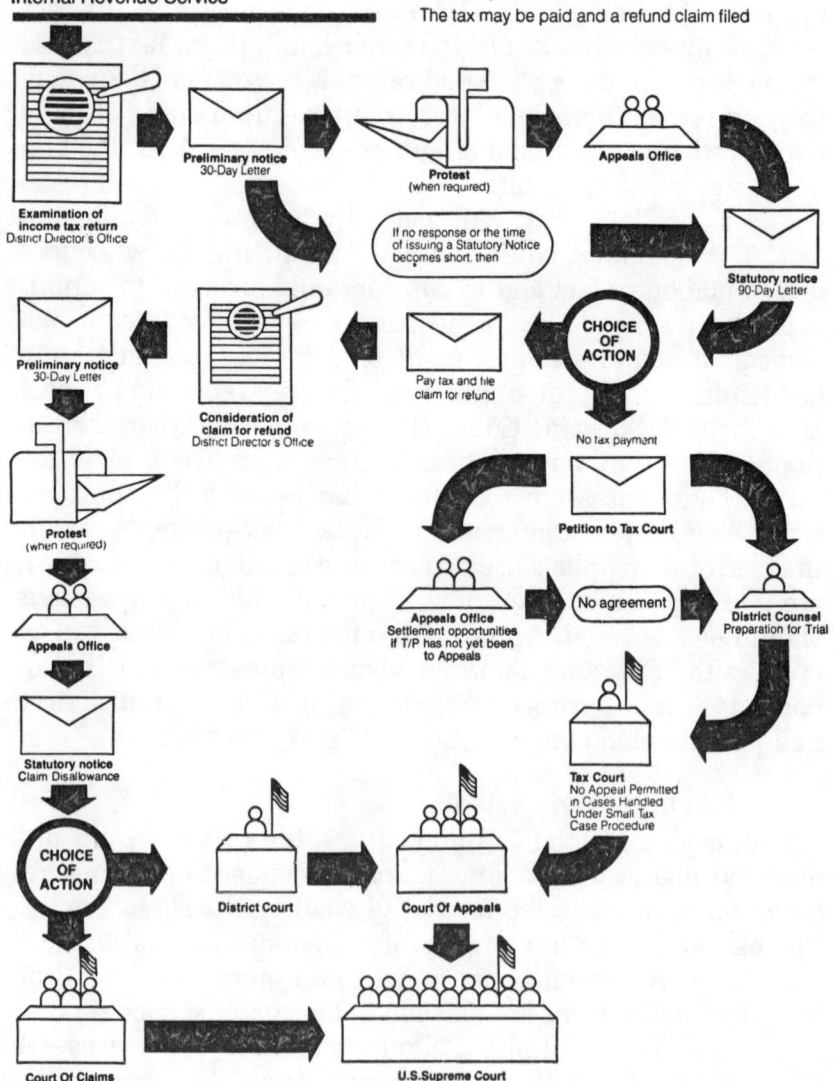

those going to conference were settled without judicial proceedings. During that year, the IRS conceded about 30 percent of the tax deficiency initially assessed. Considering only the agreed cases that were settled without trial, the IRS conceded an even larger percentage of the initial deficiency assessment. The result of judicial proceedings in tax matters at the trial court level during 1978 have been summarized in Table 15–1.

TABLE 15–1

	Complete taxpayer victory (percent)	Split decision (percent)	Complete IRS victory (percent)
Tax Court	11	38	51
District courts	26	11	63
Court of Claims	26	11	64

The point of these statistics is simply to impress upon the reader the following important conclusions:

1. The chances that any particular tax return will be selected for audit are something like 1 in 50.
2. The chances that any error in a tax return will be discovered are even less than 1 in 50 because the IRS agents obviously cannot detect every error on every return examined.
3. If a return is audited, the overwhelming odds are that the taxpayer and the IRS will be able to settle any dispute without a judicial hearing.
4. If the IRS and the taxpayer do resolve a disputed item without a judicial hearing, the probabilities are that the IRS will agree to accept less than the amount of the initial deficiency assessed.
5. If a dispute proceeds to trial, the chances are about four out of ten that the taxpayer will win at least some portion of his or her case.

These conclusions are important for several reasons. First, they should explain why a competent tax adviser may not be impressed by the argument that something must be right just because a taxpayer has always done it that way and the IRS has never objected. Second, the statistics should explain why there is no real reason to panic when a taxpayer first learns that he or she is being audited. Third, the statistics should explain why the level of taxpayer assistance may be substantially less than ideal without the taxpayer ever being aware of this. Critics have often suggested that a surgeon's worst mistakes are buried, undiscovered. There can be little doubt that that observation holds true for many a tax adviser.

Taxpayer Assistance

Taxpayer advisory services have become a big business in the United States. It is estimated that there are currently more than 250,000 people offering their services to the public as tax advisers. Surprising as it may seem to many readers, most of these experts remain almost wholly unregulated. In a world in which those who cut hair and fingernails can operate only by government license and regulation, it is surprising indeed that tax advisory services remain an open frontier.

Questions of Competence

Most alleged tax experts can be divided between "regulated agents" and "unenrolled practitioners." The regulated agents can be further subdivided into (a) attorneys, (b) certified public accountants, and (c) "enrolled agents," or persons who are neither attorneys nor CPAs, but have passed a special tax examination given by the Treasury Department. Attorneys and certified public accountants are automatically admitted to practice before the IRS, based upon their regular professional examinations and license. Of the estimated 250,000 people offering tax advisory services, approximately 90,000 are regulated and 160,000 are unenrolled practitioners. The 90,000 are regulated by Treasury Circular 230, as well as by the codes of ethics of the professions involved; the 160,000 are free to operate without risk of sanction other than the normal risk of civil and criminal liability, to which everyone is subject, and some relatively minor preparer penalties that have been imposed since 1976. Although the latter group is free to claim almost anything that it wishes, the IRS will not allow an unenrolled practitioner to represent a taxpayer in an administrative conference.

Until the last few years, neither CPAs nor attorneys could advertise at all. This meant, of course, that those who were most likely to be capable of providing a valid tax advisory service were precluded from claiming their expertness, whereas those who had little or no special knowledge were entirely free to proclaim publicly anything that they wished. Under these conditions, the taxpayer might safely conclude that only anyone who could advertise or who could list himself as a tax expert in the Yellow Pages was probably not highly qualified as a tax expert, whereas anyone who could not make such claims just might be so qualified. The necessary "probably" and "might be" in the preceding sentence do little to add to a taxpayer's confidence in selecting a qualified tax adviser. Obviously, some unenrolled agents have reasonable skills in tax matters, while some who have proved their right to be licensed as attorneys or as certified public accountants are totally inept in matters of taxation. During the past few years, several states have granted attorneys with special expertise in selected areas, including taxation, the right to proclaim their special abilities to the world. It is hoped that the accounting profession will someday grant this same opportunity to its members. And, when that does happen, let us hope that certification will be by examination, not by self-proclamation, as it is with most attorneys to date. Until then, the buyer of tax advice must be wary of the service he or she receives.

A common misconception. Most people erroneously believe that the formal education required of an attorney and a CPA includes a heavy background in taxation, especially federal income taxation. As a matter of fact, most colleges and universities offering a major in accounting require only one three-semester-hour course in taxation and most schools of law require no minimal study of taxation. Between 20 and 25 percent of the time devoted to the practice portion of the nationally administered CPA examination is usually devoted to income tax questions. Although some state bar examinations still include tax questions, other states have removed all tax questions from the bar examinations. Notwithstanding the minimal standards for formal tax education, a substantial number of certified public accountants and attorneys have become extremely competent in matters of taxation. Their general education in related subjects has been combined either with special graduate education in taxation or with heavy practical experience in tax problems. These professionals are, beyond any doubt, those best qualified to advise others on all matters of taxation. The major problem for the taxpayer seeking competent assistance is the fact that in most states there is no easy way to distinguish between highly qualified advisers and poorly qualified advisers. Someday, it is hoped in the near future, all of the state and federal professional associations in law and accountancy will recognize the need to certify tax specialists for the benefit of everyone concerned.

A worthless guarantee. Some tax experts guarantee a taxpayer that they will pay for any technical errors made in their preparation of a tax return. The reader should observe that these guarantees extend only to the correct reporting of the facts as they are related to the preparer of the tax return. If the facts are erroneously reported, the preparer obviously cannot be held responsible for any additional tax imposed in a subsequent audit. More important, however, there may be a tendency of the "guaranteed" preparer to resolve all questionable items in favor of the government. To the extent that such a tendency exists, the guarantee becomes less than worthless. The guarantee actually may cost the taxpayer more than it saves. A real tax expert would explain all questionable issues to the taxpayer and allow the taxpayer to make the final decision on how those items will be reported. The taxpayer is, of course, entitled to know the expert's opinion of what he or she would do in the same circumstance, before reaching a conclusion. Given that kind of tax advisory service, a taxpayer cannot hold the expert responsible for an incorrect decision. Nevertheless, this would be the author's preferred way of resolving all doubtful issues. Even though a true tax expert may not be able to guarantee that the IRS and/or the courts will agree with a professional opinion on a difficult tax issue, an expert is very sensitive to the need to give consistently good tax advice and charges accordingly. The time required to reach a sound conclusion is the basis for the fee.

What is a taxpayer to do? The reader may well wonder how to find and recognize qualified taxpayer assistance if advertisements cannot be trusted and if it is not safe to assume that each and every CPA and attorney is knowledgeable in tax matters. The only certain method of locating qualified tax assistance known to the author is through personal reference. In other words, the only safe way to locate your first qualified tax adviser is to ask another taxpayer who has found out. Individuals who have been in business for a considerable period of time have encountered the need for qualified taxpayer assistance on a number of occasions, and they are usually willing to share their experiences with a fellow sufferer. Sometimes, on the basis of bitter personal experience, they will be able to tell you who is not qualified, as well to suggest tax advisers whom they deem competent.

Once a taxpayer has made an initial contact with a qualified tax adviser, the taxpayer must decide what kind of service is needed and desired. Assuming that the taxpayer is engaged in a continuing business, it is the author's opinion that a taxpayer cannot be getting adequate service unless the taxpayer and the adviser are engaged in frequent communication with each other. The taxpayer must understand that an adviser will have to know *all* of the details of every proposed transaction at the *earliest possible* moment if he or she is to perform satisfactorily. Really qualified tax experts maintain the highest possible ethical standards and keep all client communications and records confidential. Therefore, the taxpayer has nothing to lose and everything to gain from sharing detailed plans with a tax adviser. A tax adviser who does nothing more than file tax returns on a timely basis is not rendering an adequate service to a continuing business. A good adviser will make numerous suggestions for change, as well as answer all of the taxpayer's inquiries. Such an adviser will also expect to be paid a reasonable fee for the work done.

Questions of Cost

Most individuals have a natural reluctance to seek the advice of a competent tax adviser until long after the need for assistance has first been observed. The apparent reason for this reluctance is the belief that the fees charged by such advisers are usually exorbitant. Although it is true that good tax advisory service is expensive, it is seldom exorbitant, for several reasons. First, in most instances, a competent tax adviser will save the client substantially more in taxes than the charges for advice. Thus the taxpayer usually comes out ahead, not behind, in dollars. Second, the tax adviser's fees are themselves tax deductible; hence, the cost of that service is shared by the government on a ratio determined by the taxpayer's marginal tax bracket. The higher the marginal tax bracket, the lower the real cost of the tax adviser's service. Third, most tax advisers bill their clients on the basis of hourly rates. These rates may range from $20 to $200 per hour for a qualified tax adviser. The taxpayer, however, generally need not fear that the adviser will be anxious to bill for the largest possible number of hours at the highest possible billing rate. Good tax advisers are so scarce that they cannot begin to handle the work that naturally gravitates to them. Consequently, the more competent the adviser (and therefore the higher the billing rate), the more likely it is that he or she will either refer a problem to another firm or to a less experienced individual within a firm if a problem really does not warrant personal attention. Far from trying to acquire more clients, many of the qualified tax advisers known to the author are trying to reduce the number of clients they advise. Some charge a minimum fee to discourage the taxpayer with too small a problem. Fortunately, however, a competent adviser will always advise a client of any minimum fee before beginning work on a project. In summary, therefore, the author's advice to the reader is to aim too high rather than too low. Taking too simple a problem to an overly qualified tax adviser has a way of correcting itself in most cases; taking too complex a problem to an underqualified tax adviser has a way of becoming very costly in the long run, even though the real cost may not be discovered for several years.

The Tax Future

No one, including the author, has a particularly clear view of what the future holds with regard to taxes. Successful tax planning must nevertheless take possible future tax changes into consideration. If the tax rates are going to increase significantly next year, we should all accelerate taxable income into this year and defer all possible tax deductions until next year. If the investment credit is to be suspended anytime soon, taxpayers should consider the possibility of placing orders for certain equipment earlier than they might have otherwise. The prescriptions come easily if only we know the prognosis.

A few things seem reasonably certain. In absolute terms, the income tax will either remain at its present size or grow; there is little chance that it will be reduced substantially anytime soon. In relative terms, the income tax may lose stature with the introduction or expansion of other taxes. Even if defense spending can be controlled, the growing demands for increased health, education, and welfare services at the federal, state, and local levels seem destined to increase the aggregate governmental budget. The traditional state and local taxes simply cannot keep pace with these growing demands. Therefore, the federal government is destined to share a larger and larger portion of state and local government expenditures through revenue-sharing measures. Continued inflationary pressures will make federal deficit spending at the present rate an unacceptable alternative in the long run. For all these reasons, we can only anticipate a continuation of the heavy income taxes we have come to know since World War II.

Major tax reform bills have been proposed by both the Republicans and the Democrats within the past few months. The only thing that they seem to agree on is the need to reduce taxes and increase investment spending. Unfortunately, no one can agree on the best route to the desired end. President Reagan supported the Kemp-Roth proposal—calling for a 10 percent reduction in personal tax rates each year for three years—during the 1980 campaign. He also supported major business tax cuts similar to the 10:5:3 depreciation proposals. Some Democratic congressmen are saying that these proposals are too inflationary and, therefore, they support less drastic tax proposals. We can anticipate a lengthy debate of the merits and demerits of every proposal. With the elections over and the Republicans in clear control of the Senate, there is reason to anticipate support for some proposals that the Democratic leadership had previously rejected, particularly the concept of indexing. Inflation is constantly increasing the amount of taxable income reported by all taxpayers—individual, corporate, and fiduciary. Although taxable income is increasing rapidly, real disposable income is declining steadily because the government continues to take a larger and larger share of the reported income by operation of the progressive rate schedules. All government bureaucrats and politicians are well aware of this "fiscal dividend." The only question is how to "correct" the basic problem: through semi-automatic indexing or through periodic tax reductions. For obvious reasons, many politicians prefer periodic tax reductions because they like to tell voters that they have just enacted a tax cut. However it is finally arranged, the next tax cut is likely to be in the vicinity of $30 to $35 billion and include a significant reduction in the income tax on business profits because there is a general consensus on the need to increase investment spending. And increasing investment spending usually means decreasing the tax on business income. Some modified version of 10:5:3 depreciation (discussed briefly in Chapter 8) seems a very likely prospect. So are small reductions in capital gains taxation and some reduction in personal income taxation. Further modification of the Social Security tax is an equally likely candidate for revision in the short run. Major tax reforms—such as the introduction of VAT, the value added tax, to reduce our heavy dependence on income taxation and social security levies—are much more in doubt, even though it still has the support of a few leading tax legislators in Congress.

To what extent the congressional leaders, the administration, or the Treasury Department's bureaucracy initiates congressional action, and to what extent that action stems from a general political and social unrest, remains uncertain. The author's best guess is that political constraints will make a truly massive modification of the income tax impossible until the U.S.A. faces another major crisis, such as World War III or a great depression. Frequent revision of those provisions intended primarily to stimulate critical economic variables, such as rapid depreciation, the investment credit, and rapid write-offs, will continue in the interim.

Most major tax revisions enacted into law during the past few years have been made retroactive to the date on which they were first discussed publicly in a congressional committee. The reader should therefore get accustomed to following proposed tax legislation through daily newspaper accounts and weekly magazine reports. Any proposal that appears to harbor potential tax consequences for the reader or a business should be called to the immediate attention of a tax adviser. And a really good tax adviser will take it from there.

Code Section Index

§37, 26
§56, 219
§57, 220
§74(a), 27
§74(b), 26, 27
§79(a), 26, 145–46
§101, 25, 148
§101(d), 28
§102, 25, 28–29, 34
§103, 25
§104, 25
§105, 25
§106, 25, 146–47
§107, 25, 30–31
§108, 25
§109, 25
§110, 25
§111, 25
§112, 25
§113, 25
§114, 26
§115, 26
§117, 26, 29–30
§118, 26
§119, 26, 147–48
§120, 26, 147
§121, 26
§122, 26
§123, 26
§124, 26, 148–49
§125, 26, 149
§126, 26
§127, 26, 149
§128, 26
§162, 31
§167(a), 195–96

§248, 350
§267, 340, 341
§278, 228
§279, 294
§306, 358
§318, 358, 367
§341, 358, 364, 365
§341(b)(1)(A), 123
§351, 260–61, 286, 367
§354, 288, 289
§355, 284, 289
§356, 288
§357, 288, 289
§358, 288, 290
§361, 288, 289
§362, 288, 290
§368(a)(1), 277, 287
§368(a)(1)(B), 277
§382, 40
§401, 159–60
§446, 333
§446(a), 339
§453, 294
§464, 228
§482, 358
§482, 367–68
§501(c)(3), 328
§531, 359
§532, 358
§533, 359
§534, 359
§535, 359
§536, 359
§537, 359
§541, 362
§542, 358, 362

§543, 362
§544, 362, 367
§545, 362
§546, 362
§547, 362
§621, 26
§643(b), 10
§704(b), 237
§706(c), 237
§872(b), 26
§892, 26
§893, 26
§911, 26
§912, 27
§933, 27
§936, 93
§1031, 255–57, 259, 275
§1033, 266, 267
§1034, 269
§1035, 270
§1036, 271
§1037, 271
§1039, 269, 270
§1231, 103, 104, 125, 132, 133–34, 234
§1239, 134, 262
§1244, 59, 132–33
§1245, 234
§1250, 270
§1348, 221
§1563(a)(2), 52
§1563(c), 367
§2033, 308
§2613(a)(1), 10

Topical Index

A

Accelerated deductions, 231
Accident insurance, 165
Accounting methods, 17–18, 36–37, 333–34
  accrual basis, 36, 334, 338–42
  cash basis, 17–18, 334–38
  completed contract method, 334, 342–43
  installment method, 334, 343–45
  modified cash basis, 336
Accounting principles, matching concept, 36, 37
Accounting procedures and conventions, 345
  convenient assumptions, 347–48
  fiscal year, 348
  income averaging, 351–52
  inventory costing, 345–46
  records, 348–50
  unit of account, 346–47
Accounts receivable, 105
Accrual method of accounting, 36, 334, 338–39
  considerations in electing, 341–42
  required usage of, 339
  special limitations, 339–41
Accumulated earnings tax, 73, 359–61
Adjusted gross income (AGI)
  deductions for, 62–63
  deductions from, 63–65
Administrative reviews, 375
ADR (asset depreciation range) system, 207
Adverse ruling, 263
Affiliated groups of corporations, 51–52
Aggregate income of business owner, 70
Agricultural investments, as tax shelter, 190–91, 228

Airplane, company, as company benefit, 151–52
Airline passes, as company benefit, 153–54
Alimony, deduction of, 63
Allocation of cost, 124–26
Allocation of income and deductions, 267–69
Almond trees, as tax shelters, 228
Amortization, 108
  rapid, 202, 270
Annuity
  taxability of proceeds of, 28
  taxpayer's rights in, 310
Artistic compositions, exclusion of, from capital assets, 100, 104, 105
Asset depreciation range (ADR) system, 207
Assets; see Capital assets; Fixed assets and Noncapital assets
Assignment of income, 23–24
Athlete, taxation of income earned by, 23
Attorneys, role of, as tax advisors, 21–22, 189, 380, 381
Audits
  selection of returns for, 373–74
  settling of disputes in, 374–80

B

Bad debt deduction, 32
Bailout of accumulated corporate income, 293–94
Bailout of preferred stock, 365–66
Bargain purchases, 153
Barter transaction, 249
Base country corporations, 90
Basis rules, importance of, 327–28
Beneficiary, 57

Benefits
  direct versus indirect status of, 20–21
  nontaxable, 145–55
  tax-deferred, 155–65
Bonds, taxation of interest coupons, 24
Boot
  cash as, 249
  in nontaxable transaction, 249
  treatment of, in corporate reorganization, 289–90
Boot relaxation rule, 283
Boot requirement, 249–51, 256, 262
Bootstrap sale of corporation, 366
Borge, Victor, 34
Branch operations of multinational business, 90
Brizendine, Everett, 28
Brother-sister corporation, 51, 52, 54
Building trades industry, use of almost-collapsible corporation in, 124
Buildings, construction of, as tax shelter, 189
Business
  deduction of expenses related to, 32
  disposition of, 86–87
Business form, tax aspects of selecting
  disposition of business, 86–87
  earned income, 77–84
  employee status, 76–77
  fluctuating income, 87–88
  gaining a special tax deduction, 84–86
  maximum reinvestment of income, 70–73
  retention of special income characteristics, 74–75
  special considerations for multinational businesses, 88–94
  utilization of net operating losses, 75–76
Business losses, deduction of, 63
Business purpose doctrine, 356–57
Buy-sell agreements, 292–93

C

Cafeteria plans, 149
Capital assets
  definition of, 99–100
  definitional manipulation of, 117–34
  determination of tax basis of, 107
  as property in nontaxable transaction, 253–54
  status of, as determined by relationship between asset and taxpayer, 106
  time dimension of, 116–17
Capital expenditures, 108, 206–7

Capital gains and losses
  advantages of, 96–99
  combination of short- and long-term, 96, 113
  conversion of ordinary income to, 233–34
  corporate quagmire, 127–32
  defining the boundaries of, 99–106
  in the disposition of a business, 86–87
  in the disposition of a fixed asset, 209–10
  favorable interest rate in installment sales, 126–27
  favorable price allocation in property transactions, 124–26
  and low-income housing, 269–70
  measurement of, 96, 106–13
  modification of use involving more than one taxable entity, 121–24
  modification of use involving single taxable entity, 117–21
  and need for tax planning, 116
  and residence sales, 267–69
  separation of, from ordinary gain for tax purposes, 96
  statutory exceptions to normal rules, 132–34
  taxation of, 82–83
  as tax loophole, 95–96
  tax treatment of net capital losses, 114–15
  tax treatment of, for real or depreciable property used in trade or business, 103, 104, 118–21
  timing considerations of, 134–42
  use of capital losses to offset gains, 76
  utilization of special rules when losses exceed gains, 96
  year-end security review, 135–41
Capital improvements, 109
Carry-back, 39, 115
Carry-forward, 39, 114, 162
Carry-over basis, 251, 288, 290
Carry-over credit, 162
Cash, as boot, 249
Cash basis of accounting, 17, 36, 37
  advantages, 337–38
  popularity of, 334–35
  specific limitations, 335–37
Cash-equivalence rule, 18
Cash-receipts test, 17–18
Cash salary, 165, 166
Casual sales by nondealers, 344
Cattle breeding, 182
Change-in-use opportunity, 125
Change-of-business test, 40
Charitable contributions, 32, 34, 64

Charitable gifts, 305, 328–31
Children, earned income of, 85–86
Citrus groves, 182, 228
Clergy, gifts to, as part of gross income, 28
Cohan rule, 348, 349
Collapsible corporation, 87, 123, 265, 364–65
Commissioner v. Newman, 3
Common law state, tax treatment of married couple in, 42–43
Community property state, tax treatment of married couple in, 42–43, 308
Company homes, 148
Compensation, 143–45; *see also* Salary
  techniques providing for immediate corporate deduction and benefit that is never taxed to employee, 145–55
  techniques providing for immediate corporate deduction and immediate tax to employee, 165–70
  techniques providing for immediate corporate deduction and tax-deferred benefit to employee, 155–65
  techniques providing no corporate deduction but tax to employee, 171–73
Complete liquidation, 131
Completed contract method of accounting, 334, 342–43
Component depreciation, 200–1
Consolidation, of corporate entities, 277
Constructive ownership of stock, 366–67
Constructive receipt, 18–19
Contemplation-of-death rule, 309
Contingent acquisitions, 292–93
Coors, Adolph and Joseph, 148
Copyrights, 100, 104, 105
  as excluded from capital assets, 100, 104, 105
  taxation of income attributable to, 23–24
Corporate entity
  avoidance of, 235–38
  and earned income, 77–83
  employee status of owner of, 76–77
  special tax deductions for, 84–86
Corporate income, extraction of, 129–32
Corporate insolvency, 287
Corporate quagmire, 127–34
Corporate reorganization
  and contingent acquisitions, 292–93
  debt-financed acquisitions, 294
  importance of, 276

Corporate reorganization—*Cont.*
  and liquidation-reincorporation, 293–94
  and net operating losses, 292
  recognition of gain or loss in, 288–90
  special problems of, 291–94
  tax consequences of, 288–91
  treatment of liabilities, 289
  type A reorganization, 277–79, 290, 291, 292
  type B reorganization, 279–81, 291, 292
  type C reorganization, 281–84, 290, 291, 292
  type D reorganization, 284–86, 291
  type E reorganization, 284, 287
  type F reorganization, 284, 287–88
  and unwanted assets, 291–92
Corporate taxpayers
  advantages of capital gains for, 98
  correct tax treatment for net capital losses, 114–15
  economic reality of, 51–52
  legal definitions in, 52–56
  as legal entity, 48–51
  special deductions available to, 60–62
  as taxable entity, 47–48
Corporate tax rate shelter, 73
Corporations
  controlled groups of, 51–55
  formation of, as nontaxable transaction, 260–62
  liquidation of, 265
  nontax advantages and disadvantages of, 69
  purchase of employee benefits by, 20–21
  reorganization of, 262–65; *see also* Corporate reorganization
  tax rate structure of, 49, 50
  tax treatment of, 47–48
Cost allocation method, 195
Cost allocation opportunity, 125
Cost depletion, 203–4
Courts, role of, in tax questions, 12, 375–77
CPA (certified public accountant)
  role of, in handling income from criminal activities, 22
  role of, as tax advisor, 380–81
Curtesy rights, 309

D

Dealer sales, 343–44
Death benefits, 148
Debt-financed acquisitions, 294

Declining-balance method of depreciation, 197–98, 199, 201
Deductions
  accelerated, 231
  charitable, 300
  comparison of, with expenses, 33–36
  definition of, in tax parlance, 5–6
Deferred compensation plan, 170–71
Deferred vesting, 163
De minimus amount, 5
Dependent exemption deduction, 32
Depletion methods, 203–6
Depreciable property, 101–2
Depreciation
  comparison of methods of, 198–99
  component, 200–1
  first-year deduction for, 201–2
  increase of amount allowed when economic stimulation is needed, 177
  methods of, 195–96
    declining balance, 197–98, 199, 201
    double-declining, 199
    straight line, 196–97, 198–99
    sum-of-the-years' digits, 197, 199
    10:5:3, 202–3, 386
  restrictions in use of methods of, 199–201
  switching of methods of, 199
  for the traditional tax shelter, 233–34
Depreciation deduction, 32
Diamond A. Cattle Company v. Commissioner, 357
Direct exchange, 249
Direct tax credit, 35
Discount bonds, 100, 105–6
Disguised compensation, 154–55
Disguised dividends, 171–72
Disposition, form of, 209–10
Dividend-received deduction, 32, 60–62, 71, 71n
Dividends, deductibility of, to owner versus individual stockholders, 71
Domestic International Sales Corporation (DISC), 60, 92–93
Donative transfer tax, 9–10, 295; see also Estate taxes and Gift taxes
Double income taxation, 48–49, 70–71, 264
Double-declining balance (DDB) method of depreciation, 198
Dower rights, 309

E

Earned income, 70, 77–83
  of children, 85–86
Economic policy considerations, 35

Educational assistance, 149
Employee benefits; see also Benefits
  employee discounts, 152–54
Employee Retirement Income Security (1974) (ERISA), 155, 161, 164, 173
Employee status, tax advantages and disadvantages of, 76–77
Employee stock ownership plan (ESOP), 194–95
Energy Tax Act (1978), 194–95
Entertainer, taxation of income earned by, 23
Entertainment expenses, tax treatment of, 150–51, 152
Equipment leasing, 232–33
Estate, as form of fiduciary taxpayer, 56
Estate taxes, 9, 307
  addition of taxable gifts, 313–14
  basic provisions of, 307–16
  deductions from, 311–13
  exemptions from, 311–13
  gross estate, 308
  history of, 295–96
  illustration of, 316
  importance of marginal tax rate for, 325–27
  integration of, with income and gift taxes, 322–32
  planning considerations for, 316–22
  tax credits, 314–16
  tax rates, 314
Estimated tax payments, 218–19
Exchange value credit account, 259
Exclusions, 4–5
Executives, compensation received by, 144
Expenses
  comparison of, with deductions, 33–36
  theoretical mismatching of with revenues, 227–31

F

Fair market value (FMV)
  of assets, 187–88
  of gift, 111, 299
  of noncash payments, 19
  of property, 111, 310
Family tax planning; see also Estate taxes and Gift taxes
  components of, 295–96
  importance of basis rules, 112–13
Farming syndicates, and tax shelters, 228
Favorable price allocation
  for installment sales, 126–27
  in property transactions, 124–26
Fellowships, 29–30

TOPICAL INDEX **393**

Fiduciary taxpayers
 advantages of capital gains for, 96–97
 correct tax treatment of net capital losses for, 114
 as taxable entity, 56–57
 tax rate schedules for, 67
Field audit, 374
Fifo (First-in, first-out) inventory costing method, 345, 346
50-percent identical ownership test, 55
Financial Accounting Standards Board, 339
First-year depreciation allowance, 35
Fiscal dividend, 385
Fiscal year, 348
Five-year rule, 284
Fixed annuity, 163
Fixed assets
 alternative treatments available for, 178
 capital gain or ordinary income in disposition of, 206–7
 classification of, as tax shelters, 224
 comparison of tax effects on investment decisions, 210–16
 construction or creation of, 189–91
 definition of, 177
 depletion methods of, 203–6
 depreciation of, 195–203
 determination of taxpayer's basis in, 224–27
 direct purchase of, 185
 disposition of, 128–29, 209–10
 economic success of investment in, 184
 expenditures during use of, 206–7
 indirect acquisition of, through stock ownership, 186–88
 indirect purchase of, 185
 investment credit recapture, 209
 and the investment tax credit, 191–95
 leasing of, 185, 188–89
 rapid amortization provisions for, 202, 270
 tax factors pertinent to acquisition of, 185–95
 tax factors pertinent to disposition of, 207–10
 volatility of tax rules governing acquisition, use, and disposition of, 177
Foreign country, taxation of income earned by U.S. citizen in, 89
Foreign entity, income paid by, as subject to U.S. income tax, 22
Form 1040, 58, 335
Form 1065, 58
Form W-2, 335

G

Gain or loss
 potential need to recognize in nontaxable transaction, 249–51
 recognition of, in corporate reorganization, 288–90
Gas industry, tax shelters in, 189–90, 228–30
Generation-skipping tax, 318–21
Gifts and inheritances, 28–29
 charitable, 328–31
 tax basis of property acquired by, 110–11
Gift taxes, 9
 basic provisions of, 297–303
 charitable deductions, 300
 charitable gifts, 305, 328–31
 cross gifts, 305–6
 exempt gifts and deductions, 300–1
 gross gifts, 297–300
 history of, 295–96
 illustration of, 303–4
 integration of, with income and estate taxes, 322–32
 marital deduction, 300–1
 planning considerations for, 304–7
 serial gifts, 306–7
 systematic giving, 304–5
 tax credits, 302–3
 tax rates, 301–2
Global income tax, 22, 89
Government bonds, 4, 29
Gregory v. Helvering, 356
Gross income
 accounting methods used, 17–18, 36–37
 assignment of, 23–24
 constructive receipt of, 18–19
 deductions from, 31–40
 definition of, 16
 exclusions, 24–31
 form of payment, 19–20
 and illegal gains, 21–22
 indirect benefit concept, 20–21
 as positive element in income determination, 15
 and the realization criterion, 16–17
 source of payment, 22
Group legal services, 147
Group term life insurance, 145–46

H

Hand, Learned (Justice), 2
Heads of households, 43–44, 67
Health and accident plans, 146–47, 165

Highest and best use value, 311
Hobby expenses, deductibility of, 32–33, 34
Holding company, creation of, 283
Hornung, Paul, 27, 28
H. R. 10 plans, 172–73, 174
Hybrid organizations, tax treatment of, 58–59

I

Identical ownership, 53, 54
Illegal gains, taxability of, 21–22
Income
  assignment of, 23–24
  classification of, 7
  definition of, 35, 226
  fluctuations of, 87–88
  maximum reinvestment of, as business consideration, 70–73
  measurement of, for tax and financial accounting purposes, 177
Income averaging, 87–88, 351–52
Income-producing property, 47
Income-producing venture, 32–33
Income taxes
  amount of revenue from, 9
  dominant role of, in U.S., 9
  as global tax, 22, 89
  importance of marginal tax rate for, 323–25
  integration of, with gift and estate taxes, 322–32
  withholding system, 218–19
Indirect benefit concept, 20–21
Indirect taxes, 9
Individual retirement accounts (IRA), 173–74
Individual taxpayers
  advantages of capital gains for, 96–97
  correct tax treatment of net capital losses for, 114
  definitional problems, 46
  head of household, 43–44
  important differences in tax treatment of, and corporate entities, 84
  married couple, 42–43
  planning opportunities, 46–47
  single persons, 44–46
  special considerations for, 62–63
  as taxable entity, 41–42
Inflation, and retirement, 518–19
Inheritances, tax treatment of, 28–29, 111–13,
Installment method of accounting, 334, 343–45
Installment sales
  favorable interest rate in, 126–27
  use of, in sale of capital assets, 141–42

Intangible drilling and development costs, 229, 231
Interest expense deduction, 32, 64
Interest-free loans, 154–55
Internal Revenue Code; see Code Section Index
  and classification of taxable entity, 41
  complexity of, 10
  constant revision of, 10–11
  definition of capital assets by exception, 99–100
  statutory changes in, to deal with multinational corporations, 92
Internal Revenue Service, 12–13
  audit staff, 374
  conferee agents, 375
  district offices, 374–75
  forms and booklets of, 372
  regional offices, 374
  revenue agents, 374
  service centers, 372–73
  special agents, 374
Intent, role of, in nontaxable transactions, 274–75
Inter vivos trust, 57
Inventory costing conventions, 345–46
Inventory items, 99, 100–1
Investment interest, and cash basis of accounting, 338
Investment properties, exchange of, 255–60
Investment tax credit, 35, 177, 191–95, 209–10, 232–33, 350,
Involuntary conversions, 266–67

J

Joint income tax return, 42–43
Joint ownership, and determination of gross estate, 308
Joint tenancy, 308
Joint venture, 41
  modification of use of property on timely basis, 117
Judicial doctrines
  business purpose, 356–57
  step transactions, 357–58
  substance over form, 354–56
Judicial reviews, 375–77
Jury trial, no provision for, in tax court, 376–77

K–L

Keogh plans, 172–73

Land development, as tax shelter, 190
Last-in, first-out (Lifo) inventory costing method, 345, 346

TOPICAL INDEX 395

Laws of descent and distribution, 317
Leasing, of fixed assets, 185, 188–89
Legal entities, 48–51
Letters, as not capital assets, 100, 105
Leveraging, 224–27
Lewellen, Wilbur, 144
Liabilities
  assumption of, 257–58, 273
  repayment of, 129–32
  treatment of, in corporate reorganization, 289
Life insurance
  exclusion of benefits from gross income, 28, 309
  group-term, 145–46
  as part of qualified retirement plan, 165
Life interest, 318
Lifo (last-in, first-out) inventory costing method, 345, 346
Like-kind exchanges, 255–60
Limited partnership, use of in tax shelters, 236–37
Liquidating distribution, 356–57
Liquidating dividend, 87
Liquidation, of corporation, 265
Liquidation-reincorporation, 293–94
Literary compositions, 100, 104, 105
Litigation, in type D reorganization, 284–85
Lodging, as benefit, 147–48
Long-term capital gain deduction, 63
Long-term capital gains and losses, 74, 113, 137–38
Losses
  exchange of productive-use or investment properties, 255–60, 275
  involuntary conversions, 266–67
  net capital, 114–15
  net operating loss (NOL), 38–39
  paper, 255
  personal, 38, 117–19
  proper tax treatment of, 37–40
Losses deduction, 32
Low-income housing, 269–70
Lump-sum distribution, from qualified retirement plans, 156–57

M

Marginal tax rates
  on corporations, 70
  estate tax considerations, 325–27
  importance of, 323–27
  income tax considerations, 323–25
  maximum tax considerations, 325
  personal service income, 78–79

Marital deductions
  estate tax, 311, 312, 325–26, 327
  gift tax, 301–2, 313–14
Marriage, effect of, on tax rate, 7
Marriage tax, 44–45
Married individuals
  as taxable entity, 42–43
  tax rate schedules for, 66
Matching concept, 36, 37
Maximization of taxable entities, 6
Maximization of tax deductions, 5–6
Maximization of tax exclusions, 4
Maximum reinvestment of income, 70–73
Maximum tax on personal service income, 325
Max tax, 325
Meals and lodging, as company benefit, 147–48
Medical expenses, deductions for, 64
Memorandums, as not a capital asset, 100, 105
Mergers, of corporate entities, 277
Minimization of tax liability, 6
Minimum tax, imposition of, on tax preferences, 219–21
Modified cash basis of accounting, 336
Mortgaged properties, 230–31
Movies, investment in, as tax shelter, 231
Moving average, 345
Moving expenses, deduction of, 63
Multinational business
  branch operations, 90
  corporate business, 89–94
  Domestic International Sales Corporation, 92–93
  possessions corporation, 93
  subsidiary corporations, 90–92, 286
  unincorporated businesses, 89
Multinational transactions, 22
Multiple-corporate entities, 82
Multiple-family corporations, 56
Musical compositions, exclusion from capital assets, 100, 104, 105

N

Net capital gain, 89–90, 96, 97, 233–34
Net capital losses, 114–15
Net income, 227
Net operating loss (NOL)
  carry back, 87–88
  reorganization of corporations, 292
  tax treatment of, 38–40
  utilization of, 75–76
Net tax base, 8
Net tax payable, 8

Nobel prize, income from, as excluded from gross income, 27
Nonbusiness property, 102
Noncapital assets, 99–106
 disposition of, 128–29
Noncash payments, taxation of, 19–20
Noncash salary, 166
Nonemployee trade or business expense, deduction of, 62
Nonqualified stock options, 166–70
Nonrecourse debt, 225
Nonresident aliens, taxability of, 22, 90
Nonroutine transactions, 18
Nontax considerations, 7, 69
Nontaxable entity, 41
Nontaxable exchange provisions, 141
Nontaxable transactions, 249
 between corporation and its shareholders, 260–65
 boot requirement, 249–51, 256, 262
 carryover tax basis for, 251–54, 255, 261
 characteristics of, 248–54
 exchange of investment properties, 255–60
 exchange of productive-use properties, 255–60
 fair market value, 250
 formation of corporation, 260–62
 importance of, 247
 involuntary conversions, 266–67
 liquidation of corporation, 265
 low-income housing, 269–70
 mortgaged properties, 230–31
 planning considerations in, 271–75
 potential need to recognize some gain, 249–51
 qualified property, 249
 reorganization of corporation, 262–65
 replacement property, 271–73
 residence sales, 267–69
 role of intent in, 274–75
 three-cornered exchange, 271–73
 time contraints in, 254
 transfer of tax basis in, 251–54
Notes receivable, 105

O

Obsolescence, 196
Office audit, 374
Oil industry, tax shelters in, 189–90, 228–30
One-time elections, 350–51
Ordinary income
 conversion of, to capital gain, 233–34
 in disposition of a fixed asset, 209–10

Ordinary and necessary business expenses, 31
Organization expenses, amortization of, 350
Other income, 7
Outside sales expenses, deduction of, 63
Owner-operator of business
 earned income of, 77–83
 modification of use of assets for capital gains and losses treatment, 117–24

P

Paper gains and losses, 136, 248, 255
Parent-subsidiary corporations, 51–52
Parsonages, rental value of, as excluded from gross income, 30–31
Partial liquidation, 130–31
Partnership, 41
 creation of, 69
 employee status in, 76, 143
 modification of use of property on timely basis, 117
 net operating losses, utilization of, 75–76
 selection of, as business form, 69
 treatment of, for tax purposes, 58, 74, 75, 76
Patents
 as capital assets, 104–5
 taxation of income from, 23–24
Pension plans; see also Qualified pension plans
 deduction of contributions to, 63
 qualification of, 158–60
 taxpayer's rights in, 310
Percentage depletion, 35, 204–6
Percentage depletion allowance, 235
Perks, 81
Perquisites, 150
Personal assets, capital gain or loss on sale or exchange of, 117–21
Personal exemption deduction, 85; see also Zero bracket amount
Personal expenditures, 32–33
Personal holding companies, constructive ownership of stock in, 366–67
Personal holding company tax, 84–85, 361–64
Personal residences
 conversion of property from or to, 120–21
 sales of, 267–69
 by senior citizens, 269
Personal service taxable income, 7, 77, 78, 87, 221, 325
Personal use property, 308

Phantom income, 226
  tax liabilities on, 227
Phantom stock plan, 170
Pig theory, 354
Possessions corporation, 93
Powers of appointment, 309
Preferred stock bailout, 365–66
Prepublication ventures, as tax shelter, 231
Present value concept, relationship of, between tax laws and simple economics, 179–84
Price allocations, favorable
  for installment sales, 126–27
  for property transactions, 124–26
Price gerrymandering, 91
Privileged communications, concept of, 21–22
Prizes, exemption of, from gross income, 27
Productive-use properties, exchange of, 255–60
Professional service corporations, 143–44
Profit-sharing contributions, deductions of, 63
Profit-sharing plans
  qualification of, 158–59
  taxpayer's rights in, 310
Progressive tax rates, 6
Property
  change in form or substance of, and use of realization criterion, 17
  favorable price allocation in transactions of, 124–26
  ownership of, as providing opportunity for tax avoidance, 2, 3
  tax basis when acquired by gift, 110–11
Property tax, revenue from, 9
Public assistance payments, as excluded from tax base, 25
Puerto Rico, 93
Pulitzer prize, income from, as excluded from gross income, 27
Purchased property, tax basis of, 107–10

Q

Qualified pension plan, 155, 156–62, 173, 331
Qualified profit-sharing plan, 155, 156–62
Qualified property, in nontaxable transaction, 249
Qualified SEP-IRA plans, 174
Qualified stock bonus plans, 156–61, 162–65, 331

R

Rapid amortization provision, 202, 270
Rapid depreciation allowances, 35
Raw land, investments in, 234
Real estate, tax shelters in, 230–31
Real estate investment trust (REIT), 60
Real property
  exclusion of from capital assets, when used in trade or business, 99, 101–4, 117
  investment in, as tax shelter, 225
Realization, as necessary condition to recognition of profit, 247
Realization criterion, 16–17
Reasonable determination, of total compensation package, 171–72
Recapitalization, 287
Receivables acquired in trade or business, 100, 105
Records, need for, 348–50
Refunds, tax, 39, 348
Regulated agents, 380
Regulated investment company, 60
Reimbursed business expenses, as deductions, 63, 77
Reincorporation of liquidating corporation, 293–94
Reinvestment of capital, 70–73
Related tax papers, 18, 366–67
Rent or royalty expenses, deductibility of, 63
Repairs, 206–7
Replacement property, 271–73
Research and development, 32, 231
Residences; see Personal residence
Resident aliens, 22
Retail sales, 345
Retirement income funds, and family tax planning, 331–32
Returns, tax
  assistance in preparing, 380–84
  audits of, 373–80
  filing requirements, 372–73
Revenue Act (1924), 356
Revenue Act (1976), 230
Revenue Act (1978), 51, 56, 83, 123, 148, 174, 225
Revenues, theoretical mismatching of with expenses, 227–31
Rigged transactions, 119–20

S

Salary; see also Compensation
  cash as, 165, 166

Salary; see also Compensation—Cont.
  as compensation for service rendered, 28
  deductibility of owner's, 71
  reasonableness of, 81–82
Sales tax, 4, 9
Salvage value, 196
Savings accounts withdrawal penalties, 63
Scholarship and fellowship grants, exclusion of from gross income, 29–30
Security Exchange Commission, 155
Self-employed individuals
  distinction between employees and, 143
  estimated tax payments of, 218–19
  individual retirement accounts (IRA), 173–74
  options of, for tax savings, 2, 76–77, 172–74
Senior citizens, sale of residence by, 269
Serial gifts, 306–7
70-30 basis, 37, 133
Short-period return, 348
Short sales, 138–40
Simplified employee pension plan (SEP-IRA), 174
Single individuals, as tax entity, 44–46
Small business corporations, 59–60
Small business investment corporations (SBICs), 59
Social policy considerations, in determining gross income, 25–36
Social security payments, exclusion of, from tax base, 25
Social security taxes, 9, 386
Soil and water conservation expenditures, 32
Sole proprietorship, 41
  creation of, 69
  deductibility of routine business expenses of, 62
  employee status of owner, 76, 143
  opportunities of, to modify use of property on timely basis, 117
  treatment of, in financial accounting, 57
  treatment of, for income tax purposes, 57–58, 74, 75, 76
Special use value, 311
Specific identification, 345
Spin-off, 286, 356
Split-off, 286
Split-up, 286
Standard deduction, 85; see also Zero bracket amount
Starker, 259

Starks, Greta, 28
State inheritance taxes, 315
State retirement program, taxability of employee's participation in, 18–19
Statutory depletion, 203
Step transaction doctrine, 357–58
Stipends, taxability of, 29–30
Stock bonus plans, qualification of, 158–59
Stock options, 166–70
Stock redemption, 130
Stockholders
  nontaxable transactions between corporation and, 260–65
  tax treatment of distributions to, 129–32
Straight-line method of depreciation, 196–97, 198–99, 234
Subchapter C, 262
Subchapter R, 59
Subchapter S corporations, tax treatment of, 59–60, 74–75
Subsidiary corporations, 90–92, 286
Substance over form doctrine, 354–56
"Substantially all" requirement, 282
Sum-of-the-years'-digits method of depreciation, 197, 199
Surviving spouse status, 46

T

Tax advisor
  consulting fees of, 237
  need for, 11, 21, 24, 195
  role of, 386
Tax attorney, 21–22
Tax avoidance, 3, 13–14
Tax base, 6
Tax basis
  of capital assets, 107
  of inherited property, 111–13
  of property acquired by gift, 110–11
  of purchased property, 107–10
  transfer of, in nontaxable transactions, 251–54
Tax complexity, 1
Tax constraints, 69–88
Tax court, 12, 375–77
Tax credit, 8–9
  on estate taxes, 314–16
  on foreign income tax paid, 89
  on gift taxes, 302–3
Tax cuts, 385–86
Tax deductions, 15, 32, 64
Tax evasion, 13–14, 19–21
Tax-exempt income, 34, 74
Tax future, 384–86

Tax haven countries, 90
Tax incentive, 323
Tax laws, 144, 179–84
Tax liability, 6–7
Tax litigation, 12, 375–77
Tax loopholes, 87, 134, 358
Tax on marriage, 44–45
Tax planning
  basic terminology of, 3–9
  complexity of, 1
  elements of, 10–13
  importance of statutory interpretation on, 30–31
  importance of taxable entity to, 46–47
  and maximization of all tax exclusions, 4
  morality of, 2–3
  success of, 11
  use of human test in, 13
Tax preferences
  alternative minimum tax on, 222–23
  interaction between, and maximum tax, 221–22
  minimum tax on, 219–21
Tax rate, definition of, 6–7
Tax rate schedules, 66–67
Tax Reform Act (1969), 51, 55, 56, 82, 190, 256–57
Tax Reform Act (1976), 37, 83, 92, 191, 204, 225, 310, 317, 353
Tax returns; see Returns
Tax shelters, 223
  advisability of, 237–38
  in agriculture, 228
  capital requirements of, 235
  confusion concerning, 217–18
  and creation of personal holding company tax, 84–85
  illustration of, 238–46
  ingredients of, 223–38
  investment in, as legal alternative, 217
  need for professional advise on, 237
  in oil and gas industries, 228–30
  in real estate, 230–31
  short- and long-term implications of, 218
  special tax provisions for, 231–35
  and use of limited partnership, 236–37
Tax shields, classification of, 144–72
Tax traps, 353–54
  judicial, 354–58
  and role of intent, 274–75
  statutory, 358–69
Taxable entities
  acknowledgement of three, 41
  modification of use involving more than one, 121–24

Taxable entities—Cont.
  modification of use involving single, 117–21
  and the taxable income concept, 60–67
Taxable estate, 6
Taxable gifts, 6
Taxable income, 6, 15–16, 31, 60–67, 250
Taxable profits, 250
Taxes, types of, 9–10
Taxing process, 370–71
  compliance considerations, 372–80
  filing requirements, 372–73
  as human process, 370
  level of, 371
  returns selected for audit, 373–74
  settling disputes in, 374–77
Taxpayer assistance, 380
  competence of, 380–83
  cost of, 383–84
Taxpayers, number who pay no taxes, 2
Tenancy by the entirety, 309
Tenancy in common, 308
10 : 5 : 3 depreciation, 202–3, 386
Testamentary trust, 57, 318
Thin corporations, 131
Three-cornered exchanges, 271–73
Time constraints, in nontaxable transactions, 254
Time-preference value of money, effect of tax laws on, 181–84
Tips, inclusion of, as gross income, 28
Tollgate tax, 93
Trade
  deduction of expenses related to, 32
  exclusion of property used for, from capital assets, 99, 101–4, 117
Transportation,
  expense deductions for, 63
  to and from place of employment, as company benefit, 148–49
Travel, correct tax treatment of expenses, 63, 77, 150–51, 152
Treasury Circular 230, 380
Trust corpus, 318
Trustee, role of, 57
Trusts, 56, 57, 318
28-72 basis, 37, 133

U

Unfunded equivalent of pension plan, 170
Unified gift and estate tax credit, 315–16
Unincorporated business as multinational business, 89

Unincorporated service-and-capital business personal service taxable income, 79–80
Unit of account, 346–47
U.S. Gypsum, 304 F. Supp. 627, 94
U.S. Supreme Court, 12, 377
Unreasonable accumulation of income, 73, 360
Unwanted assets, 291–92
Useful life of assets, 350–51

V

Variable annuity, 163–64
Variable tax credit, 8
VAT (value added tax), introduction of, 386
Vesting, 161, 163
Videotapes, investing in, as tax shelter, 231

Voting-stock-for-voting-stock requirement, 281

W

Wash sales, tax treatment of, 136–37
Weighted average, 345
Western Hemisphere Trade Corporation (WHTCO), 94
Will
  death with valid, 317
  death without valid, 317–18
  use of equalization clause, 326–27
Windfall Profits Tax Act (1980), 83

X–Y–Z

Year-end security review, 135–40
Zero bracket amount, 32, 77, 85
Zero bracket amount deduction, 63–65

This book has been set VIP, in 11 and 10 point Melior, leaded 2 points. Chapter numbers are 11 and 36 point Melior Bold. Chapter titles are 18 point Melior Bold. The size of the type page is 26 by 45 picas.